Wilhelm Furtwängler

Wilhelm Furtwängler rehearsing the Berlin Philharmonic
Orchestra in London, November 1948

Wilhelm Furtwängler

ART AND THE POLITICS OF THE UNPOLITICAL

ROGER ALLEN

THE BOYDELL PRESS

First published 2018
The Boydell Press, Woodbridge

ISBN 978 1 78327 283 9

The Boydell Press is an imprint of Boydell & Brewer Ltd
PO Box 9, Woodbridge, Suffolk IP12 3DF, UK
and of Boydell & Brewer Inc.
668 Mt Hope Avenue, Rochester, NY 14620–2731, USA
website: www.boydellandbrewer.com

A CIP catalogue record for this book is available
from the British Library

The publisher has no responsibility for the continued existence or accuracy of URLs
for external or third-party internet websites referred to in this book, and does not
guarantee that any content on such websites is, or will remain, accurate or appropriate

This publication is printed on acid-free paper

Designed and typeset by BBR Design, Sheffield
Printed and bound in Great Britain by TJ International Ltd, Padstow

MIX
Paper from
responsible sources
FSC® C013056

For Pamela

CONTENTS

ILLUSTRATIONS

*The author and publishers are grateful to all the institutions and individuals listed
for permission to reproduce the materials in which they hold copyright. Every
effort has been made to trace the copyright holders; apologies are offered for any
omission, and the publishers will be pleased to add any necessary acknowledgement
in subsequent editions.*

ABBREVIATIONS

Full citations are given in the bibliography

AZN   Wilhelm Furtwängler, *Aufzeichnungen*

CM   Wilhelm Furtwängler, *Concerning Music* (English translation of *Gespräche über Musik*)

FM   *Furtwängler on Music*, Essays and Addresses translated and edited by Ronald Taylor

GM   Wilhelm Furtwängler, *Gespräche über Musik*

GSD   Richard Wagner, *Gesammelte Schriften und Dichtungen*, 10 vols

NBKS   Wilhelm Furtwängler, *Notebooks* (English translation of *Aufzeichnungen*)

PW   *Richard Wagner's Prose Works*, translated and edited by W. Ashton Ellis, 8 vols

SPK   Furtwängler Nachlass der Staatsbibliothek zu Berlin – Preußischer Kulturbesitz, Musikabteilung mit Mendelssohn-Archiv

TW   Wilhelm Furtwängler, *Ton und Wort*

VMS   Wilhelm Furtwängler, *Vermächtnis*

PRELUDE

In February 1948 Wilhelm Furtwängler returned to conduct in England for the first time since the end of World War II. He appeared with the London Philharmonic Orchestra in no fewer than ten concerts in London, Birmingham, Leicester, Watford and Wimbledon. He then travelled to Argentina, Switzerland and Italy before returning to London in September of that year for a complete cycle of Beethoven symphonies given with the Vienna Philharmonic Orchestra in the Royal Albert Hall.

The most significant of these visits by far was that which he made in November 1948 with his 'own' Berlin Philharmonic Orchestra. This renowned but politically compromised ensemble had earlier been invited to visit England by an Anglican clergyman, John Collins (1905–82), Chaplain and Dean of Oriel College in the University of Oxford, until promoted in 1948 by Prime Minister Clement Attlee to a Canonry of St Paul's Cathedral in London. Collins was a vigorous social reformer and strong opponent of nuclear weapons who in the years after the end of hostilities worked tirelessly for international reconciliation between the former wartime enemies. In September 1947 he made a two-week-long visit to Germany where, apparently on an impulse, he invited the Berlin Philharmonic to make a tour of England under the direction of both the young Sergiu Celibidache and Furtwängler.[1]

There were many diplomatic, administrative, organisational and financial difficulties to be overcome; but these eventually proved surmountable and the tour arranged for November 1948. The first concert was originally scheduled for 3 November in the notoriously difficult acoustic of London's St Paul's Cathedral; but at the last minute the cathedral authorities had a change of heart and the event was relocated to the cavernous Empress Hall in Earl's Court. As the commentator of the London-based news agency Visnews Ltd put it in the breathless newsreel style of the time:

1   Diana Collins, *Partners in Protest: Life with Canon Collins* (London: Victor Gollancz Ltd, 1992), p. 160.

The 103 musicians of the Berlin Philharmonic Orchestra conducted by the renowned Dr Wilhelm Furtwängler rehearse Brahms' Fourth Symphony for their concert in the Empress Hall, Earls Court. The Orchestra had been invited by the Dean of Oriel College, Oxford as gesture of reconciliation.

The programme was exclusively of Austro-German music: J. S. Bach's Orchestral Suite No. 3 in D; Beethoven's Piano Concerto No. 4 in G (Op. 68) with the English pianist Dame Myra Hess as soloist; and Brahms' Symphony No. 4 (Op. 98). The participation of Myra Hess was especially significant. During the war she had famously organised a series of concerts at London's National Gallery as a morale-boosting exercise in support of service personnel. John Collins had initially approached her with some diffidence, but as soon as she understood the purpose of the concert she agreed to perform. Now Myra Hess, symbol of wartime resistance, and Wilhelm Furtwängler, the public face of German music during the Nazi period, appeared together as symbols of a spirit of reconciliation between Great Britain and Germany. The effect of the concert was overpowering. One critic remarked that 'Dame Myra Hess's playing had a touch of crusader's fire'. Another wrote: 'Scarcely anyone in that vast audience can have remained unmoved at the visible symbol of reconciliation when, after memorable performance, Dame Myra Hess and Wilhelm Furtwängler stood to receive applause hand in hand.'[2]

In all Furtwängler gave four concerts of Bach, Beethoven, Schubert, Brahms and Richard Strauss in London, Liverpool, Birmingham and Oxford. The orchestra was warmly received wherever it travelled and the tour was a significant turning point not only in the rehabilitation of the politically compromised Furtwängler but also in the restitution of relationships between Great Britain and Germany. Sadly, because of a dispute between the Musicians' Union and the BBC, the concerts were not broadcast and no complete recordings are known to exist; but something of the visceral power of the music-making can be experienced in a surviving newsreel film-clip of Furtwängler rehearsing the end of the Brahms Symphony in preparation for the London concert.[3]

Though much of the focus in this footage is on the orchestra, in the shots of Furtwängler we see and hear an evident master at work, exercising absolute control over the players, who were familiar enough with his requirements to need no more than occasional eye contact. The trembling arms and famously indecisive beat seem to advertise a kind of daemonic 'possession' by the music, whose very essence seems visibly matched by his considerable

2   Ibid., p. 168.
3   <https://www.youtube.com/watch?v=leYbb5KZYDg> (accessed 10 November 2017).

height and powerfully modelled head resting upon a long neck. Furtwängler
the master conductor had lost nothing of his power to mesmerise orchestra
and audience alike with the volcanic intensity of his music-making. The spirit
of German music appears to animate and flow through his physical gestures.
Here all the power and ambivalence of German Music as represented by
Wilhelm Furtwängler, officially exonerated from blame yet indelibly
associated in the public imagination with the Third Reich, is strongly
projected. The purpose of what follows will be to probe that ambivalence,
accepting Furtwängler as the master musician he was, while considering the
historical and ideological foundations of that mastery in ways that, rather
than follow the well-trodden path of establishing what he did or did not do
for the Nazi regime, respond to more recent scholarship on the antecedents
and aftermath of the Third Reich.

ACKNOWLEDGEMENTS

The author would like to thank the following for their assistance in the preparation of this study: the late Frau Elisabeth Furtwängler (1910–2012), for granting initial access to the material held in the Furtwängler estate, Zentralbibliothek Zürich, and for permission to translate extracts from Furtwängler's writings and photographic material held in the Furtwängler Nachlass; Prof. Dr Andreas Furtwängler for renewing that permission; Peter McMullin of Blackwell's Music Shop, Oxford, for help in obtaining many of the German scores and texts necessary for this study; Sue Palmer for intensive coaching in the German language, checking translations and helping to unravel some of Furtwängler's more complicated syntax; the late Ronald Taylor for permission to quote extracts from *Furtwängler on Music*; similarly to Shaun Whiteside for permission to quote from his translation of the Furtwängler *Notebooks*; James Treadwell, for advice in matters of literary theory; Jean Christoph Gero, Director of the Musikabteilung, Preußischer Kulturbesitz, Staatsbibliothek zu Berlin, for his assistance both before and during research visits made to consult the portion of the Furtwängler Nachlass held in Berlin; the staff of the Musikabteilung, Zentralbibliothek Zürich for prompt assistance in answering queries and providing material; and to Silver Hesse (Zurich) for permission to reproduce the caricature of Furtwängler, Goebbels and Richard Strauss by Gregor Rabinovitch. I am also grateful to my colleagues the Master, Mark Damazer, and the Fellows of St Peter's College, Oxford, for granting me sabbatical leave to bring this project to completion; to my colleagues in the Faculty of Music, University of Oxford, for their continued interest and support; and especially to my former student Matthew Thomson for so ably covering my academic duties during my absence.

My especial thanks go to my former teacher Michael Nicholas, who long ago when I was a schoolboy in Northampton loaned me his EMI LP recording of *Tristan und Isolde* and first made me aware of Wilhelm Furtwängler; to my close friend and colleague Chris Walton, sometime director of the Musikabteilung, Zentralbibliothek Zürich, for generous hospitality in Zurich when this research was in its early stages, for suggesting so many fruitful lines of enquiry and for consistently keeping up a uniform and gentle pressure when the project was displaced by other things and was in danger of disappearing completely below the horizon. Michael Middeke, Editorial Director of the Boydell Press, provided the motivation I needed to dust off my original research and return to it after a fallow period during which I left Furtwängler in abeyance and pursued other interests. His assistant, Megan Milan, and Boydell's Production Manager, Rohais Haughton, promptly answered my many queries and gave constant support during the publication process. My Oxford friends Margaret Bent, and Barbara Eichner, Christian Leitmeir and their son Martin, gave me continuous encouragement along the way. The late Brian Hitch was indefatigable in his assistance with making sense of Furtwängler's more abstruse German syntax. Bojan Bujić suggested readings and answered enquiries concerning the more obscure corners of the æsthetic and philosophical systems in which Furtwängler was so deeply embedded. Peter Pulzer helpfully guided my investigations in the labyrinthine complexities of late-nineteenth- and early-twentieth-century German political history over tea at All Souls college. Nicholas Attfield gave expert input from his specialist field, the 'Conservative Revolution' in early-twentieth-century German music. My Germanist colleague and academic neighbour Kevin Hilliard patiently answered my many questions about Goethe in particular and subtleties of meaning in German texts in general. Nicholas Attfield, Hilda Meldrum Brown and Barry Millington kindly read early drafts of the complete text, gave invaluable input from their respective fields of expertise and through their enthusiasm for the project encouraged me to keep going. My former student Peter Hall carefully prepared the music examples extracted from the full scores. My Oxford mentor Peter Franklin suggested many of the original critical lines of enquiry and has since its inception taken an enthusiastic and close personal interest in this work. His scrupulous criticisms, suggestions and detailed comments on the penultimate draft immeasurably improved the final version. To them all I express my most grateful thanks. All mistakes and errors are, of course, my own, for which I take full responsibility. Lastly, I have to express my warmest thanks to my wife Pamela. Without her dedicated support and help so unstintingly given over so many years, this study simply would not have been begun, let alone brought to completion. This book is dedicated to her.

In addition to the above, the author is grateful to and pleased to acknowledge the following copyright holders:

- *Furtwängler on Music*, tr. Ronald Taylor, Copyright 1991, Scolar Press. Reproduced by permission of Taylor & Francis Books UK.
- Ries & Erler (Berlin) for permission to prepare music examples from the full scores of Furtwängler's symphonies.
- Zentralbibliothek Zürich for permission to reproduce material held in the Furtwängler Nachlass.

PREFACE

Wilhelm Furtwängler (1886–1954) is both a monument to a grand tradition and an example of how the phenomenon of the Great Man can distort the perception of history. The aim of what follows is therefore to penetrate the aura that presently surrounds the icon of a particular 'Great Conductor' and engage with the phenomenon he represented: that of an artist driven by an ideological world-view which determined everything he did and which drove him to extremes of both perversity and greatness.

Furtwängler has entered the historical memory primarily as a supreme interpreter of the central repertoire of the Austro-German canon of musical masterworks. His extensive legacy of sound recordings, whether captured live through radio broadcasts or made in the studio, are the main routes of access to his art. They are now almost universally available and are regularly remastered and reissued in various formats. As a body of work these recordings are freighted with historical meaning: for the historian of performance they are a direct record of past orchestral and operatic practice; for the cultural historian, the live recordings in particular document significant historical events, for example the 1936 Bayreuth Festival, concerts given during the war years (such as Beethoven's Ninth Symphony given in Berlin on 22 March 1942), or those from the period after the defeat of Germany in 1945 when Furtwängler was permitted to resume his conducting activities following the conclusion of de-Nazification proceedings. The catalogue is far too extensive for even a cursory treatment to be remotely comprehensive. Representative examples taken from the relevant period will nevertheless here be examined as primary historical evidence.

Film sources of Furtwängler are limited but also of considerable value. The image showing the conductor shaking hands with Goebbels following the conclusion of the last movement of Beethoven's Ninth Symphony on the eve of Hitler's birthday on 19 April 1942 is a powerful reminder of how the Nazis made propaganda out of art. Furtwängler conducting Wagner's *Meistersinger* overture as part of a 1942 *Strength through Joy* (*Kraft durch Freude*) film before a rapt audience of seemingly absorbed industrial workers brought Wagner out of the opera house and onto the factory floor as a means

of cultural morale-boosting.[1] The clip already mentioned of a rehearsal of the
last movement of Brahms' Fourth Symphony in London (2 or 3 November
1948) made during the first tour abroad of the Berlin Philharmonic together
with film of a complete performance of Strauss' *Till Eulenspiegel* (extracted
from a film entitled *Der Botschafter der Musik* produced in 1951) are reminders
of the rehabilitation process of German musical culture and of Furtwängler
himself in the post-war period. If, as the saying has it, a picture is worth a
thousand words, then these images have much to tell.

Furtwängler's reputation as a conductor and interpreter of the works of
others is so embedded in the historical memory that his output as a composer
is often overlooked. In this respect he was not so much a lion of the podium
following the model of his predecessor Arthur Nikisch but part of a much
older Kapellmeister tradition, stretching back to Wagner and Mendelssohn,
of composers who conducted their own works and the works of others.
Furtwängler's claim that he considered himself a composer first and a
conductor second does not entirely stand up to scrutiny. As Chris Walton has
observed, Furtwängler's bursts of intense compositional activity coincided
with periods when his conducting activity was constrained either by circum-
stance or design.[2] This is certainly true of his three quasi-Brucknerian
symphonies, especially No. 2 in E minor, begun in the final stages of the
war and completed during the early part of his post-war exile in Switzerland
(1944–45), and the Third Symphony in C sharp minor. (Furtwängler was
still engaged on revising the finale to this equally large-scale work when
he died in 1954.) Furtwängler's symphonies are today very seldom played;
and even if they are given occasional outings it is only as curiosities and
because they are by a famous conductor rather than as part of any ongoing
repertoire. The First Symphony was never performed in Furtwängler's
lifetime and, as we shall see in Chapter 8, there is evidence to suggest that
he never regarded it as finished. Furtwängler himself made a commercial
recording of the Second Symphony and there are live performances, though
in inferior sound, captured in Vienna (22 February 1953) and Stuttgart (30
March 1954). Even a Furtwängler champion of the international standing of
Daniel Barenboim could not succeed in bringing Furtwängler the composer
into the mainstream repertoire. His commercial recording with the Chicago
Symphony Orchestra (12–15 December 2001) of the Second Symphony is
the best extant recording of any Furtwängler work, but remains *sui generis*:
a curiosity rather than an important rediscovery of an unjustly neglected

1   All film sources are fully referenced in Appendix 3.
2   See Chris Walton, 'Wilhelm Furtwängler and the Return of the Muse', in *Lies and
    Epiphanies* (New York: University of Rochester Press, 2014), pp. 94–109, here pp. 95–7.

masterpiece. It is ironic that it was the Chicago Symphony Orchestra under a conductor of Jewish origin who made this recording: in 1948 Furtwängler withdrew his acceptance of an invitation to conduct a series of concerts in Chicago on account of the hostility of a group of musicians that included the pianists Vladimir Horowitz and Artur Rubinstein.

Yet Furtwängler's music, and the Second and Third Symphonies in particular, should not be dismissed out of hand as symphonic dinosaurs: they are significant cultural statements with a good deal to tell. First, in spite of their prolixity and unwieldy structure, they both contain music of great expressive beauty. The slow movement of No. 3 (the concluding movement if it is performed without the unrevised finale in the manner of the incomplete Bruckner Ninth) is a threnody that inhabits the same world as Strauss' *Metamorphosen* (1945), a work Furtwängler conducted infrequently but memorably in the post-war years. Secondly the question must be asked why Furtwängler composed three symphonies in a self-consciously Romantic idiom broadly following a Brucknerian model at this point in time. Even by the conventions of fifty years earlier they are conservative in style. There is no attempt to engage with the chromatic idioms of later Wagner or Bruckner. The harmonic language is steeped in the tonally more secure world of Schumann and Brahms. A relevant compositional voice seems to be that of Hans Pfitzner who, as we know from Furtwängler's letters, occupied his thoughts a good deal during the period in which these works were composed. To what extent were the Second and Third Symphonies in particular cultural memories in dialogue with the grand Austro-German symphonic tradition as Furtwängler perceived it, in the context of Europe after World War II?

What is less well known, particularly in the English-speaking world, is that Furtwängler wrote extensively on music and associated matters. The principal published sources of his formally composed writings are two anthologies. The first and most extensive is *Ton und Wort: Aufsätze und Vorträge 1918–1954* (*Sound and Word: Essays and Addresses 1918–1954*). This publication was authorised by Furtwängler during his lifetime and consists of a collection of essays, articles and lectures arranged in chronological order that encompasses almost the entire span of his professional and creative life. It contains the majority of his extended essays and is the principal resource for the study of his writings. Included are studies of Bach, Beethoven, Bruckner, Brahms, the music theorist Heinrich Schenker, and his most extensive essay 'The Case of Wagner, freely after Nietzsche' ('Der Fall Wagner, frei nach Nietzsche', 1941). The second anthology is the posthumously published *Vermächtnis: Nachgelassene Schriften* (1956). The title, roughly translated as *Legacy: Posthumous Writings*, is a clear reference to the eponymous poem by Goethe with its closing reference to 'devising

patterns for noble souls as the highest calling': it consists of a collection of
diary jottings arranged chronologically followed by a series of fragmentary
writings and more substantial essays.[3] The third important collection of
Furtwängler's writings, *Wilhelm Furtwängler, Aufzeichnungen 1924–1954*
(1980), was edited by Elisabeth Furtwängler and Günter Birkner; English
translation by Shaun Whiteside, edited and with an introduction by Michael
Tanner, *Wilhelm Furtwängler: Notebooks 1924–1954* (1989).[4] Throughout his
life Furtwängler carried a notebook in which he recorded his thoughts (in
what for him was an aphoristic style) on artistic, philosophical and musical
matters. These personal jottings were never intended for the public eye: as
such they are a cultural document of the first importance and of incalculable value to the historian. However, in the form in which they are presently
available they are highly problematic for the published edition represents no
more than a selection from Furtwängler's complete diaries. For the purposes
of the present study careful comparisons have therefore been made between
the entry in question and the manuscript sources.

The same critical difficulties apply to the volume edited by Frank Thiess,
Wilhelm Furtwängler: Briefe (1964; Vierte Auflage, 1980), for this again
represents only a selection of Furtwängler's correspondence, held in the
Berlin State Library (Staatsbibliothek zu Berlin). The collection by Thiess
is useful as far as it goes, for it contains the early exchanges between the
young Furtwängler and Bertel von Hildebrand; these letters are the principal
source for a study of the origins of the world-view which was to infuse his
writings and, with the important exception of the change in his attitude
towards Wagner, predominate in his thinking for the remainder of his life.[5]
A further publication to appear under Furtwängler's own name is *Gespräche
über Musik* (1948), translated into English as *Conversations about Music* by
L. J. Lawrence (1953). This consists of a series of transcripts of seven conversations on predetermined musical subjects which took place in 1937 between
Furtwängler and Walter Abendroth. In 1947 Furtwängler added a further
chapter in which he considers the problems of modern music. This book is
the most concentrated source of his musical æsthetic and is described by the
author Hans-Hubert Schönzeler as 'Furtwängler's musical *Credo*'.[6]

The Furtwängler Nachlass is divided between the Zentralbibliothek
Zürich and the Staatsbibliothek Berlin. Manuscripts and typescripts of most,

3   See Goethe, *Vermächtnis*, in translation by David Luke in *Goethe: The Penguin Poets*
    (Harmondsworth: Penguin Books, 1964), pp. 276–8.
4   For a review of *Aufzeichnungen* by Carl Dahlhaus, see *Frankfurter Allgemeine Zeitung*, 6
    December 1980.
5   For a review of *Briefe*, see *Neue Zürcher Zeitung*, 28 November 1964.
6   Hans-Hubert Schönzeler, *Furtwängler* (London: Duckworth, 1990), p. 163.

though not all, of Furtwängler's published articles and essays are contained in the portion of the Nachlass held in Zurich. In some cases these articles exist in several different versions; as will become clear in the course of this study, comparison between the various versions can be revealing. The Zurich material was deposited together with the musical manuscripts in 1970 by Elisabeth Furtwängler, who rather ruefully comments in her memoir of her husband: 'I would have preferred it if this material could have gone to a German library, but only Zurich expressed interest.'[7] In addition to the primary source material for Furtwängler's compositions, published articles and essays, there is a comprehensive collection of newspaper articles and reviews relating to Furtwängler's career; an invaluable resource which saves the historian endless archival research in newspaper offices and archives. A full list of Furtwängler's extant compositions and writings can be found in *Wilhelm Furtwängler in Diskussion*, edited by Chris Walton, Jürg Stenzl *et al.* (1996), pp. 85–132. The portion of the Nachlass containing Furtwängler's extensive correspondence, together with further copies of the formally composed writings etc. is held in Musikabteilung mit Mendelssohn-Archiv, Preußischer Kulturbesitz, Staatsbibliothek Berlin. The Furtwängler literary estate has been extensively consulted during the course of this study; in addition to the unpublished material, the published articles and essays to be found in *Ton und Wort* and *Vermächtnis*, many of which are not yet translated and are therefore not available to the English reader, have received careful critical attention. Representative translations of two published articles on Heinrich Schenker (1947) and Hans Pfitzner (1948) are included in Appendix 1.

The bibliography of late-nineteenth- and early-twentieth-century German political and cultural history is of course extensive. I mention a few studies that have left a particularly strong impression. Golo Mann's *History of Germany in the Nineteenth and Twentieth Centuries* (1958) is a classic and stands alone. Of more recent books Erik Levi's *Music in the Third Reich* (1994) is indispensable, as are groundbreaking studies such as Michael Kater's *The Twisted Muse* (1997) and Pamela Potter's *Most German of the Arts: Musicology and Society from the Weimar Republic to the End of Hitler's Reich* (1998). Richard Evans' authoritative writings on the Third Reich, in particular his assessment of Hitler's Cultural Revolution in *The Coming of the Third Reich* (2003), are invaluable; Peter Pulzer's concise *Germany 1870–1945* (1997) is a model of clarity and precision in the treatment of complex historical issues; Saul Friedländer's *Nazi Germany and the Jews: The Years of Persecution 1933–39* (1997) is a model of disinterest and balanced historical judgement. New

7   Elisabeth Furtwängler, *Über Wilhelm Furtwängler* (Wiesbaden: Brockhaus, 1979), p. 25.

perspectives and lines of enquiry suggested by Nicholas Cook's *The Schenker Project* (2007), Alexander Rehding's *Music and Monumentality* (2009) and meta-discussions of absolute music such as Mark Evan Bonds' *Absolute Music: The History of an Idea* (2014) provided a particularly strong impulse to return to work on Furtwängler. There is a general bibliography of all works consulted at the end of the volume.

The intention in what follows is to approach a critical, intellectual biography by tracing the progress and development of Furtwängler's thought from its foundation in late-nineteenth-century traditions of *Bildung* through the cultural and moral dilemmas of the Nazi period to the post-war years in which the beleaguered idealist found himself adrift in an alien cultural environment. Chapter 1 therefore investigates the historical and cultural background to Furtwängler's privileged upbringing in the traditions of *Bildung*. In Chapters 2 and 3 Furtwängler's early reception of Beethoven is considered together with the catalytic effect of his initial acquaintance with the work of the theorist Heinrich Schenker and his empathy with Schenker's organicist methodology. Chapter 4 investigates how these ideas shaped Furtwängler's approach to musical performance and also how the inherent ideological subtexts in much closely related contemporary theory shared the intellectual premises that shaped developing nationalistic ideologies. Chapters 5 and 6 examine how this performance æsthetic, with its almost obsessive concern with the idea of organic cohesion, coincided with much of the artistic and political ideology of Nazism, how such ideology inter-sected with the kind of artistic experience Furtwängler strove to achieve in performance and how this in itself helped support the Nazi state and gave it cultural credibility. Chapter 7 investigates Furtwängler's intellectual and artistic position in the period immediately following the collapse of the Third Reich; in his writings he called for a return to the ideology of the Wilhelmine period as the only way of restoring true cultural values. Chapter 8 investi-gates why after a long gap Furtwängler returned to composition and in the last years of his life produced three large-scale symphonies in a tendentiously Romantic idiom. Finally, Chapter 9 examines the two most important essays from the last year of his life, which show how, in essence, his world-view remained unchanged from that which was so firmly established in his formative years. Each chapter begins with a brief sketch of relevant historical and biographical details sustaining a necessary narrative thread and creating a framework in which the relevant writings may be appropriately contextu-alised. A chronology showing dates of significant events, articles and compo-sitions is included on pp. xxiii-xxxi.

NOTE ON TRANSLATIONS

In the case of Furtwängler the study of primary source material, whether published or archival, is beset with difficulties. Equally daunting are the problems encountered by the non-native German speaker in attempting to penetrate and understand Furtwängler's thought patterns: his world-view is thoroughly Germanic and rooted in the linguistic patterns and syntactical traditions of the nineteenth century. He wrote in the German tradition of idealistic philosophy as seen at its most complex in the writings of Kant and Hegel. The problems facing the translator are therefore formidable. It is fortunate that the late Ronald Taylor, sometime Professor of German in the University of Sussex, translated a compilation from both *Ton und Wort* and *Vermächtnis* which was subsequently published as an anthology entitled *Furtwängler on Music* (1991).[1] Taylor has rendered the English reader an invaluable service. In his brief introduction he draws attention to the problems encountered in translating Furtwängler's originals into intelligible English prose without obscuring some of the textual references. In a letter to the present author dated 9 February 1998 he wrote: 'One sometimes feels like banging one's head against the wall in the face of his foggy prose. The most useful tool for dealing with it is sometimes not a torch but a machete, which in the end does him a service, I think.' In the present study translations are either by the author or, where a translation by Taylor of a Furtwängler essay exists, his helping hand has been gratefully accepted. Nevertheless, careful line-by-line comparisons with the German originals have been made and in some cases Taylor's version has been modified accordingly in order to restore resonances obscured in the interests of making a readable translation. All such modifications are identified in footnotes. A similar practice has been followed with regard to Shaun Whiteside's translation of the *Notebooks*. This process of comparison can reveal thought patterns and allusions that are not always immediately obvious in translation, an example of which can be found in the extended notebook entry on Bach's *Matthäus Passion* (1939). Furtwängler

1   For a review of *Furtwängler on Music* by Chris Walton see *Music and Letters*, vol. 74, no. 3 (1993), pp. 466–7.

writes 'wer es nicht selbst fühlt, wird es nicht erreichen' (whoever does not feel it himself will not achieve it).[2] This is a clear reference to Goethe's *Faust*, Part I: 'wenn ihrs nicht fühlt, ihr werdets nicht erjagen' (give up pursuing eloquence, unless you can speak as you feel).[3] To Furtwängler, as to most educated Germans of his generation and cultural background, *Faust* was the foundation of his literary heritage. His writings are infused with Faustian references which, though a natural part of his expressive language, are not always immediately obvious in translation.

Furtwängler's thought does not lend itself to easy summary: for this reason direct quotation, sometimes at length, has proved a necessary tool. It has not, however, been the intention simply to provide an anthology of extracts from the writings: the primary purpose here is to place the major published essays and articles in historical context in such a way that a developing critical exegesis becomes possible. It is hoped that what can appear to be rather empty and prolix passages of æsthetic theorising will here be readable as cogent indicators of an evolving intellectual biography of some historical significance. Where there is a possibility of ambiguity, key German words, and in some cases entire phrases, have of necessity been included. It must, however, be said that ambiguity of expression, or sometimes just sheer verbosity, is a recurring problem when examining Furtwängler's writings. In all cases the whereabouts of the original German text is specified.

2   AZN, p. 176; NBKS, p. 108.
3   Goethe, *Faust*, Part I, line 534, tr. David Luke (Oxford: Oxford World's Classics, 1987).

CHRONOLOGY

Date	Wilhelm Furtwängler Life and Works	Significant Historical, Cultural and Literary Events
1853 30 June	Adolf Furtwängler (father) born in Freiburg	
1863 14 September	Adelheid Wendt (mother) born in Karlsruhe	
1864 11 June		Richard Strauss born in Munich
1868 19 June		Heinrich Schenker born in Wisniowczyki, Austrian Galicia
1869 5 May		Hans Pfitzner born in Moscow
1871 18 January		Proclamation of the German Empire at Versailles
1875 6 June		Thomas Mann born in Lübeck
1876 August		First Bayreuth Festival
1883 13 February		Death of Richard Wagner in Venice
1886 25 January	**Wilhelm Furtwängler born in Berlin**	
1887		Ferdinand Tönnies, *Gemeinschaft und Gesellschaft*
1888 9 March		Death of Kaiser Wilhelm I; succeeded briefly by Friedrich III then by Wilhelm II
1889 20 April		Adolf Hitler born in Braunau am Inn, Austria

Date	Wilhelm Furtwängler Life and Works	Significant Historical, Cultural and Literary Events
1894	Appointment of Adolf Furtwängler to Munich University. Family moves to Munich	
1896		Death of Anton Bruckner in Vienna
1897		Death of Johannes Brahms in Vienna
1899		H. S. Chamberlain, *Foundations of the Nineteenth Century*
1901		Thomas Mann, *Buddenbrooks*
1902	Visits Florence with Ludwig Curtius and the Hildebrand family	
1905		H. S. Chamberlain, *Kant*
1906 19 February	Conducts first orchestral concert with Kaim Orchestra of Munich	
1906–07	Zurich	
1907 10 October	Death of Adolf Furtwängler in Athens	
1907–09	Munich Court Opera with Felix Mottl	
1909–11	Strasbourg Opera with Hans Pfitzner	
1910		Friedrich Huch, *Enzio*
1911–15	Lübeck: Chief conductor of *Verein der Musikfreunde*	
1911	Reads Heinrich Schenker's *Beethoven's Ninth Symphony*	
1912		H. S. Chamberlain, *Goethe*; Heinrich Schenker, *Beethoven's Ninth Symphony*
1914 28 July		Austro-Hungary declares war on Serbia. Outbreak of World War I
3–4 August		Germany declares war on France Britain declares war on Germany

Date	Wilhelm Furtwängler Life and Works	Significant Historical, Cultural and Literary Events
1915	Essay: 'Timely Reflections of a Musician' by Wilhelm Furtwängler (Lübeck)	
		Chamberlain, *Politische Ideale*
1915–20	Mannheim: *Hofkapellmeister*	
1917 12 June		Pfitzner: *Palestrina*, premiere in Munich conducted by Bruno Walter
6 November	Conducts Bruckner's Eighth Symphony Article: Anton Bruckner's Eighth Symphony	
14 December	First appearance with Berlin Philharmonic Orchestra	
1918		Thomas Mann, *Reflections of a Non-Political Man*
	Essay: 'Remarks on Beethoven's Music'	
		Oswald Spengler, *Decline of the West*, vol. 1
9 November		Abdication of Kaiser Wilhelm II
11 November		Armistice between hostile powers. 'Stab in the back' legend attributes German defeat to betrayal by Republicans.
1919	Conductor of Vienna Tonkünstler Orchestra concerts	
		Hans Pfitzner, *New Aesthetic of Musical Impotence*
	Essay: 'Remarks on Wagner's *Ring*'	
3 May	First meeting with Heinrich Schenker	
28 June		Treaty of Versailles imposes severe reparations on Germany
11 August		Weimar Republic constitution adopted (to 1933)

Date	Wilhelm Furtwängler Life and Works	Significant Historical, Cultural and Literary Events
1920 August	Conductor of Frankfurt Museumskonzerte in succession to Willem Mengelberg. Relinquishes position in Mannheim	
1921	First appearances with Leipzig Gewandhaus Orchestra	
1922		Oswald Spengler, *Decline of the West*, vol. 2
23 January	Subsequently succeeds Nikisch as Conductor of the Leipzig Gewandhaus (until 1928) and Berlin Philharmonic Orchestras	Death of Arthur Nikisch
27 January		Pfitzner, *Von Deutscher Seele* (Op. 28), premiere in Berlin
25 March	First appearance with Vienna Philharmonic Orchestra	
1924		Thomas Mann, *The Magic Mountain*
July/August		Reopening of Bayreuth Festival
1925 (1927)		Adolf Hitler: *Mein Kampf*
1929		Hans Pfitzner, *Das dunkle Reich* (Op. 38)
1930 27 and 28 May		Toscanini conducts New York Philharmonic Orchestra in Berlin
	Notebook entry: 'Toscanini in Germany: An article on the true situation of German music-making in 1930'	
August		Bayreuth Festival: Toscanini conducts *Tannhäuser* and *Tristan*
November/ December	Essay: 'Interpretation: a Question of Musical Destiny'	
1931	Appointed Musical Director of Bayreuth Festival	
23 July	Festival debut conducting *Tristan und Isolde*	

Date	Wilhelm Furtwängler Life and Works	Significant Historical, Cultural and Literary Events
1932 19 April	Address: 'Classical Music in Crisis'	Fiftieth anniversary of the Berlin Philharmonic Orchestra
1932 28 June	Essay: 'Um Bayreuths Zukunft', article giving reasons for resignation as Music Director of the Bayreuth Festival	
1933		Posthumous publication of Wilhelm Dilthey's *On German Poetry and Music*
30 January		Hitler comes to power
13 February		Thomas Mann, Address: 'The Sufferings and Greatness of Richard Wagner'
21 March	Day of Potsdam: conducts *Die Meistersinger* at Berlin Staatsoper	
11 April	Publication of open letter to Goebbels in defence of Jewish artists forced to leave Germany	
16 May	Address: 'Johannes Brahms: Address for the Johannes Brahms Festival in Vienna, 16–21 May'	
1934 11–12 March	Conducts Hindemith's Symphonic Suite, *Mathis der Maler*	
25 November	Article: 'The Case of Hindemith'	
4 December	Resigns all official posts	
17 December	Essay: 'German Music Problems'	
1935	Compromise reached with Goebbels	
February/ March	Resumes conducting. Memorandum: 'When I wrote my article about Hindemith'	
1936 19 July	Bayreuth Festival: *Lohengrin*	

Date	Wilhelm Furtwängler Life and Works	Significant Historical, Cultural and Literary Events
1–16 August		Eleventh Olympiad held in Berlin
September to February 1937	Sabbatical from conducting. Resumes composition	
1937	*Conversations about Music* with Walther Abendroth	
4 March	First Performance of Violin Sonata No. 1 In Leipzig	
May	Conducts two cycles of the *Ring* in London (Covent Garden Coronation Season)	London: Coronation of King George VI
6 June		Regensburg Valhalla: Hitler unveils bust of Bruckner. Speech by Goebbels
26 October	First Performance of Symphonic Concerto for Piano and Orchestra in Munich with Edwin Fischer	
1938 13 March		Hitler annexes Austria
May/June	Last appearances at Covent Garden: two cycles of the *Ring*	
27 December	Last appearance at Paris Opera: *Siegfried*	
1939 5 July	Address to the German Bruckner Society	
1 September		Hitler invades Poland
3 September		Britain declares war on Germany
1940		Hans Pfitzner, Symphony in C (Op. 46)
19 Feb	Symphony No. 1. First Performance of Violin Sonata No. 2 in Munich	
1941 April	Essay: 'The Case of Wagner, freely after Nietzsche'	
1943 26 June	Marries Elisabeth Ackermann, neé Albert	

Date	Wilhelm Furtwängler Life and Works	Significant Historical, Cultural and Literary Events
July	Conducts *Die Meistersinger* in Bayreuth	
1944 16 March	Concert in Prague with the Berlin Philharmonic Orchestra	
July	Conducts *Die Meistersinger* at Bayreuth	
	Begins composition of Symphony No. 2 in E minor	
1945 23 January	Last concert with the Berlin Philharmonic Orchestra until 1947	
29 January	Last concert with Vienna Philharmonic Orchestra until 1947	
7 February	Escapes to Switzerland	
12 April		Richard Strauss completes *Metamorphosen*
30 April		Death of Adolf Hitler in Berlin
8 May		End of the war in Europe
29 May		Thomas Mann Lecture: 'Germany and the Germans', Library of Congress, Washington
18 October	Completes composition of Symphony No. 2	
1947	Address: 'On the Centenary of Mendelssohn's Death'	
	Essay: 'Heinrich Schenker: A Contemporary Problem'	
	Additional chapter added to *Conversations about Music*	
		Thomas Mann, *Doctor Faustus*
27 April	Ratification of de-Nazification proceedings. Cleared of all charges of collaboration	

Date	Wilhelm Furtwängler Life and Works	Significant Historical, Cultural and Literary Events
25 May	First Concert with the Berlin Philharmonic Orchestra in Berlin since the defeat of Germany	
1948–49		Hans Pfitzner, Composition of *Urworte, Orphisch*, Op. 57 (unfinished)
1948	Essay: 'On the Works of Hans Pfitzner'	
22 February	First Performance of Symphony No. 2 in E minor in Berlin	
3–7 November	Concerts in Great Britain with Berlin Philharmonic	
1949 22 May		Death of Hans Pfitzner in Munich
8 September		Death of Richard Strauss in Garmisch-Partenkirchen
1950 22 May	Conducts premiere of Richard Strauss' *Four Last Songs* in London with Kirsten Flagstad	
1951 March	Essay: 'Bach'	
29 July	Conducts Beethoven's Ninth Symphony at the reopening of Bayreuth	Reopening of Bayreuth Festival under the direction of Wieland and Wolfgang Wagner
20 August	Salzburg Mozarteum, Address: 'Beethoven and Us'	
1952 June	Records *Tristan und Isolde* in London with Kirsten Flagstad, Ludwig Suthaus and Philharmonia Orchestra	
1954	Essay: 'Form and Chaos' (originally, 'The Musician and his Public')	
July and August	Salzburg Festival: *Don Giovanni* and *Der Freischütz*	
22 August	Lucerne Festival: Beethoven's Ninth Symphony	

Date	Wilhelm Furtwängler Life and Works	Significant Historical, Cultural and Literary Events
6 October	Completes recording of *Die Walküre* in Vienna	
15 November	Essay: 'All Greatness is Simplicity'	
30 November	**Death of Wilhelm Furtwängler, Clinic Ebersteinberg, near Baden-Baden**	
4 December	Funeral Service at the Church of the Holy Spirit, Heidelberg, followed by burial in the Bergfriedhof.	
1955 12 August		Death of Thomas Mann in Zurich
1956 26 January		First Performance of Symphony No. 3 (movements 1–3), conducted by Joseph Keilberth

INTRODUCTION

In me there are two souls, alas, and their
Division tears my life in two.
One loves the world, it clutches her, it binds
Itself to her, clinging with furious lust;
The other longs to soar beyond the dust
Into the realm of high ancestral minds.[1]

The life of Wilhelm Furtwängler (1886–1954) spans three failed attempts
to create a German national state. The young Furtwängler spent his
journeyman years and began his professional career during the final years of
the Wilhelmine Empire (1871–1918), that overweening political construct of
Chancellor Otto von Bismarck – so sharply caricatured by Heinrich Mann
in his novel *Man of Straw* (*Der Untertan*) – which came to an inglorious
end in the cataclysmic upheavals of World War I and the aftermath of the
shock defeat of 1918.[2] The older Furtwängler rose to prominence in the
experimental years of the Weimar Republic (1919–33), a brave but ultimately
unsuccessful attempt to found a modern democratic state that imploded and
opened the door for the rise of Nazism. His most notable achievements as
a performing artist were as a high-profile representative of the totalitarian
Third Reich (1933–45), during which years he gave performances of works
from the central Austro-German canon of musical masterworks that helped
give a carapace of cultural authority to a barbaric regime. The final nine years
of his life were passed in attempting to come to terms with the very different
context of post-war Europe, and through performances, recordings and the
composition of large-scale symphonies rehabilitate the politically compromised culture of which he had been so prominent a representative.

It is clear from the above brief outline that the life of Wilhelm Furtwängler
brings us very close to great historical themes of the age. Unsurprisingly,

1 Goethe, *Faust*, Part 1, lines 1112–17, tr. David Luke.
2 Heinrich Mann, *Der Untertan* (Leipzig: Kurt Wolff Verlag, 1918); Eng. edn, *Man of
   Straw* (London: Hutchinson & Co., 1946).

therefore, the question that casts a long shadow over his reputation is that of his relationship with the Third Reich. Furtwängler always claimed that art, and by association he himself as an artist, was above politics; yet as historian Richard Evans has pointed out

> of all the myths of German history that have been mobilised to account for the coming of the Third Reich in 1933, none is less convincing than that of the 'unpolitical German'. Largely the creation of the novelist Thomas Mann during the First World War, this concept subsequently became an alibi for the educated middle class in Germany which could absolve itself of the blame for supporting Nazism by accepting criticism for the far less serious offence of failing to oppose it.[3]

As Thomas Mann writes in *Reflections of a Non-Political Man* (*Betrachtungen eines Unpolitischen*, 1918): 'German culture resists being politicised. The political element is lacking in the German concept of culture.'[4] Or, as Nicholas Attfield more succinctly puts it, that culture which gave rise to 'conservative politics masquerading as a-politics'.[5] In one sense the notion of 'art above politics' reverted to a form of pre-Romantic artistic absolutism stemming from the Weimar classicism of Schiller.[6] In the case of musicians of a conservative cast of mind, this took the form of resistance to any moves that would threaten the autonomy of music as a special art. In any event, the conservative-nationalist 'non-political' German of the Weimar period tended towards an 'illiberal' anti-modernism rooted in the Romantic traditions of the previous century rather than the values of Western liberal democracy.

The historian Fritz Stern has described the character of the Imperial Germany in which Wilhelm Furtwängler was nurtured as 'illiberal'. 'By illiberalism I mean not only the structure of the political regime, suffrage restrictions or class chicanery, but a state of mind.'[7] Characteristic of this state of mind among the educated middle classes was a veneration of culture (*Bildung*) rooted in the traditions of German idealism; it was this admiration

3   Richard Evans, *The Coming of the Third Reich* (London: Allen Lane, 2003), p. xxv.
4   Thomas Mann, *Betrachtungen eines Unpolitischen* (Berlin: S. Fischer Verlag, 1918), p. 79; Eng. edn, *Reflections of a Non-Political Man*, tr. Walter D. Morris (New York: Frederick Ungar, 1983), p. 78.
5   Nicholas Attfield, *Challenging the Modern: Conservative Revolution in German Music 1918–1933* (Oxford: OUP, 2017).
6   Friedrich Schiller, *On the Aesthetic Education of Man*, tr. Reginald Snell (Bristol: Thoemmes Press, 1994). Also James Garratt, *Music Culture and Social Reform* (Cambridge: CUP, 2010), p. 52.
7   Fritz Stern, *The Failure of Illiberalism: Essays on the Political Culture of Modern Germany* (New York and Oxford: Columbia UP, 1955; republished with a new preface, 1992), p. xxvi.

of culture as something apart that 'became the rhetoric with which the unpolitical German denounced the mass society, democracy, liberalism and modernity of the Weimar Republic'.[8] As the Nazis tightened their grip on all aspects of cultural life through the process of co-ordination (*Gleichschaltung*), Furtwängler became inextricably caught in the tangled web of interconnecting threads that bound the grand Austro-German musical tradition to conservative cultural ideology; by consistently claiming that art was 'non-political' and above politics, he effectively politicised art. As we shall see, despite undisputed acts of heroism regarding the Third Reich, often at no small risk to himself, any claim that he was some kind of Parsifal-like innocent abroad, caught dangling in the cross-winds of history, does not stand up to scrutiny.[9] His retreat into diffuse speculation and the supra-rational elevation of experience over thought links him to a culture that, although ostensibly non-political, needs a 'carapace of power to shelter it from politics'.[10] This protection was provided not by democracy but by an 'illiberal' authoritarianism that was to find its most extreme form in Nazi Germany. Yet just as it is tempting to dismiss the claim of Furtwängler the 'unpolitical' as unsupportable, it is equally too easy to categorise him as one of the educated 'illiberal' Germans who was by inclination anti-democratic and therefore helped to create the political climate in which Nazism established itself. No single template fits so complex and self-contradictory an individual; hence the importance of a study that neither takes, nor attempts to take, uncritical admiration or, worse still, moral censure as a frame of reference.

The period between the proclamation of the empire in 1871 and the turn of the century saw profound shifts in the social and economic structures of the emerging German nation state.[11] Wilhelmine society was highly complex and is not easily understood in terms of pre-constructed historical models retrospectively applied. In any case, Wilhelm Furtwängler was exceptional in that he was possessed of creative ability of an high order; to that extent he stands apart and resists definition. It can be tendentious, not to say misleading, to apply a conceptual template where convenient as a means of identifying conservative-nationalist ideologies that led inexorably towards the rise of Nazism. In the case of a figure such as Furtwängler there is the additional temptation of allowing his high-profile position in the Third Reich

8   Ibid., p. 18. See also Richard Evans, ed., *Society and Politics in Wilhelmine Germany* (London: Croom Helm Ltd, 1978), p. 115.
9   See e.g. Hans-Hubert Schönzeler, *Furtwängler* (London: Duckworth, 1990), p. 69.
10 Roy Pascal, *From Naturalism to Expressionism: German Literature and Society 1880–1918* (London: Weidenfeld & Nicolson, 1973), p. 115.
11 See Evans, ed., *Society and Politics in Wilhelmine Germany*, esp. Introduction and Ch. 5.

to shape the historiography of the study. The reality, as we shall see, was much more complicated.

As the writer Alan Bennett has observed, 'there is no period so remote as the recent past'; yet it is on these constantly shifting historical sands of the recent past that we have to attempt to understand Furtwängler.[12] Anything to do with Furtwängler defies simple answers; his contradictions and ambiguities reflect the dark labyrinth of a complex epoch in European history that is as yet imperfectly understood. It is enormously difficult to revisit the Germany of the late Wilhelmine Empire and the Weimar Republic from the standpoint of the early twenty-first century, since everything is refracted through the prism of 1933–45 and weighted with a sense of post-Holocaust unease. This can all too easily result in a skewed historiography that distorts figures such as Furtwängler. As with his close contemporary Richard Strauss, so much critical discussion of Furtwängler has been, and in many respects still is, dominated by the blunt question of to what extent he was or was not a Nazi sympathiser.[13]

The challenge facing the writer on Furtwängler is above all to aid understanding. To cite Richard Evans once again: 'If the experience of the Third Reich teaches us anything, it is that a love of great music, art and literature does not provide immunisation against violence, atrocity or subservience to dictatorship.'[14] What follows will therefore consider Wilhelm Furtwängler within the historical context of the times in which he lived and worked. It is essentially a study of his thought and practice through examination of primary sources rather than a life and times narrative; it will give only as much biographical information as is necessary to track his career as one of the most significant and influential executive musicians of his own or any other day. It is essentially a study of the politics of the unpolitical: how the avowedly apolitical artist, who unquestionably did a great deal to resist the more blatant excesses of the Nazis, was in his public and private utterances a protagonist of the strongly conservative, anti-democratic, supra-rational world-view which in its most extreme and perverted form was so intertwined with and inseparable from the official ideology of a totalitarian regime.[15]

12 See Alan Bennett, *The History Boys* (London: Faber & Faber, 2004), p. 74.
13 See Pamela Potter, 'Strauss and the National Socialists: The Debate and its Relevance', in Bryan Gilliam, ed., *Richard Strauss: New Perspectives on the Composer and his Work* (Durham, NC: Duke UP, 1992), pp. 93–113.
14 Evans, *The Coming of the Third Reich*, p. xxiii.
15 The term supra-rational is used here and throughout in the sense of a world-view that transcends or achieves a higher rationality rather than ideas of the non-rational or irrational. In *Doktor Faustus* Thomas Mann writes of the 'Sphäre das Dämonische und Widervernünftige' (Stockholm: Fischer Verlag, 1947, p. 9). 'Widervernünftige' is especially difficult to translate into English. H. T. Lowe-Porter (*Doctor Faustus*

Furtwängler's significance is that he was a meeting point for so many strands in German culture. Therefore the present study is offered in the hope that it may go some way towards establishing him as a historical figure that, like the fictitious Adrian Leverkühn in Thomas Mann's novel *Doctor Faustus*, may be studied not simply as a Nazi or a non-Nazi but as a representative educated German. The reference in the title to Thomas Mann's early *Reflections of a Non-Political Man* (*Betrachtungen eines Unpolitischen*) is intentional.[16] At the time of World War I Mann and Furtwängler shared a good deal of common intellectual ground; however, when the Nazis came to power in 1933, as a comparison between their respective public addresses on Brahms and Wagner shows, they were beginning to diverge. In the post-World War II years Furtwängler's formal and private utterances are full of pleas for a return to the Wilhelmine culture and artistic values of nineteenth-century *Bildung*, while Mann, in *Doctor Faustus*, provides an all-too-clear analysis of the destructive forces latent in that very culture for which Furtwängler was such an impassioned and persuasive advocate. We might ask, as did the writer Neville Cardus, to what extent is it true to describe Wilhelm Furtwängler as a 'Faust who lacked the ironic corrective of a Mephistopheles'?;[17] or as Mephisto puts it in his ironic description of himself in Goethe's *Faust*, Part I: 'Part of the Power which would constantly do evil, and constantly does good.'[18]

(London: Martin Secker & Warburg, 1949), p. 4) renders it as 'irrational', but there's a suggestion in the 'wider' of willed perversity, of gloating defiance, that neither 'irrational', 'non-rational' or 'supra-rational' can quite capture. I am grateful to Kevin Hilliard for clarification of this point.

16 Thomas Mann, *Betrachtungen eines Unpolitischen* (1918); Eng. edn, *Reflections of a Nonpolitical Man*.

17 Neville Cardus, *Full Score* (Cassell: London, 1970), p. 141.

18 Goethe, *Faust*, Part I, lines 1335–6. This is in itself an ironic reference to Romans Ch. VII, v. 21 'when I would do good, evil is present within me' (King James Bible, 1611).

CHAPTER 1

WILHELM FURTWÄNGLER: THE HISTORICAL, CULTURAL AND INTELLECTUAL BACKGROUND

'The Germans', said the new undergraduate, a grass blade in his mouth, 'have a two-track mind and an inexcusable habit of combination; they always want one thing and the other, they want to have it both ways. They are capable of turning out great personalities with antithetic principles of thought and life. But then they muddle them, using the coinage of the one in the sense of the other; mixing everything all up and thinking they can put freedom and aristocracy, idealism and natural childlikeness under one hat. But that probably does not do.'[1]

The Historical Background

At the time of Wilhelm Furtwängler's birth on 25 January 1886 the newly founded Second German Reich was in the process of consolidating its national identity and sense of purpose under the leadership of Kaiser Wilhelm I and Chancellor Otto von Bismarck. The increasing wealth and power of the capitalist state was a result of rapid industrialisation and internal expansion that in turn encouraged a corresponding increase in the domestic population and a growth in the size of important urban centres. In this *Gründerzeit* (the period which saw the foundation and growth of the German state following the proclamation of the empire in 1871) the complementary spheres of finance and industry merged and the state became the central organ of the economy. Capitalists, financiers and merchants determined the economic life of the nation, but as yet the business of government remained in the hands of the pre-capitalist and economically declining aristocracy, the Prussian 'Junkers', or land-owning nobility who maintained an almost

1   Thomas Mann, *Doctor Faustus*, p. 84.

feudal system of management of large estates in the north-eastern provinces. The commercially minded middle class had gained in influence as a result of growth and expansion, but within this social and economic group the educated and intellectually gifted, or *Bildungsbürger*, occupied a privileged position: in spite of the prevailing materialistic outlook the tradition of respect for the scholar which resonated from Germany's pre-industrial past, the age of Kant, Wilhelm and Alexander von Humboldt, and Hegel, lived on.

Wilhelm Furtwängler belonged to what might broadly be termed the *Bildungsbürger*, or educated upper middle classes of Wilhelmine Germany. In order to understand the culture that formed him, it is important to draw a distinction between the *Bildungsbürger* and the catch-all generic term most commonly used to describe the middle classes: the bourgeoisie. According to Marxist thought, the bourgeoisie was a nineteenth-century social phenomenon that came to prominence as a result of the rapid industrialisation and commercial expansion of post-unification Germany. As a social grouping the bourgeoisie was primarily concerned with commercialism, property and industrial production as a means of generating wealth. In contrast the predominantly Protestant *Bildungsbürger* were of earlier, pre-industrial origin and defined more by education and culture than economic status.[2] The idea that individual potential was best realised through a classical education, or *Bildung*, was derived from Enlightenment thought. As Klaus Vondung puts it, 'to the *Bildungsbürger*, Bildung ultimately appeared to be the immortal gift of Kant, Humboldt, Fichte, Schelling, Hegel, of Goethe and Schiller, in order that the concept of the perfectibility of mankind might be made apparent'.[3] Education was an organic process in the sense that the individual is in a state of continuous development. By the time of the Wilhelmine era characteristics that could be associated with *Bildungsbürgertum* included an academic education, social exclusivity and a quasi-aristocratic thinking that generated a sense of cultural elitism. The *Bildungsbürger* were well represented in academic life. As will become apparent, Professor Adolf Furtwängler's eminence in the field of classical archaeology and his decision to educate his son Wilhelm apart from others in

2   There is no satisfactory English equivalent of the German terms *Bildung* and *Bildungsbürger*. They have much deeper cultural resonances than can be rendered by the terms 'education' and 'educated middle classes'. The terms have therefore been left untranslated.

3   Klaus Vondung, ed., *Das wilhelminische Bildungsbürgertum: Zur Sozialgeschichte seiner Ideen* (Göttingen: Vandenhoek & Ruprecht, 1918), p. 36. See especially Michael Naumann, 'Bildung und Gehorsam: Zur ästhetischen Ideologie des Bildungsbürgertums', pp. 34–52.

order to enhance his sense of intellectual superiority, not to say exclusivity, is strongly *Bildungsbürgerlich* in intent.

The importance of this cultural background and tradition of education in nurturing Wilhelm Furtwängler cannot be overestimated; the rich tradition of *Bildung* provided him with the mental furnishings that were to shape his thought and nourish his artistic achievements. Goethe, Schiller and the traditions of Weimar Classicism were as central to his existence as Bach and Beethoven: Goethe's *Faust* was as deeply embedded in his world-view as Beethoven's Ninth Symphony. Literature contemporary with Furtwängler also provides instructive additional perspectives on his origin and background. One of the themes running through the later chapters of Thomas Mann's early novel *Buddenbrooks* (1901), subtitled *The Decline of a Family*, is the growing tension between the mercantile class of the bourgeoisie and pre-industrial *Bildungsbürgerlich* values. Mann describes the eponymous Thomas Buddenbrook as 'a merchant, not a scholar. He had not completed a classical *Gymnasium* course, he was not a lawyer and above all had not received an academic education.'[4] In the case of the Buddenbrook family, the materialism of the commercially minded *haute bourgeoisie* is gradually challenged by the traditions of the *Bildungsbürger* introduced through Senator Thomas Buddenbrook's marriage to the cultivated and musical Gerda. In contrast to the scholarly Professor Adolf Furtwängler, the patrician Senator Thomas Buddenbrook is determined that commercial values should prevail. It was his intention that his musically inclined and rather delicate son Hanno, heir to the business, was to be a merchant: Hanno does not therefore receive a classical education at the *Gymnasium*; his father 'was convinced he was doing the boy a kindness in relieving him of the unnecessary Greek'.[5] Another way of understanding this distinction between the traditions of *Bildung* and the commercialism of the bourgeoisie is through the differentiation made in contemporaneous political thought between community and civil society, or *Gemeinschaft* and *Gesellschaft*. *Gemeinschaft* is a community formed through an organic process deeply rooted in culture and tradition; *Gesellschaft* is civil society based on materialism and commerce. As the political theorist Ferdinand Tönnies puts it in Book 1 of his influential treatise *Gemeinschaft und Gesellschaft*, first published in 1887, a year after Wilhelm Furtwängler's birth, '*Gemeinschaft* must be understood as a living organism in its own right, while *Gesellschaft* is a mechanical aggregate and artefact.'[6]

---

4   Thomas Mann, *Buddenbrooks*, Eng. tr. by H. T. Lowe-Porter (London: Secker & Warburg, 1924), p. 494 (translation modified).
5   Ibid., p. 500.
6   Ferdinand Tönnies, *Gemeinschaft und Gesellschaft*; Eng. edn, *Community and Civil Society*, tr. and ed. Jose Harris and Margaret Hollis (Cambridge: CUP, 2001), p. 19.

On 9 March 1888 the venerable figurehead of German unification, Kaiser Wilhelm I, died, to be succeeded briefly by his son, the terminally ill Friedrich III. Friedrich's death on 16 June of the same year made way for the young, egotistical and impulsive Wilhelm II. Wilhelm's subsequent dismissal of Bismarck in 1890 resulted in a change of mood among many of the educated middle classes: the architect of the German Empire was gone; the sense of pride in the achievements of the 1870s in creating a unified state gave way to growing dissatisfaction at what was regarded as an accelerating cultural decline resulting from economic expansion. In 1893 the sociologist Max Weber gave his inaugural address at the University of Heidelberg in which he offered a penetrating analysis of the state of German society of the time: 'It is not peace and human happiness that we have to bequeath to our descendants but the preservation and cultivation of our national peculiarity ... the social unification of our nation that modern economic development has blasted asunder.'[7] But Weber considered the middle classes as yet unready to lead the state: they were politically immature, having been kept too long in waiting during the long years of Bismarck's rule. Two years later in 1895, now newly appointed Professor of Sociology at the University of Freiburg, Weber again wrote:

Part of the upper middle class longs only too obviously for the appearance of a new Cæsar who will protect it against the emergence of classes from below, and from above against social and political impulses of which they suspect the German dynasties.[8]

Economic expansion also had a lasting effect on late-nineteenth-century musical culture. The development of the commercial aspects of music, as exemplified by the rise of the publishing industry, played a leading role in transforming not only the economic foundation of musical life but also the nature of musical taste. By the mid nineteenth century the growing distrust of the cult of virtuosity and anything resembling mode or fashion had fully transformed music into a 'high' art. Influenced both by the Beethoven paradigm and the increasing use of the organic metaphor as a measure of artistic worth, this tendentious form of romantic idealism venerated the pantheon of Austro-German composers from Bach to Beethoven, against whose music all new works should be judged.

7   Quoted in Peter Pulzer, *Germany, 1870–1945: Politics, State Formation and War* (Oxford: OUP, 1997), pp. 50–1.
8   See Golo Mann, *Deutsche Geschichte des 19. und 20. Jahrhunderts* (1958); Eng. edn, *The History of Germany Since 1789*, tr. Marian Jackson (London: Chatto & Windus, 1968; pbk reprint, 1996), pp. 208–9.

The Austro-German Canon

The emergence of the canon of Austro-German musical masterworks in the early years of the nineteenth century was to some extent a result of a process of dislocation implying the gradual disappearance of the social contexts in which the canonical 'works' had been created.[9] Music thus became a non-social, metaphysical phenomenon, its 'meaning' transferred from a specifically representational external to a non-representational internal function. This idea, described by Carl Dahlhaus as the 'Metaphysic of Instrumental Music' and Lydia Goehr as the 'Separability Principle', shaped the perception and reception of the canon for much of the nineteenth and the early part of the twentieth century.[10] Wilhelm Furtwängler was to be one of its most persuasive protagonists.

One of the earliest works to hold an undisputed place in the canon was to be of central importance to Furtwängler: J. S. Bach's *Matthäus Passion*, famously 'rediscovered' by Mendelssohn in 1829 and relocated from a liturgical to a secular context. Such dislocations intensified the process by which musical artworks began to acquire iconic properties. However, this lofty example of Lutheran theology, realised in a large-scale musical design of complex instrumental textures and grand chorale fantasias, was something of an exception: the genre which most naturally served as the gravitational centre of the canon was that of the instrumental symphony and of chamber and solo works governed by the dialectic of the sonata principle. The emergence of the canon was paralleled by a corresponding shift in educated æsthetic perception away from the desire for artistic experience as a 'reflection of inner emotion' to the concept of the autonomous musical object as a phenomenon which existed entirely by virtue of its own internal musical logic; the musical object as a paradigm of Kant's 'thing-in-itself', yet knowable through experience *a posteriori*. The elevation of the musical object to the status of a work of fine art further increased its standing. In Hegel's view a work of fine art 'cuts itself free from any servitude in order to raise itself to the truth which it fulfils independently and conformably with its own ends alone. In this freedom is fine art truly art.'[11] Thus the concept

---

9   For a fuller discussion of this point, see Susan McClary, 'The Blasphemy of Talking Politics in the Bach Year', in Richard Leppert and Susan McClary, eds, *Music and Society* (Cambridge: CUP, 1987), pp. 13–62.
10 Carl Dahlhaus, *Die Musik des 19. Jahrhunderts* (1980); Eng. edn, *Nineteenth-Century Music*, tr. J. Bradford Robinson (Berkeley; London: University of California Press, 1989), pp. 88–96.
11 Quoted in Lydia Goehr, *The Imaginary Museum of Musical Works* (Oxford: Clarendon Press, 1992), p. 158; citing Hegel, *Æsthetics: Lectures on Fine Art*, tr. T. M. Knox (Oxford: OUP, 1975), vol. I, p. 7.

of the autonomous musical process came into being, the essence of which was to be found in absolute instrumental music, divorced from text and existing for its own sake and on its own terms. This stage in the development of the æsthetic perception of the artwork is cogently summarised by Carl Dahlhaus: 'In highbrow æsthetics – which thereby moved away from popular æsthetics – sensibility and the search for feeling gave way to a metaphysic based on Edmund Burke's and Immanuel Kant's theory of the Sublime in order to do justice to absolute instrumental music and to capture in words the æsthetic experience of the listener.'[12] As E. T. A. Hoffmann wrote in his essay on 'Beethoven's Instrumental Music' (1813), music 'is the most romantic of all the arts – one might almost say, the only genuinely romantic one – for its sole subject is the Infinite'.[13]

Hoffmann's central claim is that music belongs in the domain of the infinite; the autonomous musical artwork is therefore capable of transcending the commonplace and penetrating the realm of the ideal. This supra-rational quality of transcendence attributed to the musical work of fine art enabled it to go beyond the worldly and particular to the spiritual and universal.[14] Theoretically, the domain of the infinite, to which music gave access, had nothing in common with the external world of the senses. It therefore followed that the significance of the musical artwork lay not so much in its capacity to evoke an emotional response or represent worldly phenomena but rather in its ability to explore and reveal a higher world. Instrumental music, with its lack of particularised content, assumed the mantle of the genre best suited to transcend the particular and specific.

At the same time the elevation of the musical object from contextualised commodity to the status of a fine art engendered a parallel shift in the perception of the creative artist. The musical artwork capable of penetrating the domain of the infinite could only come into being through the operation of a more powerful agency than the activities of a self-contained human agent. The creator of the fine artwork became an idealised figure whose creations mirrored divinely inspired order and truth. A starting point for this process is arguably the publication in 1802 of Johann Nikolaus Forkel's biography of J. S. Bach. In his exordium to his work he wrote:

> Bach united with his great and lofty style the most refined elegance and the greatest precision in the single parts that compose the great whole. He

---

12 Dahlhaus, *Nineteenth-Century Music*, p. 89.
13 Oliver Strunk, *Source Readings in Music History* (New York; London: W. Norton, 1998), p. 755.
14 For an exegesis of the concept of musical transcendence, see Dahlhaus, *Nineteenth-Century Music*, pp. 88–96.

thought the whole could not be perfect if anything were wanting to the
perfect precision of the single parts; and this man, the greatest musical poet
and the greatest musical orator that ever existed, and probably ever will
exist, was a German. Let his country be proud of him; let it be proud but at
the same time, worthy of him![15]

The historical and ideological reception of Bach in the nineteenth century
is described by Carl Dahlhaus as 'one of the central processes in the history
of nineteenth-century music'.[16] In 1850 the Bach Gesellschaft had been
founded with the objective of publishing a complete critical edition of the
works of J. S. Bach (*Vollständige kritische Ausgabe aller Werke Johann Sebastian
Bachs*) in commemoration of the first centenary of the composer's death.
In 1880, six years before Furtwängler's birth, the musicologist Philip Spitta
published the final volume of his Bach biography, and during the Wilhelmine
and Weimar years interest in Bach intensified as part of the newly unified
Germany's search for a cohesive cultural identity.

The canonisation of Bach by Forkel and his successors and the elevation
of the Beethoven symphony into the *opus metaphysicum* of high art represent
two of the cornerstones of the emergent canon. As the century progressed this
association of ideas became increasingly volatile and the concept of musical
autonomy, with its associated qualities of metaphysical transcendence,
diverged into two broadly parallel streams. On the one hand the formalists
rejected the idea that music encoded and referred to things outside itself. The
content of a musical work consisted purely of a series of tonally moving forms
(tönend bewegte Formen). The æsthetic object (form) became apparent
through the operation of the musical process (content). Such was the position
defined by Eduard Hanslick in *On the Musically Beautiful* (*Vom Musikalisch-
Schönen*, 1854).[17] On the other hand there was the Schopenhauerian idea that
music symbolised or even expressed the Will whose ceaseless Becoming had
ultimately to be overcome. Schopenhauer's 'ideal' is the ultimate denial of
the Will. This concept permeates Wagner's later works, most notably *Tristan*

15 J. N. Forkel, 'On Johann Sebastian Bach's Life, Genius and Works', *The Bach Reader*,
    ed. Hans T. David and Arthur Mendel (New York: W. Norton, 1945), pp. 352–3. See
    also Bernd Sponheur, 'Reconstructing Ideal Types of the "German" in Music', in
    Celia Applegate and Pamela Potter, eds, *Music and German National Identity* (Chicago
    and London: University of Chicago Press, 2003), pp. 36–58, here pp. 48–52.
16 Dahlhaus, *Nineteenth-Century Music*, pp. 30–1.
17 'Tonally moving forms' is the English translation of Hanslick's phrase in common use:
    see Eduard Hanslick, *On the Musically Beautiful*, tr. Geoffrey Payzant (Indianapolis:
    Hackett Publishing Company, 1986), p. 29. An alternative is 'forms moving through
    sound', which is perhaps closer to Hanslick's meaning. See Bojan Bujić, ed., *Music in
    European Thought* (Cambridge: CUP, 1988), pp. 11–39.

und Isolde (1859), and was to find its most articulate and persuasive literary protagonist in the young Friedrich Nietzsche who in *The Birth of Tragedy* (*Die Geburt der Tragödie*, 1872) defined the polarity of the Apolline and Dionysian as an allegory of the tension of form and content.

Wagnerian Thought and Practice

In the last quarter of the nineteenth century the increasing influence of Wagnerian thought and practice became ever more apparent. Wagner's ideas on the art of symphonic and operatic performance profoundly influenced the practice of the late nineteenth and early twentieth centuries. In 1865 he submitted a report to Ludwig II of Bavaria outlining his proposals for the establishment of a music school in Munich in which he expressed his thoughts on the current state of musical education and performance in Germany:

> We possess classical works but we are not in possession of a classical style for the execution of these works. Does Germany possess a school at which the proper execution of Mozart's music is taught? Or do our orchestras and their conductors manage to play Mozart in accordance with some occult knowledge of their own? If so whence do they derive such knowledge? Who taught them it?[18]

The establishment of such an institution would have given Wagner an ideal medium through which to disseminate his ideals of performance. In his essay 'The Case of Wagner, freely after Nietzsche' ('Der Fall Wagner, frei nach Nietzsche', 1941), Furtwängler laments the fact that the project never came to fruition. 'It never became possible to found a conservatoire under his directorship – an undertaking which would have made no great demands on state funds and would have brought incalculable benefits to the musical life of Germany.'[19] In the essay 'On Conducting' (Über das Dirigiren, 1869) Furtwängler believed that Wagner had laid down the principles of the art of interpretation; in particular the comprehension of 'melos' by the conductor is the sole guide to the correct tempo:

18 Richard Wagner, 'Bericht an Seine Majestät den König Ludwig II von Bayern über eine in München zu errichtende deutsche Musikschule', in GSD, vol. 8, pp. 125–76; Eng. edn, 'A Music School for Munich', PW, vol. 4, pp. 171–224. See also 'On Conducting', tr. Edward Dannreuther (London: William Reeves, 1887), Appendix A, p. 109.
19 See Furtwängler, TW, pp. 123–4; Eng. edn, FM, p. 67.

The right comprehension of the *melos* is the sole guide to the right tempo; these two things are inseparable: the one implies and qualifies the other [...]. The whole duty of a conductor is comprised in his ability always to indicate the right tempo. His choice of tempo will show whether he understands the piece or not. With good players, again, the true tempo induces correct phrasing and expression, and conversely, with a conductor the idea of appropriate phrasing and expression will induce the conception of the true tempo.[20]

Foremost among the artists who were initially responsible for the promulgation of Wagner's ideas on matters of performance practice, and in particular the reception of the musical artwork, was Hans von Bülow (1830–94).[21] Bülow, who conducted the first performances of *Tristan und Isolde* (1865) and *Die Meistersinger von Nürnberg* (1868), eventually broke with Wagner following the composer's well-publicised affair with and subsequent marriage to his wife Cosima; but he continued to exert a pioneering influence as one of the foremost executive musicians of his time. Between 1880 and 1885 he transformed the provincial Meiningen orchestra into a world-renowned ensemble; on 21 October 1887 he gave the first of a series of concerts with the recently formed Berlin Philharmonic Orchestra that was to establish this fledgling ensemble as the 'benchmark orchestra of the greater Germany'.[22] In his book *Das Berliner Philharmonische Orchester* the historian Werner Oehlmann writes:

> With the first Philharmonic concert of the 1887/88 season, which took place on Friday 21 October 1887 and included Haydn's Symphony No. 102 in B flat, Mozart's *Jupiter* and Beethoven's *Eroica* Symphonies, it was clear that a new epoch, not only for the Philharmonic Orchestra but for Berlin's concert life in particular and [the art of] symphonic interpretation in general, had begun.[23]

As a result of his estrangement from Wagner and his circle Bülow played no part in bringing the later operas before the public; his activities in Meiningen and Berlin were principally concerned with symphonic music and he became a fervent champion of Brahms. Nevertheless, there were others who were only too willing to carry the Wagnerian banner; the composer's ideas on

20 Richard Wagner, 'Über das Dirigiren', in GSD, vol. 8, pp. 274–5; Eng. edn, 'On Conducting', in PW, vol. 4, pp. 303–4. Cited here from 'On Conducting', tr. E. Dannreuther (London: William Reeves, 1887), p. 20.
21 See Alan Walker, *Hans von Bülow: A Life and Times* (New York: OUP, 2010); Kenneth Birkin, *Hans von Bülow: A Life for Music* (Cambridge: CUP, 2011).
22 See Norman Lebrecht, *When the Music Stops* (London: Simon & Schuster, 1996), p. 63.
23 Werner Oehlmann, *Das Berliner Philharmonische Orchester* (Kassel: Bärenreiter Verlag, 1974), p. 28.

performance practice and the presentation of classical music were further disseminated by the school of executant musicians which emerged from the musical powerhouse created by the foundation of Bayreuth and influenced by principles of interpretation outlined by Wagner in 'On Conducting', such as fluctuating tempo, expressive rubato and a creative approach to the printed score. Hans Richter (1843–1916), Anton Seidl (1850–98) and Felix Mottl (1856–1911) were among those who formed the 'Nibelungen Chancellery' ('Nibelungen Kanzlei'), the collective name given to the group of musicians who assisted Wagner at the festivals of 1876 and 1882.

The first important musical gathering at Bayreuth had taken place on 22 May 1872 when Wagner marked the occasion of the laying of the foundation stone of his Festival Theatre (Festspielhaus) by personally conducting a performance of Beethoven's Ninth Symphony given by the elite of Germany's musicians. Among the orchestral violinists on this occasion was the young Arthur Nikisch (1855–1922), the charismatic figure who was to become the first 'star' conductor in the modern sense of the term and to whose position as undisputed leader of the German musical establishment Wilhelm Furtwängler was to succeed in 1922. Nikisch toured with the impresario Angelo Neumann and took part in the early performances of Wagner's *Ring* in important European cultural centres. After a period as director of the Boston Symphony Orchestra from 1889 to 1893 he returned to Europe as director of the Budapest Opera (1893–95) in succession to his younger colleague Gustav Mahler, and in 1895 he became director of the Leipzig Gewandhaus concerts, a post which he held in conjunction with that of chief conductor of the Berlin Philharmonic Orchestra until his death in 1922. Furtwängler heard Nikisch conduct in Hamburg in 1912 and from that point on became a member of the Nikisch circle, regularly attending his after-concert suppers. He revered him as his artistic mentor and greatly admired his powers of musical expression and control over an orchestra. In the essay 'The Tools of the Conductor's Trade' (1937) he wrote:

> I was able to observe at first hand the secret of the power of Arthur Nikisch. He could make an orchestra sing – an extremely rare gift. This quality was not confined to comparatively straightforward contexts where the music consisted of broad, sweeping melodies. In classical music it also permeated the infinite variety of phrases where the unbroken vocal line – the 'melos', as Wagner called it, – constantly changed its position and its pitch, moving from one orchestral part to another, often within one and the same bar. The 'melos' remains as important as ever for grasping the meaning of the work in question but its thousand different disguises make it the more difficult to recognise.[24]

---

24 'Vom Handwerkszeug des Dirigenten', VMS, pp. 97–106; Eng. edn, 'The Tools of the Conductor's Trade', FM, pp. 16–22.

When Furtwängler became Chief Conductor of the Berlin Philharmonic Orchestra he inherited the artistic mantle of both Nikisch and Bülow: he thus became the legatee of an artistic tradition which originated with Wagner himself and was closely associated with the practices and influence of Bayreuth.

Wagner's ideas were also to have a profound and long-lasting effect in the political sphere in which Furtwängler moved and worked. By the early 1870s the original idea of a democratic festival, conceived in the aftermath of the failed revolutions of 1848–49, had become an impossibility in the changed political and economic circumstances of Bismarck's post-unification German Reich. Wagner's dream of an ideal, non-political German art, the 'heil'ge deutsche Kunst' of *Die Meistersinger*, that transcended politics, was a powerful boost to the notion of a German *Sonderweg*, or special path, rooted in the supra-rational ideology of romanticism and nourished by the growing tide of conservative anti-modernity.[25] Wagner's voluminous and abstruse political writings were a compendious source of *völkisch* or *Gemeinschaft* ideologies that were considered particularly German.[26] From the first festival in 1876 and the continuation from 1882 onwards Bayreuth became not only an artistic magnet but also an ideologically charged summer meeting place for the old ruling elites. After Wagner's death the cultural conservatism of Bayreuth hardened inexorably into a strongly anti-democratic, reactionary ideology promulgated largely by the group that gathered around Wagner's widow. Prominent among this 'Bayreuth Circle' were two of Cosima Wagner's sons-in-law, the art historian Henry Thode, who married Daniela von Bülow, and the English-born author and Germanophile Houston Stewart Chamberlain (1855–1927), husband of Eva Wagner. Chamberlain's writings in particular were to prove a powerful means of disseminating conservative-nationalist ideologies.[27]

25 For more on the idea of *Sonderweg*, see Bernd Sponheur in *Music and German National Identity*, pp. 52–6.
26 See Ernst Hanisch, 'The Political Influence and Appropriation of Wagner', in Ulrich Müller, Peter Wapnewski and John Deathridge, eds, *The Wagner Handbook* (London and Cambridge MA: Harvard UP, 1992), pp. 186–201, here p. 191.
27 See Houston Stewart Chamberlain, *Politische Ideale* (München: F. Bruckmann, 1915). Also Saul Friedländer, *Nazi Germany and the Jews: The Years of Persecution 1933–39* (London: Weidenfeld & Nicolson, 1997), pp. 89–90; Roger Allen, entries on The Bayreuth Circle (pp. 34–5) and Houston Stewart Chamberlain (pp. 78–80) in Nicholas Vazsonyi, ed., *The Cambridge Wagner Encyclopedia* (Cambridge: CUP, 2013).

The Organic Metaphor and the Idea of the 'Whole'

Then they have the parts and they've lost the whole,
For the link that's missing was the living soul.[28]

As with Furtwängler, Chamberlain's world-view was increasingly expressed in organic terms. This construct, based on notions of organic growth, was an important metaphor for the philosophy of history and the nature of society in nineteenth-century Germany. Moreover, as the century progressed the 'organic' and the idea of the 'whole' increasingly became ideologically charged expressions in what Nicholas Cook succinctly describes as the 'classic idiom of cultural conservatism'.[29] In its nineteenth-century guise it developed from the ideas first articulated by Johann Gottfried Herder (1744–1803) and continued by Goethe and Hegel. Herder expressed his 'organic' vision of history and society in metaphors of the natural world, which in turn exercised a strong influence on Goethe in the development of his scientific theory.[30] The organic world-view perceives society and its characteristic products 'in terms of the biological metaphor of a living organism'.[31] The process of growth takes place through time; the component parts of the organism depend upon one another; the individual parts are therefore inter-dependent and functionally interrelated. In Hegel's view the organic unity of a musical work is a measure of value and artistic worth. In his influential Lectures on Aesthetics he writes:

If the work is a genuine work of art, the more exact the detail [and] the greater the unity of the whole. [...] Inner organization and overall coherence are equally essential in music, because each part depends on the existence of others.[32]

28 Goethe, *Faust*, Part I, lines 1938–9, tr. David Luke.
29 Nicholas Cook, *The Schenker Project* (New York: OUP 2007), p. 187.
30 See David L. Montgomery, 'The Myth of Organicism: From Bad Science to Great Art', in *The Musical Quarterly*, vol. 76 (1992), pp. 17–66. See also G. W. F. Hegel, *Grundlinien der Philosophie des Rechts* (1821); Eng. edn, *Philosophy of Right*, tr. S. W. Dyde (London: G. Bell, 1896; pbk reprint, New York, 1996), pp. 240–350. In Hegel's complex view of history, organic society, or *Volksgeist*, is thought to have a life of its own. 'In that direction lies totalitarianism and racism': R. S. Downey in Ted Honderich, ed., *The Oxford Companion to Philosophy* (Oxford: OUP, 1995), p. 636; also Peter Singer, *Hegel* (Oxford: OUP Past Masters, 1983), pp. 42–3.
31 *Oxford Companion to Philosophy*, p. 636.
32 Cited in Le Huray and Day, *Music Aesthetics in the Eighteenth and Early-Nineteenth Centuries* (Cambridge: CUP, 1981), p. 227.

The idea of the 'whole' entered political discourse in the *Addresses to the German Nation* delivered between 1807 and 1808 at the newly founded university of Berlin by Johann Gottlieb Fichte (1762–1814). Fichte's rhetoric was influential in the growth of a sense of national identity as a response to the Napoleonic occupation of German lands. In the thirteenth address he declared that: 'Those who speak the same language are linked together [...]; they understand each other and are capable of communicating more and more closely with one another, they belong together, they are by nature one indivisible whole.'[33] Hegel expanded this theoretical metaphor into an applied political philosophy where the microcosm of the individual functions as a component part of the macrocosm of the state. In *The Philosophy of Right* (*Grundlinien der Philosophie des Rechts*, 1821) he writes: 'This substantive unity is its own motive and absolute end. In this end freedom attains its highest right. This end has the highest right over the individual, whose highest duty in turn is to be a member of the State.'[34] At the other end of the century, in the seminal work of political thought, *Community and Civil Society* (*Gemeinschaft und Gesellschaft*, 1887), Ferdinand Tönnies describes 'the whole as not merely the sum of its parts; on the contrary the parts are dependent on and conditioned by the whole, so that the whole possesses intrinsic reality and substance'.[35]

The idea of the 'whole' and of organic growth was central to Wagner's conception of drama, and especially that of the *Ring*. In the third part of the treatise *Opera and Drama* (1851) he describes the genuine drama as 'an organic Being [organisch Seiendes] and Becoming [Werdendes], evolving and shaping itself from inner necessity'.[36] In the justly famous letter to Liszt of 20 November 1851, in which he outlines the development of the entire *Ring* from its initial conception in 1848 to the eventual formulation of the four-opera design, Wagner writes 'every unbiased human feeling must be able to grasp *the whole* through its faculties of artistic perception, because only then can it properly absorb the least detail'.[37] In Furtwängler's thought, his organic world-view was literary in origin and most immediately derived from Goethe's natural science as poetically expressed in the poems *The Metamorphosis of Plants* (*Metamorphose der Pflanzen*, 1798), *The Metamorphosis*

33 J. G. Fichte, *Sämmtliche Werke* (Berlin: Veit und Comp., 1845–46), vol. 7, p. 459. See also H. S. Reiss, *Political Thought of the German Romantics 1793–1815* (Oxford: Basil Blackwell, 1955), here p. 102.
34 Hegel, *Philosophy of Right*, p. 240.
35 Tönnies, *Community and Civil Society*, p. 21.
36 GSD, vol 4, p. 204; PW, vol. 2, p. 350.
37 *Selected Letters of Richard Wagner*, tr. Stewart Spencer, ed. Barry Millington (London: J. M. Dent, 1987), p. 237.

of Animals (*Metamorphose der Tiere*, 1798) and in the oracular and well-nigh untranslatable *First and Last Words: Orphic* (*Urworte, Orphisch*, 1817): 'Und keine Zeit und keine Macht zerstückelt / Geprägte Form die Lebend sich entwickelt', roughly paraphrased in translation as 'and no time nor power can destroy the form that has been impressed on evolving life'.[38] For Goethe the human being was a single whole involving both mind and body; nature was a continuously evolving chain of being. In the conversation between Goethe and Eckermann, recorded as having taken place on 20 June 1831, Goethe speaks of a musical work, in this case Mozart's *Don Giovanni*, as:

> a spiritual creation, in which the details as well as the whole, are pervaded by one spirit, and by the breath of one life; so that its creator did not make experiments and patch together and follow his own caprice, but was altogether in the power of the daemonic spirit of his genius, and acted according to orders.

For Furtwängler the concept of the organic is so all-pervading that it can be regarded as an 'idée fixe'; it represents an inflexible constant that formed the foundation of his world-view. Closely associated with the organic is Goethe's notion of the 'daemonic', an idea 'derived from the ancients'.[39] The 'daemonic' has no connotations of the diabolic, as in the English sense of the word: rather it is a numinous, supra-rational force of artistic inspiration that is closely linked to the romantic category of creative genius. The closest English equivalent is to be found in Wordsworth's poem *Lines Composed a Few Miles above Tintern Abbey* (1798): 'A motion and a spirit that impels all thinking things, all objects of all thought, and rolls through all things.' Goethe's *Urworte, Orphisch* has *Dämon* as a superscription in Greek capitals over the first verse. In Book 20 of his autobiography *Dichtung und Wahrheit*, Goethe defines the daemonic as 'a power, not contrary to the moral order of the world athwart it', and the people who incarnate it radiate an 'enormous force' and 'exert unbelievable power over all creatures, even over the elements'.[40] In an earlier conversation with Goethe on 11 March 1828 Eckermann recorded Goethe as saying that 'all artistic certainty can be

---

38 Goethe, *Schriften zur Morphologie*, FA (Frankfurter Ausgabe), vol. 24, pp. 439–40; reprinted with commentary by Goethe in *Ästhetische Schriften 1816–1820*, FA, vol. 20, pp. 492–7. Eng. tr. by David Luke, *Goethe: The Penguin Poets* (Harmondsworth: The Penguin Poets, 1964), pp. 147–54, pp. 302–3.
39 'Dieses Wesen [...] nannte ich dämonisch nach dem Beispiel der Alten' (FA, vol. 14, pp. 839–40). See also Angus Nicholls, *Goethe's Concept of the Daemonic: After the Ancients* (Rochester NY: Camden House 2006), pp. 2–31.
40 FA, vol. 24, p. 841. As cited in Ritchie Robertson, *Goethe: A Very Short Introduction* (Oxford: OUP, 2016), p. 82.

associated with a divine and godlike influence that exists beyond all earthly power and that he [Goethe] sees as being related to the daemonic'.[41] Wagner uses the term in the same sense when he somewhat disparagingly writes in his essay 'On the Application of Music to Drama' (1879) of 'the excesses to which his highly gifted daemon drove Berlioz'.[42]

The Faust Tradition

In common with Goethe, and later Wagner and Nietzsche, a conceptual goal that was to be at the centre of Furtwängler's existence was that of a dialectical fusion of German romantic art with the classical genius of the Greeks. This desire for classical discipline and restraint, symbolised by Goethe in the cultural union of the chronologically disparate cultures of Ancient Greece and modern Germany through the marriage of Faust and Helen in *Faust*, Part II, was embedded in the ideals of *Bildung*. In the *Notebooks* in 1943, Furtwängler writes:

> Goethe says: 'Classical is that which is healthy, Romantic is that which is ill.' I say: A Classicist is one who expresses something clearly and plainly, a Romantic one who does so unclearly, ditheringly and with far too many words. I love Classicists.[43]

If the idea of the organic was an idée fixe in Furtwängler's world-view, then Faustian thought was a leitmotif woven into his discourse that mutated and changed according to need. Faust was a literary icon of powerful symbolic significance in Wilhelmine culture, and, as Alexander Rehding succinctly points out, 'had long been seen as the quintessential "German character"'.[44] The legend first appeared in the *Faustbuch* (Frankfurt, 1587), the creation of an anonymous author who amalgamated magical tales from a variety of sources and assigned them to one Johann Faust, a dilettante who acquired his magic powers by entering into a satanic pact. The *Faustbuch* originated from the final quarter of the sixteenth century, an age of discovery and revival of classical scholarship.[45] The figure of Faust thus embodies the quest for the expansion of knowledge through secular

---

41 Goethe, FA, vol. 39, p. 657.
42 Wagner, GSD, vol. 10, p. 180; PW, vol. 6, p. 179.
43 Furtwängler, AZN, p. 230; Eng. edn, NBKS, p. 141.
44 Alexander Rehding, *Music and Monumentality* (New York: OUP, 2009), p. 170.
45 For a discussion of the literary sources of *Faust*, see Eliza Butler, *The Fortunes of Faust* (Cambridge: CUP, 1952; pbk reprint, Stroud, Gloucs.: Sutton Publishing Ltd, 1998).

enquiry and the emancipation of the individual from institutional demands and prescribed patterns of thought; as such it fired the imagination of the young Goethe (1749–1832) who was preoccupied with the legend for most of his creative life. The sixteenth-century Faust was a disillusioned scholar; Goethe's Faust is a figure of infinitely greater depth and subtlety. Faust seeks both sensory and cognitive apprehension of the underlying principles governing the existence of the universe. He enlists diabolical help in order to extend his personal boundaries and encompass the entire realm of human experience; he has a highly developed capacity for the supra-rational feeling which apprehends the presence of cosmic forces transcending reason. In the posthumously published *Faust*, Part II (1832) Faust becomes a more abstract figure than that of Part I (1808), representative of his own epoch and its search for cultural, scientific and political meaning. Faust is a truth-seeking intellectual with an insatiable desire for knowledge whose search for ideal beauty as represented in the figure of Helen can be seen as analogous to the artist's search for higher knowledge through the creative process: *Faust*, Part II, Act II can in one sense be seen as an exploration of the nature of creative genius as illustrated by the figure of Homunculus in his search for corporeal form.

From the outset *Faust* had been associated with music through settings by composers such as Schubert, Schumann and even the young Wagner.[46] In *The Foundations of the Nineteenth Century* H. S. Chamberlain introduces the musical element of Goethe's *Faust* into the culturally conservative discourse of the Wilhelmine period:

> *Faust* is altogether music; not only because, as Beethoven says, music flows from the words, for this is only true of individual fragments, but because every situation from the *study* to the *chorus mysticus* has, in the fullest sense of the word, been musically conceived.[47]

Wilhelm Furtwängler was to seek Faustian access to higher levels of consciousness through an ever-deepening knowledge of the central canon of German musical works as a performer, composer and writer. His formally composed essays are shot through with resonances of and references to Goethe's *Faust*. For example, in his essay 'Bruckner' (1939) he speaks of 'the

---

46 See Hilda Meldrum Brown, *The Quest for the Gesamtkunstwerk & Richard Wagner* (New York: OUP, 2016), Ch. 3, pp. 59–84.

47 H. S. Chamberlain, *Die Grundlagen des neunzehnten Jahrhunderts* (München: F. Bruckmann, 1899), here 4th edn, 1903, p. 987; Eng. edn, *The Foundations of the Nineteenth Century*, tr. John Lees (London: The Bodley Head, 1910), 2 vols, vol. 2, p. 543.

grey area of theory' (alles ersichtlich graue Theorie), a reference to the scene with the student in *Faust*, Part I: 'Grey, my friend is all theory, and green is the golden tree of life' (Grau, teurer Freund, ist alle Theorie, und grün des Lebens goldner Baum).[48] In an essay dating from the final months of his life, 'All Greatness is Simplicity' (Alles Grosse ist Einfach, 1954) he refers to Goethe sensing in the figure of Faust the presence of 'the daemonic' (das Dämonische) the force that drives each individual towards his preordained destiny.[49] Furtwängler saw his own creative life in these terms. He was imbued with the spirit of Faust: that powerful symbol of *Bildung*, a supra-rational seeker after higher knowledge whose creative life extended into the rational, mechanistic age of the *Neue Sachlichkeit* – or New Objectivity.

The fusion of classic and romantic ideas was no less central to the early work of Friedrich Nietzsche (1844–1900) and in the Wagner-inspired *The Birth of Tragedy* (*Die Geburt der Tragödie*, 1872) he had promulgated the non-rational idea that: 'We shall have gained much for the science of æsthetics when we have succeeded in perceiving directly, and not only through logical reasoning, that art derives its continuous development from the duality of the Dionysiac and the Apolline.'[50] Nietzsche's formulation ultimately derives from the Socratic opposition of 'mythos' and 'logos' and is rich with Faustian resonance.[51] The paradoxes and contradictions in Nietzsche's own character and thought were marked: he disliked romantics yet equally disliked the industrialists and militarists of Imperial Germany; he distrusted German 'profundity' yet lamented the fact that Germany no longer produced profound thinkers.[52] These vacillatory and self-contradictory aspects of his thought were later to be equally characteristic of Furtwängler.

By the end of the century the constant resort to the organic metaphor and ideas of the daemonic were not only indicative of conservative patterns of thought but had become inexorably associated with elements of an increas-ingly tendentious interpretation of Charles Darwin's theory of evolution. This can clearly be seen in, for example, H. S. Chamberlain's study of Goethe (1912), which includes a substantial discussion of the Organic (das Organische) in apposition to the Inorganic (das Anorganische). Chamberlain concludes with what he describes as an indispensable discussion of the

48 TW, p. 118; FM, p. 115.
49 TW, pp. 253–68; FM, pp. 160–8.
50 Friedrich Nietzsche, *Die Geburt der Tragödie* (1872); Eng. edn, *The Birth of Tragedy*, tr. Shaun Whiteside (London: Penguin, 1993), p. 14.
51 Plato, *Phaedo*, tr. and with commentary by R. Hackforth (Cambridge: CUP, 1955), p. 61.
52 See Friedrich Nietzsche, 'Peoples and Fatherlands', in *Beyond Good and Evil* (1886), tr. R. J. Hollingdale (London: Penguin, 1973), pp. 170–91.

relationship between Goethe's theories of nature and the evolutionary dogma (Evolutionsdogmen) of Darwin and his successors.[53] The use of the metaphor was more generally apparent in the widespread use of evolutionary terms, for example struggle, organic, biological, etc., as tropes in cultural discourses, not least in the writings of Wilhelm Furtwängler. This form of Social Darwinism was socio-political rather than scientific and regarded the existence of all life to be the result of a struggle; an important constituent of this *Lebensphilosophie* is the idea of a leading design, an ideal purpose which has determined that one state or another, one race or another, should prosper and rule over others. Ernst Haeckel (1834–1919), biologist, philosopher and the leading German exponent of Social Darwinism writes that Darwin 'has taught us to recognise in the "struggle for existence", the powerful force of nature, which, for millions of years, has exerted supreme and uninterrupted control over the entire course of the world's organic evolution'.[54]

This was the network of ideas that formed Wilhelm Furtwängler's world-view, or *Weltanschauung*. There is no precise English equivalent of this ideologically laden German term, which is most conveniently but inadequately rendered into English as 'world-view'. This literal translation does not carry what H. S. Chamberlain, drawing on the organic metaphor, describes in his study *Immanuel Kant* (1905) as having resonances of 'religion and mythology, altogether human, but developed in all manner of different directions, with a network of roots nourished by art and science, by philosophy and mathematics'.[55] What is clear is that this all-pervading world-view derived from the organic and daemonic drove Furtwängler's entire system of musical thought; and in so doing engaged directly with key philosophical, historical, political and ideological debates of the age that comprised conservative cultural and nationalist ideologies within the broad usage of the organic metaphor. These debates formed part of the extensive discourses that lent themselves to appropriation by the forces of nationalism within the conservative 'illiberalism' of post-Bismarckian Germany.

53 Houston Stewart Chamberlain, *Goethe* (München: F. Bruckmann, 1912). Here Ungekürzte Volksausgabe zum Goethe-Jahr 1932, pp. 359–75; esp. p. 374.
54 Ernst Haeckel, *Die Welträthsel* (Bonn: Emil Strauss, 1900), pp. 121 and 311–14; Eng. edn, *The Riddle of the Universe at the Close of the Nineteenth Century*, tr. Joseph McCabe (New York: Harper & Brothers, 1900), pp. 104 and 269–71; quoted in Joachim Remak, ed., *The Nazi Years, A Documentary History* (Englewood Cliffs, NJ: Prentice Hall, Inc, 1969), pp. 2–4.
55 See Houston Stewart Chamberlain, *Immanuel Kant* (München: Verlagsanstalt F. Bruckmann AG, 1905), pp. 16–17; also *Die Grundlagen des neunzehnten Jahrhunderts*, p. 736; Eng. edn, vol. 2, p. 242.

Heinrich Schenker

The musical theorist who more than any other developed the organic world-view not only into an analytical system but also into a form of æsthetic ideology was Heinrich Schenker (1868–1935). This formidable musical thinker was to exercise a lasting if ambiguous influence on Furtwängler. On 6 February 1933, when at the height of his fame and prestige as a conductor, he wrote to the critic Ludwig Karpath (1866–1936): 'I consider Schenker the most important music theorist of the present day and am of the opinion that his music-theoretical work [...] belongs to the greatest and most significant achievements of our time.'[56] The purpose of Schenker's analytical methodology was, in short, to 'shore up the masterworks, and the laws of tonal construction that they embody, against wilful misinterpretation on the part of a world in decline'.[57] Many of the ideas that were to characterise Furtwängler's thought are present in Schenker's early essay 'The Spirit of Musical Technique' (1895), which includes a section entitled 'Moods, Forms and the "Organic"'.[58] Elements of the evolutionist thinking which pervades these constructs and which are so characteristic of Social Darwinism appear in his discussion of 'The Biological Nature of Form' in the early treatise, *Harmonielehre* (1906):[59]

> The motif is led through various situations. At one time its melodic character is tested; at another time, a harmonic peculiarity must prove its valour in unaccustomed surroundings; a third time, again, the motif is subjected to some rhythmic change: in other words, the motif lived through its fate, like a personage in a drama.[60]

In this he follows Wagner who draws a similar analogy between Shakespeare's treatment of his characters and Beethoven's development of motivic material

---

56 Ian Bent, David Bretherton and William Drabkin, eds, *Heinrich Schenker, Selected Correspondence* (Woodbridge: The Boydell Press, 2014), p. 219. The majority of citations from Schenker can also be referenced online at <http://www.schenkerdocumentsonline. org> (accessed 16 November 2017).

57 As cited in Nicholas Cook, 'Heinrich Schenker, Polemicist: a reading of the Ninth Symphony Monograph', *Music Analysis*, vol. 14, no. 1 (1995), p. 90.

58 Heinrich Schenker, 'Der Geist der musikalischen Technik', tr. William Pastille, in Cook, *The Schenker Project: Culture, Race and Music Theory in Fin-de-Siècle Vienna* (New York: OUP, 2007), pp. 319–32.

59 Heinrich Schenker, *Harmonielehre* (1906); Eng. edn, *Harmony*, ed. and annotated by Oswald Jonas, tr. Elisabeth Mann Borgese (Chicago: Chicago UP, 1954; pbk reprint, Cambridge, MA: MIT Press, 1973), p. 4.

60 Ibid., p. 13.

in his essay 'Beethoven' (1870).[61] This is not to say that the music is expressing an extrinsic dramatic programme; rather the process is intrinsic to the music itself. Schenker's promulgation of the idea of musical form as a function of biological processes is here in its early stages. Later in the *Harmonielehre* he develops the concept, which is expanded to include elements of Social Darwinism and its resultant hegemonic musical ideology: 'How do the vitality and egotism of man express themselves? First of all, in his attempts to live fully in as many relationships as the *struggle for life*[62] will permit and, second, in the desire to gain the upper hand in each one of these relationships – to the extent that the vital life forces measure up to this desire.'[63]

Schenker's early work contains elements that were to influence the development of his analytical methodology. His interest in the compositional process was such that from the early years of the century until his death he gradually developed a theoretical system in which he sought to elucidate the 'idea' of German music, to discover and explain the laws which govern musical masterworks and to penetrate and account for the processes common to the creators of those works. It was this aspect of the theorist's approach that so strongly appealed to Furtwängler and which was to have such a lasting influence on the development of his thought and on his work as a performing musician.

Schenker considered that cognition of the phenomena of musical creativity was beyond the reach of philosophical enquiry. In a diary entry for 18 May 1916 he writes:

> Hegel does not realise that artistic truth is merely a matter of the fulfilment of artistic law. All further considerations have nothing to do with the inner truth contained in works of art. This is true not only of music, where this concept is probably at its most difficult and persuasive, but also of poetry and painting. These inner laws are and remain the secret of genius and this alone. Hence philosophers and æstheticians are groping around in the dark.[64]

Understanding of the creative process was only possible through close engagement with the works themselves by means of a system of musical analysis. Through this process 'the composer reveals the innermost nature

---

61 See Roger Allen, tr. and ed., *Richard Wagner's 'Beethoven' (1870)* (Woodbridge: The Boydell Press, 2014), esp. pp. 143–9.
62 Author's italics.
63 Heinrich Schenker, *Harmony*, p. 84.
64 See Hellmut Federhofer, *Heinrich Schenker nach Tagebüchern und Briefen in der Oswald Jonas Memorial Collection* (Hildesheim: Georg Olms Verlag, 1985), p. 275.

of the world and expresses the profoundest wisdom in a language that his reasoning faculty does not understand'; a constant thread derived from Schopenhauer, which ran through the thought of both Schenker and Furtwängler.[65] It was therefore largely inevitable that the principal object of the analyst's attention was, and was to remain, the works of Beethoven. E. T. A. Hoffmann's essay of 1813, contemporaneous with the formulation of Goethe's scientific theories in *On Morphology* (*Zur Morphologie*) provided the initial motivation in passages such as the following:

> In Shakespeare, our knights of the æsthetic measuring-rod have often bewailed the utter lack of inner unity and inner continuity, although for those who look more deeply there springs forth, issuing from a single bud, a beautiful tree with leaves, flowers and fruit; thus, with Beethoven, it is only after a searching investigation of his instrumental music that the high self-possession inseparable from true genius and nourished by the study of the art stands revealed.[66]

The notion that the musical object existed as a structure of ideas transcending its various interpretations called for an attempt to be made to elucidate the meaning of what had taken place in the music.[67] Hoffman's use of the organic metaphor recalls Goethe's scientific theories as expressed through his interest in morphology. These ideas were to recur in the work of A. B. Marx (1795–1866), whose development of a methodical system of musical analysis was symptomatic of the search for a deeper comprehension of the phenomenon of the musical artwork.[68] As with Furtwängler, Goethe was also a primary source of many of Schenker's initial ideas. Much of Schenker's later terminology, for example *Ursatz* and *Urlinie*, recalls the titles given by Goethe to his prototypical forms, or *Urtypen*: the generating animal for fauna was an *Urtier*; the generating plant for flora was an *Urpflanze*.[69]

The developing system of musical analysis, which received its initial motivation from the desire to understand and communicate the ideas contained in Beethoven's works, devolved during the latter part of the

65 See Artur Schopenhauer, *Die Welt als Wille und Vorstellung*, §52 (1819); Eng. edn, *The World as Will and Representation*, tr. E. J. F. Payne (New York: Dover Books 1966), vol. 1, p. 260.
66 Oliver Strunk, *Source Readings in Music History*, pp. 755ff.
67 For a summary of this process see Dahlhaus, *Nineteenth-Century Music*, p. 11.
68 For an overview of Marx's reception of Goethe's ideas, see Lotte Thaler, *Organische Form in der Musiktheorie der 19. und beginnenden 20. Jahrhunderts* (München and Salzburg: Katzbichler, 1984).
69 For an overview of Goethe's impact on Schenker, see William Pastille in Heidi Siegel, ed., *Schenker Studies* (Cambridge: CUP, 1990).

nineteenth century into two distinct methodologies which may be termed the analytic principle and the hermeneutic principle. The analytic principle sought to 'explain' Beethoven by attempting to discover the musical laws governing his compositional process; hermeneutics attempted to describe the subject matter or concepts depicted by the musical work and thus explain its processes in narrative terms. Schenker and the young Furtwängler were at one in their adherence to the analytical, formalist approach: both revered Beethoven and shared a strong, if inconsistent antipathy towards Wagner as theoretician, who practised the hermeneutic approach with conviction.[70] Schenker's gradual development of a theoretical system of musical analysis based on the organic metaphor was to be a lifelong preoccupation. In the introduction to his final work, *Free Composition* (*Der freie Satz*, 1935), he summarised his approach: 'I here present a new concept, one inherent in the works of the great masters; indeed it is the very secret and source of their being: the concept of organic coherence.'[71]

Anti-Semitism

Heinrich Schenker was an assimilated Jew who originated from Galicia. It is therefore ironic that his mission to shore up the Austro-German canon of musical masterworks coincided with the gathering momentum of an idea which was in many respects fuelled by the same search for cultural identity: anti-Semitism. In the wake of the nineteenth-century emancipation, the Jewish population in Germany had gradually become assimilated into the middle classes and had readily joined the flow from rural areas to the rapidly expanding urban centres; yet paradoxically this process of assimilation had in itself prompted a hardening of the anti-Semitic position, as can readily be seen in Thomas Buddenbrook's conversation with his sister Antonie that took place in the 'Spring of 1868': 'I have heard of such things, mostly in Hesse, where a few of the landed gentry are in the hands of the Jews. Who knows what sort of cut-throat [Halsabschneider] it is that has poor Herr von Maiboom in his clutches?'[72] One of the consequences of the post-unification economic crisis of 1873 was that the Jews were increasingly seen as represent-ative of all the negative, un-German features of modernity: commercialism,

70 See, for example, Wagner's description of Beethoven's String Quartet in C sharp minor (Op. 131) in *Beethoven*, pp. 121–5.
71 Heinrich Schenker, *Neue musikalische Theorien und Phantasie*, vol. 3: *Der freie Satz* (Wien: Universal Edition, 1935); Eng. edn, *Free Composition* (New York: Schirmer Books, 1979), p. 9.
72 Thomas Mann, *Buddenbrooks*, p. 375.

materialism, and so on. Among the most strident protagonists of anti-Semitic thought was Adolf Stöcker, court chaplain to the Kaiser, who founded the Christian Socialist party in 1878.[73] His appeal to the middle classes was to those of its members engaged in commerce and resentful of the success of Jewish firms and financial institutions. The high point of Wilhelmine political anti-Semitism came in 1893 when anti-Semitic parties elected no less than sixteen deputies to the German Reichstag. In neighbouring Austria Karl Lueger was so successful in mobilising anti-Jewish sentiments that in 1895, in spite of the personal opposition of the Emperor Franz Josef, he was elected mayor of Vienna. The development of anti-Semitism within musical culture can be traced to the anonymous publication in 1850 of Wagner's 'Judaism in Music' (Das Judentum in der Musik), a tract motivated in part by resentment of the Jewish composer Felix Mendelssohn's fluent and easy technical facility. Wagner later republished the essay in 1869 under his own name together with a substantial appendix. To Heinrich von Treitschke, the official Prussian historian, Jewry similarly posed a threat to the German national ethos; moreover, the new science of Darwinian anthropology added a specious aura of scientific respectability to anti-Semitism. It was this portfolio of ideas that was adapted by Gobineau and other racial theorists to divide humanity into Aryan and Semitic subspecies, thus changing the identity of the Jews from a religious to a racial minority.[74] Such thinking was grist to the Wagnerian mill and in the years immediately prior to his death in 1883 Wagner gave a further boost to the anti-Semitic position by publishing a series of essays and articles known as the Regeneration essays.[75] The English Germanophile Houston Stewart Chamberlain (1855–1927) continued this line of thought in his lengthy, portentous but widely read book, *The Foundations of the Nineteenth Century*.[76] This compendium of conservative-nationalist thinking, which includes ideologically laden discussions of Art as a 'whole' and music as a specifically 'German' art, tendentiously reduces all of European cultural history to a struggle between Aryan and Semitic races.[77] Among

73 See Golo Mann, *The History of Germany Since 1789*, p. 236.
74 Arthur Comte De Gobineau (1816–82): French diplomat and publicist; one of the most influential precursors of racist dogma.
75 See, for example, 'Religion and Art' ('Religion und Kunst') and supplements. This essay originally appeared in the *Bayreuther Blätter* (October 1880), and was reprinted in volume 10 of GSD; Eng. tr. PW, vol. 6.
76 *Die Grundlagen des neunzehnten Jahrhunderts* (F. Bruckmann: München 1899); Eng. edn, *The Foundations of the Nineteenth Century*, tr. John Lees (London: The Bodley Head, 1910).
77 For differing perspectives on European anti-Semitism from the Franco-Prussian war to the rise of Hitler see: David Goldberg and John Rayner, *The Jewish People: Their History and Religion* (London: Penguin, 1989), pp. 157–72; Daniel Jonah Goldhagen,

Chamberlain's enthusiastic readers was Kaiser Wilhelm II, who praised this specious conflation of racial dynamics and German imperial ambition as a wake-up call to the German nation: in Chamberlain's version of world history modern Germans and the Imperial Reich were the inheritors of all great cultures and civilisations of the past. The most significant effect this had on cultural discourse was to infuse racial anti-Semitism with Social Darwinism. Anti-Semitism was therefore no longer a minority position but an integral part of the warp and weft of cultural life which carried the imprimatur of the highest levels of the artistic establishment, especially Bayreuth, and exercised an important influence on contemporary conservative thought.

Wilhelm Dilthey

The reaction of the educated middle class to the ever-increasing materialistic impact of industrial expansion was seen in the field of philosophy and æsthetics as a reaction against the domination of liberal humanism by scientific, positivistic modes of thought. In this context the work of Wilhelm Dilthey (1833–1911) is significant. Dilthey was Professor of Philosophy at the University of Berlin at the time of Wilhelm Furtwängler's birth and through his lectures exercised considerable influence. As we shall see, there is some evidence in Furtwängler's writings that he was familiar with Dilthey's system. Dilthey began from the premise that the natural sciences, which so strongly influenced contemporary philosophical thinking, were not a suitable means by which to study works of art or issues arising from them. He also contended that Hegelian historicism was too rigid a system to take into account the lived experience on which artistic experience should be founded. Dilthey's æsthetic mediates between the classical formalism of Hanslick and the emotionalism of Wagner. His musical writings represent a small but significant part of his philosophical system and in his *On Musical Understanding*, c.1906 (the year of Furtwängler's first orchestral concert), he defines his system of musical hermeneutics as 'an act of understanding, thus broadening the previous concept of explaining'.[78] The dynamic, changing quality of life embodied in the human soul (Seelenleben) and the triad 'Experience – Expression – Understanding' (Erlebnis – Ausdruck – Verstehen), can be paralleled in

---

Hitler's Willing Executioners: Ordinary Germans and the Holocaust (New York: Alfred A. Knopf, 1996), Chs 2 and 3; Saul Friedländer, *Nazi Germany and the Jews*, vol. 1, esp. Chs 1–3.

78 *Das musikalische Verstehen*. For a concise introduction to Dilthey's thought, see Bujić, ed., *Music in European Thought 1851–1912*, pp. 365–7.

musical terms as creation – performance – reception: Erlebnis, the act of living through – of recreating the vision of the composer expressed in a musical work which is in itself a creative process; Ausdruck, the expression in art of a lived experience through the process of time, or in musical terms, the act of performance; and Verstehen, an act in which 'all mental powers are engaged in the process of grasping and reliving the experience of another person', or the act of reception. This fundamental tripartite idea has its antecedence in Hegelian dialectical thought: Thesis – Erlebnis – Conception; Antithesis – Ausdruck – Performance; Synthesis – Verstehen – Reception; there are also clear echoes of Kantian critical philosophy in that the power of reason is an essential component of the act of Verstehen, which is not entirely an intuitive process.

Dilthey's hermeneutic system grew out of a world-view that presupposed the acceptance of the idea of German artistic hegemony; there are in addition strong resonances of both the organic world-view and the theories of Gestalt psychology in that the process of 'Verstehen' involves cognition of the relations between the whole and its constituent parts.[79] Ideas of unity and coherence are central to Dilthey's philosophical system. In *The Nature of Philosophy* (*Das Wesen der Philosophie*) Dilthey introduces 'The Category of Selfsameness (of the Whole, of Unity, of Substance)'; 'Die Kategorie der Selbigkeit (des Ganzen, der Einheit, der Substanz)'. As with 'Weltanschauung', 'Selbigkeit' is a concept difficult to render in English. The nearest equivalent is 'Selfsameness', but, as with 'world-view', this does not capture the elusive resonances of the German term. Dilthey claims that through the category of selfsameness (or self-reference as a form of identity) 'all differences and changes are combined in an experienced but non-conceptual unity'.[80]

As Stephen McClatchie observes, the basis of Dilthey's thought was 'idealistic in that it strove for transcendence'.[81] This is particularly evident in a collection of essays from Dilthey's last decade that were posthumously published in 1933 under the collective title *Of German Poetry and Music: On the Study of the History of the German Spirit* (*Von Deutscher Dichtung und*

---

79 For a useful introduction to the principles of Gestalt psychology, see Christian von Ehrenfels, 'Über Gestaltqualitäten', *Vierteljahrschrift für wissenschaftliche Philosophie*, vol. 14 (1890), pp. 249–92; Eng. tr., Barry Smith, ed., *Foundations of Gestalt Theory* (München and Vienna: Philosophia Verlag, 1988), pp. 82–123.

80 Wilhelm Dilthey, *Das Wesen der Philosophie* (Stuttgart: Philipp Reclam Jun., 1984), p. 173. See also Jacob Owensby, *Dilthey and the Narrative of History* (Ithaca and London: Cornell UP, 1994), pp. 89–92.

81 Stephen McClatchie, *Analyzing Wagner's Operas: Alfred Lorenz and German Nationalist Ideology* (New York: University of Rochester Press, 1998), p. 34.

Musik. Aus Den Studien Zur Geschichte Des Deutschen Geistes). These include studies of 'The Germanic World', 'Courtly Poetry and the National Epic', and 'The Great German Music of the Eighteenth Century: Schütz, Bach, Handel, Haydn, Mozart and Beethoven'.[82] The posthumous publication of these essays at the end of the Weimar Republic and the beginning of the Nazi period is a striking indication of just how easily this kind of lofty transcendent idealism drawn from the traditions of *Bildung* lent itself to tendentious appropriation by the forces of conservative nationalism.

■　■　■　■　■

Such, in brief, is the historical, cultural and intellectual background that nurtured the young Wilhelm Furtwängler. The various philosophical and musical strands of thought outlined above, and which were to converge in him, nourished among the conservative-nationalist elite a developing sense of national pride and identity to the point where the former became a potent symbol of the latter. It was therefore to a certain extent inevitable that in the early years of the twentieth century such ideas should gradually harden into hegemonic ideology of cultural elitism; a process accelerated by the humiliation of Germany's capitulation at the end of World War I. As Thomas Mann was later to write in his essay 'Germany and the Germans' (1945), 'historical misfortune, the sufferings and humiliation of a lost war, nourished this seed'.[83] What had formerly been a lofty form of non-political artistic idealism became increasingly infused with conservative political thought, partly as a reaction to the shock of defeat in 1918 and the subsequent liberalism, or cultural Bolshevism, of the experimental democracy of the Weimar Republic.

82 Wilhelm Dilthey, *Von Deutscher Dichtung und Musik* (Leipzig und Berlin: Verlag und Druck von B. G. Teubner, 1933), pp. 189–298.
83 See Appendix 2.

CHAPTER 2

CHILDHOOD AND YOUTH (1886-1911)

Gustav Heinrich Ernst Martin Wilhelm Furtwängler (born 25 January 1886) was the eldest child of Adolf Furtwängler (1853–1907) and Adelheid Wendt (1863–1944). The Furtwänglers were of south German agrarian origin while the Wendts came from a north German small-town background of academics, schoolteachers and civil servants. Wilhelm Furtwängler was of the generation that came to maturity in the period following the rapid industrial expansion in Germany in the 1870s and 80s. This, as we have seen, was a time of changing attitudes among the educated middle classes of the *Bildungsbürgertum*. The overt materialism and commercialism of the *haute bourgeoisie* associated with industrialisation prompted a growing desire to reclaim a sense of pre-industrial cultural heritage and identity. This phenomenon was to some extent epitomised by the Furtwängler family. Adolf Furtwängler was a respected classical archæologist who at the time of Wilhelm's birth held the post of director of the Museum of Antiquities in Berlin, before moving in 1894 to an appointment as Professor of Archæology and the director of three museums in Munich. Around the same time that he made the move from the Prussian to the Bavarian capital Adolf Furtwängler re-established his agrarian roots through the purchase in 1896 of Haus Tanneck, a small country house on the Tegernsee near Bad Wiessee, where the young Wilhelm was able to pursue his passion for the natural world and outdoor sports. Adolf Furtwängler's reputation had been made by his distinguished contribution to the excavations at the site of Olympia in 1878. As was the case with other German scholars of the humanities, he was driven by that nineteenth-century German fascination with the Ancient Greeks engendered by Goethe's Weimar Classicism and Wilhelm von Humboldt's vision for a classically based education and given a public face by such contrasting examples as the colonnades of Friedrich Schinkel's Berlin and Ludwig I of Bavaria's portentously positioned Bavarian reconstruction of the Parthenon: the Regensburg Valhalla of 1848. Both in their different ways were tendentious expressions of a search for a culturally enhanced national identity through the association of modern Germany with Ancient Greece.

The family of Wilhelm's mother, Adelheid Wendt, came from a solid north German *Bildungsbürger* background. Wilhelm's maternal great-grandfather Karl Heinrich Wendt was a senior education official in the royal Prussian State who numbered among his pupils none other than the future unifier of Germany, Otto von Bismarck. In 1867 Wilhelm's maternal grandfather Gustav Wendt moved from his north German homeland to the south-western city of Karlsruhe in order to introduce the Prussian educational system to the state of Württemberg. Gustav's wife, Wilhelm's maternal grandmother Anna Dohrn, was of a long-established and very well connected family. The Wendt household was one of the most musically cultured in Karlsruhe in which 'Wagner was Beelzebub and Brahms a God!' Brahms was a regular guest and on one occasion played his recently completed *Requiem*, which was not yet known in Karlsruhe. Adelheid recalled in later years the visits of the 'good uncle with the white beard'. It was Georg Dohrn, a second cousin of Adelheid Wendt and a leading figure in the musical life of Breslau, who was to play such an influential role in launching Wilhelm Furtwängler's early musical career.

The young Wilhelm spent his formative years in Lutheran Berlin, the capital of the Reich, which on the one hand retained its strong protestant Prussian traditions and on the other embodied many of the economic, social and political features of the new Germany typified by the growing influence of the mercantile middle class. The move to Munich placed him within the more liberal cultural atmosphere of the catholic-dominated Bavarian capital. Munich at that time retained many pre-industrial features but did not entirely escape the effects of growing industrialisation in the process of finding its place within the newly ordered greater Germany. From an early age, he was imbued with the riches of ancient Greek culture, which became a seminal influence in his development and in which he retained a lifelong interest. As his sometime secretary, Berta Geissmar, later recalled in her autobiography: 'The journeys father and son took together to Greece and Italy during Furtwängler's youth opened his eyes to the world of ancient Greece and Rome, and to the Renaissance, which meant so much to him during his whole life.'[1]

The surviving letters from Furtwängler's childhood and youth are evidence of the close-knit and privileged cultured environment in which he was nurtured. It is clear that his was a serious temperament and his mind was from a very early age preoccupied with musical matters. In a letter to his paternal grandmother Christiane the eight-year-old boy wrote:

[1]   Berta Geissmar, *The Baton and the Jackboot* (London: Hamish Hamilton, 1944), p. 14. See also Elisabeth Furtwängler, *Über Wilhelm Furtwängler*, pp. 114–15.

1   Wilhelm Furtwängler aged thirteen

I like it better here in Munich than in Berlin; I can ice-skate and I am learning to play the piano. When the summer arrives Papa has told me that he will take me walking in Italy. I am looking forward to this so much as the Doctor says it will help Mama to get well again. I have also composed a new piano piece, which I will send to you.[2]

Of all the early exchanges of letters that which is most revealing of his youthful precocity is between the teenage Furtwängler and Bertel von Hildebrand, the youngest daughter of the sculptor Adolf von Hildebrand (1847–1921). The Hildebrands were a well-known Munich family who frequented the same cultural circles as the Furtwänglers. They owned a villa in Florence, San Francesco da Paola, and it was here in 1902 that Wilhelm spent an extended period with his tutor Ludwig Curtius, experiencing and absorbing at first hand the art and architecture of the Italian Renaissance as described in a series of letters to his father. It appears that the young Wilhelm and Bertel von Hildebrand even at one point contemplated marriage; but the couple grew apart in early adulthood and Bertel later married the composer Walter Braunfels (1882–1954). Wilhelm clearly considered Bertel his intellectual equal and took full advantage of the opportunity to exchange views on artistic and cultural experiences in a series of letters that give an account of his development from boyhood through adolescence to early manhood.[3] These are no ardent outpourings of youthful affection: the writer emerges as a detached young man of a lofty, distinctly idealistic cast of mind.

Munich, 14 June 1901

I can well understand why you don't like Schubert. It is also very true that he is decidedly more Romantic than Classic, but Romantic in the best sense. He is certainly greater than Schumann and Brahms. Admittedly his works contain a certain amount of that sentimental sweetness which is what makes the works of later composers so unbearable. (When I hear something of Mendelssohn and particularly Schumann I immediately want to run away.) But with works such as the B minor or C major symphonies,

---

2   The originals of Furtwängler's youthful letters to his family are held in the Furtwängler Nachlass der Staatsbibliothek zu Berlin – Preußischer Kulturbesitz (SPK), Signatur 55, Nachl. 13, Kasten 13. See also Frank Thiess, ed., *Wilhelm Furtwängler: Briefe* (Wiesbaden: F. A. Brockhaus, Vierte Auflage, 1980), p. 15. Unless otherwise stated, all translations of Furtwängler's letters are by the author.

3   Further information may be found in the Programme Book for the 2. Wilhelm Furtwängler Tage, University of Jena, 26–29 November 1998, which contains a substantial essay on the young Furtwängler's connections with the Hildebrand family (pp. 14–52). The essay accompanied a lecture on the same subject given by Frau Dr Sigrid Esche-Braunfels.

the D minor or G major quartets, there is none of this. Schubert did not invent his own form, as is the case with Beethoven and Haydn, so what then are the antitheses on which he bases his art? On the one hand there is feeling, which I cannot express any more clearly than being the Nature of Art; on the other there is the 'Form', not the external structure of Sonata form but the form created by the feeling itself. Whether or not this form is unconscious, irregular, independent and unartistic; whether it functions only for the expression of feeling or stands as a complete artwork only the artist knows. He knows what he has created, if he has created a 'World'. The word 'World' certainly has many shades of meaning and formerly I have thought little about it. But when one does form an opinion it is indeed a noble thought. I think it is important to understand the relationship of specifics to the world in general, to know what one has before oneself and to understand the concept of beauty. This is clearer in Schubert's art than in all subsequent music. It is true that he has something of the Bohemian about him but this does not affect his deeper character. There are Hungarian traits in Brahms. I must admit that I find his songs very beautiful but I must again emphasise that nothing can be compared to Beethoven. With his wonderful inner sense of form and lyrical expression, he stands alongside Goethe, which Schubert does not. But farewell. All love and tender greetings from your Willi.[4]

This letter written by the fifteen-year-old Furtwängler is significant as it contains in essence the elements which were to dominate his world-view for his entire creative life: the dislike of 'sentimental sweetness' and anything that detracts from the musical expression; the preoccupation with matters of musical form; the placing of Beethoven at the head of his personal musical pantheon; these attitudes were to remain central to his personal musical æsthetic. Shortly afterwards he impressed his relatively conservative ideas still further on Bertel when he wrote to revise his previously stated view of Wagner:

Munich, 26 June [1901]

I received both your letters this morning. I can't say that I am pleased for I see now how unutterably stupid I was to write to you and say that I admire Wagner. I honestly didn't think that you would react as you did, although I must admit that if you had written to me in the same way it would have had a similar effect. I am surprised that you could believe it of me. I thought it was clear from the way I wrote that I was joking. Have I not said again and again, that to me nothing can stand above Beethoven; certainly not Wagner, who I do not consider to have been a true artist. Recently I met an

4   SPK Berlin, 55 Nachl. 13, W. Furtwängler, Kasten 6; *Furtwängler: Briefe*, pp. 29–30.

enthusiastic Wagnerian who maintained that *Tristan* was the greatest of all artworks. I could not say to him that I simply cannot endure Wagner under any circumstances.[5]

The correspondence is by no means confined to musical matters. In the summer of 1901 Furtwängler expresses his enthusiasm for the dramatic art of Shakespeare and Goethe and the visual art of Rubens in a series of letters that demonstrates an extensive cultural knowledge and experience unusual even for a fifteen-year-old of his educated background.

[No address] 15 July [1901]

I have now completed my essay on Rubens; it is not particularly successful. The small picture, in which he depicts himself walking in the garden with his wife, I find magnificent. The *Rape of the Daughter of Leukippes* is also wonderful in formal design. I was recently in the Secession, where there is a Renaissance exhibition, and there was another magnificent picture by Rubens. It is a very simple conception, just three donkeys feeding on turnips. In the background is nothing but a tower and a bleak skyscape, which heightens the effect of the donkeys.

Do you find that there are similarities between the art of Goethe and Shakespeare? The young Goethe certainly creates characters of tremendous strength; Götz von Berlichingen and Werther are certainly Shakespearian in conception. But later, as in *Tasso* for example, he does not create a tragedy in the manner of *King Lear*. He also has nothing of Shakespeare's humour and he was not interested in depicting humanity. He wants to express the universal, the beautiful and the consummate in the manner of Homer and the Greek poets. I find it difficult to express this in words. I can only sense it. Perhaps this too is a false idea.[6]

Goethe is becoming increasingly important to him and he is steeping himself in the works of Shakespeare. The German romantics raised the celebrated English dramatist to the status of an icon; knowledge of his plays was an important part of the cultured, humanistic tradition in which Furtwängler was raised. Four days later he develops his enthusiasms in more detail in a long letter to Bertel.

Tanneck, 19 July [1901]

Your letter has given me a great deal of pleasure and no little amusement. It is already late in the evening, the sun has just gone down and I am here

5   Ibid., pp. 30–1.
6   Ibid., p. 32.

at my favourite place by the lake. It is quite charming, for the evening sun is reflected in the glassy surface but the heavens and the distant shoreline are obscured by mist. But how I wish I were in Italy, by the sea, for it must be even more beautiful there. I am reading Goethe's *Italian Journey* with great enthusiasm. It is magnificently written, so wonderfully clear and yet so profound.

But I have only recently begun it, today in fact, and I am therefore not yet very far advanced. Up to now my reading has been confined to Shakespeare and I have acquired good background knowledge of his works. I only brought a few books with me which were insufficient to last me for my entire stay so I have re-read some of them. I found *Cymbeline* and *Winter's Tale* particularly impressive. The latter, which in some ways is similar to *The Tempest*, I find utterly charming. *All's Well that Ends Well* is also very fine. Is that not based on a Novelle by Boccaccio? It occurred to me that I had read it before but I can't recall exactly where. My admiration for Shakespeare increases daily; such magnificent power and strength is unique.[7]

In the best traditions of *Bildungsbürgertum*, the young Wilhelm Furtwängler's education took place outside of any formal system and was entrusted by Adolf Furtwängler to two of his students: Ludwig Curtius (1874–1954) and Walter Riezler (1878–1965). They were representatives of the tradition of cultivated humanism that flourished in Munich around the turn of the century. Their interests were widely different yet complementary, and their impact on the young Furtwängler was to be lasting and profound. Curtius, who later acquired a reputation as a distinguished archæologist, enriched his knowledge of antiquity; while Riezler guided his musical education in much the same way that in Thomas Mann's *Buddenbrooks* the provincial organist Herr Edmund Pfühl guided that of the young Hanno Buddenbrook.[8] It was Riezler in particular who laid the foundations that were to be the bedrock of his creative life and which were to be strengthened by early professional contact with musicians of the cast of mind of Hans Pfitzner. His first fully professional tutor in music was Anton Beer-Walbrunn (1864–1929), a distinguished Professor of Music in Munich who quickly recognised Furtwängler's exceptional abilities. In 1900 he began a course in advanced harmony and counterpoint with Josef Rheinberger (1839–1901), a composer of organ music and at that time director of the Munich Academy of Music. Rheinberger directed the young Furtwängler towards an intensive study of Beethoven's string quartets but in other respects his approach was somewhat austere and reactionary. Rheinberger revered the classics but to him music

7   Ibid., pp. 33–4.
8   See *Buddenbrooks*, Part 8, Ch. 6, pp. 405–14.

ceased with Beethoven; the German Romantics with Wagner at their head were anathema. Furtwängler needed a more progressive musician to guide him into the world of contemporary musical thought; in 1901 Max von Schillings (1868–1933) became his composition teacher.

Schillings, a Rhinelander, was a musical pedagogue who studied in Bonn and eventually settled in Munich. He served as an Assistant Stage Conductor at Bayreuth in 1892 and assumed the position of Chorus Master in 1902. In the Autumn of 1908 he became musical assistant to the Intendant of the Stuttgart Court Theatre, conductor of the Royal Concerts and director of operatic productions; from 1911 to 1918 he served as General Music Director at Stuttgart before taking control of the Staatsoper in Berlin in 1919. He was at the centre of German musical life during the period of Furtwängler's musical apprenticeship. Shortly after Schillings' death in 1933 Furtwängler published a brief article 'In Memoriam Max von Schillings' in which he describes the effect that this wide-ranging, eclectic musician had on his development:

I was fifteen years old when I first made the acquaintance of Max von Schillings. It was before his Stuttgart period and at that time he was living as a private individual in Munich. He had already written his *Pfeifertag* and was considered alongside Strauss and Pfitzner as the most important successor to Wagner. I had as yet no interest in what was later to become my career, that of Kapellmeister. I came to him simply as a musician and composer. He took an interest in me and I became his pupil. At that time I went to him every few weeks and stayed for several hours, often until late into the afternoon. I was a passionate, 'absolute' musician from the strict school of Rheinberger and for Schillings, as a new-German composer and Wagnerian, it was not easy to temper the determined views of the young with his mature artistic experience. However, he spared no time and effort and always showed great kindness as well as a vigorous sense of dedication and purpose. His ability was as great as the personal warmth and kindness of heart that was so characteristic of him. He was one of the few representative composers of the epoch and he felt he had much to give to the development of German music. It is this aspect of his nature which had such a far-reaching influence and which will be so sorely missed. I myself received from him both as man and artist many decisive and meaningful impressions and directions, for which I will always be deeply grateful.[9]

From Schillings Furtwängler received a heady synthesis of Beethovenian and Wagnerian influences that combined with the strict discipline of

9   TW, pp. 72–3 (author's translation).

Rheinberger's pedagogy to provide him with a firm musical foundation on which to develop his ideas. Schillings was also a fervent German nationalist and anti-Semite who allied himself to the musical conservatives who opposed the Weimar regime (1920–33). He later became a willing tool of the Nazi propagandists. During the early months of the regime he became a member with Furtwängler of a commission of leading musicians whose function was to supervise and censor the programmes of all music organisations in Berlin. At the time of his death in July 1933 he was establishing himself as an important influence on Nazi artistic policy.[10]

Furtwängler studied the central repertoire of the piano literature with Frau Regine Sulger-Gebing, the wife of a lecturer at the University of Munich. Instruction in piano playing was considered an essential part of the musician's education. A fluent keyboard facility was indispensable for the study of music and, in the time before the dissemination of music by means of broadcasting and mechanical reproduction, piano arrangements of orchestral scores for two, four or even eight hands were the means by which music entered the home. As Hanno Buddenbrook's mother Gerda tells Herr Pfühl, 'familiarity with the piano, as a means of summarizing the richest and most varied structures, as an incomparable instrument for musical reproduction, means for me a clearer, more intimate and comprehensive engagement with the music'.[11] Or as Wendell Kretschmar was later to instruct the young Adrian Leverkühn, 'the piano, properly speaking, is the direct and sovereign representative of music itself in its intellectuality, and for that reason one must learn it'.[12] There is no direct evidence that the young Furtwängler ever considered becoming a concert pianist, although he clearly attained a high level of proficiency. For him the piano was and would remain the most direct means of access to the innermost substance and processes of music.

Wilhelm vividly describes this broadening of his musical horizons in a series of letters to his paternal Aunt, Minna Furtwängler:

Munich, 4 December 1901

My studies continue as last year, piano lessons with Frau Sulger, then violin lessons and the conclusion of my study of counterpoint with Beer.[13] I have taken great care with this because of its usefulness. With Frau Sulger I am studying Beethoven's E flat major concerto. It is a wonderful piece,

---

10 See Erik Levi, *Music in the Third Reich* (London: Macmillan, 1994), pp. 17–18.
11 *Buddenbrooks*, p. 409.
12 *Doctor Faustus*, p. 62.
13 Anton Beer-Walbrunn (1864–1929).

far superior to the Brahms concertos. Recently I visited Schillings; we conversed for over two hours and I played to him both my Fantasia and my Sextet. He really is an excellent man, so sensitive and full of understanding. He had nothing new to say to me, but I intend to go to him every few weeks and discuss matters with him. He says that he is reluctant to be too critical in case I find it discouraging, but on the whole he is very civil towards me.[14]

Munich,
20 December 1901

I am now playing a new Beethoven Sonata, the one in D major, op 10 No 3. It is a wonderful piece and certainly far superior to Brahms's C major sonata, of which I play the adagio. This appears to be Frau Sulger's favourite piece; but I find early Brahms of indifferent musical quality, an unhappy mixture of Schumann and Beethoven. Tomorrow I am going to visit Schillings again and I am rather apprehensive. I am just going to talk to him and this time I am not expected to perform. My Sextet, however, is to be played at the Hildebrands and I will have to direct. I am trying to produce occasional pieces, so now for a Christmas song, and then perhaps a Kyrie or something for Choir and organ. I am studying the *Missa Solemnis* with great enthusiasm. It seems to me that this work represents a far-reaching development in musical style. It is perhaps the greatest work in the whole of music. I am also writing an extended essay about *Die Meistersinger*.

P.S. I have now attended a performance of *Die Meistersinger*, and sadly it has made no impression on me whatsoever.[15]

Munich, 26 January 1902

Yesterday was my sixteenth birthday. With Frau Sulger I am now studying a new Beethoven sonata, op 110 in A flat major. This does not please me as I know the piece at least as well as Frau Sulger and I find it too easy. Even the Scherzo presents no technical challenges. However, she seems content with my progress, much more so than I am. I am also playing a wonderful Bach partita, the B flat major, and a Mozart sonata. Frau Sulger considers that Beethoven's E flat major concerto is too difficult for me so I am not playing it for the time being. I disagree with her and I intend to take it to Florence in order to practise it there. Our plans to visit Florence are now more certain. I know that you have your doubts, as my piano studies will suffer a modest interruption. However, this disadvantage is offset by the many advantages.

14 *Briefe*, pp. 34–5.
15 Ibid., pp. 35–6.

2   Furtwängler in 1902 aged sixteen

It is clear that the young Furtwängler was developing clearly defined views on musical matters which were to remain essentially in place throughout his adult life; although his view of Wagner, a composer towards whom he maintained a consistently ambivalent attitude, was already changing. In a letter to Bertel he wrote:

> Tanneck, 31 July 1903

> You write to me of a disagreement with Baltus[16] about Beethoven, Wagner and myself. I believe I understand perfectly well what your father meant when he called Wagner constructive. It is only in *Meistersinger* that Wagner has achieved a degree of musical excellence, which can be compared with Beethoven. He is certainly a long way removed from my music, for he sought mood and atmosphere and I seek feeling in music. I have recently become acquainted with *Parsifal*, his last opera (we have a piano score here). Here the prevailing mood is one of evil, which is most unpleasant. It is a more gigantic step backwards than *Meistersinger*, for example. But I have to say it must have a colossal effect in the theatre, though not on everyone. You would certainly find it fearfully tedious.

> I am not prepared to make a sweeping condemnation of Wagner. It is important not to be blinded by his errors to his considerable merits. Besides, before judging Wagner it is necessary to know him. To me he now appears next to Schubert the greatest after Beethoven.[17]

Perhaps, like Hanno Buddenbrook's mentor Edmund Pfühl, Furtwängler was gradually beginning to realise that Wagner's music was not as 'foreign to his inner self' as he had previously thought.[18]

The richness and intellectual breadth of the education evident in these youthful letters also found an outlet in an extensive series of compositions. Of the 120 items in the Wilhelm Furtwängler *Werkverzeichnis*, 109 were completed before the composer's twentieth birthday.[19] Among a wide range of solo instrumental and chamber works are to be found settings of texts by romantic German poets; in particular those by the author who appealed most strongly to his musical imagination and had acted as the touchstone for so many of the cultural trends which shaped the contemporary *Zeitgeist*: Johann Wolfgang von Goethe (1749–1832). The Furtwängler Nachlass contains three complete songs and two further fragments for voice and piano to texts

16 George Baltus (1874–1967), painter. Brother-in-law of Bertel von Hildebrand.
17 *Briefe*, pp. 38–9.
18 *Buddenbrooks*, p. 408.
19 See Chris Walton, Jürg Stenzl *et al.*, eds, 'Wilhelm Furtwängler in Diskussion', *Werkverzeichnis Wilhelm Furtwängler* (1996).

WILHELM FURTWÄNGLER

by Goethe.[20] In addition the manuscripts of three extended choral works to Goethe texts are extant, all of which were composed before the end of 1903 when Furtwängler was approaching his eighteenth birthday.

The first of the choral works, *Die erste Walpurgisnacht* (1897 to 27 January 1898), bears the inscription, 'Dem Onkel Adolf zum 70. Geburtstag, 27 Januar 1898 gewidmet'.[21] Later there followed a setting of the Chorus of Spirits from *Faust*, Part I.[22] This was begun in Florence during the visit referred to in the letter to Bertel von Hildebrand and evidently cost Furtwängler a good deal of trouble, for he wrote to his mother:

4 April 1902

At present I am still composing the chorus from *Faust* (Schwindet ihr dunkeln Wölbungen droben), or rather I have started all over again. This is my third attempt. I want to avoid too much emphasis on the supernatural element, which so often provides the dramatic contrast in Goethe, and bring out the rich poetic vibrancy of thought which is all too often oversimplified. I have done this by excising many of the minor chords and the music is now predominantly in a powerful major tonality.[23]

The most extended of these Goethe settings is the *Religiöser Hymnus* (WF 106) for Soprano and Tenor soloists, Chorus and Orchestra (1903) in which Furtwängler sets lines from the closing scene of *Faust*, Part II.[24]

Furtwängler's youthful correspondence with Bertel von Hildebrand and his early compositions reflect patterns and paradigms inherited from across the broad cultural spectrum outlined in Chapter 1. One factor emerges as fundamental: the phenomenon of the musical object that exists for its own sake and on its own terms.[25] The autonomous musical work is paramount. In all his early discussions of musical matters Beethoven is the absolute

20 Ibid., pp. 85–132. Manuscript sources Zentralbibliothek Zürich, Nachl. W. Furtwängler: WF 57, *Erinnerungen, op. IV, No. 1* (28 June 1897); WF 75, *Ganymed* (1898?) Fragment; WF 88, *Wanderers Nachtlied* (November 1900) Fragment; WF 90, *Auf dem See* (1900); WF 100, *Herbstgefühl* (between April and June 1902 in Florence).
21 Zentralbibliothek Zürich, Nachl. W. Furtwängler 9, 1–2.
22 Ibid., 22a. Goethe, *Faust*, Part I, lines 1447–505.
23 SPK Berlin, 55 Nachl. 13, W. Furtwängler, Kasten 12. See also the inset booklet that accompanies a recording of the works (1993).
24 Zentralbibliothek Zürich, Nachl. W. Furtwängler 23a. Goethe, *Faust*, Part II, text selected from Dr Marianus' petitions to Mary, lines 11997–2103.
25 For an understanding of how Furtwängler's thought engages with ideals and discourses of Absolute Music, see Mark Evan Bonds, *Absolute Music: The History of an Idea* (New York: OUP, 2014).

standard by which all other music is judged. To Furtwängler the Beethoven symphony is the *opus metaphysicum* of instrumental music.

In the long letter of 14 June 1901 cited above, the sixteen-year-old Furtwängler considered questions of musical form and its function. Mendelssohn and Schumann, for example, are rejected on account of their 'sentimental sweetness'. However, in his implied rejection of the æsthetic of feeling he shows certain ambivalence and his discussion of Schubert tacitly accepts the idea, which he earlier described as essential to his own compositional procedures, that form may be a result of the function of the musical content. The sonata idea as exemplified in the works of Beethoven remained paramount. Of particular interest is the reference to the *Missa Solemnis*. Furtwängler's study of this 'Ur'-text of musical transcendence predated the composition of his early religious choral works. The high tessitura of the *Religiöser Hymnus* (1903) is suggestive of the choral sonorities of Beethoven's mass. The Hildebrand correspondence is also laced with disparaging references to the composer who at this stage in his life represented Furtwängler's musical nemesis: Richard Wagner. At first, as we have seen, he rejected Wagner unconditionally; it was to be one of the ironies of his career that he, an autonomist in matters of musical form, should at a later stage come to be a perceived paradigm of expressive performance practice following in the Wagnerian tradition. Wagner's thematicising of dramatic content in musical terms was at this point an alien concept: to him music could express only itself. However, his attitude towards Wagner began to change as he conceded that, although this amalgam of the arts fell below his ideal, it might have some merit.

Apprenticeship

In 1905 Georg Dohrn (1867–1942), a cousin of Furtwängler's mother Adelheid, assisted Wilhelm in obtaining his first professional position as repetiteur at the Stadttheater in Breslau (the present-day Wrocław in Poland). As an accomplished pianist with an advanced facility for reading scores at sight, the nineteen-year-old Wilhelm was well equipped for the task and gained some useful practical experience in the craft and business of opera performance. This existence was in stark contrast to his comfortable upbringing, but it had the advantage of engendering a nascent interest in conducting through direct contact with the professional world of performing musicians active as singers and orchestral players. Adolf Furtwängler, ever keen to encourage and support his son's musical ambitions, therefore hired the Kaim orchestra of Munich for a concert to be given on 19 February

1906 and conducted by the now twenty-year-old Wilhelm. The ambitious programme, strikingly prescient of the mature Furtwängler's core repertoire, consisted of Beethoven's overture *The Consecration of the House* (Op. 124), Furtwängler's own Symphonic Adagio in B minor and Bruckner's monumental but incomplete Ninth Symphony, presumably in the performing version by Ferdinand Loewe. This year in Breslau was followed by a further year in 1906–07 as repetiteur and assistant conductor at the Stadttheater in Zurich, where one of his predecessors was the current conductor of Bayreuth's *Parsifal*, Karl Muck (1859–1940) before returning for a two-year period in 1908 to 1909 at the Munich Hofoper, then under the direction of Felix Mottl, a legendary Wagnerian who, as a member of the 'Nibelungen Chancellery', had been one of the composer's associates at the first Bayreuth Festival in 1876.

The most significant encounter of these early journeyman years was undoubtedly with the composer and conductor Hans Pfitzner (1859–1949). Pfitzner was at that time director of the Strasbourg opera where Furtwängler spent two seasons from 1909 to 1911 as third assistant Kapellmeister, conducting a variety of repertoire and generally broadening his experience in a major repertory opera house. Pfitzner exercised a strong and continuing influence on the young Furtwängler, who a decade later was to conduct some of the earliest performances of the opera, or 'musical legend' *Palestrina*. There is ample evidence of Furtwängler's early admiration for Pfitzner: a letter dated 10 December 1911 indicates that he was present on an occasion when the composer (in true Wagnerian fashion) read the recently completed libretto of *Palestrina* to a small circle of friends. Afterwards he wrote to Pfitzner, '*Palestrina* was to my joyous satisfaction the most beautiful fulfilment of all my hopes. Never before have you expressed your nature more clearly and comprehensively.'[26] Furtwängler is presumably referring here to a reading of the libretto given either in Munich on 13 August 1911 or Strasbourg on 19 October 1911. As he continues in the same letter to describe a concert given on 6 December in Strasbourg it seems likely that he is referring to the Strasbourg reading.[27] Four years later, on 19 July 1916 (and before the first performance) Furtwängler wrote to Pfitzner from Tegernsee:

> Eight days ago in Munich I was introduced to your *Palestrina*. It is difficult to express in a few words just what a profound effect the work made on me. It appears to me to be your greatest and most mature work and one of the most movingly human artworks which has probably ever been written.[28]

26 Furtwängler to Pfitzner. SPK Berlin, 55 Nachl. 13, W. Furtwängler, Kasten 25.
27 See John Williamson, *The Music of Hans Pfitzner* (Oxford: OUP, 1992), p. 137.
28 Furtwängler to Pfitzner. SPK Berlin, 55 Nachl. 13, W. Furtwängler, Kasten 25.

The documentary evidence of Furtwängler's three seasons in Strasbourg working with Pfitzner is sparse, but the conductor Bruno Walter (1876–1962) recounts in his memoirs how 'a young musician, who was one of Pfitzner's assistant conductors, impressed me as being a gifted and singular personality. He was Wilhelm Furtwängler, at that time twenty-three years old.'[29] As we shall see, Hans Pfitzner remained a presence in Furtwängler's musical universe throughout the years of his pre-eminence as a conductor, and, after a period of some distance between the two, increasingly occupied his thoughts during his later years when he was attempting to come to terms with and find his place in the very different cultural environment of post-Nazi Germany.

Enzio: Ein musikalischer Roman (Friedrich Huch)

The years from 1905 to the end of his time working with Pfitzner in Strasbourg in 1911 may be described as the young Wilhelm Furtwängler's apprenticeship, or journeyman years. This was a formative period in his development as a musician as he acquired a working knowledge of the craft of music-making and gained crucial early experience as a conductor. As is evident from his correspondence, his cultural experience was by no means confined to the German tradition; in addition to his musical knowledge he was well acquainted with Shakespeare and had a particular empathy for the visual arts. As we have seen, he owed this broad, general culture to the influence of his two tutors, Ludwig Curtius and Walter Riezler. It was Riezler in particular who influenced the young Furtwängler's thinking about Beethoven. An unusual corroborative source of the young Furtwängler's opinions, together with a probable indicator of Riezler's views, is to be found in the novel Enzio by Friedrich Huch.[30] Huch (1873–1913), a cousin of the more famous Ricarda (1864–1947), lived in Munich and worked as a freelance author, writing popular novels which dealt with the psychology of childhood and youth. In addition to Riezler's claims for the authenticity of

---

29 Bruno Walter, *Theme and Variations*, tr. James A. Galston (London: Hamish Hamilton, 1947), p. 204.
30 Friedrich Huch, *Enzio: Ein musikalischer Roman* (Leipzig: Josef Singer Verlag, 1910). See also Helene Huller, 'Der Schriftsteller Friedrich Huch: Studien zu Literatur und Gesellschaft um die Jahrhundertwende' (Inaugural Dissertation zur Erlangung des Doktorgrades der Philosophischen Fakultät der Ludwig-Maximilians-Universität zu München, 1974), pp. 288–9; Programme book for 1. Wilhelm Furtwängler Tage, University of Jena (6–9 November 1997), pp. 53ff. All translations from *Enzio* are by the present author.

this source, further evidence is supplied by Karla Höcker, the author and personal confidant of Furtwängler, who states that:

> Furtwängler began at that time to write on musical subjects, above all on Beethoven. Most revealing are the notes that he gave to his friend Friedrich Huch shortly before 1910 for the latter's novel *Enzio*, whose story concerns music. What Furtwängler wrote in that connection reveals what he recognised as the truth even in his early youth: that Beethoven was the centre of his spiritual world.[31]

Huch was resident in Munich around the turn of the century and became a close friend of the young Furtwängler. Riezler claims that in *Enzio* Huch based the character of Richard on a synthesis of the characters of himself and Furtwängler and that certain statements on musical matters made in the context of musical discourse within the novel are verbatim Furtwängler. Huch inscribes the title page of Riezler's personal copy of *Enzio* 'Walter Riezler von F.H.'.

The pencil annotation by Riezler reads:

> Für meine Nachkommen: diese Widmung bedeutet nicht etwa, wie man meinen könnte, da? Fr. Huch <u>mich</u> gemeint hat, als er die Gestalt des Enzio schuf. Sondern: mit der Figur des Richard meinte er mich, in einer seltsamen Vermischung mit Zügen, die er von Wilhelm <u>Furtwängler</u> nahm, von dem übrigens die Ausführungen über Musik <u>wörtlich</u> stammen. W.R.[32]

> For my descendants; this dedication does not mean, as one could easily think, that Friedrich Huch had <u>myself</u> in mind when he created *Enzio*. But in the character of Richard he told me that he has combined the peculiar characteristics of myself and Wilhelm <u>Furtwängler</u>, from whom, incidentally, the [annotated] remarks about music are quoted <u>verbatim</u>. W.R.

The origin of the relevant passages was presumably either spoken conversation or written material prepared by Furtwängler for his tutor; the passages attributed to Furtwängler are clearly marked in Riezler's own hand. The following extracts are sufficiently close to the previously cited correspondence with Bertel von Hildebrand to support Riezler's claim. The first composer to come under scrutiny is J. S. Bach.

31 Booklet notes for Furtwängler's recording of Bruckner Symphony No. 5, 28 October 1942.
32 Handwritten inscription on the title page of the copy of *Enzio* in the Zentralbibliothek Zürich. Shelfmark AWD 3124. Author's translation. Reproduced by kind permission.

Friedrich Huch: Enzio

3　Title page of Friedrich Huch's *Enzio*, inscribed by Walter Riezler

I fully understand your dislike of writing fugues. Certainly, it is important to know how a fugue is constructed but it is no longer necessary to imitate the style of Bach. It is the external form of a fugue rather than the specific thematic content which can heighten a particular effect and, as in the case of the Gloria of Beethoven's *Missa Solemnis*, express supreme joy. Bach captures the feeling within a stiff, unyielding [musical] mould. To me it is as if he wrote without the listener in mind; when he began his great works, e.g. the *Matthäus Passion*, he immediately penetrated to the heart of the matter. There is no introduction, no development, his pieces are so constructed that he could almost finish at any point in time he chose. He does not draw to a conclusion, he simply stops; there is no heightening of intensity, no internal contrast within his works, only elaboration. It is wonderful but also rather one-sided. There is hardly any other music in which the musical effect depends on the compositional technique to such an extent that one is actually conscious of the 'craftsmanship'. His pieces are good to play; they have a similar, toughening effect on the musical soul as gymnastic activity does on the body and at the same time the considerable ethical content becomes apparent. It is as if his music develops in the same manner as a natural object created by the living God, but one does not ask: Why has he created that? He stands in the same relationship to contemporary man as the countryside does to those who live in towns.[33]

The fugue is considered as a musical device that serves a specific expressive, intellectual end rather than as an autonomous musical object. Furtwängler was to modify his evaluation of Bach's major works in later years, especially the *Matthäus Passion*, but *Enzio* suggests that he originally viewed the work from a Beethovenian perspective as if, in order to meet his ideal, it should contain elements of 'symphonic' development. He laments the fact that to him Bach's works lack internal contrast but again is considering the idea of musical contrast from a symphonic perspective as an extension of the principle of sonata dialectic. Furtwängler does not in any sense view Bach as a dramatic composer; the *Matthäus Passion* is considered as 'absolute' music rather than a work whose form is determined by dramatic content.

The view of Mozart attributed to Richard/Furtwängler is ambivalent, somewhat deprecatory and takes no account of the composer's operatic output:

He is so much of his period that he must be accepted on his own terms. There is no other standard by which he can be measured. If I was not a musician I would perhaps regard him more highly than any other; but I protect myself from him and keep my distance. There is nothing in

33 *Enzio*, pp. 217–18.

him to which I can relate and which increases my own understanding. Unconditional surrender to him is the only thing possible and only rarely am I capable of that.[34]

Furtwängler's relationship to Mozart was to remain ambivalent; he was to include comparatively few of his works in his concert programmes and, in spite of notable performances of *Don Giovanni* at the Salzburg Festival in the last years of his life, several compositions with which he might have had a temperamental affinity received scant attention (e.g. the *Jupiter Symphony*). The most extensive observations in *Enzio* naturally concern Beethoven.

I said before, nothing in Mozart that I reject could possibly increase my understanding. For me, in spite of all modern music, in spite of Wagner, Berlioz, Bruckner and Brahms, there is only one musician who stimulates me for his work is on an entirely different level: Beethoven. His music is unique and absolute. He is the standard against which all others are measured. His music is pure and speaks only of itself. In spite of the unruly nature of his temperament he has a passion for the direct, the legitimate and the natural. He transcends his passing moods and brings to his work a natural form of self-expression. This integrity is in striking contrast to the mood of today; because of this we can learn more from him than from any other composer.[35]

The way that Beethoven has shown us is not relative but absolute.[36]

At this point Riezler's annotations indicate a break of some six lines in the direct quotation. It continues as follows:

The essence of artistic creativity and what makes every great artwork akin to a heroic deed is struggle. Artistic productivity can only come about as the result of struggle.[37] The artist is a mixture of both active and passive characteristics; it is as if two separate powers are at work in his breast. The struggle begins with the first sounds and motives that the musician discovers: he is now not the servant of one but of two masters for he must not only fulfil his own will but also that of previous creators. It is as if all musical motives and inventions have their own laws and that each in their

34 Ibid., p. 218.
35 Ibid., pp. 219–20.
36 Ibid., p. 293. Italicised sentence underlined by Riezler.
37 The German word used here for struggle is the familiar 'Kampf'. The concept of 'struggle' is here more that of 'Steigerung', or intensification: 'a struggle towards perfection which governs the development of each organism'. See Ritchie Robertson, *A Very Short Introduction to Goethe*, p. 32. The word 'Kampf' had not yet acquired the ideological resonances it was later to accrue.

own fashion will fulfil themselves according to their own necessity. Each has its own will, its own voice. To hear, to recognise and to follow this voice is the task of the artist and we see this most clearly in the greatest artworks: it is as if they were not created by human hands but develop in the manner of a living object. It is like a tree that grows of its own accord. It cannot be made to grow and develop its living nature by watering and giving it nourishment: it lives by virtue of its own absolute essence. It is the same with a work of art. It requires of the artist a degree of modesty and humility which is rare today but it also engenders a sense of joy and contentment of spirit which is only achieved by a very few. This spirit enables us to resist the unjust claims and tolerate the contempt and mockery of the world and, in spite of the most fearful solitude, to be content. Of such an artist can it truly be said that his art is his religion.[38]

These passages are cited at length for here, in this concept of artistic creativity as a result of struggle, we encounter the Faustian duality of 'two souls within a single breast' and the living plant as a metaphor for the artwork. Here too is the reverence for artistic creation that was so characteristic of the tradition of *Bildung*. The attribution is corroborated by their similarity to passages in one of Furtwängler's early published essays. In the article 'Remarks on Beethoven's Music' ('Anmerkungen zu Beethovens Musik', 1918) he writes:

In the midst of the tempest, held in the grip of a raging passion, he retains his steely control, his singularity of purpose, his unshakeable determination to shape and master his material down to the very last detail with a self-discipline unparalleled in the history of art. Never has an artist, driven by an irresistible creative force, felt so intensely the 'law' that underlies artistic creation, and submitted to it with such humility.[39]

Yet again Beethoven is at the centre of the young Furtwängler's musical universe: the idea of musical autonomy, the absolute nature of the musical object, is paramount. The discussion of the fundamental laws that govern all music echoes the Platonic theory of forms; such laws are absolute and exist independent of experience and are therefore, in the Kantian sense, *a priori*. Specific musical objects are a reflection of these absolutes and knowledge of them is gained through experience. Such knowledge is therefore empirical or *a posteriori*. The musical absolute appears to have various qualities at different times according to experience; but it preserves its own absolute nature throughout these phenomenal changes. Individual works which

38 Op cit., pp. 294–6.
39 Zentralbibliothek Zürich: Nachl. W. Furtwängler: S 3; TW, p. 9; FM, p. 33.

are a reflection of this prototype, Kant's 'thing-in-itself' or Goethe's *Urphänomenon*, cannot therefore be distorted by 'human capriciousness'.

Enzio was published in October 1910, by which time Furtwängler was aged twenty-four. In spite of Riezler's inscription, it is important to exercise a degree of caution in ascribing the cited passages directly to Furtwängler, for in the process of writing they passed through the novelist's imagination; but what is significant is that they reflect the æsthetic outlook of a member of the educated elite with an emerging musical talent of an high order at around the time he directed his first orchestral concert in 1906. As such *Enzio* is an important and revealing cultural statement. Such a position represented a synthesis of Shakespearian humanism, the philosophical idealism of Kant, the musical supremacy of Beethoven, the scientific theories of Goethe and an emerging organic world-view that all combined in a Faustian striving for an ideal form of beauty as the catalyst for artistic creativity. The elements of the thoroughgoing education in the traditions of *Bildung*, later to be identified with calculated ironic detachment by Thomas Mann in *Doctor Faustus* as one of the catalytic factors in the release of extraordinary creative powers, together with their inherent dangers, are all present in this one high-minded, artistically driven individual.[40]

40 Thomas Mann, *Doctor Faustus*, especially Chs 8 to 14.

CHAPTER 3

LÜBECK AND MANNHEIM (1911-20)

What I saw growing out of the burgherly character was not the hard bourgeois, but the artist.[1]

Furtwängler's rise to musical pre-eminence in Germany was rapid. It took a mere thirteen years for him to progress from the journeyman position of third assistant conductor to Hans Pfitzner at the Strasbourg Opera from 1909 to 1911 to that of one of the leading musical directors in Germany when in 1922 he assumed the late Arthur Nikisch's mantle as head of the Leipzig Gewandhaus and Berlin Philharmonic orchestras. Yet this rise took place against a background of turbulent political upheaval during which Germany experienced the end of the Wilhelmine Reich, the carnage of World War I, the shock defeat of 1918 and the faltering attempts at democracy under the nascent Weimar Republic.

Furtwängler's first substantive appointment was as chief conductor in the ancient Hanseatic town of Lübeck from 1911 to 1915, where the nature of his work was largely determined by the cultural tastes and values of the patrician families of the *Bürgertum* whose social ethic and customs provided Thomas Mann (1875–1955) with such rich material for his 1901 novel *Buddenbrooks*. In a retrospective look back at the Lübeck of his youth Mann later wrote

I think back to the corner of Germany [...] which formed the first framework of my existence: it was the old Lübeck, near the Baltic, once the Bailiwick of the Hansa, founded before the middle of the twelfth and elevated by Barbarossa in the thirteenth century to be a free imperial city. The extraordinarily beautiful Town Hall, which my father frequented as a Senator, was completed in the year in which Martin Luther nailed his theses to the gate of the castle church in Wittenberg; i.e., at the onset of the modern era. Just as Luther, the reformer, was in his manner of thinking and in his soul a man of the Middle Ages and wrestled with the Devil all

1   Thomas Mann, *Reflections of a Non-Political Man*, p. 101.

his life, in the same way one could stroll in the Protestant Lübeck that had become a republican member of Bismarck's Reich, and still move in the atmosphere of the gothic Middle Ages. In saying this I am thinking not only of the sharply-pointed image of a town with gates and walls, of the humorously macabre shudderings evoked by the Death-Dance painting in the Marienkirche, the crooked, enchanted alleys which were often named after the old Craftsmen's guilds, of the bell-founders, butchers and of the picturesque town houses. No, in its very atmosphere something remained of the state of mind of that time: let's say the last decades of the fifteenth century, the hysteria of the closing years of Middle Ages, something of a latent spiritual epidemic.[2]

For Furtwängler his time in Lübeck was a period of assimilation of the many influences which had come to bear on him during his formative years, as well as a time when he gained a good deal of practical experience of the craft of conducting; as a result his youthful compositional activity largely gave way to the demands of his burgeoning career as a performing artist.

It was the Lübeck novelist Ida Boy-Ed (1852–1928), a friend of Furtwängler's mother Adelheid and an early supporter of Thomas Mann, who encouraged the young Wilhelm to try for the appointment in Lübeck as conductor of the *Verein der Musikfreunde*. He was very much the outsider among the four shortlisted candidates, but notwithstanding a certain amount of confusion surrounding his candidacy, he made an instantaneous impression at the audition (*Probekonzert*) and emerged from the competition as the unanimous choice for the position. He was initially reluctant as he considered himself too inexperienced for such a task, but after further persuasion from Frau Boy-Ed he accepted. His statutory duties required him to conduct eight symphony concerts and two oratorio performances each season together with a number of popular concerts consisting of lighter fare. The programmes of Furtwängler's four seasons in Lübeck are illuminating with regard to his developing repertoire. The symphony concerts show increasing predominance of the Beethoven symphonic canon culminating in his first ever performance of the Ninth Symphony (Op. 125) at the concluding symphony concert of the 1912–13 season on 26 April 1913. There are isolated performances of (for him) comparative rarities such as Tchaikovsky's Symphony No. 6 (29 March 1913), Sibelius' *Finlandia* (30 October 1912) and, more significantly for the future development of his repertoire, Bruckner symphonies began to make an appearance: No. 7 on 9 November 1912; No. 8 on 28 March 1914; and No. 4

2 Thomas Mann, 'Germany and the Germans': see Appendix 2. See also Ronald Hayman, *Thomas Mann* (New York: Scribner, 1995; pbk edn, London: Bloomsbury, 1997), pp. 511–12.

on 5 December 1914. Among the choral works performed were the Mozart *Requiem* (4 and 5 April 1912) and J. S. Bach's *Matthäus Passion* (9 and 10 April 1914 and 1 and 2 April 1915). It may have been the preparations for his performances of the *Matthäus Passion* that prompted Furtwängler to enquire in a letter to Karl Straube (1873–1950), the Cantor of St Thomas's Leipzig: 'Is your edition of the *Matthäuspassion* finished yet? Next time [presumably at the next rehearsal] I must begin to study it with the choir.'[3] Illness forced Furtwängler to withdraw from planned performances of Brahms' *Ein deutsches Requiem* on 20 and 21 March 1913; he was replaced by his predecessor in Lübeck, Hermann Abendroth. Although Furtwängler's position in Lübeck did not include opera, he sufficiently impressed the authorities in the city to be invited as a guest to conduct two works that were to become central to his operatic activity: *Die Meistersinger* (20 November 1913) and *Fidelio* (23 March 1915); and a work which ironically was a lasting favourite of his near contemporary Hans Knappertsbusch (1888–1965), Otto Nicolaï's *The Merry Wives of Windsor*.

The years in Lübeck were crucial in the course of Furtwängler's artistic development. An informative first-hand account of the socially awkward yet charismatic young Kapellmeister, by now in his mid-twenties, is given in a series of letters from Lübeck 'Musikfreundin' Frau Lilli Dieckmann to her mother. In September 1911, shortly after Furtwängler's arrival, she not only gives a vivid description of the effect the 26-year-old had when absorbed in music but also an insight into the prevailing culture of *Bildung*.

When he begins to speak, we see at once that this is a spirit of rare refinement and breadth of culture; and when he sits at the piano his entire artistic soul opens up. [...] His entire being is absorbed in music. He played Beethoven's Sonata Op. 109 and the effect was shattering. It was as if he was creating it himself as a key to his soul.[4]

Lilli Dieckmann was one of the few who were close to Furtwängler during this time and it was in her company that he first heard Arthur Nikisch conduct in Hamburg.[5] As we have seen in Chapter 1, Nikisch exercised a profound influence on Furtwängler.

3   SPK Berlin, 55 Nachl. 13, W. Furtwängler, Kasten 33; *Briefe*, pp. 47–8. Letter undated, probably late 1913.
4   For a selection of Lilli Dieckmann's correspondence with her mother see Martin Hürlimann, ed., *Wilhelm Furtwängler. Im Urteil seiner Zeit* (Zürich: Atlantis, 1955), pp. 131–48, here p. 133. Also Lilli Dieckmann, Anhang L.D., Erinnerungen an Wilhelm Furtwängler's Lübecker Zeit 1911–15, SPK Berlin, 55 Nachl. 13, W. Furtwängler, Kasten 10.
5   Ibid., p. 137; letter of February 1912.

Heinrich Schenker's Monograph on
Beethoven's Ninth Symphony

It was in 1911, the year of his appointment to Lübeck, which was the year after the publication of Friedrich Huch's *Enzio*, that Furtwängler encountered at first hand the work of Heinrich Schenker when he made an intensive study of the theorist's monograph, *Beethoven's Ninth Symphony* (*Beethovens neunte Sinfonie*).[6] Schenker was to have a lasting influence on the development of Furtwängler's thought and approach to musical performance. At the other end of his career in 1947 he wrote a retrospective appreciation of Schenker in which he recalled the impact that this reading had made on him:

> The first work that became widely known was a monograph on Beethoven's Ninth Symphony. This book fell into my hands in Lübeck in 1911 when I was beginning my career as a Kapellmeister and immediately aroused my passionate interest.[7]

Schenker's monograph was published in 1912, a year after Furtwängler states that he first encountered the work. Writing in 1947 after the passage of thirty-five years it is possible that his memory was at fault; but it is more likely that he was made aware of Schenker's work prior to publication by his mother's cousin, the conductor Georg Dohrn (1867–1942), an enthusiastic admirer of Schenker's writings and an early champion of Furtwängler as a conductor.[8] Like many of his fellow assimilated Jewish Germans, Schenker was virulently nationalistic and identified strongly with the Wilhelmine Reich. As with Furtwängler, his thought was bound by the parameters of the Austro-German canon of musical masterworks: he underscored his almost Messianic belief in the hegemony of this tradition by dedicating the Ninth Symphony monograph 'to the memory of the last master of German composition: Johannes Brahms'. For many nineteenth-century Europeans the Ninth Symphony was the *non plus ultra* of the canon and as such acted as a polemical axis around which many of the ideological vicissitudes of the century revolved. In the process, Schenker believed that the purely musical content had become obscured under thickening layers of hermeneutic discourse: Schenker's aim in writing his monograph was therefore to remove

---

6   Heinrich Schenker, *Beethovens neunte Sinfonie* (1912); Eng. edn, *Beethoven's Ninth Symphony*, tr. John Rothgeb (New Haven and London: Yale UP, 1992).
7   Furtwängler, TW, p. 199. See Appendix 1 for a translation of the complete text.
8   See Ian Bent, David Bretherton and William Drabkin, eds, *Heinrich Schenker: Selected Correspondence* (Woodbridge: The Boydell Press, 2014), pp. 251–4.

this obfuscation and 'reclaim the work for "absolute" music'.[9] He was strongly critical of Wagner's programmatic interpretation of the symphony; he even went so far as to accuse him of misunderstanding the 'work' in the process of evolving his conception of music drama:

> In particular, if, as is evident here, the otherwise so original and consequential Wagner has so completely misunderstood the Ninth Symphony precisely in respect to the most crucial artistic points – for example, in respect to voice leading, structure, orchestration, style, and so forth – then must this not automatically discredit all the consequences he has drawn with such unprecedented passion from his own misunderstandings in support of an alleged progress based on the idea of superseding absolute music?[10]

Furtwängler may have found this polemical style excessive; yet he had his own serious misgivings about Wagner and empathised with the spirit of Schenker's approach, even if the virulence of some of Schenker's statements was exaggerated and inelegant to one of his *bürgerlich* sensibilities.[11] The most influential factor, however, was the central thrust of the argument in which Schenker, through his developing organicist methodology, explores the function of the musical process within the parameters of the fluctuating dialectical relationship between form and content. He portentously paraphrases the opening of St John's Gospel by stating unequivocally that 'in the beginning was content', and posits the view that form is a result of the demands of the musical content:

> A musical content that is so perfect in itself as that of the Ninth Symphony uncovers laws of tonal construction that most other human beings do, indeed, carry within their own bosoms, but only the genius, by dint of natural gifts, can actually make manifest! [...] Thus, while for the genius a specific content could produce only this specific shape and none other, the theorists grasp the content *a posteriori* only through a form arbitrarily abstracted by them, but one in which no manner of necessity rules.[12]

It was this uncompromising approach to musical form as being defined by the composer's creative processes that earned Furtwängler's enthusiastic approval:

---

9   See Nicholas Cook, *Beethoven: Symphony No. 9* (Cambridge: CUP, 1993), p. 83.
10 Schenker, *Beethoven's Ninth Symphony*, p. 18.
11 For an alternative reading of Schenker's polemics in relation to Wagner's view of the Ninth Symphony see Nicholas Cook, 'Heinrich Schenker, Polemicist: a reading of the Ninth Symphony Monograph', *Music Analysis*, vol. 14, no. 1 (1995), pp. 89–105.
12 Schenker, *Beethoven's Ninth Symphony*, pp. 4ff. See also Goethe, *Faust*, Part 1, line 1237, 'In the beginning was the deed' (tr. David Luke).

Here for the first time there were no hermeneutics, no irrelevances but the question was asked, simply and directly, what really stands before us in Beethoven's Ninth Symphony? No questions regarding the formal structure were asked, which today are the cause of so much misunderstanding; there was no attempt made to place the work in historical context, but rather the composer's creative process was examined which is the source of the organic cohesion of the work as a whole and which so profoundly affects us all.[13]

The organic world-view of Heinrich Schenker, still at this point at an early stage of its development, found a ready adherent in Furtwängler. His musical education as directed by Riezler, together with his own study of Beethoven and his early experiences as a conductor, made him receptive to the idea that a musical work functioned through the working of processes inherent within itself.

'Timely Reflections of a Musician' (1915)

This idea is developed at much greater length in Furtwängler's first extant essay on musical matters: 'Timely Reflections of a Musician' (Zeitgemässe Betrachtungen eines Musikers). Given Furtwängler's broad cultural education and interests, the title could be an ironic reference to Nietzsche's four *Untimely Reflections* (*Unzeitgemässe Betrachtungen*), published between 1873 and 1876, in which Nietzsche's use of the term 'untimely' in his title implies an attack on public opinion as an arbiter of artistic taste and worth.[14] This is certainly a thread that runs throughout Furtwängler's lengthy and often portentous discourse. The only extant primary source is undated but bears the authorial inscription 'von Wilhelm Furtwängler in Lübeck'.[15] The posthumous anthology *Vermächtnis* gives the date 1915, the year of Furtwängler's final season in Lübeck and his move to Mannheim. It is a prolix but revealing attempt to rationalise and justify his position in relation to the cultural and intellectual context in which he was working. The original source is impossible to identify. It exists only as an extract from a journal or newspaper and bears a superscription taken from Goethe's *Annalen* (1803): 'Die Totalwirkung bleibt immer das Dämonische, dem wir huldigen'

13 Furtwängler, TW, p. 199.
14 See Nietzsche, *Untimely Reflections*, tr. R. J. Hollingdale (Cambridge: Cambridge Texts in the History of Philosophy, 1997), p. xlvi.
15 Zentralbibliothek Zürich, Nachl. W. Furtwängler: S 121. See VMS, pp. 57–82; FM, pp. 123–37.

– Goethe.[16] (The total effect is always that of the daemonic, to which we pay homage.) It is likely that Furtwängler was familiar with the Lübeck literary scene through his mother's connection with the novelist Ida Boy-Ed. It is therefore noteworthy that the publication of this article anticipates by three years that of Thomas Mann's similarly entitled *Reflections of a Non-Political Man* (*Betrachtungen eines Unpolitischen*, 1918). In the series of essays contained in *Reflections* Mann sets up a dichotomy between the organic culture of community (Gemeinschaft) and the commercially motivated rationalism of civilisation (Gesellschaft). German culture is throughout aligned with the supra-rational. Non-political art is set against ideological artifice; paternalistic and authoritarian community is contrasted with democratic civilisation. As with Mann, Furtwängler's wartime nationalism is encoded in his views on German art as regenerative of national character rather than in any openly nationalistic sentiments. Mann was later to change his views, although significantly he never retracted *Reflections of a Non-Political Man*. The categories identified, which include a lengthy discourse on the characteristics of *Bürgertum*, determined much of his later thinking about Germany and the Germans that was to find ultimate expression in the novel *Doctor Faustus* (1947). Furtwängler's 'Reflections', on the other hand, set out a conservative agenda for much of his thinking about German music and art that was to remain largely unchanged for the rest of his life.

At this point in his career Furtwängler was twenty-nine years old; yet already in this essay there is a strong sense of the cultural conservative at odds with the prevailing artistic trends of his day. The opening paragraph leaves the reader in no doubt as to the authorial purpose:

> The following lines are written from the point of view of an artist. It is not usually the artist's task to consider art in general terms. [...] The reason I am doing so is that the current situation unfortunately demands a degree of clarity and certainty about artistic matters that was unnecessary in earlier and happier times. In the state of unbelievable conceptual confusion that prevails today, the artist needs a measure of reassurance to help him preserve his integrity in this one-sided, over-intellectualised environment.[17]

The line of descent to this essay from the remarks attributed to Furtwängler by Huch in *Enzio* is apparent in the opening statement as it subsequently unfolds: the notion, derived from Goethe, of intensification (*Steigerung*) as

---

16 This superscription, with its reference to the daemonic, is redacted from the text later included in VMS.

17 VMS, p. 57; FM, p. 123 (translation revised).

a struggle towards perfection is now giving way to the Darwinian idea of struggle (*Kampf*) as a metaphor for artistic creation.[18] The energy that fuels the creative act is released by the conflict of forces present in the compositional material. To Furtwängler the creative act consists in harnessing this energy and channelling the dialectical process:

> The artist's task is to harness the forces inherent in this substance to a single common purpose. Before he sets to work on it, it is in a wild, natural, unordered state. [...] As the composer regards the elements of the raw material at his disposal, he sees an endless series of possibilities in his struggle both to unite the various stresses and tensions in that material, with its underlying laws of rhythm, harmony and so on, and to produce his final cohesive artwork.[19]

If the creative act is a matter of releasing latent energy, then the continuing existence of the artwork depends on maintaining a state of equilibrium between two distinct levels within the work itself:

> When we look more closely at this process, we find we can distinguish two levels. On the first each individual element combines with those adjacent to it to form larger elements, these larger elements then combining with others and so on, a logical outwards growth from the part to the whole. On the other level the situation is the reverse: the given unity of the whole controls the behaviour of the individual elements within it, down to the smallest detail. The essential thing to observe is that in any genuine work of art these two levels complement each other, so that the one only becomes effective when put together with the other. Not until today, when the essential unity of the two levels has dissolved, have we been in a position to perceive the distinction between them.[20]

Furtwängler examines the dual nature of the inherent process. The logic of the movement from individual unit to larger element governs the organic growth of the artwork; yet conversely the behaviour of the individual element is governed by the 'whole'. Furtwängler's observations are at the same time both organicist and structural; in Schenkerian terms he moves both from background to foreground and foreground to background. The function of the musical process is dependent on the maintenance of a state of equilibrium between these two levels within the work. It is at this point in the structural layering within the work that form and content counterbalance

---

18 Ritchie Robertson, *Goethe: A Very Short Introduction*, p. 32.
19 VMS, p. 58; FM, p. 123 (amended).
20 Ibid., pp. 58–9; pp. 123–4.

each other. The form of the work is defined through 'the given unity of the
whole controlling the behaviour of the individual elements'; the content
is determined by 'individual elements combining to form larger elements;
a logical outwards growth from the part to the whole'. Furtwängler is here
articulating the concept which Schenker was later to define as the middleground; the point at which the surface processes of the music intersect with
the controlling fundamental structure, or *Ursatz*. The comparison with
Schenker's approach is instructive. Whereas, in the preface to *Beethoven's
Ninth Symphony*, Schenker assigns prominence to content, asserting that
form is a result of the musical process, Furtwängler maintains that form has
a generative, and content a controlling function. The point at which the two
processes intersect is the motivating point for the re-creative or interpretative
act of performance.

The creative process, however, is to Furtwängler merely the means by
which the initial vision of the artwork is given corporeal existence. The
influence of the ideas of Gestalt psychology is again apparent in the view that
the artwork is initially conceived as a whole and the purpose of the creative
work is to realise this vision:

> The artistic process that has at its starting-point the unity of the whole
> rests on the concept of a more-or-less complete vision of that whole. For
> the artist at work – work being, in this context, not a state, a condition but
> a dynamic activity of struggle [Kampf] and victory [Sieg] – this vision is
> the goal he seeks to attain. [...] Only at the end of the journey, therefore,
> will the vision emerge in its totality, not only for the listener, the receiver of
> the work of art, but also – and this is the vital point – for the composer, the
> creative artist himself.[21]

The latent ideology inherent in the use of the Darwinian concept of the
dynamic activity of struggle and victory as a metaphor for creative activity
is particularly instructive, given that this essay was written at a time of
heightened national enthusiasm for World War I. Furtwängler continues his
exegesis of the musical process by considering the intrinsic properties of the
raw materials of music. Rhythm is the only element with the representational
qualities capable of portraying an actual event; it is this that makes musical
naturalism theoretically possible. Naturalism and its realisation in the form
of programme music are of secondary importance to Furtwängler, for 'the
sound of a single concrete harmony transports us at once into the realm
of art, far from the world of objective reality'.[22] This transcendent position

21 Ibid., p. 60; pp. 124–5.
22 Ibid., p. 63; p. 126.

defines Furtwängler's perception of the essence and nature of the musical object as an autonomous, self-contained entity with an organic life of its own:

> The existence of music as an art is linked to the capacity to experience a sound, any sound, as something self-contained, something with a life of its own, a piece of living reality. Only from such a starting point is it possible to conceive the existence of objective æsthetic form. The musical forms that have developed in the course of history are only the rich and diverse manifestations of a law whose basic expression is the cadence. The works of the great masters, the fugues of Bach, the symphonies of Beethoven, are all subject to this formal law, a law laid on them by nature.[23]

Here Furtwängler promulgates an idea that is neatly congruent with the Schenkerian concept of prolongation, or the extension of the cadence over a large time span. This proto-typical musical movement from dominant to tonic generates a wide range of musical styles. For historical artistic development to be genuine it must conform to the organic idea of evolutionary growth, drawing its energy from the forces latent within the musical substance, as exemplified by cadential progression:

> All genuine development, right down to the present day, derives on the one hand from the expansion and enrichment of the relationships arising from these basic conditions, and on the other from a growing concentration and intensification of the innate forces within them. These forces are taken for granted and their existence would only be questioned if we were to decide to express ourselves in a different tonal system – a system of quartertones for example. Such a system could not, however, develop from our present system, any more than an apple tree could be grafted on to an oak.[24]

In addition, as Oswald Spengler was shortly to declare, genuine artistic growth is incompatible with the idea of sudden change; the political, social and æsthetic maelstrom of the second decade of the twentieth century was therefore antithetical to the concept of artistic growth as Furtwängler understood the term. Organic cohesion within the autonomous whole, bounded by the laws of tonality, was the *sine qua non* of the worth of a musical work.

Within this overall context Furtwängler considers the nature of the creative process itself. The 'act' of creation occurs when the artistic vision intersects with the energy latent within the musical substance. The momentum of the

23 Ibid., p. 64; p. 126.
24 Ibid., p. 64; p. 127.

creative process is sustained through the operation of the laws of organic growth:

> Consciousness [Bewußtsein] thus holds within itself the terms of the relationship between the artistic material and the vision this material is to embody – that is to say, the artist ultimately discovers through his own labours how to give expression to this feature and that. Once acquired, this is knowledge he can never lose; it will remain with him through all his future works. Consciousness is thus the equivalent of reaching, more or less involuntarily, the end of the creative process.[25]

The self-renewing creative process is always self-contained and finite within the context of the individual autonomous artwork: the status of the individual work is thus assured. Furtwängler develops this concept by considering the idea of the autonomy of the artwork as part of the overall process of organic growth:

> What originally had its own purpose now becomes a link in a new chain; it becomes a means to an end and loses its independent status. This is the way in which all progress, all development takes place, both in the general and in the particular. This, of course, refers specifically to the individual units of expression within the body of the work of art and not to the work as a whole, which is an end, a goal in itself, and cannot be treated as a part of something new.[26]

Sudden and abrupt change imposed from without was antithetical to the concept of organic growth; development was a continuous process. Yet in addition to the function of the specific artwork within the concept of overall development it also has independence proportionate to the integrity and power of the original concept:

> All this is a matter for the individual artist. The more capable he is of giving full creative form to his subject matter, the more complete and fulfilled will be the life enjoyed by his works, the more self-sufficient and independent of their creator. He, in turn, will have greater freedom to shape each succeeding work from a completely new point of departure: nothing will be left over from the preceding work, in which everything, so to speak, has been used up.[27]

25 Ibid., pp. 65–6; pp. 127–8 (amended). The translation of 'Bewußtsein' is particularly problematic in this context. The concept of consciousness here appears to be synonymous with the idea of the creative process.
26 Ibid., pp. 66–7; p. 128.
27 Ibid., p. 67; p. 128.

The concomitant idea of artistic individuality follows from the concept of autonomy. Individuality is a matter of consistency; consistency in the treatment of and approach to the use of materials is the means by which the artist creates his own style and his own world. The substance may differ but the method remains constant.

The organic world-view conditions and defines Furtwängler's concept of the flow of history; Hegelian historicism underpins the comparison of historical development with the growth of harmonic language. There are no sudden shifts; one style flows naturally out of the content of another:

> These are the elements which make possible the development of art independently of, and, as it were, over the head of the individual artist. In contrast to his basic approach to his material [...] these individual elements undergo a process of development in which the earlier elements are subsumed, cancelled out by the subsequent material. Thus a modern composer cannot take over the harmonic range of Wagner, say, or Schumann, let alone Mozart, because the harmonic material itself has developed – irresistibly, automatically, from inner impulsion. It is a development no one can resist or escape, and constitutes what one calls the style of a particular epoch.[28]

The absolute paradigm of the organic process is to be found in the works of Beethoven. It is the perfection of organic cohesion and the perfect state of equilibrium between the whole and the parts which constitutes the Beethovenian ideal, a state not even achieved by Haydn and Mozart: their perceived failure consistently to meet and achieve this ideal resulted in what should be regarded as diminished artistic integrity and an imperfect understanding of the full potential of the material with which they were working:

> Up to the time of Beethoven musical development had taken place according to the tacit assumption that the work of art emerged like an organism. [...] Whereas Beethoven, following both his basic attitude to his material and the nature of his genius, sought to bring out the whole with even greater clarity and power, his contemporaries such as Weber, but even more his successors in the Romantic movement, turned away from this approach. The concept of the work of art as an organic whole crumbled in their hands. The Romantics remained faithful to it only in small forms, and it was not long before the grand ideals of the past were forgotten altogether.[29]

28 Ibid., pp. 68–9; p. 130.
29 Ibid., pp. 70–2; pp. 130–1 (amended).

This passage could almost have been written by Heinrich Schenker as a preface to one of his theoretical works. The main buttresses of the Schenkerian edifice are in place: the organic ideal reaches its zenith in Beethoven; the Romantics moved away from the governing principles of the organic whole, thus the Romantic epoch represented a debasement of artistic values. It is striking how thoroughly and completely Furtwängler not only shared the same assumptions which gave rise to Schenker's system but also had absorbed Schenkerian thinking as a result of his reading of *Beethoven's Ninth Symphony*. It is therefore not surprising that he now proceeds to discuss the figure who both for Schenker and himself posed the biggest problem and who represented the greatest challenge to the musical principles rooted in the organic world-view: Richard Wagner.

> Then came Wagner, with a new view of the whole, creating a new unity in the form of drama and adding a whole series of new material elements. The nature of the whole as seen by Wagner gave rise to a more intense exploitation of the material, an intensity encouraged by the fact that this exploitation was less concerned with the logical sequence of the elements in a purely musical sense. But as a result the material as such was all the more quickly exhausted, and Wagner's successors, who lack his own very personal sense of unity sustained by drama, now face total bankruptcy. They are not interested in a unity created by following the laws of the musical material itself, like that sought by Brahms in taking his lead from the classical composers of the past, and the unity offered by Wagner is not open to them, since they work only as composers, not as creators of a *Gesamtkunstwerk*. Viewed in this light, the path that leads to programme music – in its naturalistic form in opera, in its conceptual form in the music of the concert hall – seems the only one remaining, if the necessity for any kind of form is not to be totally negated.[30]

Furtwängler was later to express similar views in his later essay of 1919.[31] Wagner's artistic cohesion was not the result of the organic logic latent in his material – rather it was an extrinsic unity of dramatic rather than purely musical origin. It was Furtwängler's view that, without the powerful unifying force of Wagner's artistic imagination, successive composers lacked artistic integrity. Brahms is singled out as an exception to this rule for he followed the Beethovenian path. Furtwängler further develops his view that a fall from a state of organic grace represents a decline in standards of artistic integrity:

30 Ibid., pp. 71–2; p. 131 (amended).
31 See present work, pp. 76–8.

No longer is it the whole that controls the behaviour of the parts. No longer does the vision go hand in hand with the forces contained in the material; rather, it is the latter that has come to dominate the vision, determining the form of the whole and thus the vision itself. The parts have consumed the whole, with the result that not only is there no longer a whole but there are also no longer any parts, because these can only exist so long as there is a whole to which they can refer. Everything exhausts itself in the individual moment, no heed being paid either to what has gone before or to what follows. The consequence is a concentration on the effectiveness of the moment, effectiveness for its own sake, in harmony, in rhythm, in orchestration, and through numerous charming effects [Reizwirkungen].[32]

Overall form is no longer the primary factor; the content goes further than determining the form, it actually precipitates its disintegration. The equilibrium between form and content, or the whole and the parts, no longer exists. The importance of the individual moment is therefore exaggerated; the fact that effect becomes an end in itself rather than a function of the continuing musical process contributes to the dissolution of form.

Furtwängler continues to stress the Gestalt-inspired idea of the paramount importance of artistic vision or *Einfall* (inspiration). The vision encapsulates the act of creation itself; the interaction of the whole with the material, or form with content, constitutes, and through a release of latent energy motivates, the musical process through which the artwork is brought into being. It is the integrity and intensity of the artistic vision that determines greatness in art. The vision defines the material:

For this overall form itself is the expression of the artist's vision, and although the vision can only become reality through its interaction with the material [...] it cannot possibly be derived *from* the material. The vision is the most direct, most immediate expression of the artist's relationship to the world. As such it lives its own life in the artist's mind, without thought of realisation in formal terms, although, as we have seen, it only achieves its realisation through the act of formal creation.[33]

It is this lack of artistic vision that Furtwängler considers to be the chief fault of his time: the musical process has become an end in itself; it is a manufactured rather than a creative act. This does not constitute artistic progress, rather it leads to an accelerating process of decline:

32 VMS, pp. 72–3; FM, p. 132.
33 Ibid., pp. 73–4; p. 133 (amended: author's emphasis).

Artists of today categorically deny that the material is dependent on, and conditioned by the vision, or that the parts are dependent on the whole. In fact, they deny that there is a whole. This leaves them with only the parts. [...] The significant features of a work of art, including the great works of the past, are now identified as residing only in the techniques employed. [...] They cannot grasp what history would teach them – that every complex of material forces is in the last analysis only a means towards the realisation of a vision, the creation of a living world, which is the sole purpose of all artistic activity.[34]

Again Furtwängler justifies his position with a critique of Wagner and in so doing he provides a brief and cogent summary of Wagnerian thinking:

The basic, ever-recurrent content of his writings may be summarised in two sentences: firstly, I am a poet, not a composer, and secondly, the language that expresses the profoundest truths of the human soul is music. Put another way, this paradox, real or apparent, means: the total vision of my work is of a different nature, i.e. poetic, from that of the means, i.e. musical, through which it is to be realised.[35]

Poetry is the source of Wagnerian form; music is the material, the means through which the form is realised. What, asks Furtwängler, has been the long-term effect of this æsthetic on musical art? In answering his own question Furtwängler endorses Nietzsche's critique of Wagner; he is essentially a miniaturist:

One thing that immediately strikes us when we look at Wagner's music is its complete lack of traditional forms – Liedform, sonata and so on. Viewed solely as a piece of music, a work by Wagner is sheer chaos, with no beginning, middle or end but simply an accumulation of small self-contained sections. Where such formal elements are found, as in his early works, in *Parsifal* and, as part of the historical content, in *Die Meistersinger*, they do not emerge naturally from the heart of the work but are treated either in an arbitrary, fragmented manner or agglomerated in the style we associate with Baroque. Yet in spite of this the effect left by an opera of Wagner's is not one of chaos but one of absolute precision and singlemindedness.[36]

To Furtwängler the source of the precision is that Wagner's music brings the poetic idea to life; each work has an individual style of its own. It is the governing poetic idea which is generative in an organic sense; the more

34 Ibid., p. 75; p. 133 (amended).
35 Ibid., pp. 76–7; p. 134 (amended).
36 Ibid., p. 77; pp. 134–5.

cohesive and unified the central poetic idea the greater the organic integrity of the work. It is not so much Wagner himself, so he believed, but the so-called assimilation of his ideas by those who followed him that has set music upon the present unsatisfactory path. Those who have rejected Wagner on absolutist grounds reject him for the best of reasons: Wagner's work represented a distortion and misappropriation. It was those who regarded Wagner's music as absolute music in itself who predetermined this decline:

> When musicians began to regard Wagner's music as absolute music it was inevitable that a revolution in their attitudes would follow. What had formerly been rejected now began to be seen as a new form of freedom, a release from the laws of thematic and harmonic composition, from the strict observance of rules of organically developed form and from other constraints that had been felt to be so burdensome. [...] The most important aspect of the situation was that understanding of the meaning of music now took a new turn. They no longer felt the necessity for an organic musical whole, and the destruction of this concept opened the way to the developments we see in modern times, when music has been handed over to the forces of so-called progress.[37]

Furtwängler concludes his essay with 'a few observations on the subject of performance'.[38] In his view it is the inadequacy of contemporary intellectual and spiritual life which is having an adverse effect on the quality of musical performance:

> This circumstance seems deeply rooted in the general artistic conditions of the age. We are the same people as performers that we are as creators; we both produce and reproduce; the currents, trends and dangers characteristic of the music of our own time reveal themselves in the way we regard music of other ages. The inability to feel the fundamental expressive content of a work through its entire course, from beginning to end, is at its most glaringly obvious in those works of whose living example we stand in greatest need today. It is those works that receive the worst performances because they are the very ones that make the greatest spiritual demands on the performer.[39]

Performance is a re-experiencing of the process of organic growth that takes place in the creation of an artwork.[40] Furtwängler rejects as inappropriate

---

37 Ibid., pp. 79–80; pp. 135–6.
38 Ibid., p. 80; p. 136.
39 Ibid., pp. 80–1; p. 136 (amended).
40 Furtwängler's conception of the phenomenon of musical performance here suggests the ideas of Wilhelm Dilthey.

both the historical approach, i.e. that an artwork is representative of a specific historical period and is contained within the parameters of that period, and the personal approach whereby an artwork becomes a means of personal expression on the part of the individual performer.

> Proof of this can be found everywhere, most frequently in performances of the 'classical' Masters – Bach, and especially Beethoven. There are two broad approaches. One is the 'historical' approach – that is to say, these works are seen as belonging to an historical period which is over and done with and has no direct relevance to the present age. After hearing a work performed in accordance with such a view, we find ourselves left with not the slightest doubt that it has indeed no relevance to the present age. It has that kind of slick elegance against which Wagner protested and which appears to be enjoying a revival today. Any passionate outbursts that might be considered to be in bad taste are studiously avoided, as is any appeal to present-day expectations. As a result all 'expression' is effectively banished from the performance.
>
> The other approach is to thrust one's own 'personality' to the fore and seek, as a modern man, to turn the classics into modern works. Here, by means of a characteristically modern urge to pack as much expression into each individual moment as possible, one can see even more starkly how ill-equipped we are for the task. In both cases the reason is the same: the inability to identify the sources of that expressive power that flows through and permeates every part of the living organisms that are these works.[41]

To Furtwängler the expression is in the act of performance itself which therefore assumes a much more lofty purpose; it is a continuation of the ongoing organic process of artistic creation.

'Timely Reflections of a Musician' may be regarded as a governing text for Furtwängler's entire creative life. This little-known, early essay written by a rising young conductor on the threshold of his career has here been cited and considered at length as it is a arguably the single most significant document in understanding the development of Furtwängler's thought from its roots in a nineteenth-century musical aesthetic governed by the organic world-view. It is a tough, unyielding read: prolix in style, tortuous in expression and often repetitive in argument. Yet it is no exaggeration to say that it sets the artistic and intellectual agenda for the rest of Furtwängler's career. It defines an ideological position from which he never essentially deviated for the rest of his life. It is significant that it was written in Lübeck, with its strong Lutheran traditions. There is no evidence that Furtwängler had any specific

41 VMS, p. 81; FM, pp. 136–7 (amended).

denominational allegiances, but like Thomas Mann's Senator Thomas Buddenbrook, it is evident that he was 'full of the Protestant's passionate, relentless sense of personal responsibility'.[42] For all the authority of its manner, however, 'Timely Reflections' bears the stamp of one accustomed to diffuse speculation and rumination rather than rigorous philosophical enquiry. Furtwängler probed the essence of the works he sought to bring before the public from the standpoint of a creative artist. From the outset of his career he had a strong sense of mission. The performer had a priestly function; his purpose was to act as a channel through which the energy latent in a musical composition flowed.

Hofkapellmeister in Mannheim (1915–20)

Furtwängler's Lübeck performance of *Fidelio* on 23 March 1915 was attended by a delegation from the city of Mannheim headed by the outgoing Hofkapellmeister Artur Bodanzky (1877–1939), recently appointed to the New York Metropolitan Opera. As a result, and in spite of the shortcomings of the *Fidelio* performance, Furtwängler was nominated as Bodanzky's successor. In September 1915 he became first conductor of the Mannheim Opera and of the concerts of the much older institution of the Musical Academy (Musikalische Akadamien), founded in 1779. Mannheim enjoyed a long cultural tradition and prided itself on the excellence of its musical life as demonstrated by the high standards of orchestral playing established in the mid eighteenth century by Johann Stamitz. In contrast to the patrician Hanseatic merchants of Lübeck, Mannheim's artistic values were defined by a cultural elite of lawyers, bankers and merchants, typical of which were the Geissmars. Leopold Geissmar, head of the family, was a wealthy banker of Jewish descent and an amateur violinist. Leopold had a passion for music and possessed a collection of fine instruments, including the Vieuxtemps Stradivarius. His daughter Berta, who later became Furtwängler's personal assistant and managed his affairs until forced to emigrate in 1936, describes the Mannheim public as 'in the habit of looking on its *Hofkapellmeister* as a kind of demi-god: he was general property, and all he said and did was the talk of the day'.[43]

Although in 1915 Germany was at war, Berta Geissmar's memoir describes cultural life as continuing:

42 *Buddenbrooks*, p. 523.
43 Geissmar, *The Baton and the Jackboot*, p. 13.

4   Furtwängler in Mannheim, 1915–20

'This was the musician's look; vague and vacant precisely because it abodes in the kingdom of the purer, profounder, more absolute logic than that which shapes our verbal conceptions and thoughts' (Thomas Mann, *Buddenbrooks*, p. 406).

The last [1914–18] war was in no sense a total war, and during those four years cultural and artistic life was kept up in Germany. The authorities saw to it that those really indispensable for the maintenance of cultural life, of opera, drama and concerts, were exempt from whole-time war work.[44]

Furtwängler's primary duties were as director of the opera. He made his Mannheim debut on 7 September 1915 with *Fidelio* and during his first season expanded his repertoire to include operas by the early German Romantic composer Marschner (*Hans Heiling*), his former teacher Max von Schillings (*Mona Lisa*), his mentor Hans Pfitzner (*Der arme Heinrich*) as well as works that were to accrue special significance for him at the other end of his career: *Don Giovanni* and *Der Freischütz*. He expanded his Wagner repertoire to include *Der fliegende Holländer*, *Tristan*, *Parsifal* and the complete *Ring* cycle, which he conducted in its entirety for the first time in March 1916. This momentum continued into the 1916–17 season during which the music of Richard Strauss features strongly (*Ariadne auf Naxos* and *Salome*) together with that of the young Erich Korngold (*Violanta* and *Der Ring des Polykrates*). All this represents a formidable workload for a Kapellmeister who had arrived two years previously with only three operas in his repertoire.

It was through his work as a performer that the ideas formulated in 'Timely Reflections of a Musician' were given practical realisation, for in addition to his duties at the opera Furtwängler was also responsible for the Academy Concerts (Akademiekonzerte). This was a series of subscription concerts given by personnel largely drawn from the opera orchestra that gave the young conductor the opportunity to extend his repertoire by performing canonical symphonic works as well as rarities by Siegmund von Hausegger and Max Reger. Bruckner's monumental Eighth Symphony was first programmed during the 1917–18 season; Furtwängler wrote a feature article for a local newspaper in which he introduces the work to the musical public. This is the earliest extant article by Furtwängler on Anton Bruckner. The article survives only as a fragile newspaper cutting. It is not possible to ascertain from the source either the precise date of publication or the title of the newspaper in which it appeared. However, there is a brief postscript to the article: 'Bruckner's Eighth Symphony today begins the second Musical Academy. The public is requested to be punctual and not delay the beginning of the concert.' Furtwängler first gave the symphony in Mannheim at the second Academy Concert on 6 November 1917. It seems safe to assume that the article was written to introduce this performance.[45]

---

44 Ibid., p. 12.
45 Zentralbibliothek Zürich, Nachl. W. Furtwängler: S 5. Author's translation.

Anton Bruckner's Eighth Symphony
by
Wilhelm Furtwängler (Mannheim)

The Eighth Symphony is the last work that Bruckner was able to complete. It is, if one disregards the torso that remains of the Ninth, the most powerful and personal record of him that we possess. It is the largest in his series of gigantic symphonies; gigantic in conception, gigantic in the growth of ideas and the power and scope of feeling. It is a thoroughly heroic world[;] pure superhuman content here confronts us. The sombre prevailing mood which pervades the work gives to it a quality of tragic truthfulness which in some passages, particularly in the finale, appears to intensify the apocalyptic visions. In the middle comes the wonder of the Adagio, the ultimate concept of peace, transfiguration, indescribable rest and harmony. I have difficulty in putting this into words and I feel myself wholly incapable of describing the effect which this work has on me and conveying something of its meaning.

Some expert musicians – either prejudiced through convention or hypnotised by classical conceptions of form – consider Bruckner's music to be lacking in structural cohesion; as is so often the case, they cannot see the wood for the trees. They consider only the undeniable formal clumsiness which is, incidentally, easy to rectify. They forget the certainty with which the dominating thoughts dictate the formal structure. Admittedly, it is the responsibility of the performance to make this into a living experience but there are other considerations. Bruckner's music is not thought of as suitable for the public of today, for whom a concert is one social experience more or less and an opportunity for the type of conversation that takes place in most theatres. In addition Bruckner does not create for the 'pure' specialist musician, any more so than does Wagner (this today stirs up pitiful opposition towards him against which he is helpless). Just as there is no militaristic content in his music neither is there any sense of fatigue or hedonistic artificiality, which in music is only created by a combination of nerves and intellect. Bruckner turns, as does all great art, to humanity and only to this; to him the essence of a musical work is to experience its central core of feeling. Whoever is unable to do this should remain at a distance. The immense stature of this music highlights the flimsy mediocrity of so much of our concert life today.

Here in less abstract form is a summary of the ideas that Furtwängler had already considered at length in 'Timely Reflections of a Musician'; he concentrates his thoughts in order to impress his ideas on the concert-going public. The concept of the apocalyptic visions stimulating the growth of ideas which determine the formal structure is realised through the act of performance which itself transforms this process into a living experience of the central core of feeling at the heart of the work. The quasi-religious metaphors of peace, transfiguration, indescribable rest and harmony (Frieden, Verklärung, eine unbeschreibliche Ruhe and Harmonie) suggest that even at this point in his career Furtwängler regarded Bruckner as a source of revealed truth. He is particularly anxious to emphasise that there is no militaristic content, nor any undercurrent of decadence in this music; here is Furtwängler assuming, during the last year of the Great War, the lofty role not of a mere representative but of a high priest of *Kultur*. The lasting significance of this view of Bruckner will become apparent later.

'Remarks on Beethoven's Music' (1918)

The social and political catharsis of the Great War (1914–18) naturally defined and conditioned the context in which Furtwängler was working and writing. In his censure of modern musical culture he does not mention specific individuals by name but his remarks were made at a time when the ideas of Schoenberg and his school were reaching an ever-widening audience. The dissolution of tonality evident even in such early works as *Verklärte Nacht* Op. 4 (1899) and the First Chamber Symphony Op. 9 (1906) provoked in some quarters the reaction in favour of pre-Wagnerian tonality, which prompted Schenker to dedicate his work *Beethoven's Ninth Symphony* to 'the memory of the last master of German composition, Johannes Brahms'. Schenker considered that the art of musical composition was now defunct: it was an art of the past.

An early essay dating from the Mannheim years, 'Remarks on Beethoven's Music' (Anmerkungen zu Beethovens Musik) shows how thoroughly Furtwängler had absorbed the methodology and didactic principles of Schenker's *Beethoven's Ninth Symphony*, but not necessarily its polemics.[46] First, Furtwängler considers the 'absolute' nature of Beethoven's music: 'With its roots in itself, self-contained and self-sufficient, his music is ultimately impervious to any attempt to understand it from without.' Like Schenker he is dismissive of the hermeneutic approach to an understanding of Beethoven:

> Instead of looking for Beethoven in his works, approaching the numerous confusing aspects of his personality from the centre, i.e. from his music, people have been trying to 'explain' his music in terms of personal characteristics and thus make it more 'intelligible'.

46 VMS, pp. 7–14; FM, pp. 32–7.

Although in this case Furtwängler does not specify a particular author, he seems to be referring to the critical methodology of Paul Bekker, whose influential study of *Beethoven* (1911) is representative of the hermeneutic approach to Beethoven criticism.[47] In so doing he anticipates by two years the Bekker contra Pfitzner debate, in which these contrasting approaches came into direct conflict.[48] Bekker and Schenker were at opposite ends of the spectrum in their respective views. Furtwängler was firmly of the Schenkerian persuasion; in a diary entry for 15 April 1920 Schenker records how Furtwängler reproached him for not attacking Bekker with sufficient vigour.[49] Furtwängler's criticism of Wagner's reception of Beethoven, however, is more subtle and refined than that of Schenker. There is none of the coarse vitriol that infuses Schenker's polemic; such a mode of expression would have been totally alien to Furtwängler's cultivated *bürgerlich* nature. He even goes so far as to credit Wagner with being the first to realise the implications of organicist thought in the matter of performance:

> Only one thing will help the performer – the most important thing of all – namely, for him to feel his way into the structure of the work as an entity, as a living organism. [...] Wagner was the first to point to the practical implication of this organic experience of the structure of Beethoven's works. Foremost among them is the use of rubato, that almost imperceptible yet constant variation of tempo which turns a piece of music played rigidly according to the notes on the printed page into what it really is – an experience of conception and growth, of a living organic process.[50]

'Remarks on the Music of Wagner's *Ring*' (1919)

In Furtwängler's early writings the organic metaphor features as a measure with which to assess the artistic worth of musical works. Here in his linking of tempo fluctuation as means of realising the organic process of composition his reader is reminded of Wagner's prescriptions in his essay 'On Conducting'

47 Paul Bekker, *Beethoven* (Stuttgart and Berlin: Deutsche Verlags-Anstalt, 1911); Eng. edn, tr. M. M. Bozman (London: J. M. Dent, 1925).
48 See Peter Franklin, 'Audiences, Critics and the Depurification of Music: Reflections on a 1920s Controversy', *Journal of the Royal Musical Association*, vol. 114, Part 1 (1989), pp. 80–91.
49 Hellmut Federhofer, *Heinrich Schenker nach Tagebüchern und Briefen in der Oswald Jonas Memorial Collection*, p. 111.
50 Zentralbibliothek Zürich, Nachl. W. Furtwängler: S 4, in *Mannheimer Theaterjahrbuch*, vol. 1 (1919). TW, p. 12; FM, pp. 35–6.

(Über das Dirigieren, 1869). After he had directed his first cycle of *Der Ring des Nibelungen* in Mannheim, Furtwängler wrote an essay, 'Remarks on the Music of Wagner's *Ring*' (Anmerkungen zur Musik von Wagners Ring des Nibelungen), in which he developed the ideas on the function of music in Wagnerian drama as previously expressed in 'Timely Reflections'. In his comparison of the *Ring* with *Tristan und Isolde* and *Die Meistersinger* the organicist inference is clear:

> The differences between the *Ring* and Wagner's other works are not all that easy to identify. If we take *Tristan* or *Die Meistersinger*, we are aware from the very beginning of something which gives the whole work, heterogeneous though it is, a quite extraordinary unity. There is an all-enveloping atmosphere that permeates every pore of the work, a mysterious nucleus from which energy spreads to every corner. This is the source of the characteristic musical style peculiar to each individual work. Starting in the Prelude, a microcosm of the meaning of the work as a whole, it retains its power to the very last bars. But the *Ring* has no such central nucleus.[51]

A concept central to the organic view of the artwork is that the content of a musical work originated from and was infused by a single idea as a source of musical energy. *Tristan* and *Die Meistersinger* conformed to this ideal; the *Ring* did not. Furtwängler develops this line of thought by considering the function of the network of leitmotifs in the *Ring*:

> Strictly speaking, in the context of the drama as a whole these motifs derive their meaning only from their first appearance, accompanying the events on the stage. They stand isolated, they do not lead anywhere, do not generate a creative atmosphere around themselves, like the main themes of so many works. They are in the nature of mnemonics, or units of construction.
>
> Nowhere is this technique of the leitmotif more consistently employed than in the later sections of the *Ring* cycle. The music acquires an out-and-out decorative character, seen especially in the orchestration – hence the size of the orchestral forces employed. Unlike in the other operas, where his principal concern is with the production of an all-enveloping, homogeneous

---

51 TW, p. 15; FM, p. 62. This passage is clearly a critique of Wagner's own description of his compositional method as outlined in *A Communication to my Friends* (*Eine Mitteilung an meine Freunde*, 1851). Wagner writes: 'I remember, before I set about the actual working-out of *The Flying Dutchman*, to have drafted first the Ballad of Senta in the second act, and completed both its verse and melody. In this piece I unconsciously laid the thematic germ of the whole music of the opera: it was the picture *in petto* of the whole drama, such as it stood before my soul. [...] In the eventual composition of the music, the thematic picture thus evoked, spread itself quite instinctively over the whole drama, as one continuous tissue.' PW, vol. 1, p. 370.

musical sound, Wagner here aims at the creation of a wealth of individual effects, exploiting the colours of the tonal palette in all their characteristic brilliance. The music has abandoned all attempt to retain its absolute, self-sufficient character and avoids as far as it can all forms of a purely musical nature. Its design is loose, often non-committal, sometimes consisting of little more than fragments stuck together in a rough-and-ready way.[52]

This view is essentially an extension of the views expressed in his early letters; but the subsequent experience of detailed study and the act of performance enabled Furtwängler to rationalise and articulate the conceptual and specifically musical difficulties he experienced with Wagner's *Gesamtkunstwerk*. Furtwängler's attitude towards Wagner's work remained self-contradictory throughout his life. At this point, in 1919, the underlying reason for this ambivalence begins to emerge: Wagner's work approaches his ideal only when the music grows organically from a single poetic idea.

Pfitzner's *Palestrina*

Furtwängler maintained an apparent catholicity of taste. He regularly included contemporary works in his programmes and was to give the first performance of the newly revised version of Schoenberg's *Five Orchestral Pieces* (*Fünf Orchesterstücke*) at the Leipzig Gewandhaus on 7 December 1922, and the *Variations for Orchestra* (*Variationen für Orchester*, Op. 31) in Berlin on 2 December 1928. In spite of this, he never essentially departed from the position that tonality and the sonata principle were the only valid foundations of musical expression. Such, too, was the position of Hans Pfitzner (1869–1949), Furtwängler's superior at the Strasbourg opera from 1909 to 1911, whose musical legend *Palestrina* (1917) he greatly admired. As previously recounted, he first became acquainted with the text of the opera early during his tenure in Lübeck. A letter to the composer of 19.7.1916, over a year before the premiere, suggests that his first encounter with the music was at the Munich residence of Pfitzner's biographer, Paul Cossman. Clearly the musical score was not easily available for the letter concludes: 'May I include a request. Could I obtain a piano score so that I do not always have to walk to Cossman.'[53]

The premiere of *Palestrina* was given at the Prinzregententheater, Munich, on 12 June 1917 conducted by Bruno Walter. Furtwängler first conducted the work himself on 28 March 1920 followed by five further performances

---

52 TW, p. 17; FM, p. 63.
53 SPK Berlin, 55 Nachl. 13, W. Furtwängler, Kasten 25.

that were among his last as director of the Mannheim Opera. The ideological subtext of the work is that of the erosion and devaluation of artistic values by what Thomas Mann described in his book *Reflections of a Non-Political Man* as the 'melancholy march of the new'.[54] As Mann's son Golo points out, Thomas Mann did not want to forsake his German past of 'music, reverie and love of death'. Mann put forward the specious view that German politics must be non-political: the war had been essentially a conflict between ideals of German *Kultur* against the democratised civilisation of the West.[55] In summary Mann's argument was a thinly veiled 'defence of the German authoritarian state'.[56] He lauds Pfitzner and his *Palestrina* as an example of an attempt to 'bolster German Romantic art in the face of increasing politicisation, the encroaching collapse of the Hohenzollern Empire and the emergence of European democracy'. Mann, however, was later to distance himself from the anti-democratic position of the *Reflections* while Pfitzner was to become increasingly strident in his promotion of the extremes of æsthetic and political conservatism. In his polemic against the rising tide of musical modernism *The New Aesthetic of Musical Impotence* (*Die neue Aesthetik der musikalischen Impotenz*, 1920) he wrote, 'now something has happened to our holy art which was in earlier times unthinkable. Musical impotence is now permanently explained and supported by theory. Music no longer needs to be beautiful. The composer no longer needs inspiration.'[57]

Renewed Contact with Heinrich Schenker

This was the heady world of ideological and political ferment in which Wilhelm Furtwängler rose to artistic pre-eminence. As with other artists, the experience of being at war heightened his sense of nationalism; something which was to be reinforced through further contact with Heinrich Schenker.[58] Although Furtwängler had first encountered Schenker's ideas in 1911 it was not until 1919 towards the end of his tenure in Mannheim that

54 Thomas Mann, *Betrachtungen eines Unpolitischen* (1918); Eng. edn, *Reflections of a Non-Political Man*, pp. 297–314.
55 For more on the antithesis between civilisation and *Kultur*, see Fritz Stern, *The Politics of Cultural Despair*, p. 196; 'The Political Consequences of the Unpolitical German', in *The Failure of Illiberalism: Essays on the Political Culture of Modern Germany* (New York: Columbia UP, 1992).
56 Golo Mann, *History of Germany*, p. 370.
57 See Hans Pfitzner, *Die neue Aesthetik der musikalischen Impotenz* (München: Süddeutsche Monatshefte GmbH, 1920), p. 11.
58 Heinrich Schenker, *Selected Correspondence*, pp. 294–317.

the two encountered each other personally. The meeting was arranged by
Dr Paul Hammerschlag, director of the Austrian Credit Institute for Trade
and Industry, who on 2 May 1919 wrote to Schenker:

> Yesterday evening Herr Kapellmeister Furtwängler was with me and
> he spoke of you and your work in the warmest possible terms. He also
> expressed a wish to meet you personally. [...] I think perhaps that you will
> be interested to meet this excellent musician.[59]

The meeting took place on 3 May 1919 and marked the beginning of a working
relationship based on mutual respect rather than uncritical admiration.
Schenker had a high regard for Furtwängler's musical achievements but
considered him to be superficial and lacking in musical understanding;
Furtwängler admired Schenker's single-mindedness even though he did not
fully share his views, particularly with regard to Bruckner and Wagner. They
met frequently in Vienna – at Schenker's home, in the company of mutual
acquaintances or in restaurants. Schenker, clearly considering Furtwängler
to be a rising conductor who would put Schenkerian ideas into practice, was
unsparing with his artistic advice. Furtwängler accepted it willingly and took
every opportunity to express his thanks which in 1931 took the form of a
personal donation of 3,000 marks in support of the publication of volume 3
of *Das Meisterwerk in der Musik*.[60]

In a diary entry of 4 May 1919 following his first meeting with Furtwängler,
Schenker describes his initial impressions of the conductor:

> Furtwängler appeared to be about thirty years of age. [...] He had been
> introduced to my book six years previously whilst working in Lübeck and
> was well acquainted with my contacts in Germany. In any case, he was
> willing to involve himself in my current mission.[61]

The idea of mission is a common thread running through Schenker's
writings; he was clearly anxious to enthuse the up-and-coming Furtwängler

59 Hellmut Federhofer, *Heinrich Schenker nach Tagebüchern und Briefen in der Oswald
Jonas Memorial Collection*, p. 107. All translations from Federhofer are by the author.
The original text and alternative translations of these documents may also be accessed
at <http://www.schenkerdocumentsonline.org>.
60 Furtwängler's name occurs in Schenker's diaries approximately one hundred times.
The Schenker archive, held as part of the Oswald Jonas Memorial Collection by the
University of California, Riverside, contains twenty-two letters and two cards from
Furtwängler dated between 1919 and 1937, two years after Schenker's death. Latterly
Furtwängler directed his communications to the theorist's widow. See Federhofer,
pp. 106–7.
61 Ibid., p. 107.

with similar proselytising zeal. On 4 November 1919 Schenker attended his first concert directed by Furtwängler (Beethoven's *Egmont* stage music and the Fifth Symphony). The diary entry in which he records the event is representative of his critical approach: 'There is no doubt that the young conductor is superior to Weingartner, Nikisch and Strauss, so it is only to be regretted that he does not penetrate more deeply into the composition.'[62] The following day, 5 November, Schenker wrote to congratulate Furtwängler on his success.[63] In a letter written on 18 or 19 November Furtwängler later replied, 'I must confess that there is no-one whose approval of my work so pleases me as yourself, for there is no-one today whose knowledge of Beethoven approaches yours'.[64]

The Schenkerian concept of the *Urlinie* is first mentioned in connection with Furtwängler in a diary entry for 15 April 1920. On this occasion Schenker's pupil, Hans Weisse, acted as intermediary between the two: 'Dr Weisse brought greetings from Furtwängler together with an invitation to a forthcoming performance of the Ninth Symphony. He recounted how he had acquainted Furtwängler with the concept of the *Urlinie*.'[65] Schenker attended the performance in question which took place on 28 April 1920; his critical approach to Furtwängler's art is again clear from his comments:

> The conductor does not yet understand that an increase in tension comes from an accelerando rather than a crescendo and that this heightens the effect of moving towards a specific destination. In the last movement the vocal parts were sufficiently prominent and the chief difficulty was therefore overcome.[66]

Schenker's exegesis of musical texts for Furtwängler continued throughout the period of their acquaintance. On 19 November 1922 Schenker records how he showed Furtwängler the *Urlinie* of Brahms' Third Symphony, Bach's *Little Preludes*, Beethoven's *Appassionata* (Op. 57) and the Sonata in E major (Op. 109). The meetings in Vienna between Schenker, Furtwängler and other members of the circle sometimes became heated. On 11 April 1925 Schenker records a discussion that had a pronounced polemical content:

---

62 Ibid., p. 109.
63 SPK Berlin, 55 Nachl. 13, W. Furtwängler, Kasten 31. The full text of Schenker's letter, transcribed by Christoph Hust and translated by Ian Bent, may be found at <http://www.schenkerdocumentsonline.org>.
64 Federhofer, *Heinrich Schenker nach Tagebüchern und Briefen*, p. 109.
65 Ibid., p. 111.
66 Ibid., p. 112.

During the meal we touched upon technical questions, principally those relating to the sonata. We had not previously suspected just how ignorant Furtwängler is on these matters. He hardly understands sonata form at all!!

He stands up for Bruckner – a composer towards whom he considers me an opponent. He thinks that Bruckner is a composer who has something specific to say. It is futile for him to try and clarify the spiritual content of Bruckner's works. He seems to think that spiritual fulfilment is only possible through abnegation of personality. In short, Furtwängler speaks as a dilettante and both Weisse and I have the greatest trouble in conversing with him on artistic matters. In spite of this he remains the leading conductor. After the meal we went into the music room where the Bruckner debate continued. In the course of this he behaved as an undisguised anti-Semite. I have to say that I agreed with his reasons even though I staunchly upheld my own Jewish point of view.[67]

This comment by Schenker is one of the few direct references to Furtwängler as an anti-Semite. It is a pity that no indication is given of the reasons with which Schenker himself agreed. On 9 September 1925 Schenker perceptively draws attention to the many contradictions in Furtwängler's character: 'Furtwängler: "deutschnational" and international; a classicist who also performs Stravinsky and Schoenberg. [...] In spite of the fact that Furtwängler is a mass of contradictions, he considers himself to be without contradiction.'[68]

The entries in Schenker's diaries are the principal source of information regarding the relationship between himself and Furtwängler. There is also a heavily corrected draft of a letter dated 13 November 1931, in which Schenker expressed his gratitude to Furtwängler for his donation towards the cost of publishing volume 3 of *Das Meisterwerk in der Musik*.[69]

You are well aware that the musical community is in disarray. You have made your position with regard to gramophone recordings and the radio quite clear; but a still more important reason is that we have lost touch with our musical heritage. Handel and Bach both belonged to the same historical period but neither of these geniuses could appear within the third or fourth centuries of our present epoch. We must develop in the practice of Art a stronger sense of tradition for the only honest art is rooted in tradition. It is a fundamental mistake of our age to believe that a genius of the past is only for its own time and has no relevance for the future. We must make every effort to correct this misunderstanding. A religious genius such as

67 Ibid., p. 116.
68 Ibid., p. 117.
69 Ibid., p. 106.

Moses cannot be said to be dead when today millions of orthodox Jews stand in his name against the world. No doubt the Jews have fundamentally misunderstood their own bible – a misunderstanding from which even Jesus wanted to free them – and yet: *theirs is the mistake* through which they were and are bound to Moses. They still look towards him for salvation, so strong is the power of genius. Consider these examples: has Jesus been superseded? He is still an ideal towards which men strive and will remain so in the future. Has Plato been superseded? At times he has been mocked but the central core of his thought remains intact. Personally I am in no doubt that in future centuries nothing will remain of the Germans but their great musical geniuses whose holy honour will be guarded in the same way as the Jews have guarded their Old Testament throughout the ages.[70]

This letter could only enhance Furtwängler's view of himself as a musical genius charged with guarding the honour of German art. His personal contact with Schenker strengthened the position he adopted in the 'Timely Reflections of a Musician'. This earlier essay represented an assimilation of the ideas of Schenker's *Beethoven's Ninth Symphony* into his overall musical outlook and in particular the paramount importance of the organic metaphor, as it was understood at that time, as a means of penetrating to the heart of the creative process. After World War I, Furtwängler held the view common among the educated middle classes that German musical culture had been irreparably damaged by the national humiliation imposed on Germany by the Treaty of Versailles; he therefore joined the vanguard of conservative musical intellectuals determined to preserve as an active force the Austro-German spirit as enshrined in the canon of musical masterworks. It was part of Schenker's thinking that the function of interpretation was to sustain the existence of the masterworks, for content was a product of interpretation and musical content could therefore only be communicated through the act of performance. Interpretation was vital for the continuance of the creative force.

Furtwängler thus allied himself with the conservative, anti-modernist movement in music which increasingly was directing its polemical fire at the ideas of Schoenberg, Stravinsky and their followers. Although he performed a small number of Schoenberg's works in the 1920s his close alliance with Schenker leaves little doubt as to where his true sympathies lay. Schoenberg himself held Schenker in open contempt. In 1923 he wrote:

70 Ibid., p. 126. For more on this letter in particular and on the relationship between Furtwängler and Schenker in general, see Christoph Hust, "'How desolating to have to say that he is and will be the premier conductor of our time!'": Heinrich Schenker and Wilhelm Furtwängler', in *Journal of Schenkerian Studies*, vol. 4 (2010), pp. 3–14.

The main thing impressing the decline or downfall of our art and culture
on all these Spenglers, Schenkers, and so forth, has been an awareness of
themselves as totally lacking in creative talent.[71] A natural and very simple
reaction to such findings would have been contempt for themselves, not
even for others comparably impotent. [...] Nowadays, according to such
prophets – the only ones 'with honour' in anyone's country – the creative
disposition no longer exists; what does exist, plentifully, is critical trash
such as themselves, and these are the only ones still to have ideas, to possess
creative gifts, even – the only geniuses, then.[72]

The epiphany of 1911 when Furtwängler first encountered Schenker's work
was later strengthened by personal contact. Most importantly, Schenker
enhanced his understanding of organic growth through the concept of the
Urlinie, the *Ursatz* and *Fernhören* (roughly translated as 'distance' or 'structural
hearing'). The content of a musical work should be realised through the act
of performance as a series of exfoliations of the *Ursatz*. Thus to Furtwängler
there was no such thing as a definitive musical text. Each performance of a
work was in a sense a process of recomposition; it had to have a strong element
of improvisation and at the same time reveal the deep underlying structure of
a work. Organic cohesion was what gave a work its validity. Schenker acted as
a powerful catalyst in the development of this concept, although Furtwängler
was too independent minded not to retain a strong sense of critical distance
from the complete Schenkerian package. In his retrospective tribute he
criticised Schenker for lack of clarity (somewhat ironically in view of his own
convoluted prose style) and for the concept of the *Urlinie*, which he considered
insufficiently thought through. It was the concept of *Fernhörens*, or structural
hearing, that left the longest lasting impression.

The ideas first encountered in Schenker's *Beethoven's Ninth Symphony*
brought together many of the diverse strands in Furtwängler's thinking at
a crucial point in his career as a performer: they aided his understanding of
the inner processes of music, enhanced his understanding of the concept of
the organic and strengthened his already unassailable belief in the supremacy
of the Austro-German tradition. Hegemonic ideology with a strong element
of nationalism was never very far below the surface of Schenker's work. His
ideas were founded in a close study of the masterworks of the German canon

71 Oswald Spengler (1880–1936): philosopher of history whose major work, *Der Untergang
    des Abendlandes* (1918–22), published in English as *The Decline of the West*, had consid-
    erable influence on the development of Nazi ideology. See also Erich Heller, 'Oswald
    Spengler and the Predicament of the Historical Imagination', in *The Disinherited Mind*
    (London: 1952; pbk edn, Harmondsworth, 1961), pp. 159–72.
72 Arnold Schoenberg, *Style and Idea*, tr. Leo Black, ed. Leonard Stein (London: Faber &
    Faber, 1975), p. 203.

and in the mind of the educated middle classes the 'idea' of German music increasingly acted as a focus of national identity. As a result, the concept of organic growth in music became associated with the prevailing conservative world-view. There was thus a strong ideological subtext to the application of the organic model to the emergent methodology of music analysis.[73]

In 1915 Houston Stewart Chamberlain published his influential and widely read tract, *Politische Ideale*.[74] As in his biography of Goethe previously discussed, Chamberlain's world-view drew heavily on the organic model: Chamberlain 'viewed the state as a natural, organic entity, a reflection of the "individuality" or genius of the nation'.[75] Chamberlain warned the German people against taking what he regarded as 'the false path of Social Democracy' no matter what the outcome of the 1914–18 conflict might be. Moreover, Chamberlain's increasingly strident pronouncements carried the imprimatur of Bayreuth and were highly regarded by the conservative musical establishment. The parallel between Chamberlain's conception of the ideal state and the methodology and underlying ideological subtext of Schenker's system of analysis is therefore significant. Central to Chamberlain's political philosophy was the idea of a strong leader who would create the nation state based on the organic model: in 1915 he had called for 'an iron broom to sweep Germany clean'.[76] Schenker believed that such a figure was necessary in music. As early as 1894 he had put forward in an article his blueprint for the rescue of the musical world from what he considered to be the chaotic conditions prevalent in the closing decade of the nineteenth century. His use of biblical paraphrase is intended to give his words canonical authority:

Is any amelioration possible in such a repugnant set of circumstances? [...] A brilliant and inspiring teacher would have to appear, a teacher in the broadest and most beautiful sense of the word, an educator, composer, critic and philosopher, just as were Guido of Arezzo, J. S. Bach, Schumann and Wagner in their time; a man who would 'go into the temple of art, and cast out all them that sell and buy in the temple, and overthrow the tables of the moneychangers, and the seats of them that sell doves, And say to them, It is written, My house shall be called a house of prayer'.[77]

---

73 Schenker's terminology is shot through with ideological overtones that are easily obscured in translation. This is largely a result of the fact that in the post-World War II period Schenker's ideas were taken out of context by the English-speaking world, particularly in America. In the process his language was sanitised and largely de-Germanified.

74 Houston Stewart Chamberlain, *Politische Ideale* (München: F. Bruckmann, 1915).

75 Geoffrey Field, *Evangelist of Race* (New York: Columbia UP, 1981), p. 371.

76 Chamberlain, *Politische Ideale*, p. 101. See also Geoffrey Field, *Evangelist of Race*, p. 421.

77 Heinrich Schenker, 'The Music of Today' (1894), tr. Jonathan Dunsby, in *Music Analysis*, vol. 7, no. 2 (1988), p. 134.

The development of Schenkerian thought is thus paradigmatic of the process through which nineteenth-century musical culture rooted in the traditions of German Idealism became irrevocably associated with conservative-nationalist political ideologies. It was inevitable that Furtwängler became enmeshed in the conservative musical revolution of which Schenkerian thought was an indicative constituent. As a result of his increasingly high profile as a conductor shortly to be appointed to lead two of Germany's most prestigious orchestras, Wilhelm Furtwängler became the public face of the Conservative Revolution in German music.[78]

78 See Fritz Stern, *The Politics of Cultural Despair*, p. xiv: 'The term conservative revolution denotes the ideological attack on modernity, on the complex of ideas and institutions that characterise our liberal, secular and industrial civilisation.'

CHAPTER 4

FURTWÄNGLER IN THE WEIMAR REPUBLIC (1919-33)

Social democracy was anathema to him; he spoke of it with fear and loathing.[1]

Art is an undemocratic thing. And yet it turns to the people.[2]

Conductor's Lament!

It should be an art, but it is an exhibition, a spectacle.[3]

By the end of the 1920 Mannheim season Furtwängler's burgeoning reputation meant that he was in increasing demand as a guest conductor in the most important musical centres of Germany and Austria. In 1919 he secured his first appointment in Vienna as director of the Tonkünstler Orchestra; on 2 April 1920 he made a guest appearance with the orchestra of the Berlin State Opera before being appointed director of the Berlin Staatsoper concerts as successor to Richard Strauss; in September of the same year he succeeded Willem Mengelberg as director of the Frankfurt Museumskonzerte. It is unsurprising that with this increased activity his position in Mannheim became unsustainable; he could no longer commit to the demands of running a repertory opera company. He therefore ended his period of tenure as Hofkapellmeister in Mannheim in order to follow the path of a guest conductor and have greater freedom to accept engagements elsewhere. This freelance existence was, however, to be short-lived. Arthur Nikisch, head of both the Leipzig Gewandhaus and Berlin Philharmonic Orchestras, died on 23 January 1922. Acclaimed guest appearances with both orchestras led to Furtwängler's appointment as Nikisch's successor at the head of these influential ensembles. At the age of just thirty-six, Wilhelm

---

1   *Buddenbrooks*, p. 594.
2   Furtwängler, notebook entry of 1929, cited in VMS, p. 9.
3   AZN, p. 34; NBKS, p. 16.

5   Furtwängler at Tanneck, c.1920

Furtwängler was the pre-eminent conductor of the newly democratic Weimar Republic.

The immediate post-World War I years were uncertain times for the conservative nationalists. The 'colliding worlds' of authoritarianism and social democracy, the breakdown of law and order in Bavaria, the growing fear of a Bolshevik revolution inspired by events in Russia and the faltering attempts at establishing democratic government under the Weimar consti- tution engendered a deep sense of unease among the anti-democratic elites rooted in nostalgia for the authoritarian certainties of a lost Bismarckian age.[4] As Mann, citing Rousseau, wrote in *Reflections*:

> Monarchical form of government, he says, is the one that is natural for human beings. [...] Every dangerous human undertaking, every ship must obey *one* supreme commander. [...] Republics, however are unnatural, artificially made and the result of *reflection* – which is enough for this anti-intellectual intellect, this antirationalistic reason to condemn them straight out.[5]

On 15 August 1922, Furtwängler wrote to Ludwig Curtius that 'political life in Germany is a matter of indescribable concern'.[6] A year later on 3 September 1923 he wrote to Frau Edith Curtius that 'I am constantly thinking of the terrible political situation now prevailing in Germany'.[7]

Oswald Spengler's *Decline of the West* (1918–22)

Indicative of this pervading mood of cultural pessimism was the publication in 1918 and 1922 of the two parts of one of the defining texts of the 'Conservative Revolution': Oswald Spengler's monumental *Decline of the West*.[8] Like Houston Stewart Chamberlain, Spengler was a dilettante in the sense that his

---

4 The portmanteau phrase 'colliding worlds', which so neatly sums up the prevailing situation in early 1920s Germany, is borrowed from Mitchell Cohen, 'To the Dresden Barricades: the genesis of Wagner's political ideas', in Thomas Grey, ed., *The Cambridge Companion to Wagner* (Cambridge: CUP, 2008), p. 47.
5 Mann, *Reflections*, p. 89.
6 SPK Berlin, 55 Nachl. 13, W. Furtwängler, Kasten 9. Furtwängler, *Briefe*, p. 61.
7 Ibid.; *Briefe*, p. 63.
8 Oswald Spengler, *Der Untergang des Abendlandes: Umrisse einer Morphologie der Weltgeschichte. Erster Band, Gestalt und Wirklichkeit* (München: C. H. Beck'sche Verlags- buchhandlung, 1918); *Zweiter Band, Welthistorische Perspektiven* (1922). Annotated English translation in one volume by C. F. Atkinson, *The Decline of the West* (London: George Allen & Unwin, 1932).

mind had a broad sweep that attempted to encompass the entire spectrum
of Western cultural history. In brief, Spengler's pessimistic assessment of the
Western world saw history as an organic process of cyclic progression. The
nineteenth century is seen as the winter of a cultural cycle that began around
AD 900 with the Nordic Sagas or Eddas, Western legends of the Saints such
as Bernard of Clairvaux (founder of the Cistercians) and Francis of Assisi;
in the nineteenth century this culture is superseded by an inferior form of
industrial, materialistic civilisation which, according to Spengler, resulted
in the extinction of the spiritual creative force. As noted earlier, in *Phaedo*
Plato reports the Socratic distinction between the faculty of the imagination
(mythos) and description (logos). Mythos is creative, poetic, organic, supra-
rational; logos is rational and governed by the rules of dialectical argumen-
tation. The creative supra-rational 'mythos' has now been overridden by
the rational, materialistic 'logos'. Among the figures Spengler identifies as
responsible for this decline are Darwin and Marx, for their materialistic world
outlook; and Schopenhauer, Wagner and Nietzsche for their 'unmathematical'
philosophy. In the words of the critic Erich Heller the organisms of history are
'frozen into rigid forms by the metaphysical winter of their old age. It is this
petrified stage of a culture that Spengler calls "civilisation".'[9]

As was common with German intellectuals of the time, Spengler had
acquired a broad musical background. This is readily apparent in the central
chapters of volume 1 of *The Decline of the West* in which he discusses concepts
of the Apollonian, the Faustian and the 'Magian' soul.[10] Spengler does not
follow Nietzsche in creating a binary opposition between the Apolline and
the Dionysiac; rather he draws a distinction between the Apolline and the
culturally more resonant Faustian. Spengler is quite specific about what
he means by Faustian: the prime symbol of the Faustian soul is 'pure and
timeless space'. To Spengler music is the ultimate Faustian art 'raised by
Corelli, Handel and Bach to be the ruling art of the West'. After identifying
the violin as the instrument that 'the Faustian soul has imagined and trained
for its last secrets' Spengler goes on to say that:

> in chamber music, Western art as a whole reaches its highest point. Here
> our prime symbol of endless space is expressed as completely as the
> Spearman of Polycletus expresses that of intense corporeality. [...] We

9 Erich Heller, *The Disinherited Mind*, p. 144.
10 This use by the translator of the word 'Magian' is significant. The original German
   is 'magische', which would conventionally be translated as magical; 'Magian' carries
   overtones of the biblical Magi, those mysterious Kings from the East who followed
   signs and portents in the heavens and responded to warning visions. This captures a
   good deal of the subtext that runs through Spengler's discourse.

know ourselves in the presence of an art beside which that of the Acropolis is alone worthy to be set.[11]

Spengler's view of music in what he regards as a post-cultural age is unsurprising and quickly told. Faustian art dies of senility.

> What is practised as art today – be it music after Wagner or painting after Cézanne, is impotence and falsehood. [...] We go through all the exhibitions, the concerts, the theatres, and find only industrious cobblers and noisy fools. [...] a faked music filled with the artificial noisiness of massed instruments.[12]

Spengler's *Decline of the West* is a formidable read that requires considerable staying power to navigate its weighty prose and pessimistic outlook. Along with Chamberlain's equally portentous *Foundations of the Nineteenth Century* it is a time-specific text of considerable historical interest. It is easy to dismiss both Chamberlain and Spengler as products of dilettantism; but, sophistry notwithstanding, they demonstrate a formidable grasp of the broad sweep of history and both enjoyed considerable vogue in their time. Spengler's *Decline of the West* is thus a useful tool in gaining critical purchase on the cultural pessimism of figures such as Furtwängler and Hans Pfitzner. There are clear correspondences with the young Furtwängler's 1915 essay 'Timely Reflections of a Musician', discussed in Chapter 3, and Pfitzner's strident polemic *The New Aesthetic of Musical Impotence*, published shortly after volume 1 of *Decline of the West*. In his generally pessimistic view Pfitzner shares a good deal of common ground with Spengler; as indeed does his 1917 opera, or 'musical legend' *Palestrina*, with its metanarrative of a cultural epoch coming to an end.[13]

Hans Pfitzner, *Von deutscher Seele* (1922)

If Spengler's *Decline of the West* was a defining text in the Conservative Revolution against cultural disintegration, its musical equivalent might be said to be Hans Pfitzner's *Von deutscher Seele*, an extended setting of texts by Joseph Eichendorff (1788–1857) for four soloists, large orchestra, organ and chorus. Pfitzner completed the score on 8 August 1921. We know that Furtwängler greatly

---

11 Spengler, *Decline of the West*, p. 231.
12 Ibid., pp. 293–4.
13 As expressed, e.g., through the chilling invocation of the Masters of the Past who urge resistance: 'your earthly task, Pierluigi, is not yet accomplished' (dein Erdenpensum, Pierluigi, is noch nicht getan). Pfitzner, *Palestrina*, Klavier-Auszug (Berlin: Adolphe Fürstner, 1916), pp. 131–48.

admired the work: on 26 December 1921 he wrote to Pfitzner: 'It is of all the works we so far have from you perhaps the greatest.'[14] This enthusiasm was not just for Pfitzner's benefit. A few days later on 31 December 1921 Furtwängler wrote to Ludwig Curtius: 'I must bring to your attention the new cantata of Herr Pfitzner, a full length setting of sayings and songs by Eichendorff. It is no less stirring in its way than *Palestrina*.' In Furtwängler's view it is the situation in post-war Germany that has prompted Pfitzner's musical expression of cultural decline. The same letter somewhat enigmatically continues: 'All our sufferings, and particularly the sufferings of Germany, gave to this man the path to himself, he is today what he can be; can one ask for anything more.'[15]

Von deutscher Seele was given its premiere in Berlin on 27 January 1922 by the Berlin Philharmonic conducted by the now little-known Selmar Meyrowitz, followed shortly afterwards on 28 February and 1 March by Furtwängler's own Vienna performances. Pfitzner's grandiose setting of Eichendorff's nature verses defies easy generic definition; it takes the form of a mystical pantheistic canvas, part orchestral cantata, part song cycle, part nature symphony. Pfitzner gave the cycle the title *Von deutscher Seele* as an expression of the seriousness of the German soul. Particularly notable is the death-haunted orchestral interlude 'Death as Postilion', while the serene close of Part I recalls the watchmen at the end of Act I of Richard Strauss' equally mystical *Die Frau ohne Schatten* (1919). The orchestral meditations 'Abend' and the chorale-dominated 'Nacht' in Part I and 'Ergebung' (Submission) in Part II have the character of symphonic adagio movements. The harmonic language, while rooted in late-nineteenth-century idioms, is often starkly 'modern' in its use of chromatic dissonance and orchestral effect, recalling the early Schoenberg of the *Gurrelieder* or the violence of Strauss' *Elektra*. The conclusion of the work ('Geistliche Lieder, Schifferspruch' – Spiritual Songs, Seaman's saying) has a quasi-religious character complete with consoling assurances of waves as an aid to travel and the stars as a guide; but the apparent triumphalism of the concluding D major has a hollow ring. Shadows of the war hang heavily over *Von deutscher Seele*; there is a palpable sense of *Weltschmerz* or world-weariness. The wounds inflicted by the shock defeat of 1918, the humiliation of Versailles and the establishment of the 'un-German' democratic Weimar Republic ran very deep in the conservative-nationalist soul.

It was shortly after beginning work in Lübeck that Furtwängler began to make the random jottings that formed what are now known as his *Notebooks*,

---

14 SPK Berlin, 55 Nachl. 13, W. Furtwängler, Kasten 25, emphasis in the original. The letter continues to discuss details of projected Vienna performances that took place on 28 February and 2 March 1922, and again on 2 and 3 October 1923. Furtwängler remarks that the orchestral part is 'very difficult'.
15 SPK Berlin, 55 Nachl. 13, W. Furtwängler, Kasten 9; Furtwängler, *Briefe*, p. 60.

or Diaries.[16] It is from this source that we know that he was familiar with the arguments and shared the world-view of Spengler's *Decline of the West*. Spengler is invoked by name:

> A good deal is made of the opposition between the Gothic and Antiquity – without realising that the two are one and the same but with their symbols reversed. Spengler was right to see the ancients as pertaining to the surface, the Faustian to depth. But the ancients do not lack the Faustian, and we do not lack surface.[17]

Later, at some unspecified point in 1944–45 and in a very different historical context, Furtwängler was to write: 'These are early and late people (according to Spengler) independent of age, health, talent and achievements. Art is only accessible to people in an intermediate stage. The "early" is too dull, the "late" too clever for it.'[18] It is not difficult to see the connection with Spengler's notion of cultural 'cycles' and Schenker's metaphors of musical depth in the analysis of musical masterworks.[19]

As with Furtwängler's more formally composed writings, the *Notebook* entries are shot through with recurring references to the organic nature of the musical artwork, either directly or through the use of metaphor. In a letter to Ludwig Curtius of 15 August 1922, he expresses concern that 'in the midst of the demands of the present it is more difficult to protect the living, organic form than ever it was. But without this the practice of music for me makes no sense and is of no interest.'[20] An associated idea that he discusses in some detail is the function of technique within the process of performance. Technique belongs to the musical surface; it is the mechanical means by which the interpreter realises the musical conception. Technique alone, however, cannot communicate the inner meaning of a musical work; the problem facing the interpreter is how to use technique not as an end in itself but as a means of expressing content.

> Technique is infertile knowledge. Above all, then, literal rendering. [...]
> There is a difference between treating a masterpiece either as a living plant, resplendent in its natural colours, allowing it to grow and unfold in front of the audience, or by contrast in its dried condition, in alcohol, etc.

16 Furtwängler, AZN; Eng. edn, NBKS.
17 AZN, p. 13; NBKS, p. 1 (translation modified).
18 AZN, p. 251; NBKS, p. 154.
19 For more on Schenker's metaphors of musical depth, see 'Heinrich Schenker and the apotheosis of musical depth', in Holly Watkins, *Metaphors of Depth in German Musical Thought* (Cambridge: CUP, 2011), pp. 162–91.
20 SPK, 55 Nachl. 13, W. Furtwängler, Kasten 9; *Briefe*, p. 60.

The thing to be avoided is not dissection but dissection without a consistent awareness of the living and natural context.[21]

The idea that a performance must be faithful to the spirit of the work rather than the letter of the score depends on the notion that a performance is itself an act of organic growth; it must contain an element of improvisation in the sense that the work is being created anew like a living plant. In Schenkerian terms, each individual performance consists of a series of exfoliations of the deep structure beneath the surface content.[22] The act of performance is therefore part of the continuing process of creation; it is generative in the organic sense. This improvisatory element was important in Schenkerian thinking; so too was the idea that the masterworks of the German canon depended on the process of performance for their continued existence. It followed that the performer was directly responsible for the maintenance of the tradition; hence Furtwängler could write that 'the question of how we keep the great works alive for ourselves is crucial for our musical life'.[23] In the context of the Schenkerian idea that the tradition of German composition had ended with Brahms, the nineteenth-century concept of creative genius was transferred to the twentieth-century phenomenon of the interpreter, or recreative genius. The decline of the creative artist had enhanced the responsibility of the recreative for the continued life of the masterworks of music. Musical hegemony now resided with the performer rather than the composer:

The crucial thing is that the creative artist is no longer (unconsciously) in control, and hence the growth of the importance of the recreative artist. From the point of view of the music, both conductor and orchestra are overrated – and yet the basic instinct is correct. What is overrated is technique [...]. The orchestra as an expression of the soul [Ausdruck der Seele] should never be ignored – but the standards are thrown into complete disarray by a public lacking in instinct, by sensation, desire for effect, etc.[24]

This idea of the expressive function of the orchestra as a channel of communication recalls not only Wagner's famous formulation in *Opera and Drama* of the orchestra possessing a 'faculty [Sprachvermögen] of speech', but more

---

21 AZN, p. 22; NBKS, pp. 8–9.
22 For Schenker on the duality between technique and the spirit of a work, see Nicholas Cook, *The Schenker Project* (New York: OUP, 2007), pp. 93–6.
23 AZN, p. 53; NBKS, p. 29.
24 AZN, pp. 56–7; NBKS, p. 31 (translation modified).

directly Dilthey's concept of *Seelenleben*, the ever-changing quality of life of the human soul.[25]

The notion of the modern orchestra as a means of musical re-creation – the tool which makes the act of interpretation possible – is considered by Furtwängler in a long notebook entry for 1929 headed 'The Modern Orchestra – a Contemporary Problem'. The orchestra is not just a composite musical instrument upon which the conductor plays as a soloist; it is in itself an organic whole with an intrinsic life of its own. Each player has a role to play within the section, each section has its function within the greater whole. The individual may be more or less important as the context dictates but the interdependence of the constituent parts gives the whole organic cohesion. The orchestra is an autonomous, self-contained organism with the conductor as the germ cell, or prime mover, energising the whole. Furtwängler illustrates this conception by considering the relative merits of European and American orchestras, an observation prompted by his visits between 1925 and 1927 to conduct the New York Philharmonic. The organic integrity of the orchestra is substantiated by the common national origin of its constituent parts; the intrinsic corporate empathy between the members then creates the necessary conditions for the improvisatory, spontaneous element necessary to reveal the musical truth of a work.

> An Italian, a French, a German orchestra not only has its own particular sound, but also its own particular kind of instinctive, living way of playing, in which the feeling of the individual vibrates sympathetically with the feeling of the mass, as of its own accord. This common feeling is of the greatest importance in the performance of every melody, every bar, and even a decisive conductor can only ever compensate for it to a certain degree.[26]

Over-emphasis on technical control destroys organic cohesion, creative spontaneity and the improvisatory element that is the 'source of all great, creative playing'. The function of the conductor is to awaken the common experience within this corporate body and thus realise the immanent sense of a musical work:

> The sense of the orchestra as an artistic medium is that this body, consisting of 90–100 different people, different heads and hands, becomes one instrument through which a soul, a feeling, an intuition is communicated to the listener in its tiniest details. The more it achieves this, the more

25 PW, vol. 2, p. 316; GSD, vol. 4, p. 173. For Dilthey, see the present work, Ch 1, pp. 29–31.
26 AZN, p. 61; NBKS, p. 34 (amended).

it loses the vanity of wanting to be something itself, the more it becomes the mediator, the communicator, the vessel and point of entry of the divine, speaking through the great masters.[27]

Furtwängler and Toscanini in Berlin (1930)

Furtwängler's notebook entries for this period clearly indicate that although he is seldom mentioned directly, the thinking assimilated from contact with Heinrich Schenker strengthened many of his inherited cultural ideas about the organic nature of the musical masterworks, the importance of the improvisatory element in performance and the detrimental effect of the pursuit of technical perfection on spontaneous artistic expression. This distinctly 'German' performance æsthetic rooted in the traditions of philosophical Idealism was directly challenged by the enthusiastic reception given to Furtwängler's Italian rival Arturo Toscanini (1867–1957) on his visit to Berlin with the New York Philharmonic Orchestra in May 1930. The American orchestra under their Italian conductor gave two concerts in the Philharmonie on 27 and 28 May as part of Berlin's *Kunstwoche*. In the light of Furtwängler's subsequent response, the programmes are worth giving in full:

27 May 1930: Haydn, Symphony No. 101 (The 'Clock'); Debussy, *La Mer*; Beethoven, *Leonore Overture No. 3* (Op. 72a); Pizzetti, *Rondo Veneziano*;[28] Mendelssohn, Incidental Music to *Midsummer Night's Dream*.

28 May 1930: Beethoven, *Eroica* Symphony (Op. 55); Brahms, *Haydn Variations* (Op. 56a); R. Strauss, *Tod und Verklärung*.

These concerts are the subject of a long *Notebook* entry headed 'Toscanini in Germany: An article on the true situation of German music-making in 1930'. This extended polemic amounts to an uncompromising and strident attack on Toscanini's perceived shortcomings, especially as an interpreter of the German masterworks. Toscanini became a focal point not only for Furtwängler's personal insecurity, which bordered on paranoia, but also for his conservative ideology and chauvinistic musical nationalism. Toscanini is not a German, which gives him a distinct advantage with the left-wing press; and he is not a Jew, which makes him acceptable in Munich. In this sense he is representative of the foreign element that has always been present in German musical life. After all, a century earlier such cultural giants as

27 AZN, p. 64; NBKS, p. 36.
28 Not Donizetti, as given in AZN, p. 73 and NBKS, p. 42.

Goethe and Schopenhauer were impressed with Rossini, and Toscanini now has the same effect on the present-day fickle German public. Furtwängler does find something worthwhile in Toscanini's performances: he admires the tender cantabile sound he achieves, especially in the first movement of the Haydn symphony; but this has the effect of damning with faint praise once the by now familiar tropes of Furtwängler's thinking come to the fore. Toscanini is taken to task for his 'literal [notengetreue] renderings'. The idea that the written text as fixed in the printed score is inviolate is to Furtwängler not only a meaningless cliché but a conceptual impossibility. A performance must above all else be faithful to the spirit of the work as revealed through the organic unfolding of the deep substructure. In his attempts to give a literal rendering Toscanini extinguishes the necessary element of spontaneity and thus fails to achieve the equilibrium between the whole and the parts. In a critique of the performance of Haydn's Symphony No. 101 Furtwängler writes:

> The overall impression was therefore divided, because the essence of Haydn's music and its style, that inimitable mixture of cheerful sweetness and tautened energy which makes Haydn one of the greatest masters ever to have created anything, was not forthcoming, so that the individually apparent qualities of the performance hampered each other rather than complementing and mutually supporting one another.[29]

Unsurprisingly, Furtwängler is at his most proprietorial and coruscating when considering Toscanini's Beethoven performances. He takes Toscanini to task for failing to understand the functional meaning of the modulations in *Leonore* No. 3 and for his resulting inability to communicate the spiritual and psychological content of the music:

> The functional meaning of the modulations in the long term, which in absolute music such as Beethoven's play such a different role, seems to be completely unknown to his naïve feeling for opera music. But beyond this too, there is not the slightest attempt to transmute purely musical forms into a spiritual and psychological insight.[30]

For Furtwängler it was the expressive potential of purely musical forms that was paramount. In his attack on Toscanini's performance of Beethoven's *Eroica* Symphony Furtwängler makes his position quite clear: the former's perceived shortcomings as an interpreter, we are given to understand, are

29 AZN, pp. 72–3; NBKS, p. 41.
30 AZN, p. 74; NBKS, p. 42.

unsurprisingly and in no small measure due to his lack of understanding of the organic process. In commenting upon Toscanini's interpretation of a particular passage he makes the following generalisation:

> Doubtless he has never understood the origin of this passage. But as a result the same misunderstanding recurred many times during the symphony – revealing a lack of acquaintance with and a naïve ignorance of one of the main demands of properly symphonic music, the demand for organic development, the living and organic growth of every melodic, rhythmic, harmonic formation out of what has gone before.[31]

Toscanini is essentially an Italian operatic musician: the operatic tutti and aria are his musical modes of thought. Toscanini cannot deny his own self. The sonata 'which in all its major examples is a German creation' is therefore beyond his understanding; but in Strauss' programmatic *Tod und Verklärung* 'the theatrical Kapellmeister's sense of effect was an advantage'. Furtwängler even criticises Toscanini's inexpressive conducting gestures and lack of manual talent.[32]

It is unclear whether this extensive *Notebook* entry was ever intended for publication. It is not included among Furtwängler's published or unpublished formally composed essays. The uncut original text is to be found in the handwritten 'Notizkalendar'[33] and transcribed in an incorrectly dated typescript where the stenographer has clearly had difficulty in reading Furtwängler's notoriously problematic script:[34] hence the minor Italian composer and Toscanini's near contemporary from Parma, Ildebrando Pizzetti (1880–1968), whose *Rondo Veneziano* Furtwängler loftily dismisses as unworthy of attention, is incorrectly transcribed as Donizetti, a misreading that has found its way into both published versions. The form in which it appears in the German and English editions of the *Notebooks* is abridged: the passages omitted amount to more attacks on Toscanini, accusing him of posturing, lacking in talent and a schoolmasterly (Schulmeister) insistence on precision above all else. But the most significant redaction is the epigrammatic final sentence: Toscanini's performances are described as 'Sleek portrayals, obliging, lively, springy, without tragedy, without the daemonic, full of gleaming strength, completely cold, tedious. Just like a record.' Most

---

31 AZN, p. 77, NBKS, p. 44.
32 Representative examples of the *Eroica* Symphony conducted by Toscanini (1939) and Furtwängler (1944) are given in Appendix 3.
33 Originals (1912–54) in SPK Berlin, 55 Nachl. 13, W. Furtwängler, Kasten 44.
34 Zentralbibliothek Zürich, Nachl. W. Furtwängler: S 95.

damningly of all, Toscanini's performances are without the two essentially German qualities of the tragic (Tragik) and the daemonic (Dämonie).[35]

Furtwängler's criticisms of Toscanini are driven not only by his personal insecurities and clear resentment of a rival's success on his home territory, but, more significantly for the present discussion, by his very German way of thinking about the act of musical performance. His attacks on the Italian's 'literal renderings' and over-reliance on technique stem from his belief in the conceptual impossibility of playing music according to the letter of the score without the element of spontaneous improvisation that is the lifeblood of every living performance. The supra-rational qualities of spontaneity, improvisation and organic growth in performance belong to the 'mythos'; literal rendering, precision and over-reliance on technical perfection belong to the 'logos'. It was the creative force embodied in the non-rational mythos that Goethe, 'following the example of the ancients' represented poetically as the daemonic (das Dämonische); Furtwängler's criticism of Toscanini's performances as lacking in the daemonic is therefore particularly significant and hard-hitting.[36] The ideological dichotomy of nature versus artifice seen in the opposition between the supra-rational and the overly intellectual is a later manifestation of the distinction between mythos and logos: the encoded agenda is all that is natural, that is organic growth, is good; all that is artificial, that is technique, is bad. In conservative thinking the political construct of democracy is artifice (artificial) and therefore contrary to the natural hierarchies embodied in an authoritarian system. It is the natural, the organic seen as a supra-rational unity not definable in rational terms, that is by definition unpolitical.

'Interpretation: A Question of Musical Destiny' (1930)

Later in 1930 Furtwängler penned an article in which he expressed his organic world-view in a more uncompromising fashion: 'Interpretation: a Question of Musical Destiny' (Interpretation: eine musikalische Schicksalsfrage).[37] The published versions in *Atlantisbuch der Musik* and the anthology *Ton und Wort* both give the date as 1934, after the Nazis had come to power; but the surviving typescripts in the Furtwängler Nachlass are dated 20 November

---

35 Ibid., typescript p. 12. See also Theodor Adorno, 'Die Meisterschaft des Maestro', in *Musikalische Schriften I–III, Gesammelte Schriften* (Frankfurt: Suhrkamp, 1978), vol. 16, pp. 52–67.
36 Angus Nicholls, *Goethe's Concept of the Daemonic after the Ancients*, p. 31.
37 Zentralbibliothek Zürich, Nachl. W. Furtwängler: S 53. First published in *Atlantisbuch der Musik* (Berlin, 1934); in TW, pp. 74–85.

and 5 December 1930 and thus show the article to have been written in the pre-Nazi period. The title, with its ideological resonances, makes it clear that the author is primarily concerned not only with the survival of the canonical masterworks but also with the crucial importance of the interpreter in ensuring that survival. In addition, Furtwängler introduces a political dimension into his discussion by acknowledging the fact that, for his present authorial purposes, musical and political life are inextricably interlinked:

> The relationship we have to our own past has become problematic – not least in music. As a consequence, the question of how to perform the works of the past is of greater importance than before; the interpreter as communicator of these works has acquired a fateful responsibility. The problem of interpretation is one of musical destiny. This requires our attention independently of current political matters – which are nevertheless important as they affect our everyday musical life.[38]

Furtwängler is here more uncompromising than in his previous statements. The professional interpreter is only necessary at all because there has been a break in continuity with the traditions of the past; creative artists as represented by the figure of the composer no longer define performance styles. He therefore considers it necessary to specify a set of principles which will dispel the prevailing uncertainty in matters of performance, which in itself is symptomatic of the malaise affecting all aspects of contemporary musical life. The method prescribed is predictable: a rediscovery of the principles of organic growth and cohesion.

> The starting point for the composer is nothing, or, as it might be said, chaos. His goal is the completed work. He brings form to this chaos through the act of improvisation. Improvisation is the foundation of all true music-making. This 'mental event' is a self-contained organic process. It cannot be predetermined. It has its own logic based on psychological laws, which are as compelling as any logical system. Every 'mental' event corresponds to the laws of organic life, which drive towards 'completion'. It is this process, rather than that of arbitrary convention, that generates the naturally evolving forms such as song, sonata, fugue and so forth. 'An improvisation seeking fulfilment' is the creation of musical form that remains improvisation from beginning to end.[39]

---

38 TW, p. 74 (all translations from 'Interpretation: eine musikalische Schicksalsfrage' are by the present author).
39 Ibid., p. 79.

Furtwängler's use of the German term 'improvisation' is freighted with Schenkerian resonance and fundamental to his understanding of the act of musical performance as an organic process. There is no sense in which this means that a performance is to be extemporised or, in more homely terms, 'made it up as it goes along'. Furtwängler's performances were meticulously planned beforehand through detailed study of the score; but the crucial difference is that Furtwängler conceived of a score as a living organism rather than a predetermined semiotic plan. The term 'improvisation' is used here in the sense that a musical performance is an act of unpremeditated spontaneous creativity driven by the laws of organic growth and the human will. As Ferdinand Tönnies put it, 'organic growth must be seen as spontaneous process, and so too is the development of natural or instinctive will'.[40] In Schenkerian terms the underlying deep structure of a work unfolds in performance from the fundamental or background structure (*Ursatz*) through the middleground to the musical surface, or as an 'improvisation seeking fulfilment'. 'Interpretation' bears the unmistakable stamp of Schenkerian thought and clearly demonstrates the extent to which, in spite of misgivings, Schenker's ideas of musical depth had such a profound effect on Furtwängler's ideas of performance practice. This explains why in his 1947 retrospective tribute to Schenker (to be considered later), Furtwängler identifies Schenker's concept of *Fernhörens* (or in Felix Salzer's English formulation, 'structural hearing') as so important. Simply put, 'structural hearing' means being able to hear the last note in the first across the entire span of a musical work. If a musical score is considered as a living, evolving organic entity then it follows that *Werktreue*, or literal fidelity to the letter of the score as understood by Toscanini, is a conceptual impossibility.

The problem facing the interpreter is how to recreate the original creative process in the act of performance so that the psychological and spiritual message is intact and not diminished in any way. This is what Furtwängler means by improvisation. He finds a convenient and telling metaphor in Wagner:

The process of the creation and of the re-creation of a work has nowhere been more perceptively described than by Wagner in the legend of the reforging of Siegfried's sword. Even the most skilled craftsman could not weld the shattered fragments back together. Only through the complete grinding of the whole [Ganz] to paste, returning it to the chaos of its original state before the original act of creation, can the work be newly recreated as a whole.[41]

40 Tönnies, *Gemeinschaft und Gesellschaft*; Eng. edn, *Community and Civil Society*, p. 97.
41 TW, p. 82.

This particular metaphor had powerful political resonances. In *Mein Kampf* (1925 and 1927) Adolf Hitler had also referred to the reforging of Siegfried's sword as a potent image of the longed-for reawakening of Germany. In describing the aftermath of a meeting held in Munich on 24 February 1920, Hitler wrote: 'A fire was ignited, and out of its glow there must come the sword with which the German Siegfried will restore freedom and life to the German nation.'[42] Here Furtwängler pursues the metaphor as an allegory of the phenomenon of artistic creation: the organic process is supra-rational and defies conceptual definition.

> How is it possible for the performing artist to do this, for he has been handed only the finished work? He has been given only the individual elements. How can he recognise a whole and its related mental experiences?
>
> Here we reach the limit of what can be said on this matter. It is very difficult to describe the essence of the organic process in words. This much, however, is certain: only the recognition of such a *whole* [emphasised in typescript source] whether it be through structure, the image of a mental experience, or whatever other inadequate term is used, can prevent us from sinking into a state of chaos and confusion. As long as a musical work is regarded as nothing more than a conflation of romantic 'moods' (as in the more naïve nineteenth-century literature), or as a contrived succession of empty forms (as in the equally primitive æsthetic of previous years), and not as a living organic process, then the truth of what I have said will be evident. Apart from superficial variations, there is only one approach, one manner of performance that is fundamentally 'correct'. This makes as much of a nonsense of those specious appeals to various matters of 'taste' as it does to the empty cliché of 'literal performance' [notengetreuen Darstellung].[43]

'Interpretation: A Question of Musical Destiny' was written at the time when Furtwängler was approaching the height of his power and prestige as an interpretative artist. By the time of its publication in 1934 he was to all intents and purposes Germany's *Generalmusikdirektor*, for those among his contemporaries who could be considered his equals had left the country on account of the Nazis' racial policies.[44] It is significant that his standpoint hardly differs in essence from that of the Hildebrand correspondence of

---

42 Adolf Hitler, *Mein Kampf* (1925 and 1927), p. 406. All citations are from the *Gesamtauflage* (1940); translations by the present author.

43 TW, pp. 82–3.

44 e.g. Bruno Walter (1876–1962) and Otto Klemperer (1885–1973). Erich Kleiber (1890–1956) was racially acceptable but left in protest at the Nazis' censure of Alban Berg's opera *Lulu*.

thirty years earlier.[45] He pulls no punches. The veracity and worth of the musical artwork is still measured according to his organic world-view, but now tempered not only by eighteen years of solid experience as an interpreter but also by the transformative experience of his assimilation of Schenker's analytical ideas. The article is also a clear and unequivocal demonstration of how the language of conservative-nationalist political discourse permeated Furtwängler's thought in general and his hegemonic conception of musical performance in particular: his statement that 'only one manner of performance is correct' leaves little room for any kind of challenge, let alone alternative artistic approaches such as that of Toscanini.

Bayreuth

It was not only Furtwängler who objected to the appearance of Toscanini in the German cultural heartland. In 1924 Siegfried Wagner (1869–1930), Richard and Cosima Wagner's son, had reopened the Bayreuth Festival after a silence of ten years. This was seen as something of a retaliatory blow struck by the conservative musical establishment against the ever-increasing influence of Weimar modernism; henceforth Bayreuth became a meeting place for the conservative element in musical life. As the music historian Erik Levi writes: 'During the following years Bayreuth increasingly came to represent a symbol of extreme nationalist defiance, and the Festival became a base from which to attack and undermine the Weimar Republic.'[46] Or, to paraphrase the historian Benedict Anderson, the Bayreuth Festival became 'a fine example of official nationalism – an anticipatory strategy adopted by dominant groups which are threatened with marginalisation or exclusion from an emerging nationally-imagined community'.[47]

In the same year as his triumphant visit to Berlin Toscanini was invited by Siegfried Wagner to conduct *Tannhäuser* and *Tristan und Isolde* at the 1930 Bayreuth Festival: he thus became the first non-German to conduct Wagner at Bayreuth. To the conservative-minded Bayreuth 'old guard' this amounted to an act of desecration and was one of the factors that precipitated the resignation of Karl Muck (1859–1940) as conductor of *Parsifal*. As an aspiring musical assistant, Muck had participated in early performances of *Parsifal* and could trace his roots back to Wagner himself. Both in his manner and his

45 See Ch. 2.
46 Erik Levi, *Music in the Third Reich*, p. 6.
47 Benedict Anderson, *Imagined Communities* (London and New York: Verso, 1983), p. 101.

mode of dress Muck was a survivor from the Wilhelmine age. He conducted *Parsifal* at every festival from 1901 to 1930 and was steeped in the official Bayreuth ideology of Cosima and the Bayreuth Circle. When the festival was revived in 1924 after the ten-year silence caused by World War I Muck wrote to the newly appointed conductor Fritz Busch (1890–1951): 'What matters is that you conform to the Bayreuth way of thinking and bring with you the unassuming humility and holy fanaticism of the Believer.'[48] Muck's withdrawal was symbolic of far more than just the passing of the older generation; he was regarded as the embodiment of conservative Bayreuth ideology and its associated inviolate performance tradition.

It was unfortunate that the hard-won and essentially fragile equilibrium of Bayreuth was disturbed when Siegfried Wagner died during the 1930 season; this, together with Muck's resignation, left something of a power vacuum at the centre of the festival administration. Under the terms of Siegfried Wagner's will the entire Wagner estate, together with the mantle of overall responsibility for the artistic direction of the festival, passed to his young English widow, Winifred (1897–1980), who, since September 1923, had been an enthusiastic supporter of the political agitator Adolf Hitler. Like the earlier English Bayreuther, Houston Stewart Chamberlain, Winifred was thoroughly imbued with the cultural nationalism of the Bayreuth idea and, as a result, she harboured a deep distaste for the perceived political and social disorder of the Weimar Republic. She hoped that Hitler would in time emerge as Chamberlain's 'iron broom': the authoritarian and charismatic leader capable of restoring the cultural values and social order which she, like Furtwängler, considered essential to the existence of the German state. After Siegfried Wagner's death Winifred's political extremism became more pronounced and she quickly gravitated towards the ideology of National Socialism. As a result, as her grandson Gottfried observes, by virtue of her influential position at the centre of conservative culture she made Hitler acceptable to the educated middle classes. Hitler was seen to enjoy the patronage of Bayreuth and this powerful support aided the creation of a cultural climate of opinion, which both assisted his political ascendancy and sustained him while he consolidated his hold on power.[49]

---

48 For the full text of Muck's letter, see Peter Muck, *Dr Karl Muck: Ein Dirigentenleben in Briefen und Dokumenten* (Tutzing: Hans Schneider, 2003), pp. 125–6; see also Frederic Spotts, *Bayreuth, A History of the Wagner Festival* (New Haven and London: Yale UP, 1994), p. 147; also F. Schönemann, 'Erinnerungen an Karl Muck', *Deutsche Allgemeine Zeitung*, 17 March 1940. A substantial amount of material from Muck's *Parsifal* has survived on record.

49 Gottfried Wagner, *He Who Does Not Howl With The Wolf*, tr. Della Couling (London: Sanctuary Publishing Limited, 1998), p. 212.

The year 1931 saw Winifred Wagner's first season in sole charge of Bayreuth and, to assist her as she moved to consolidate her authority, she sought to secure the services of a conductor of stature to fill the vacancy caused by the departure of Karl Muck and Fritz Busch's refusal to return. Her choice of Furtwängler was welcomed by conservatives as a Germanic counterbalance to the increasing influence of the non-German Toscanini, who had taken over from Muck as conductor of Bayreuth's sacred charge, *Parsifal*. Furtwängler was therefore appointed as musical director of the festival with authority over musical matters and policy; it was in this capacity that he made his acclaimed first appearances on 23 July 1931 conducting *Tristan und Isolde*. Tensions inevitably arose between Furtwängler and Toscanini. Their relationship soon deteriorated into one of open hostility over problems arising from a concert given in memory of Siegfried Wagner. Furtwängler's tenure as music director of the Bayreuth Festival was short-lived. His unhappy experiences of the peculiar working conditions and atmosphere together with his annoyance at Winifred Wagner's continued interference in the artistic matters, which she had promised would be subject to his sole jurisdiction, precipitated his resignation at the end of the 1931 season.[50] He gave the reasons for his resignation during the following non-festival year in a strongly worded article published in various national newspapers on 28 June 1932. Somewhat disingenuously, given the stridency of his comments on Toscanini's appearances in Berlin, Furtwängler is adamant that there was no rift between himself and Toscanini the previous year and that the Toscanini case had no bearing on his decision to withdraw from Bayreuth. 'There are still those around who are trying to make capital out of an alleged rivalry. There is no such rivalry, and there never has been. Personal relations between us were always of the very best.' For the conservative, authoritarian Furtwängler this is first and foremost a matter of authority. He gives as his reasons as differences of opinion between himself and the inexperienced Winifred: he rejects 'her claim always to have the last word in artistic matters', and asks whether Bayreuth should be governed 'as a family possession or as a national asset'.[51]

50 For an account of the negotiations which took place between Winifred Wagner and Furtwängler, together with a description of his first encounter with the Bayreuth establishment in the persons of Cosima Wagner's daughters, Daniela Thode, née von Bülow, and Eva Chamberlain, née Wagner, see Berta Geissmar, *The Baton and the Jackboot*, pp. 52–9.
51 Wilhelm Furtwängler, 'Um Bayreuths Zukunft'; here taken from *Vossische Zeitung*, 28 June 1932 and *Berliner Tageblatt*, 28 June 1932. See also Ludwig Karpath, 'Furtwängler, Toscanini und Bayreuth: Aus einem Gespräch mit Dr. Wilhelm Furtwängler', *Neue Freie Presse* (Vienna), 22 June 1932.

The Jubilee of the Berlin Philharmonic Orchestra (1932)

In 1932 another national asset, the Berlin Philharmonie, together with its resident ensemble the Berlin Philharmonic Orchestra, celebrated its Golden Jubilee. Founded in 1882, this orchestra was regarded as the ultimate authority in matters of performance of the canon of German masterworks.[52] The fiftieth anniversary of its foundation was therefore an event of some national cultural significance, especially given the political uncertainties of the turbulent final months of the Weimar Republic. Furtwängler made a speech to mark this occasion on which he took the opportunity to examine the position of musical art in general and the classical masterworks in particular within the context of the contemporary cultural scene.[53] He makes it quite clear that he considers the current situation to be so serious that the continuation of German musical life itself is under threat:

> This jubilee is taking place at a time of crisis, the like of which the modern world has not yet experienced. This is evident in our economic life as well as in artistic and intellectual matters. For this reason it is necessary for us to re-examine our cultural institutions and ask ourselves whether or not they are really essential. This process of public scrutiny has called into question the continued existence of the Berlin Philharmonic Orchestra.[54]

Furtwängler goes on to lament the fact that the chaotic economic circumstances of the closing months of Weimar are one of the prime causes of the orchestra's difficulties. He stresses the fact that its existence is of central importance to the continued spiritual well-being of the nation:

> I have said elsewhere just how much importance I attach to the preservation of music as a central part of the cultural life of us Germans. If the orchestra were to cease to exist, serious damage would undoubtedly be inflicted on German musical life. Also, it is important that the notion of music as the most original and characteristic art of the Germans is maintained and that German musical life is protected from decline.[55]

Unsurprisingly Furtwängler places a good deal of the blame for this situation on modern music and what he considers to be the general degeneracy of

---

52 See present work, p. 14.
53 'Die Klassiker in der Musik-Krise (Rede beim Jubiläum der Berliner Philharmonie 1932)', in *Unterhaltungsblatt der Vossischen Zeitung*, 19 April 1932; Zentralbibliothek Zürich, Nachl. W. Furtwängler: S 58. Reprinted in TW, pp. 60–7.
54 TW, p. 60 (author's translation).
55 Ibid., pp. 60–1.

much of the cultural life of the Weimar Republic. He closes his essay with a summary of his own position:

> And now I return to my starting point. I see in the struggle for the preservation of this orchestra, whose fiftieth anniversary occurs in the midst of an unprecedented cultural crisis, not only a struggle for the preservation of high artistic standards but also for the continued existence of our German musical life.[56]

It is by now evident that it is impossible to overestimate the ideological implications of Furtwängler's organic world-view. The notion of the musical work as an entity in which the constituent parts are interrelated and interdependent yet at the same time subservient to the whole; the notion of the organic composition of the orchestra with the conductor as the energising germ cell – these ideas all lent themselves to progressive nationalisation and have a clear parallel in the concept of the 'organic' state. The organic artwork performed by a well-disciplined orchestra can be seen as an allegory of the idealised state in which the identity of the individual is subsumed within the whole. Furtwängler's concept of the organic thus not only penetrates his entire system of musical thought; it indirectly engages with the prevailing philosophical, ideological and political debates of the age, in particular the encoding of increasingly strident conservative cultural and nationalist ideologies within the broad usage of the metaphor.

The progress of Furtwängler's thought from the early Hildebrand correspondence through 'Timely Reflections of a Musician' to the attacks on Toscanini and 'Interpretation: A Question of Musical Destiny' can be seen as a paradigm of the extended cultural discourses that lent themselves more and more to the progressive nationalisation of conservative, *bürgerlich* thought. In 1992 the British historian Richard Evans wrote:

> Furtwängler belonged essentially to the conservative-nationalist [bürgerlich] elite that did so much to undermine the Weimar Republic and bring Hitler to power in 1933. In 1929, he wrote privately that threats to what he considered 'normality included not only "Bolshevism, that fashionable religion of hatred" [...] but also politics, democracy and progress'. In the political language of the day, 'normality' meant the

---

56 Ibid., p. 67. For more on Furtwängler's speech on the occasion of the jubilee of the Berlin Philharmonic and its political implications see Fritz Trümpi, *The Political Orchestra: the Vienna and Berlin Philharmonics during the Third Reich*, tr. Kenneth Kronenberg (Chicago and London: Chicago UP, 2016), pp. 63–5.

situation that had obtained under the last Kaiser, while 'politics' meant party-politics of the sort that flourished under Weimar.[57]

In a notebook entry for the year 1929 Furtwängler wrote:

> For Germany – this statement [I am about to make] is purely historical and objective and has nothing to do with nationalism of any kind – is the actual creator of pure instrumental music in the grand style; a true symphony has never been written by non-Germans. Half-symphonists [Halbsinfoniker] such as Berlioz, Franck, Tchaikovsky, are in all essentials completely under the influence of Germany.[58]

In spite of his disavowal of any political content and insistence on historical objectivity, such opinions held by one in Furtwängler's position can hardly be read as anything other than chauvinistic and openly nationalistic. It was these sentiments that in part motivated his attack on Toscanini and fuelled the rhetoric of 'Interpretation: A Question of Musical Destiny'. The great heritage of canonical masterworks could only be entrusted to a German conductor.

Whether Furtwängler was directing polemical fire against a rival, recording private thoughts in his journal or writing a formally composed article, an increasingly tendentious form of the organic world-view is evident. It was this that became crucial to the political affiliation of the approach, for the concept ultimately developed into one of the central pillars of the idea of the totalitarian state. When Furtwängler writes 'it is only by recognising the existence of the whole that we can prevent ourselves from falling into a state of total chaos and confusion', clear and striking parallels between the respective artistic and political processes become apparent: he considered that the only release from this state of confusion was adherence to the organic model and a return to the certainties of authoritarianism. In Furtwängler's world-view the organic model not only explained the phenomenon of musical creativity but it also served to define the single, 'correct' approach to the problems of interpretation and performance; in the political arena the organic model defined the single, 'correct' approach to leadership, government and the constitution of the state. Performances of the masterworks of German music were an indispensable part of the life of that state for they helped provide the aesthetic and cultural carapace necessary for its continued existence as a living organism.

---

57 See 'Playing for the Devil: How much did Furtwängler really resist the Nazis?', *Times Literary Supplement* (London), 13 November 1992, pp. 3–4.
58 AFZN, p. 64; NBKS, p. 36.

CHAPTER 5

FURTWÄNGLER AND THE NAZI STATE I (1933-35)

By the end of the Weimar Republic, emotionally charged terms like *Volk*, *Gemeinschaft*, *Blut*, *Rasse* and *organisch* defied definition or analysis. Rather they stirred feelings of a longing for an ideal, unified German nation in an era of political and social fragmentation.[1]

There is something dubious about music. I maintain that music is ambiguous by its very nature. I am not going too far when I declare it to be politically suspect.[2]

Who can say how much suffering has been caused by the exuberant use of the organic model in politics, or the comparison of the state to a work of art, and the representation of the dictator as the inspired moulder of human lives, by totalitarian theorists in our own times.[3]

Now I know what is wrong with Germany.

Sir Thomas Beecham following a meeting with Hitler.[4]

The seizure of power by Hitler and the National Socialists in the early months of 1933 signalled the rapid establishment of a totalitarian state. As if to emphasise his importance to the state hierarchy, Furtwängler was given the title of Prussian State Councillor and later appointed as Vice President of the Reichsmusikkammer (RMK) with Richard Strauss as President. As

1 Pamela M. Potter, *Most German of the Arts* (New Haven and London: Yale UP, 1998), p. 176.
2 Thomas Mann, *The Magic Mountain* (1924), tr. John E. Woods (New York: Alfred A. Knopf, 1995), p. 135.
3 Isaiah Berlin, 'The Purpose of Philosophy', in *Concepts and Categories* (Oxford: OUP, 1980), p. 10.
4 Harold Atkins and Archie Newman, *Beecham Stories* (London: Robson Books, 1978), p. 76.

6   Furtwängler, Goebbels and Richard Strauss.
Caricature by Gregor Rabinovitch (1889–1953), undated, probably late 1934.

'He'll struggle like a bird stuck fast, I'll bind him hand and foot;'
Goethe, *Faust*, Part I, lines 1862–3 (tr. David Luke).

defined in the law of 1 November 1933, the RMK was the Music Division of the Reichskulturkammer, the central organisation that co-ordinated the creative professions such as theatre, film, literature, fine art, radio, the press and music. It was fundamental to Nazi doctrine that no area of life was outside politics or would remain unpolitical; the organic model therefore became the ideological basis of the political system on which the Third Reich was built.[5]

In order to have some understanding of this progressive nationalisation of the dominant æsthetic preoccupations of *Bildungsbürgertum*, it is necessary to examine in broad terms the social structures that resulted from the vigorous application of the organic model as a fully developed socio-political system.[6] In one sense Nazi ideology was created from a particularly tendentious and selective synthesis of Hegelian political philosophy with elements of Social Darwinism, applied with a ruthless determination. According to this world-view the Nazi state was a result of an organic process of continuous historical evolution; the leader, in the person of Adolf Hitler, was totemised as *Führer*, the inspired moulder of human lives; the state was all powerful and exercised absolute moral authority; the organic state was by definition anti-democratic and required a strong leader to impose rational order; the individual was subservient to the whole; the state provided stable conditions under which art, and particularly musical art, could flourish.[7] The extent to which the organic model was generative of so much Nazi ideology, and how culture was to be an integral part of the political process, was made clear by Hitler in *Mein Kampf*:

> Thus the highest purpose of the [völkisch] State is to ensure the preservation of those fundamental racial elements, which, particularly in the field of culture, create that beauty and dignity which is characteristic of a higher form of humanity. We, as Aryans, conceive of the State only as the living organism of a people [den lebendigen Organismus eines Volkstums]. This organism not only safeguards the preservation of the people but, through the continuing development of its spiritual and idealistic faculties, leads them to the highest form of freedom.[8]

---

5 See Erik Levi, *Music in the Third Reich*, pp. 24–34. Also Michael Burleigh, *The Third Reich: A New History* (London: MacMillan, 2000), p. 105.
6 For a broad overview of Nazi cultural policy as applied in the early part of the period, see 'Hitler's Cultural Revolution', in Evans, *The Coming of the Third Reich*, pp. 392–461.
7 See Hegel, *Philosophy of Right*, pp. 240–350.
8 Hitler, *Mein Kampf*, p. 434 (author's translation).

This statement represents the extreme politicisation of the organic world-view. It is also evident just how the organic model would later come to be used as a convenient metaphor for the tendentious justification of a pernicious racial ideology.

The concept of a strong political leader, who would free the organic state from corrosive elements, dominated the conservative-minded national imagination in the closing stages of the Weimar Republic. To those such as Furtwängler, steeped as they were in the idea of 'Germanness', the establishment of the Third Reich signalled initially a return to an author-itarian form of government which would re-establish the order and social structures of the Wilhelmine empire. With the advent of Hitler, Houston Stewart Chamberlain's plea for 'an iron broom to sweep Germany clean' became a reality.[9] A further important element in Nazi ideology was the idea of rebirth as captured in the slogan *Deutschland Erwache* (Germany Awake); the reawakening of Germany through a rediscovery of a mythical past which would serve as the foundation of the present. The slow, uninter-rupted evolution of an intellectual and cultural heritage as understood by Spengler constituted true progress; society developed and expanded through a process of renewal and enrichment which drew on this foundation. To the conservative-minded nationalists this continuity had been lost with the political upheavals following the defeat of 1918 and the establishment of the 'un-German' Weimar Republic. There was a palpable longing for a resto-ration of the certainties of authoritarian government. Many from across the social and cultural spectrum saw the advent of the Nazi state as a means by which the wound could be healed.

Associated with the concept of organic development was the notion of the creative artist as the product of generations of slowly accumulated learning and tradition. Organic continuity after Spengler's model was necessary for the appearance of genius. Creative genius, especially that embodied in the figure of the musician, was a phenomenon of the past enshrined in the canon of German musical masterworks. Musical genius was henceforth to be given continued life through the work of the recreative artist whose function it was to ensure the continuing existence of the masterworks of the past. The concept of genius was therefore now embodied in the figure of the recreative artist, in particular that of the orchestral conductor, who functioned as the leader, or energising force, of that microcosm of the organic state: the organi-cally constituted orchestra.

---

9 Houston Stewart Chamberlain, *Politische Ideale*, p. 101. 'An iron broom must sweep Germany clean: whoever has the courage to wield it will find he has all the strength of the folk behind him.'

Hostility towards modern music had intensified as the Weimar Republic moved towards its collapse. As will be seen, with the advent of Nazism a good deal of contemporary music was condemned as degenerate. The mainstay of the musical life which continued from the Weimar period into the Third Reich was a growing reverence for the German canon together with the performance of Wagner's operas at the Bayreuth Festival, which after its reopening in 1924 increasingly became a hotbed of strident nationalist and anti-Semitic ideology. The elements in Nazi cultural ideology inherited from the diverse legacy of German Romanticism emphasised the transcendent nature of music as the means by which the spirit could enter not only a metaphysical realm which existed outside of itself, but also a specifically German realm. More importantly for the political puppet masters, if film, the cinema and radio were the means by which they had access to the mind of the mass of the population at large, music was an important medium for influencing the educated middle classes. This is partly why official ideology drew so heavily on musical culture, or, as Richard Grunberger rather graphically puts it, 'from the seizure of power onwards the regime bathed the country in music as in a foetal fluid'.[10]

On 31 January 1933 Adolf Hitler told the German people that 'the National Government will again make national discipline, instead of turbulent instincts, the ruler of our lives. It will be most careful to remember those ancient institutions that are the true bearers of the power and strength of our nation.'[11] The advent of a regime whose stated intention was to exorcise the degenerate element from cultural life and restore the tradition of high *Kultur* to a place of national pre-eminence was likely to be welcomed, at least tacitly, by Furtwängler and those of the conservative elite who longed for a return to an authoritarian form of government; yet such a social grouping was unlikely to have much sympathy with the more vulgar excesses of rank-and-file National Socialism. Here the beginnings are evident of the web of contradictions that was to enfold even men like Furtwängler and Richard Strauss and cause them such difficulties throughout the twelve-year period of Nazi rule. On the one hand the nation was now ruled by a regime with no social,

10 Richard Grunberger, *A Social History of the Third Reich* (London: Weidenfeld & Nicolson, 1971), p. 513. See also William Weber, *Music and the Middle Class: The Social Structure of Concert Life in London, Paris and Vienna* (Farnham: Ashgate, 1975), pp. 75–6; Celia Applegate, 'How German Is It? Nationalism and the Idea of Serious Music in the early Nineteenth Century', in *19th Century Music*, vol. 21 (Spring 1998), pp. 274–96.
11 *Ansprache des Reichskanzlers Adolf Hitler*, Part 3: Adolf Hitler's Radio Address to the Third Reich, 31 January 1933. Source: transcript enclosed with a cassette recording prepared from original broadcast material.

cultural or intellectual pedigree that had risen to power on a tide of popular opinion backed by physical intimidation and coercion. Although this represented a longed-for return to authoritarianism, it was not accompanied by a restoration of the intricate social structures and hierarchies of the Second German Empire and was hardly likely to be congenial to Furtwängler and the educated elite. On the other hand, here was a regime which purported to value and support the art of music while severely curtailing those elements of degeneracy which conservative nationalists saw as polluting the integrity and organic cohesion of German musical life.

Furtwängler's Open Letter to Joseph Goebbels (11 April 1933)

Closely associated with this dichotomy is the problem of anti-Semitism and what exactly constituted anti-Semitic thought and behaviour. The Nazis came to power with an increasingly virulent form of anti-Semitism as one of the main pillars of their ideological framework: Jewry was a corrosive element and its presence within the organic state undesirable.[12] According to Schenker, as we have seen, Furtwängler was capable of acting in private as an 'undisguised anti-Semite';[13] yet at the outset of the Nazi period he saw the expulsion of certain Jews as detrimental to the maintenance of high artistic standards. His ambivalent, self-contradictory attitude towards the Jewish question is clearly evident in the open letter he wrote to Propaganda Minister Joseph Goebbels in protest against the removal of individual Jews from prominent positions in public life. It was written in response to the widely reported incident when Richard Strauss replaced the Jewish conductor Bruno Walter as conductor of a Leipzig Gewandhaus concert. As such it is one of the key statements that illuminate Furtwängler's often contradictory position in relation to the Nazi regime; it is thus here newly translated and cited in full.

In view of my many years in German public life and my inner attachment to German music, I hope you will allow me to draw your attention to certain happenings in our musical life which in my opinion have absolutely no connection with the restoration of our national honour – which we all welcome with enthusiasm and gratitude.

I write as an artist. Art and artists are there to unite, not divide. The only division I am willing to acknowledge is between good and bad art. A

12 See Daniel Jonah Goldhagen, *Hitler's Willing Executioners*, Ch. 2.
13 Diary entry for 11 April 1925, in Federhofer, *Heinrich Schenker nach Tagebüchern und Briefen*, p. 116.

conceptual and distasteful division is now being made between Jews and non-Jews, even against those whose political conduct has given no cause for complaint. The other crucial and decisive dividing line, that between good and bad, is all too often ignored.

Present-day musical life has been weakened by the world [economic] crisis, by the radio and by other factors; it cannot endure any further experiments. Music cannot be apportioned as other necessities of life, such as potatoes and bread. If concerts offer nothing, then audiences will stay away. The question of musical quality is therefore not only one of idealism but of survival. If the struggle against Jewry is directed against those rootless and destructive artists who seek to create effect through kitsch and empty virtuosity, then it is justified. The struggle against them and the spirit they embody – which also has its German followers – must be rigorously pursued. But if this struggle is directed against real artists, then it is not in the interests of our cultural life, because artists, wherever they may be, are much too rare to be excluded from their own land without inflicting cultural harm.

It is therefore of vital importance that men such as [Bruno] Walter, [Otto] Klemperer, [Max] Reinhardt and others be permitted to express themselves through their art.

Once more let it be said: our struggle must be against the rootless, subversive, superficial, destructive spirit; not against the true creative artist.

I therefore appeal to you in the name of German art, not to allow these actions, which it might prove impossible to reverse.[14]

This letter is entirely driven by the æsthetic and social attitudes identified in Chapter 4 under the terms *Bildungsbürgerlich* and *Gemeinschaftlich*. Furtwängler enthusiastically welcomes what he describes as the 'restoration of our national honour' before bringing the collective values of art and artifice to bear on the Jewish question. His argument is thus based on the distinction between true art and fake art, between the genuine artist and the dilettante. Individual Jewish artists representing true art should be allowed to remain in the new German state in order to ensure the continuation of vigorous artistic life; those who represent mere artifice (here colourfully described as *kitsch* promulgated by rootless and sterile performance – Furtwängler was never one to understate his case), should be excluded. Furtwängler's strongly worded edict is also a further formulation of the antithetical relationship

14 'Kunst aus deutschem Volkstum: Ein Brief an Joseph Goebbels', *Vossische Zeitung*, 11 April 1933. A heavily amended handwritten draft of this letter is to be found among the fragments in Zentralbibliothek Zürich, Nachl. W. Furtwängler: S 130; reprinted in TW, pp. 70–1.

between art and artifice that had fired his invective against the non-Jewish Toscanini in 1930.

This document throws some light on Furtwängler's attitude to the Jewish question. It is well documented and beyond doubt that Furtwängler not only defended the position of Jewish players in the Berlin Philharmonic and other orchestras, but throughout the period of Nazi rule personally assisted many other individual Jews in the face of persecution in actions which involved a good deal of personal heroism at no small risk to himself. In addition, he retained the services of Berta Geissmar, his Jewish secretary and personal assistant, for as long as possible in the face of increasing Nazi intimidation. Furtwängler was by no means a strident anti-Semite in the manner of Hans Pfitzner; all other considerations apart, one of his refined *bürgerlich* background recoiled from the vulgar excesses of Nazi anti-Semitic acts. Yet, as his letter to Goebbels makes clear, he was not altogether free from the ideological form of anti-Semitism, which perceived German Jewry as a potentially corrosive element within the organic state, and thus a threat to the integrity, and inner cohesion of national life. This form of anti-Semitism was a familiar discourse in common currency among the educated middle classes. It represented a kind of double vision that deplored the brutal suddenness with which many Jews were removed from official positions yet welcomed the cleansing of excessive Jewish influence from German cultural life.[15] It was driven by an acceptance of a particular set of ideas and values associated with *Gemeinschaft* which indicated a broad conservative-nationalist cultural stance towards the Jewish question, believing itself distanced from the visceral and increasingly destructive form of anti-Semitism promulgated by the Nazis.[16]

The Brahms Centenary Address (16 May 1933)

The fiftieth anniversary of the Berlin Philharmonic Orchestra in 1932 considered in the previous chapter had provided Furtwängler with a platform from which he could warn of the dangers to cultural life inherent in the economic and social chaos that predominated during the closing months of the Weimar Republic. In contrast, the centenary of the birth of Brahms, which occurred during the early months of Nazi rule on 7 May

15 See Saul Friedländer, *Nazi Germany and the Jews*, p. 13: 'Even some of the most celebrated German exiles, such as Thomas Mann, were not immune, at least for a time, from this kind of dual vision of events.'
16 See especially Geoffrey Field, *Evangelist of Race*, pp. 270–3; also Michael Haas, *Forbidden Music: Jewish Composers banned by the Nazis* (New Haven and London: Yale UP, 2013), pp. 222–4.

1933, gave him the opportunity to comment on the position and significance of the composer within the context of the new *Zeitgeist*. Furtwängler gave an address to the German Brahms Society as part of the opening ceremony of the Brahms Festival held in Vienna: 'Johannes Brahms: Festvortrag für das Johannes Brahms-Fest, Wien, 16–21 Mai 1933'. The Furtwängler Nachlass in Zurich contains two separate typescripts.[17] The first appears to be the script from which Furtwängler delivered the address: it bears the superscription 'Verehrte Damen und Herren', the typescript is copiously underscored in red crayon in a manner which would assist the task of reading aloud and contains emendations appropriate for public delivery. The second, dated 16 May 1933, is the source of the text as amended for publication in the *Deutsche Allgemeine Zeitung*, 28 May 1933, and in two instalments in the Vienna *Neue Freie Presse* on 28 and 31 May. The slightly modified version included in *Ton und Wort* (pp. 40–52), is incorrectly dated 1931 and within the context of this chrono-logical anthology of Furtwängler's writings is therefore out of correct order.

Furtwängler's opening remarks offer unmistakable indications of a developing political will on the part of the German nation which would be fully realised in actual terms some five years later:

> One reason why the Deutsche Brahms-Gesellschaft decided to accept the invitation from the *Gesellschaft der Musikfreunde* to transfer the celebration of Brahms's one hundredth birthday to Vienna is to take account of his relationship to that city. For Brahms, as for Beethoven, Vienna became a second home. It gave him the atmosphere and the stimulation which was so necessary for one of his Nordic nature – highly vulnerable as it was in its mixture of gruff masculinity and hyper-sensitivity.
>
> But there is a further reason why we of the German Reich chose Vienna for the celebrations. Regardless of our political masters, we should not forget, either in Germany or in Austria, that we inhabit the same cultural world. Viennese classical composers are at the same time German classical composers. Nowhere is this sense of unity and common purpose more strongly felt than here in Vienna. It is quite right to say that Brahms has become the last of the 'Viennese' German classical composers.[18]

Furtwängler takes a Pan-German view in that he considers Germany and Austria to be an indivisible cultural whole. Brahms is seen as a symbol of this common cultural identity: born in the north German Hanseatic city of Hamburg and living for most of his creative life in Vienna he represents the

---

17 Zentralbibliothek Zürich, Nachl. W. Furtwängler: S 18. The full German text as printed in *Deutsche Allgemeine Zeitung* together with references to Schenker's responses may be found at <http://www.schenkerdocumentsonline.org>.

18 TW, p. 40; FM, pp. 97–104 (amended).

fusion of these two aspects of the German creative mind. The Schenkerian view of Brahms as the last composer of the Austro-German tradition is a constantly recurring idea and is of considerable significance in the reception of German music abroad. For Furtwängler the uncontroversial respectability of Brahms enhanced the wider respectability of the German nation:

> If we want to identify the last composer to leave a permanent mark on the international standing of German music, the answer must be – excluding of course the incomparable figure of Wagner – Brahms. [...] With the exception of the cosmopolitan and internationally successful Richard Strauss, no other German composer who came after him – not his contemporary Bruckner, not Pfitzner, not Reger – has succeeded in becoming so well known beyond the borders of Germany.[19]

Furtwängler contrasts the permanence of Brahms' art with the transience of so much modern musical production; he invokes Brahms as a protagonist in his attack on what he perceived to be the shallowness of the *New Objectivity* (*Neue Sachlichkeit*). His definition of objectivity is that of the Romantic; he is redefining the concept in his own terms.

> There has been a good deal of talk in modern æsthetics of the concept of 'objectivity'. The avant garde adopted the slogan 'Neue Sachlichkeit', or 'New Objectivity' – but just about the only thing new was that the word 'objectivity' regained some of its former substance and meaning.
> Let us consider the word itself. 'Objectivity' means an immediate connection to 'objects' as such; this denotes independence from all that does not belong to the 'objects', in particular modish fashions of the moment. In this sense 'New Objectivity' is the precise opposite of what it pretends to be. In the realm of music, objectivity means a clear, precise understanding of what it is that makes music into an art. This happens when the logic of a mental event becomes a pure musical process; where in other words music and mind, mind and music, are united so completely that they cannot be separated, no matter how they are approached.[20]

19 Ibid., p. 41; p. 98.
20 Ibid., p. 43; p. 99. Furtwängler is here referring to a movement in the culture of the Weimar Republic that arose as a reaction against Expressionism. The term was first used by Gustav Hartlaub as the title of an art Exhibition staged in 1925 in Mannheim of works by artists working in a post-expressionist idiom. Hindemith is the composer most prominently associated with the movement. Among conductors Otto Klemperer at the Berlin Kroll opera (1927–31) was both attacked and praised as an exponent of *Neue Sachlichkeit*. The movement is generally considered to have ended with the advent of the Nazis in 1933. For a detailed account see Peter Heyworth, *Otto Klemperer: His Life and Times* (Cambridge: CUP, 1983), vol. 1, pp. 234–378.

Furtwängler's redefinition of musical objectivity is a clear and direct reference to the avant-garde movement of the Weimar Republic and is driven by his conservatively minded organic world-view as the touchstone of artistic value. It is therefore predictable that the validity and worth of Brahms' music should be judged according to its qualities of musical logic and cohesion. He praises Brahms for his integrity, complete lack of meretricious showmanship and any desire to create an effect for its own sake:

> He uses the orchestra with a restraint derived from the classical composers, completely overlooking Wagner's achievements, which so fascinated his contemporaries. He keeps to his concise, small-scale forms: indeed, the older he grew, the simpler, more compact, and anti-theatrical these works became, for all their latent depth and explosive force. The logical strength that prevails in his works is found only in the very greatest. It expresses only what the object (i.e. the world embodied by the work in question) requires. All things alien [Allem Fremden], all the sham attractions of what is referred to as 'a wealth of invention' [Reichtum der Erfindung] – which in reality simply means a lack of ability to concentrate – are rejected. What Brahms says he says clearly and unequivocally – because he has something to say. What a difference to most of those around him and to most of what has since been written.[21]

Sharing the same premise as dislike of effect for its own sake was a strong antipathy towards intellectual theorising. Brahms' music was paradigmatic of the distinction between the true creative act and such theorising which, with the notable exception of Schenker, Furtwängler regarded as sterile and uncreative:

> Brahms hardly ever spoke about his works. Like all truly objective artists he was clear about the distinction between the real creative deed that manifests itself in the work of art and the empty speculation [Drumherumreden] which was just beginning to become fashionable in his day, and which has since become such an intolerable feature of our so-called super-clever age.[22]

It is, however, in his view of the place of Brahms within the progress of History that Furtwängler reveals his close empathy with the concept of the organic state as a racially defined entity and the place of musical art within the developing historical continuum. The most important fact about Brahms is that he was of pure German stock and that in consequence his art is rooted

21 Ibid., p. 44; pp. 99–100.
22 Ibid., p. 47; p. 101. Furtwängler is here referring to the emerging discipline of Music Analysis.

deep within the German tradition. It is this more than any other factor that gives Brahms' art its enduring validity:

> Brahms belongs to that race of Germanic musical giants that began with Bach and Handel and continued with Beethoven. He combined colossal physical strength with great sensitivity and tenderness. In both build and character he was Nordic throughout. He seems to me to be a descendant of those Dutch or old German painters such as van Eyck and Rembrandt, whose works combine introspection and imaginative intensity with an impetuous strength and a wonderful sense of form. This affinity with the old German ways is particularly evident in his great sets of variations. His creative powers were extraordinary, and his sense of form is apparent in everything of his that has come down to us, in the briefest of letters no less than in his songs and symphonies.[23]

Furtwängler's comparison of Brahms with the artist Rembrandt and his inclusion of Rembrandt among a roll call of Dutch or old German painters may have been intended as a reference to Julius Langbehn's earlier reinvention of Rembrandt as a model German artist in his widely read and influential book *Rembrandt as Educator* (*Rembrandt als Erzieher*), first published in 1890. As the historian Fritz Stern puts it, 'one theme dominated the entire book: German culture was being destroyed by science and intellectualism and could be regenerated only through the resurgence of art and the rise to power of great, artistic individuals in a new society'.[24] In this celebration of Brahms as an icon of north German art the allegory would have been unmistakable and familiar to his audience. Furtwängler develops this theme through a discussion of Brahms' use of form. The 'Germanness' of his musical structure is, predictably, defined by its organic cohesion, a trope that is becoming synonymous with and a precondition of the idea of musical form as an ideological expression of national character and worth. It is not only this sense of national identity with which Furtwängler credits Brahms: following the tradition or respect for order he sees Brahms as the composer who gave back to German music its sense of classical cohesion and integrity. Brahms was a product of artistic evolution rather than revolution, for in musical terms he restored to the notion of progress the idea of organic continuity:

23 Ibid., p. 48; pp. 102.
24 Stern, *The Politics of Cultural Despair*, Ch. 2, 'Julius Langbehn and Germanic Irrationalism', here p. 122.

It is a typically German kind of form: a characteristic fusion of concise, highly charged content with a form of remarkable balance and clarity, not there for its own sake but for the sake of the musical 'substance'. His work gives rise to a daemonic world of fantasy – yet a world bound together within a tight organic structure. If ever there was a composer capable of countering the charge that the Germans are incapable of casting their music into classical forms, it is Brahms.[25]

It is but a short step from this notion of form as an expression of national identity, with its qualities of the daemonic and the organic, to the appropriation of Brahms as a model *völkisch* composer. Furtwängler's view is that there is nothing manufactured or meretricious about Brahms' art: it springs directly from the community of 'das Volk'.

> There is another, more specific sense in which Brahms is of importance to us today. [...] What I am thinking of is his power to make the greater community of the people [Gemeinschaft des Volkes] the source of his living existence. [...] For Brahms, like his great predecessors, had the ability to write melodies which to the very last detail were unmistakably his, but yet sounded like pure folk songs. Or, conversely, melodies that were genuine folk songs but composed by Brahms. With Mahler, for example, it was quite the opposite. Mahler's relationship to the folk song was that of a stranger, an outsider, a man who longed to find in it a refuge for his restless spirit. Taking it over as it was, he merely created 'artificial', 'imitation' folk songs. Brahms, however, was the folk, he was the folk song. He could not be otherwise, whether he was writing symphonies, quartets or songs. He could thus pour his whole personality into the space of two bars and at the same time retain his general accessibility, writing modern, original music which still appealed to the wider community [Gemeinschaft]. Wagner and Bruckner were similarly gifted, and I am in no doubt whatsoever that this represents a triumph of creativity at its highest level and in this we see the mark of genius.[26]

The values that drove Furtwängler's invective against Toscanini and his letter to Goebbels are readily in evidence in the comparison between Brahms as a creator of genuine folk song (art) and the Jewish Mahler as a composer of artificial folk song (artifice). Genuine folk song was a product of an unpolluted, organically cohesive society; the dilettante Mahler, as a supposedly rootless Jew, could only imitate folk song, whereas Brahms, who sprang from the *Volk*,

---

25 TW, pp. 48–9; FM, p. 103.
26 Ibid., pp. 50–1; pp. 103–4. For more on *Volksgemeinschaft*, see Saul Friedländer, *Nazi Germany and the Jews*, p. 116.

could create the genuine article. This ideological form of anti-Semitism, of the Jew as outsider, is a continuation of that espoused by Wagner in 'Judaism in Music' ('Das Judentum in der Musik', 1850), which represented such an important notional constituent of the organic concept of the state.

The idea of Brahms as a composer whose form is founded in natural order can be traced to notions of classical form as reflections of that order as derived from Goethe's scientific writings: 'The universal validity of Classical form is not, as earlier critics thought, merely a formal matter but an expression of nature herself. It is this union with nature that makes Brahms a classic.'[27] To Furtwängler Brahms' creative genius was entirely a result of and flowed naturally from his 'Germanness'; his art was rooted in the culture and tradition of his native land. He shared with his mentor Schenker the view that Brahms was 'the last master of German composition'.

> The people, the folk song world from which Brahms originated, was German. What he was able to do was by virtue of the strength of his Germanness – not because he wanted to be German but because he actually was German. He could do no other, and although he eagerly responded to influences from all over the non-German world, it was through his Germanness that he came to understand and conquer this world. [...] He was the last composer we have seen who so clearly demonstrated to the universality of German music.[28]

This address, given in the Austrian capital by the figure who was now regarded to all intents and purposes as Germany's *Generalmusikdirektor*, is a critically important document in understanding Furtwängler's position at the beginning of the Nazi era. It has little in the way of æsthetic content and does not engage in any depth with the phenomenon of Brahms' music in either general or specific terms. Furtwängler presents Brahms as the quintessence of Germanness and as a model *völkisch* composer whose work both epitomised and embodied the artistic ideals of the new Germany following the National Socialist revolution. His address is more of an attempt to reinvent Brahms along the lines of Julius Langbehn's earlier interpretation of Rembrandt as a model German artist; to appropriate Brahms both as a significant force in the increasing politicisation of music as a means of controlling the mind of the educated middle classes and as a useful propaganda tool in the Nazi regime's ongoing attempts to gain wider cultural credibility.

This was certainly how his address was heard and understood by one particular member of the audience troubled by the strident cultural

27 Ibid., pp. 51–2; p. 104.
28 Ibid., p. 52; p. 104.

chauvinism and overt nationalist rhetoric. On 16 May, Alban Berg (1885–1935) wrote to his wife Helene:

> Yesterday morning [16 May 1933] I was at the Universal Edition, then from 11.30 to 1.00 PM at the opening ceremony of the Brahms Festival. Miklas,[29] Dollfuss[30] (who was particularly celebrated) and Schuschnigg,[31] who also gave a speech about Brahms [were also there]; but it was Furtwängler who gave the main address and I was upset about it all day. It was a Nazi-inspired speech for *German* music, which – or so he implied – had found its last representative in Brahms. Without mentioning any names, he betrayed the whole of post-Brahmsian music, especially Mahler and the younger generation (like Hindemith). There was no reference at all to the existence of Schoenberg and his circle.
>
> It was horrible having to put up with this and witness the frenzied enthusiasm of a cretinous audience, who seemed not to realize how the Brahms *a cappella* choral songs which followed made nonsense of Furtwängler's tendentious absurdities.[32]

Berg had at this point just returned from Germany where he had been particularly struck when in Munich by the new Nazi spirit and the vulgar bombast of its associated rhetoric. He refers to this directly in an earlier letter to his wife of 23 February 1933: '*One* thing is very clear to me: we can never ally ourselves with people such as *this*.'[33] Furtwängler's special pleading for German music would have doubtless pleased the Nazi sympathisers in the audience, but must have disturbed those who, like Berg and the politicians Dollfuss and Schuschnigg, were troubled by the advent of the Nazi state and alarmed at the possible union of Austria with the new Germany. The German scholar Fred K. Prieberg, however, takes a different view. He denies that the speech shows a 'conversion to the spirit which currently prevails in Germany'; in fact he goes so far as to suggest that it is a 'wholesale rejection of that spirit'. According to his account the Brahms centenary celebrations were moved from Hamburg to Vienna on account of the fact that an unnamed racial investigator 'had made the staggering discovery that Brahms was of Jewish descent'. The purpose of Furtwängler's address was therefore

---

29 Wilhelm Miklas (1872–1956), Federal President of Austria from 1928 to 1938.
30 Engelbert Dollfuss (1892–1934), Austrian Federal Chancellor, assassinated by the Nazis on 25 July 1934.
31 Kurt von Schuschnigg (1897–1977), succeeded Dollfuss as Federal Chancellor. An opponent of the Anschluss.
32 Alban Berg, *Briefe an seine Frau* (München and Wien: Albert Langen, Georg Müller 1965), p. 628; Eng. edn, *Alban Berg: Letters to his Wife*, tr. Bernard Grun (London: Faber & Faber, 1971), pp. 413–14.
33 Ibid., p. 608; Eng. edn, p. 398.

publicly to counter this scurrilous assertion by asserting the composer's unimpeachable 'Germanness'. It is not clear how Furtwängler's endorsement of Brahms' impeccable Germanic credentials could be interpreted in the way Prieberg attempts, especially if it is to be construed as a 'rejection of the spirit which currently prevails in Germany'.[34]

'The Case of Hindemith' (25 November 1934)

Berg's assertion that Furtwängler had abandoned the younger generation of German composers is, however, not entirely borne out by subsequent events. He was by no means prepared to compromise his musical ideals and principles if challenged by what he regarded as ill-informed, uncritical and prejudicial artistic reaction on the part of the authorities. In late 1934 his spirited defence of Hindemith brought the avowedly non-political artist into direct conflict with his political masters: musical idealism into conflict with political ideology.

Paul Hindemith (1895–1963) was a leading protagonist of *Neue Sachlichkeit*, one of the experiments which had been such a prominent feature of the cultural life of the Weimar Republic and which, as is clear from the Brahms address considered above, Furtwängler regarded with deep mistrust. Hindemith reacted against what he regarded as the excesses of late-flowering Romanticism; yet, in contrast to Schoenberg, his style remained firmly rooted within the tonal spectrum. Even so, the content of his work did not conform to the strictures of Nazi ideology. The early satirical opera *Neues vom Tage* had already in 1929 attracted adverse attention on account of the scene where a naked woman sings in the bath. More generally, Hindemith's introduction of jazz rhythms into his early compositions, as such *Sancta Susanna* (1921) and the *Kammermusik* series, together with his open association with prominent Jewish artists provoked hostility from Nazi authorities.

On 11 and 12 March 1934 Furtwängler gave performances of the Symphonic Suite extracted by the composer from the opera *Mathis der Maler* to considerable public acclaim. He planned to follow this with the premiere of the complete work at the Berlin Staatsoper but, for reasons that are not entirely clear, the regime banned the opera from performance and removed

---

34 See Fred K. Prieberg, *Trial of Strength: Wilhelm Furtwängler and the Third Reich*, tr. Paul Dolan (London: Quartet Books, 1991), pp. 64–5. This account of Furtwängler's Brahms address does not appear in the German edition of Prieberg's book, only in the English translation: cf. *Kraftprobe: Wilhelm Furtwängler im Dritten Reich* (Wiesbaden: F. A. Brockhaus, 1986), p. 95.

7   Furtwängler in Potsdam, 1934

the proposed premiere from the forthcoming schedules of the Staatsoper. It is certainly true that the opera's text had considerable bearing on the situation faced by creative artists in Nazi Germany: that of the conflicted artist torn by the impossibility of creative freedom under an autocratic and politically repressive regime. The parallels with Nazi Germany are unmistakable: there is even a book-burning incident. What is far from certain, however, is just how much the authorities knew beforehand about the text of the opera, or whether they based their reactions on the prevailing hostility towards Hindemith as a 'modernist' composer. It is certainly hard to see how the *Mathis Symphony*, which in its use of folk song and chorale represents something of a reversion by Hindemith away from his 'modernist' idiom towards the romantic traditions of the previous century, could have any 'political' implications. Whatever the motivation, Furtwängler responded to what he considered to be unwarranted state interference in artistic matters by publishing a hard-hitting article in support of Hindemith.[35] Although his championship of Hindemith as a model German composer was the ostensible cause of his stance against the regime, the controversy was in one respect a more general one relating to matters of authority. Furtwängler had an infallible sense of his own position and worth which he was not prepared to compromise. His natural empathy with an authoritarian state-controlled system was at odds with his unwillingness to accept and yield to a higher authority in the artistic matters of which he considered himself the final arbiter.[36]

Furtwängler's defence begins by seeking to define the nature of Hindemith's offences against Nazi doctrine:

> In certain circles a campaign has been initiated against Paul Hindemith, the reason being that he is 'not acceptable' [nicht tragbar] to the new Germany. Why? Of what is he accused?
>
> Firstly, he is attacked for purely political reasons. It is said that he may be of Jewish descent and that he founded and for a long time played viola in the Amar Quartet, which included other Jewish members. [...]

---

35 Zentralbibliothek Zürich, Nachl. W. Furtwängler: S 31; *Deutsche Allgemeine Zeitung*, 25 November 1934. See also TW, pp. 91–6; FM, pp. 117–20. For an additional perspective on Hindemith and the Nazi response to *Mathis der Maler* see Tony Palmer's film, *Hindemith: A Pilgrim's Progress*, which contains references to Furtwängler's defence of the composer. Also Ian Kemp, *Hindemith* (Oxford: OUP, 1970), pp. 28–9.

36 Only a brief outline of the vicissitudes of the Hindemith affair is given here. The political fallout is well documented in the published Furtwängler literature. See, for example, Curt Riess, *Wilhelm Furtwängler*, pp. 120ff; Hans-Hubert Schönzeler, *Furtwängler*, pp. 69ff; Sam H. Shirakawa, *The Devil's Music Master*, pp. 179ff.

Hindemith's opponents themselves are well aware that these objections do not explain the attacks on him. The principal reason is that certain of his works are ideologically unacceptable on account of his choice of texts.[37]

Furtwängler suggests that the racial question was largely a cover for the clash of ideology inherent in Hindemith's choice of operatic texts. He defends Hindemith's libretti and subject matter on the grounds that it was in keeping with the spirit of taste of the times. The important point about the libretto of *Mathis der Maler*, which following the models of Wagner and Hans Pfitzner Hindemith had written himself, is its strong moral sense and the theme of artistic freedom imperiled by politics. It is this that is indicative of Hindemith's true character.

> Hindemith's latest opera, only recently completed, is called *Mathis der Maler*. He wrote the text himself – the only time he has acted as his own librettist. A profound sense of moral commitment is readily apparent. It is claimed that he has just responded to the changed circumstances. Apart from the fact that he would be completely incapable of reacting in such a way, the accusation is unfounded as the work was begun long before the national revolution.[38]

In the course of his consideration of Hindemith's music Furtwängler praises the composer for his talent while at the same time identifying a weakness in that his works contain a degree of fabricated passage-work.[39] This he considers a feature of the *Neue Sachlichkeit*; yet in his view it is wrong to make Hindemith a scapegoat for the excesses of this modernist æsthetic for which the protagonists of the new cultural ideology naturally had little sympathy:

> Today, in our very different age, it is easy to reject this cult [*Neue Sachlichkeit*] and make Hindemith responsible for its theoretical excesses. But it would be wrong to do so, for most of his works from this time were occasional pieces, written for effect and for practical use, rather than 'pure' composition.[40]

Furtwängler's appraisal of Hindemith soon turns to the central question of his position within the Nazi state. The composer's versatility and value to

---

37 TW, p. 91; FM, p. 117 (translation amended).
38 TW, p. 92; FM, p. 118.
39 *Gebrauchmusik*, 'music for use' or 'music for a practical purpose' is a term specifically associated with Hindemith and the *Neue Sachlichkeit*. See Erik Levi, *Music in the Third Reich*, pp. 107–19.
40 TW, p. 93; FM, p. 118.

musical pedagogy is evaluated in a way which can only be seen as emphasising his relevance to the ideals and purposes of National Socialist revolution:

> He paid close attention to school music, tirelessly seeking ways of bridging the disastrous gulf that has opened up between folk music and art music. His work in this area coincides with tendencies characteristic of our new National Socialist Germany. His *Plöner Musiktag*,[41] for instance, was a pioneering work of educational music.[42]

Furtwängler continues to define the qualities in Hindemith's music which give it both enduring artistic value and relevance to the ideals of the present day. As with Brahms, the foremost quality which he identifies is that of 'Germanness'; the strengths in Hindemith's works are a direct result of his national origin. In this respect he is placing Hindemith within the parameters of a rationale similar to that with which he justified Brahms as paradigmatic of German, and by extension, Nazi, ideals:

> His published works from his early period combine structural mastery, characteristic moderation and a particular sense of the demands of chamber music. On the one hand they show a fresh, carefree boldness and on the other they have a searching depth – particularly in the slow movements. [...] These early works – to which one could add a number from later periods, such as the song-cycle *Das Marienleben* [1923] show Hindemith (who has pure Germanic blood in his veins) [ja auch blutsmäßig rein germanisch ist] as unquestionably German – German in his honest crafts-manship and his upright nature as well as in the purity and restraint of his comparatively rare displays of emotion.[43]

Furtwängler is of the opinion that the *Mathis der Maler* symphony is paradig-matic of the very qualities which give Hindemith's music its enduring worth and its ideological validity. It does not indicate artistic subversion but represents a return to the artistic ideals which were the foundation of Hindemith's, and Furtwängler's, musical creativity:

> His most recent work, the symphony taken from the opera from *Mathis der Maler*, confirms these impressions. Since its first performance in March 1934 it has made a powerful impact wherever it has been played, particu-larly on those who could not otherwise be regarded as his friends. This

---

41 *Plöner Musiktag* is a typical piece of *gebrauchmusik*. For more on *gebrauchmusik*, see Ian Kemp, *Hindemith*, p. 23.
42 TW, p. 95; FM, p. 119.
43 Ibid.

does not imply, as I have said already, any ideological change of direction on Hindemith's part; it is rather a return to his beginnings, a return to his real self.[44]

In Furtwängler's view the vilification of Hindemith by the Nazis is therefore unjustified: in spite of the modernist excesses of his *Neue Sachlichkeit* period he is a creative composer in the German tradition whose talents the state can ill afford to lose. However, the thinly veiled subtext contained within the article, that of the question of the nature and purpose of authority, surfaces in Furtwängler's closing remarks. He asks the direct and unequivocal question which has strong resonances of his open letter to Goebbels considered earlier: 'Where will it lead if we begin to apply the methods of political denunciation to art?'[45]

Furtwängler's purpose in writing what he fully realised was a provocative article was therefore more wide-ranging than merely proffering support to a beleaguered composer and fellow artist: he is suggesting that Hindemith is a model German composer whose art is in sympathy with Nazi ideology and is therefore deserving not of official censure but of official approval and support. He warned of the inherent dangers if the creative arts, and particularly music, are appropriated for propaganda purposes; he therefore made a plea for freedom of artistic expression unhindered by political constraints, even though he was by this time well aware that unfettered artistic freedom is impossible within the rationale imposed by the organic state.

Furtwängler's championship of Hindemith in the face of official censure by the regime may be seen above all as a clash between the traditions of the educated middle classes inherited from the previous century, and the harsh reality of those traditions as now appropriated and enacted by the Nazi state. The political fallout following the publication of the article was considerable: in particular Furtwängler's final sentence warning of the consequences that would follow 'if political denunciation was applied to art' was interpreted by the regime as a direct attack on Nazi cultural policy. As a result, on 4 December 1934 Furtwängler resigned all his official posts and withdrew from public life. In an unpublished memorandum, written some two weeks later and dated 17 December 1934, Furtwängler is clearly continuing to reflect on the Nazi regime's response to his newspaper article. Although he does not refer directly to Hindemith, he is of the view that artistic judgements must be based on the works in question rather than the personality of the

44 Ibid., p. 95; p. 120.
45 Ibid., p. 96; p. 120.

artist. It is therefore preferable to allow such works to be performed so that they may be submitted to the scrutiny of the public.

> This *Volk* – which is represented in musical life by the 'Public' – but is not identical with it – may often err in detail for a moment but in the long term, never. One can therefore say that every artistic decision involved this kind of 'people's decision' in miniature. To anticipate this by means of State authority – unless it is a clear case either of rubbish, or kitsch or of anti-State cultural bolshevism – would only mean postponing the real decision.[46]

In spite of their avowed disaffection with Furtwängler, the Nazis quickly realised that they could ill afford to lose one of their most visible cultural figures. In February 1935 Furtwängler therefore reached a compromise with Propaganda Minister Goebbels whereby he would resume conducting in Germany as a guest rather than as head of a state-controlled orchestra or opera house. In reaching a *modus operandi* (or what was increasingly to resemble a Faustian pact) with the regime, Furtwängler publicly resolved the contradictions that had been created by the ideological appropriation and tendentious exaggeration of his own inherited traditions and beliefs. As an authoritarian figure himself he was compromised by the tension between his own and external authority, particularly in the artistic affairs of which he considered himself the final arbiter. It was this that in 1932 had precipitated his resignation as Music Director of the Bayreuth Festival after a conflict of authority with Winifred Wagner. It was now clear that, no matter how much he protested to the contrary, within the Nazi state art and politics were not separate and could not exist independently of one another. At some point between January and March 1935, around the time he was reaching his compromise position with Goebbels, he wrote that he regretted that what he retrospectively describes as the premature publication of his Hindemith article has had unfortunate political repercussions and unequivocally states that he in no way wished to contradict the opinion of the Führer. However, as he is in no doubt about Hindemith's artistic worth, he is confident that he can convince the Führer of the merits of the opera and is of the opinion that as the work is free of kitsch and cultural bolshevism it should be presented to the general public so that they could form a judgement. He concludes that any apparent difference between his view and that of the Führer is a tragic misunderstanding. He is quite certain that it should be possible to convince the Führer of Hindemith's credentials as a model German composer

---

46 Zentralbibliothek Zürich, Nachl. W. Furtwängler: S 25.

acceptable in the new Germany.[47] In the event, however, *Mathis der Maler* was premiered not in Germany but in Switzerland at the Stadttheater Zurich on 28 May 1938. The restrictions placed on Hindemith by the Nazis eventually forced him to emigrate, first to Switzerland and then in 1940 to the USA, where in 1946 he became an American citizen. After the war he eventually settled in Switzerland where he divided his time between teaching at the Universities of Zurich and Yale. He made limited returns to Germany, accepting, for example, an invitation to conduct Beethoven's Ninth for the opening of the 1953 Bayreuth Festival. Hindemith died on 28 December 1963 in Frankfurt.

To return to the observations of Isaiah Berlin with which this chapter began: it should by now be abundantly evident that throughout his life Furtwängler, almost to the point of obsession, sought to describe, explain and account for the phenomenon of the musical artwork through 'the exuberant use of the organic model' and its associated metaphorical constructions. His public and private writings are shot through with constant references to notions of organic cohesion, the importance of the 'whole' and copious other examples of organicist vocabulary, which, as we have noted, were by now irrevocably associated with conservative-nationalist traditions inherited from the previous century. This conditioned his world-view to the extent that, consciously or not, the parameters of the organic model determined his reaction to and view of his own function within it when it became reality in the form of the totalitarian state. It is therefore unnecessary to draw direct parallels between the state and a work of art, as Berlin suggests, for conceptually the two were regarded as indivisible: one was a reflection of the other both in form and in content; a concept that was in turn paradigmatic of the congruence of the artistic and political process.

---

47 Zentralbibliothek Zürich, Nachl. W. Furtwängler: S 128, 'Als ich mein Artikel über Hindemith schrieb', *Die Musik*, March 1935. See also Berndt Wessling, *Furtwängler* (Stuttgart: Deutsche Verlags-Anstalt, 1985), p. 293.

CHAPTER 6

FURTWÄNGLER AND THE NAZI STATE II (1935-45)

The whole is not merely the sum of its parts; on the contrary, the parts are dependent on and conditioned by the whole, so that the whole itself possesses intrinsic reality and substance.[1]

And when all said and done, he is our greatest conductor.[2]

By the spring of 1935 Furtwängler had achieved a satisfactory *modus operandi* within the Nazi state and in April resumed his conducting activities: Beethoven in Budapest and Vienna with the Vienna Philharmonic; Bach's *Matthäus Passion* with the Vienna Symphony and Julius Patzak as the Evangelist; and Beethoven in Berlin with the Berlin Philharmonic attended by Hitler, Göring and Goebbels (3 May). A visit to London quickly followed: Furtwängler conducted *Tristan und Isolde* at Covent Garden with Lauritz Melchior and Frida Leider in the title roles. In the period before the outbreak of World War II he toured extensively with the Berlin Philharmonic and made high-profile visits abroad, especially to Paris and London, where in May 1937 he conducted two cycles of *Der Ring des Nibelungen* at the invitation of Sir Thomas Beecham, as part of the season of German opera at Covent Garden given in celebration of the Coronation of King George VI. The propaganda potential of such a visit is self-evident: Furtwängler became the perceived musical representative and the visible artistic embodiment of Nazi Germany.

Furtwängler's reputation as the leading interpreter of Wagner's operas had been assured since his Mannheim days; it was therefore inevitable that as Germany's foremost conductor he should be drawn in to the appropriation of

---

1   Ferdinand Tönnies, *Gemeinschaft und Gesellschaft*; Eng. edn, *Community and Civil Society*, p. 97.
2   *The Goebbels Diaries 1939–1941*, tr. and ed. Fred Taylor (London: Hamish Hamilton, 1982), entry for 14 December 1940, p. 205.

8   Furtwängler in London outside Covent Garden Opera House, 1937

the composer by the Nazi regime. The apotheosis of Wagner as the chief icon
of Nazi high culture was completed soon after the Nazis came to power when
Joseph Goebbels ordered a performance of *Die Meistersinger* at the Berlin
Staatsoper to be given on 21 March 1933 as the climax of the celebrations
marking the Day of Potsdam, the occasion on which the Third Reich was
officially proclaimed. The powerful symbolism of the association of the centre
of the old Prussian monarchy with Wagner's most German opera signalled a
return to the authoritarian certainties of the old social and political order and
the restoration of hallowed traditions of the German past.[3] The conductor
was Furtwängler and, in order that the propaganda potential of this performance given under the leading conductor of the Reich should not be lost
to a wider audience, the third act was broadcast live. This was the first, but
by no means the last, occasion on which Furtwängler conducted Wagner
operas, and in particular *Die Meistersinger*, in a highly politicised context.
On 8 September 1935 he directed *Die Meistersinger* in the city of Nuremberg
itself as a prelude to the Party rally which began on the following day; again,
Hitler and a number of high-ranking government officials were present at the
performance. In fact *Die Meistersinger* under Furtwängler became something
of a symbol of cultural continuity throughout the twelve-year period of Nazi
rule. He gave his final performance of the opera during the Nazi years on 22
July 1944 at the last of the wartime Bayreuth Festivals.[4]

After the establishment of the Third Reich the Bayreuth Festival quickly
and to some extent inevitably became the central jewel in the national cultural
crown. It was therefore thought desirable that attempts should be made
to regain the services of the leading conductor in the Reich. Furtwängler
had made no secret of his unhappy experiences in Bayreuth during 1931
and had made public his differences with Winifred Wagner in a hard-hitting
article, 'On Bayreuth's Future' (Um Bayreuths Zukunft), published on 28
June 1932 simultaneously in the *Berliner Tageblatt* and the *Unterhaltungsblatt
der Vossischen Zeitung*. It was therefore seen as something of a triumph for
Winifred Wagner and the festival administration when, on 10 May 1935, the
press reported that Wilhelm Furtwängler would be the chief conductor for
the forthcoming Festival in 1936.[5] The notice was short and succinct: 'The
musical direction of the Bayreuth Festival is announced. For the Festival of
1936 Wilhelm Furtwängler will appear as chief conductor.' Nevertheless, the

3   See Evans, *The Coming of the Third Reich*, p. 459.
4   An almost complete Furtwängler performance of *Die Meistersinger* given as part of the
    1943 Bayreuth Festival survives on record.
5   For the announcement of Furtwängler's participation in the forthcoming Bayreuth
    Festival see *Berliner Börsen-Zeitung*, 10 May 1935; also Fred K. Prieberg, *Kraftprobe*,
    p. 234; Eng. edn, *Trial of Strength*, p. 177.

timing was propitious: it was made shortly after Furtwängler's public reconciliation with the Nazi regime which came in the wake of the rupture caused
by the Hindemith affair.

The 1936 Bayreuth Festival

The year 1936 was in many ways an *annus mirabilis* for the Third Reich: the
Eleventh Olympiad was due to be held in Berlin from 1 to 16 August and
the Nazi regime planned to exploit to the full the propaganda potential of
this prestigious international gathering. To some extent the Bayreuth Festival
was seen as a cultural prelude to the forthcoming sporting contest in Berlin;
as if to emphasise the similarity of purpose between the two events the
Reichssportführer, or director of the Olympiad, sent Winifred Wagner the
following telegram: 'In this historic moment of association between Richard
Wagner's work and the cultural background to the Olympic idea, German
sport sends you greetings as the upholder of the great tradition.'[6] Two days
later Winifred Wagner replied:

> I thank you, in your capacity as Director of German Sport, for your
> honourable words of commemoration on the occasion of the opening of
> the Bayreuth Festival. I am well aware of the historical significance of the
> association between the Olympic idea and the work of Bayreuth and I send
> my sincerest good wishes to the Olympic games.[7]

On 19 July the opening performance took place in Bayreuth of a new
and spectacular production of *Lohengrin*, produced by the Intendant of the
Berlin Staatsoper, Heinz Tietjen, and conducted by Furtwängler. This was
the centrepiece of the festival. The *Deutsche Allgemeine Zeitung* captured the
triumphalist spirit of the occasion both inside and outside the Festspielhaus:

> The Festival has begun. The town is decked with flags and there is an
> endless stream of cars ascending the Festspielhügel. The regaining of
> Furtwängler for Bayreuth together with the forthcoming Olympiad has
> encouraged more foreigners than is usual to visit the Festival. There were
> many who thought that they could purchase tickets at the box office, but
> these attempts proved futile. The best they could do was listen to the radio
> relay in a nearby restaurant.

6 *Deutsche Allgemeine Zeitung*, 20 July 1936. All translations from newspaper sources are
   by the present author unless otherwise stated.
7 Ibid., 22 July 1936.

Shortly before 4 PM vigorous cheering heralded the arrival of the Führer and Reichskanzler. Frau Winifred Wagner received her honoured guest on the steps of the Royal entrance and he in turn greeted the Mistress of the House with courtly courtesy. In the meantime the other guests had taken their place in the theatre. On the Führer's right sat Frau Wagner and on his left Frau and Dr Goebbels. Nearby Ministerpräsident Göring and his wife took their places. [...]

This performance of *Lohengrin* is equally successful in both its musical and scenic aspects. Furtwängler allows the wonderful clarity and transparency of the score to be heard; his guiding hand can be sensed in every detail. The delicate, mystical qualities, which represent the symbolic character of this work, were never obscured, even by the massive choral effects of the crowd scenes.[8]

As he made clear in *Mein Kampf*, the work meant a great deal to Hitler: 'my first opera [was] *Lohengrin*. It made an overpowering impression. From then on my youthful enthusiasm for the Bayreuth Master knew no bounds.'[9] The Bayreuth historian Frederic Spotts comments that in some aspects of its staging this *Lohengrin* was the nearest Bayreuth ever came to an overtly 'political' opera with the 'tragic love affair between Lohengrin and Elsa being paralleled by a nationalistic call to arms'. Winifred Wagner is said to have intended this production as both a tribute to Hitler personally and a public recognition of his political achievements.[10] After the performance the Führer was photographed in the company of Winifred Wagner congratulating Furtwängler and members of the cast.[11]

It was also about this time that the full potential of radio as a propaganda tool with which to influence the mind of the educated middle classes began to be realised. *Der Ring des Nibelungen* had first been broadcast from Bayreuth in 1934.[12] Two years later this powerful medium enabled the sound of this politically charged production of *Lohengrin* to reach not only domestic listeners within the borders of the Reich but also a wide international audience. On the same page as its review of the opening ceremonies, quoted above, the *Deutsche Allgemeine Zeitung* printed under the banner headline 'The World hears Bayreuth' the following fulsome account of this significant development:

8   Ibid., 20 July 1936.
9   Hitler, *Mein Kampf*, p. 15.
10 See Frederic Spotts, *Bayreuth*, pp. 187–8.
11 Two photographs, one showing Hitler and Furtwängler and the other Hitler and members of the cast, are reproduced in Geissmar, *The Baton and the Jackboot*, between pp. 216–17.
12 See Levi, *Music in the Third Reich*, p. 134.

The fact that, sixty years after the founding of Bayreuth, the entire world was able to hear the sound of a performance of *Lohengrin* taking place within his Festival theatre would have exceeded Richard Wagner's wildest expectations. In 1852 he wrote to Franz Liszt from Zurich [concerning a performance of *Lohengrin*] 'I wish it could be more widely heard: for my part I shall in all probability never hear my work.'

Now, through the genius of the Master of Wahnfried, the whole world can experience the crowning fulfilment of the Festival idea, for this *Lohengrin* is indeed an event of shattering proportions. The whole of Europe, Africa, North and South America stayed by their loudspeakers from afternoon until evening [!]; we do hope that the quality of their reception was as good as it was for us here.

It was uncanny how the unique artistic experience, which only Bayreuth can offer, was apparent from the first bar of the prelude to the end of the tragic history that is *Lohengrin*. Under Furtwängler's masterly direction the subtle clarity of the orchestral detail was never obscured by the accumulated effects. Thanks to the exemplary diction of the singers, whose voices came over the airwaves with an almost ethereal beauty, the text was audible throughout.

The broadcast successfully relayed the atmosphere and aura of this solemn occasion which was enhanced not only by the fanfares at the beginning of each act but also by the presence of the Führer. Technology successfully placed itself at the service of high culture and in addition to thanking the artists we should also express our gratitude to the technicians, who successfully fought and won this battle for peace [die eine Schlacht für den Frieden schlugen und gewannen].[13]

The author of this piece was perhaps a little optimistic in expressing the hope that the broadcast could reach such a huge intercontinental audience, and his final reference to a battle for peace is strident even by the standards of Nazi reportage. Nevertheless, it was widely heard and Furtwängler's enhancement of Nazi prestige became firmly established within the national and international consciousness. Among the listeners was Thomas Mann who, from his self-imposed exile in Zurich, summarised his reaction as follows: 'One should not have listened, should not have lent one's ears to such fraudulence, given that in principle one despises all those participating.'[14] It is due to the fact that this production was broadcast that some substantial excerpts from Act III of the performance given on 19 July 1936 have survived on record.

13 *Deutsche Allgemeine Zeitung*, 20 July 1936.
14 Thomas Mann, *Tagebücher 1935–6*, p. 334, quoted in Prieberg, *Kraftprobe*, p. 267; Eng. edn, *Trial of Strength*, p. 203.

As was seen in Chapter 3, Furtwängler's attitude towards Wagner's works was by no means straightforward. In the same year as this epoch-making Bayreuth Festival he made an entry in his notebooks in which he described how the gradual awakening of his early interest in Wagner as musician had been destroyed by his first experience of the *Ring* in performance:

Wagner as Musician

My father gave me tickets for all four performances of *Der Ring des Nibelungen* in the Munich Hoftheater. These performances, conducted by the famous Wagner conductor Franz Fischer with the best singers of the Munich stage, were certainly no better or worse than many others. And yet they thoroughly destroyed my illusion and love of Wagner for years afterwards. What I ... [*sic*] suddenly appeared as theatre.[15] The most wonderful melodic curves were trivialised, made banal by the movements of the singers and their style of singing. At once I understood Nietzsche and all the others who reject Wagner [...]. Theatre, nothing but theatre ... [...] Wagner was performed not as a poet, not as a musician, but as a man of the theatre.[16]

What matters to Furtwängler are the works themselves, and in particular the unequivocal greatness of their musical content. Here the tension created by insisting that art and politics could and should be kept separate is readily apparent. Furtwängler may declare himself to be interested in the music alone, but by performing the works he made himself an indispensable part of the total theatrical experience. It was now quite impossible to direct performances of Wagnerian opera within the highly charged atmosphere of such carefully orchestrated events as the Day of Potsdam, the Nuremberg Rallies, the 1936 Bayreuth Festival or the 1937 Coronation season of opera in London without identifying with the theatrical element in the works which were being so adroitly exploited for propaganda purposes. Furtwängler conducting Wagner served as a national and international symbol of rebirth of the organically constituted German state under Nazi rule; although unease about biological hierarchies in Wagner's musical theatre that fell short of his organic world-view remained:[17]

---

15 This is a typical example of the aphoristic and disjointed style in which Furtwängler's *Aufzeichnungen* are written. The original of this entry is to be found between pp. 99–102 of the Taschenkalender for the year 1936. In the sentence 'Was mir ... erschien auf einmal als Theater' the sentence break is clearly identifiable (see p. 100). Source (microfilm only): Zentralbibliothek Zürich, Nachl. W. Furtwängler: S 132/2.

16 AZN, pp. 133–4; NBKS, p. 81 (amended).

17 See Roger Allen, 'Furtwängler and England', in Sebastian Krahnert, ed., *Furtwängler-Studien I* (1998), 21–35; also 'Artistic Exchange or Cultural Propaganda: The

Case of Wagner

The theatre, then. The theatre is the artistic institution that can be most or least given over to 'art', that presents the whole 'art' complex most clearly and visibly. In every organism there are higher and lower organs, some serving the centre of life, of growth, others the need for expulsion [Ausscheidung], which is inseparably connected to all growth. And precisely these baser sides of all artistic work, which drag us down, are particularly well formed in the theatre by its very nature.[18]

Conversations about Music (1937)

Just how far Furtwängler's world-view (defined above as *bildungsbürgerlich* and outlined some thirty-five years earlier in the youthful correspondence with Bertel von Hildebrand) by now resonated with the prevailing political *Zeitgeist* can be seen in the content of six prearranged conversations between Furtwängler and Walter Abendroth (1896–1973), the strongly conservative and anti-Semitic Berlin music critic of the Nazi-sponsored journal *Die Musik*.[19] These conversations took place in 1937 and were subsequently published in book form, the authorial purpose of which is described by Abendroth in the introduction:

These conversations are quite genuine. They took place in Furtwängler's Potsdam home. In addition to the author and the editor, Dr Furtwängler's colleague Freda von Rechenburg was also present. The theme of each conversation was always agreed beforehand, and she kept the record. Subsequent revision has brought about few alterations from the original. The questions and openings provided by the editor were designed to give the clearest possible run to the dominant train of thought and to be severely restricted in order not to break the thread once it had been woven. [...]
     The reader will no doubt observe with particular interest how much this conscious, reflective contribution has its roots in the work of art itself, which is its starting point.[20]

Beecham–Furtwängler Exchanges 1935–8', paper presented to the Annual Conference of the Royal Musical Association, New College, Oxford, 29 March 1998.
18 AZN, p. 158; NBKS, p. 97.
19 For more on the musical press during the Nazi years, see Levi, *Music in the Third Reich*, Ch. 9, here pp. 230–1.
20 Wilhelm Furtwängler, *Gespräche über Musik* (Zürich and Freiburg: Atlantis, 1948); Eng. edn, *Concerning Music*, tr. L. J. Lawrence (London: Boosey and Hawkes, 1953). Chapters 1–6 date from 1937; Chapter 7 was added by Furtwängler as a supplementary essay in 1947. For typescripts annotated and prepared for publication see

The period prior to the outbreak of World War II saw Nazi Germany at a peak of national pride and self-confidence. *Conversations about Music* (*Gespräche über Musik*) can be said to represent the public face of Furtwängler's musical æsthetic as it stood at this time when he was regarded both at home and abroad as one of the chief artistic representatives of Nazi culture. The pre-eminence of his position is reflected in the fact that the conversations are presented in a distinctly authoritarian, *ex cathedra* manner; there is no room for spontaneous discussion or creative discourse. Hence Abendroth's questions serve a purely contextual function in that they provide the framework for Furtwängler's deliberations.[21]

Significantly, the first conversation is a study of the nature of the relationship between the artist and his audience:

> Every audience – and that includes especially our Berlin audience, since they are typically metropolitan – must be considered in the first place as a mass without a will of its own, reacting in an uninhibited way, so to speak, to every stimulus. [...] With audiences everything happens instinctively, incalculably, without complete consciousness. As far as music is concerned, there is nothing about which the so-called public knows less than about its own mind.[22]

Clear parallels are evident between Furtwängler's perception of the nature of a theatre or concert hall audience and the function of the *Volk* as the foundation of the organic state. His analysis of the collective behaviour of an audience when exposed to the powerful influence of a work of art is strongly totalitarian in outlook and could equally describe the reaction of a massed gathering when subjected to the rhetorical demagogy of a hypnotic orator of the power of Hitler or Goebbels on such an occasion as the Nuremberg rallies. He actually makes the comparison himself when reflecting on the capacity of the composer, through the medium of the executive artist, to awaken the potential of an audience:

> Let us be clear what this mutual effect of composer and audiences on one another really is. It can only come about through interdependence. Unless the composer realises the dormant potentialities of the audience, unless he tames and bends it to the work, it – and we can easily substitute 'nation' [Volk] for audience in this context – would not even become conscious of

Zentralbibliothek Zürich, Nachl. W. Furtwängler: S 44. Translations in CM revised and amended by the present author.

21 See additional items Zentralbibliothek Zürich, Nachl. W. Furtwängler: S 51, S 67, S 76.
22 GM, p. 8; CM, p. 10.

itself as such. For in the first place it is just any anonymous gathering of human beings.[23]

In artistic terms only the composer can give the audience a communal identity as an organic whole through the intensity of his artistic vision. The power of the composer's influence is so complete that the audience itself becomes an extension of the creative process, or part of the artwork itself. The transference of the concept of the interrelationship between artist and audience to the wider context of the Nazi state provides a telling analogy to describe the relationship between leader and people. Adolf Hitler, drawing a mass of people in the stadium at Nuremberg into a unified whole through the power of his oratory, is wielding the same demagogic tool with the same proselytising zeal as Furtwängler when conducting a Beethoven symphony in the Berlin Philharmonie or a Wagner opera in Bayreuth. One may use a rhetorical bludgeon, the other the rather more refined conductor's baton, but the overall intention is the same: the creation of a unified, organically cohesive whole infused and enthused with a common ideal. Hitler had emphasised the idea of a political *Führerprinzip* as one of the main ideological pillars of National Socialism.[24] The parallel concept of an artistic hegemony is clearly apparent in Furtwängler's pronouncements, but to him it is a principle intrinsic to the German canon of musical masterworks vested in the absolute authority of the works themselves. It is the hegemony of art as transforming force rather than the artist as transforming agent.

> This much is certain: these works alone succeed in turning an audience, if only for seconds, into a genuine community. They take hold of the individual in such a way that he is no longer a separate entity, but a part of his people, a part of humanity, a part of the Divine Nature operating through him.[25]

Transfer this concept of artistic transcendence, rooted as it is in the values of *völkisch* ideology, into the political arena of Nazi Germany and it becomes apparent that in the organic state the political leader and the performing artist share a common theoretical function within their respective spheres: transcendent artistic idealism and quotidian political ideology are but two sides of the same coin. In this first conversation Furtwängler is almost exclusively concerned with the nature of the relationship between the composer

---

23 GM, p. 13; CM, p. 13.
24 See Hitler, *Mein Kampf*, pp. 493ff. The National Socialist state is defined as authoritarian with power emanating from the supreme leader.
25 GM, p. 15; CM, pp. 14–15.

and his audience. The similarity of his position, albeit æsthetically idealised, with the prevailing political ideology places him in a position in which it is impossible to separate his lofty world of art from the down-to-earth arena of political reality. In the organic state the two are mutually interdependent and complementary: art gives the state a carapace of æsthetic credibility while the state provides the framework within which art can flourish.

In the second conversation Furtwängler considers the concept of musical style. In this respect, as in others, his position is largely identical to that which he laid down in his youthful correspondence with Bertel von Hildebrand and subsequently strengthened through his contact with Schenker. Biological metaphors are again part of the means of expression:[26]

> Perhaps we can express it in biological terms: nerves, senses, intellect, understanding, all had an equal share in the works of the great classical composers. The separate parts were created with and out of the whole, and the whole with the parts. Notwithstanding the fulfilment in each successive moment, the creative urge (responding to the natural feelings) was, unconsciously, of course, directed to the context as a whole.[27]

Furtwängler's principal concern is with artistic integrity; in his view, the greatest threat to this ideal is posed by the development of programme music. This concept does not conform to the organic ideal: in programme music the guiding principle of the composition, or musical structure, is extrinsic rather than resulting naturally from the operation of the intrinsic laws of musical development.

> This musical logic, as I should like to term it – pervades the entire oeuvre of the classical composers. Later it gradually becomes weaker, thinner, less cogent. When programme music came into fashion, an attempt was made, by means of an artificial rationale imposed from without, to replace the purely musical process and substitute through the programme. [...]
>
> No attention at all is paid to the whole: that is confidently left to the programme. Strauss himself was by no means unaware of this. It was of course possible by this means to achieve momentarily greater freedom of movement and to create something new. But at what price! From the purely musical point of view music was 'put together' [zusammengesetzt]. What had once been an organism became an 'arrangement' – rather like a 'flower arrangement' [Blumenarrangement]. This can often be done with a

---

26 See present work, pp. 24–7.
27 GM, p. 21; CM, pp. 18–19.

great deal of taste, but it no longer has any connection whatever with the eternal laws of music.[28]

This position is consistent with that posited by Furtwängler in 1919 when he criticised Wagner's *Ring* for its lack of musical cohesion: the *Ring* is essentially a large-scale work of programme music, a musical realisation of a succession of poetic ideas in which the function of the music is largely descriptive. In view of the fact that the conversations were from the outset intended for publication these less than complementary remarks concerning Richard Strauss call for some explanation. They may derive at least in part from an ambivalent attitude towards Strauss himself. Furtwängler had at this time recently resumed his compositional activities but the core of the modern orchestral repertoire was, and would remain, the Strauss tone poems. Since Strauss had fallen foul of the authorities, and had not been so warmly rehabilitated as Furtwängler, it is possible that Furtwängler was taking the opportunity to put down a serious rival (as composer and conductor) and celebrate his own position, formerly held by Strauss, as undisputed head of the German musical establishment. The idea of Richard Strauss as a 'flower arranger' is, to say the least, novel; although it may be that Furtwängler was making an ironic reference to Strauss' name, which can be rendered in English as a 'bunch of flowers'.

It is the third of the conversations which is in many ways the focal point of this artistic testimony. Furtwängler is unequivocal in his espousal and development of the position which by now has hardened into a form of artistic dogma: that a work is defined and limited by the organic metaphor which serves as the indicator of musical validity and worth. He illustrates his argument by examining the nature and function of a musical motif within the work as a whole. The idea of the motif serving as the equivalent to a dramatic character in a play recalls one of the central ideas in Wagner's essay 'Beethoven' (1870) and in Schenker's *Harmonielehre*: by fulfilling a dramatic function the motif is behaving according to the laws of organic development.[29]

The decisive factor which was introduced into the history of music by Haydn and which became a complete reality in Beethoven's work, was that the subject should develop organically within the work, like a Shakespearian character. [...] With Beethoven the course of a musical work is not prescribed to the same extent, although it would be entirely wrong to say that the degree of cogency in the piece is less than it is with Bach. But

28 GM, p. 22; CM, pp. 19–20.
29 Roger Allen, *Richard Wagner's 'Beethoven'*, pp. 145–51.

with Beethoven this development is not predetermined solely by the first subject; Beethoven uses several subjects; it is from the opposition of these subjects that the piece develops. These different subjects live and develop by inter-reacting with one another: nevertheless, they have to bear a destiny of their own. The work thus develops itself into a whole from parts which in themselves often present the greatest contrast imaginable. To no-one else in the whole history of music does this apply to the same extent as it does to Beethoven.[30]

The idea of different, and indeed opposing, constituent parts in a work of art having an individual destiny yet capable of being welded into a cohesive whole is associated with the concept of the autonomy of the organic artwork. The lofty, idealistic origins of this artistic philosophy become apparent when Furtwängler draws comparisons between the dramatic nature of Beethoven's musical discourse and the idealised conflict of opposing forces in the Olympian fantasy of the 'klassische Walpurgisnacht' in Goethe's *Faust*, Part II:

> In the 'klassische Walpurgisnacht' in *Faust* II Goethe represents the clash of opinions as personified by two Ionic philosophers: Thales claims that the world was created out of water (i.e. by a process of continuing evolution); Anaxogoras claims that it was created out of fire (i.e. catastrophe).[31] These theories represent two diametrically opposed concepts, obvious archetypes of a possible interpretation of nature. And there really are different kinds of organic development. There is the more feminine, or evolutionary principle, and the catastrophic, which may be called the masculine principle. The latter, too, is part of organic nature – in contrast to everything intellectual or mechanical, which operates on an entirely different level of existence.[32]

To Furtwängler the crucial point is again the distinction between art and artifice: the conflict originates in the workings of organic nature (art) which is in every way superior to 'intellectual or mechanical' processes (artifice). The organic process must be smooth, uninterrupted and free of toxic elements if the fusion of soul and matter (or form and content) within a musical work is to be achieved. In political terms the smooth and uninterrupted fulfilment of the vital functions of the state required the removal of foreign elements.

In the fourth conversation Furtwängler underlines and illustrates his general thesis through detailed and extensive reference to Beethoven. Some thirty-five years after his correspondence with Bertel von Hildebrand

---

30 GM, pp. 36–7; CM, p. 30.
31 See Goethe, *Faust*, Part II, lines 7851–72.
32 GM, pp. 39–40; CM, pp. 31–2.

Beethoven is still the summit of his personal musical Parnassus: it is in the works of Beethoven more than any other that the laws of music may be seen to have an absolute function: 'The sonata form (and its simpler prototype, the Lied, with its repetitions, etc.) are, literally speaking, in his "blood" [wörtlich gesprochen, "im Blut"]. Everything is somehow related to them, linked up with them.'[33] It is notable that Furtwängler's exegesis of Beethoven shares a good deal of common ground with that of his mentor, Walter Riezler, whose monograph on the composer had recently been published and to which Furtwängler contributed a brief Foreword. 'In Beethoven there is a spiritual force unique in German music, and by no other composer has the power and greatness of German feeling and character been more directly expressed.'[34] Riezler's *Beethoven*, described by the author as 'the fruit of forty years' study of the problem of Beethoven', contains extended discussions of the by now familiar tropes of Beethoven and Absolute Music, ideas of 'gestalt' and organic unity, and how Beethoven 'seldom gives full expression to his feelings in his sonatas and symphonies but keeps them obedient to "the law of the whole [Gesetz des Ganzen]"'.[35]

The close correlation between the organic validity of an artwork and its capacity to transcend the boundaries of human experience continues into the fifth conversation in which Furtwängler considers the nature of sonata form itself and how the classical masterpieces and the associated musical forms grew organically out of the process of improvisation. Translated into artistic terms, he is saying that the musical forms of the classical masterpieces have evolved through time by means of the operation of the laws of improvisation:

[Musical forms] grew organically, and can only be understood if viewed in this way; they always bear the characteristics of this organic process wherever they are really alive. Properly understood they represent a crystallised process of growth, and as such they are the natural precipitate from a process of improvisation. They are, in fact, improvisation.

This seems to be contradicted by the fact that there are only very few such forms in abstract music, and that these forms (fugue, sonata, song etc.) are related to one another or would seem to amount to one and the same formula in the end. But it is one of the laws of organic life that a few archetypes embrace infinite possibilities.[36]

---

33 GM, p. 49; CM, p. 38.
34 Walter Riezler, *Beethoven* (Berlin und Zürich: Atlantis, 1936); Eng. tr. G. D. H. Piddock (London: M. C. Forrester, 1938), p. 9 (author's translation).
35 Riezler, *Beethoven*, pp. 90–5. See also Mark Evan Bonds, *Absolute Music: The History of an Idea*, pp. 260–1.
36 GM, pp. 63–4; CM, pp. 48–9.

The central tenet of Furtwängler's argument is the autonomy and authority of the absolute artwork unfolding from the depth to the surface through a process of improvisation as a process of organic evolution. Both aspects were compromised if the laws of organic growth ceased to be paramount:

> On the whole we are quite ignorant of the meaning of 'form'. In our musical life today it is possible to distinguish between those who still have a remembrance of this knowledge, and those who have already lost it. This knowledge springs only from nature – for 'form', as Goethe says, is a secret to most. [...]
>
> A piece of music is no longer, as it used to be, an 'organic' process developing in accordance with the law of its own being, with a centre of gravity of its own; but is becoming, to an ever-increasing extent, a means of entertainment, lacking a centre of gravity, designed merely to offer a modicum of variety.[37]

This notion of form as an expression of ideology, with its associations of Goethe's scientific morphology and Hegelian dialectical processes, deplores the diminution of musical creativity through the imposition of external structures (artifice). The shape of an organically cohesive artwork can only evolve through the workings of the natural laws of music (art). This, as he made clear in his criticisms of Toscanini considered earlier, has its practical counterpart in the concept of virtuosity: that is, technique can obscure a paucity of musical creativity.

> This is the reason why interpretations of the great, living masterpieces of the past which are based on technical virtuosity are so dangerous in practice: they thoroughly corrupt taste. The kind of performance designed to display virtuosity, effect and variety, all of them imposed from without, is bound to stimulate corresponding characteristics in the audience. Thus the whole of music-making loses to an ever-increasing extent the weight and measure of inner necessity which hitherto – and here I speak as a German about Germany – it has always possessed. [Das ganze Musizieren verliert damit mehr und mehr an Gewicht, an jenem Maß von innerer Notwendigkeit, das es bisher – ich spreche hier als Deutscher von Deutschland – immer noch besessen hat.][38]

Nothing, in Furtwängler's view, must be allowed to obscure the inner significance of the musical utterance, the 'weight and measure of inward necessity'. Following the inherited traditions of *Bildungsbürgertum* he regards this as the

---

37   GM, p. 66; CM, p. 50.
38   GM, p. 71; CM, p. 53.

supreme quality both of the musical artwork and the soul of Germany. It must not be relegated to a subordinate position or the spiritual message may be obscured:

> Do not misunderstand me: I am not opposed to highly developed technique as such. I, too, would not want to be without its benefits. What I am against, and what gives me cause for great concern, is the chasm which has opened up between our knowledge of the technical [artifice] and that of the 'spiritual' [seelische] aspect of music [art]. In the former we may believe ourselves to be Titans and Heroes, but in the latter we are today mere children.[39]

The significance of the spiritual message of music is the subject of the sixth and final conversation in the original series. The spiritual content of a work is expressed through the operation of the eternal laws of music. According to the organic world-view, even the greatest creative artists are subject to these laws:

> If there had been no powerful laws of convention demanding universal allegiance, the great Greek tragedies could not have been written: for they were based on the revolt of the individual against eternal laws and on his destruction, as it were, as the most profound and valid acknowledgement of these laws.[40]

In addition to the notion that the creative artist must submit to the authority of the musical work, the idea familiar from the novel *Enzio* onwards is introduced that struggle (*Kampf*) is a necessary part of the creative process. Furtwängler illustrates his point by recalling Wagner's struggle against the indifference he encountered when trying to further the cause of his art:

> Wagner's struggle in this respect was the struggle of a modern artist against a modern environment. i.e. an attempt at a show-down between the artist and the present-day world. But the latter now has at its disposal far more formidable weapons than it had in the past. Whereas the past countered, as it were, with lance and sword, the present works with poison gas [Giftgas].[41]

Furtwängler is presumably here referring to the gas-choked battlefields of World War I in illustrating the point that the creative artist will not always find ready acceptance; struggle against opposition is part of the function of

---

39 GM, p. 74; CM, p. 55.
40 GM, p. 90; CM, p. 67.
41 GM, p. 92; CM, p. 68.

the artist within the organic state. He concludes by considering the place
and function of art within the historical process. Historical development,
as he terms it, is unalterable and inescapable, save by the work's transcendent aspect. Recalling Wagner's construction in the 'Beethoven' essay
of Schopenhauer's paradox as a means of identifying the inner and outer
(or conscious and unconscious) aspects of the creative mind, Furtwängler
concludes: 'Translated into terms of art, this means that every work of art has
two aspects; one turned towards its own "time" and one towards eternity.'[42]

The writer Hans-Hubert Schönzeler, author of a hagiographical study
of Furtwängler, has described *Conversations about Music* as 'Furtwängler's
musical *Credo*'.[43] If this is indeed the case then it is clear that the thought
of his artistic maturity was largely consistent with that developed in his
youth and early manhood; it had not undergone any significant change, save
of political context, over the intervening thirty-five years during which he
rose to pre-eminence as a performing artist. The main pillars of his musical
æsthetic are all contained in these conversations: authoritarianism as seen in
the artistic hegemony of the composer and his temporal representative, the
performing artist; the continuing authority of the German canon of musical
masterworks; the notion of the sonata dialectic as the leading form of musical
argument and the associated concept of musical form as an ideological
paradigm; the idea of history as a process of continuing, unbroken evolution;
the belief that art has its *völkisch* origins in the fertile soil of national
consciousness; the associated idea that music has transcendent properties
through which the boundaries of the knowable may be overcome; and, lastly,
the notion that it is both necessary and natural for the organism to rid itself
of what is not necessary for its growth. All these concepts resonated with
Nazi ideology, and as the Nazi state became ever more firmly established the
boundaries between art and politics became less and less distinct. Just how
true this was in Furtwängler's case can be seen in his approach to the work of
a composer with whom he was closely associated in the public consciousness:
Anton Bruckner.

Anton Bruckner in the Nazi Pantheon: Furtwängler's Bruckner Address (5 July 1939)

The process of the appropriation of Bruckner into the officially endorsed Nazi
pantheon of German artists reached its high point at a ceremony on 6 June

42 GM, p. 98; CM, p. 73; also Allen, *Richard Wagner's 'Beethoven'*, pp. 45–53.
43 See Schönzeler, *Furtwängler*, p. 163.

1937 when, with due solemnity and the accompaniment of the Adagio from
the Eighth Symphony, Adolf Hitler unveiled a marble bust of the composer
in Regensburg's 'Valhalla', an event described by Alexander Rehding as 'a
paragon of how the Nazis availed themselves of the monumental power of
music and image'.[44] As mentioned in Chapter 1, this portentous replica of the
Parthenon was built between 1830 and 1842 by the celebrated enthusiast for
Hellenic culture, King Ludwig I of Bavaria, in order that important cultural
figures from Germany's past might be honoured in an appropriate architec-
tural setting; the ceremonial inclusion of Bruckner in this Hall of Heroes in
the presence of the Führer and other leading members of the government
therefore represented the final step in the Nazi appropriation of the Austrian
organist-turned-symphonist. The highly politicised occasion was marked by
a series of concerts, a convention of the International Bruckner Gesellschaft
and speeches from Peter Raabe (President of the Reichsmusikkammer), Max
Auer (President of the International Bruckner Gesellschaft) and Propaganda
Minister Joseph Goebbels. Hitler presided at the ceremony by laying a wreath
in front of the bust of Bruckner, but he did not speak. It was left to Goebbels
to justify, by means of his rhetorical skills, the inclusion of Bruckner within
the artistic pantheon of National Socialism. The speech he delivered on
this occasion is highly significant for in content it amounted to a good deal
more than yet another example of government bombast; it contained clear
indicators as to how, in the Propaganda Minister's view, the ideology of the
Nazi state was embodied in the art of music.

Predictably, for a composer to be acknowledged as acceptable according
to Nazi principles, he must have an impeccable racial background. Goebbels
stresses the fact that Bruckner was from agrarian stock:

> He comes from a long line of peasants which we can trace back to the
> year 1400. Throughout his life, even after his position in his profession
> and in society had carried him to a completely different sphere, he never
> disavowed his peasant roots. His almost mystical affinity with nature; his
> steadfast and completely genuine love for his native soil and for the great
> German fatherland; the simple straightforwardness of his character, which
> was coupled with true humility yet nevertheless bore a proud awareness of
> his own accomplishments; the childlike purity of his delight in life which
> rested upon a faith in God [Gottglauben] uncomplicated by any intel-
> lectual doubts – all this demonstrates how strong and undamaged the
> heritage of his peasant roots remained in him.[45]

44 Rehding, *Music and Monumentality*, pp. 187–96, here p. 188.
45 See Helmut Heiber, ed., *Goebbels-Reden, vol. 1, 1932–1938* (Düsseldorf: Droste Verlag,
   1971), pp. 281–6. An English translation by J. M. Cooper is appended to Bryan

It is significant that Adolf Hitler took a close personal interest in Bruckner, identifying with him as a fellow Upper Austrian whose artistic hopes had been confounded by the Viennese artistic establishment. (The future *Reichsführer* had himself been rejected by the Academy of Arts when living in Vienna during the years immediately prior to World War I.) Bruckner, the humble schoolmaster of peasant origins, therefore became a convenient symbol of the Nazi doctrine of Blood and Soil (*Blut und Boden*), for his perceived *völkisch* image was in direct opposition to the mistrusted intellectual sophistication of the Viennese artistic mainstream.[46] Hitler planned to further his patronage of the composer by establishing a *Bruckner-Stiftung* at the monastery of St Florian under his own personal protection. This would serve a threefold purpose: to promote and maintain a Bruckner tradition; to be the location of an annual Bruckner festival which would equal the Wagner Festival in Bayreuth; and to house a Music Institute.[47] Thus, under the personal imprimatur of the Führer, the Upper Austrian of humble origins became a fully fledged German composer and a powerful cultural symbol of Nazi ideology. In this respect the Regensburg ceremony of 6 June 1937 was paradigmatic of the process of artistic co-ordination (*Gleichschaltung*) which anticipated and prepared the way for the political Anschluss of March 1938, when the hitherto independent state of Austria was appropriated into the German Reich.

The politicisation of Bruckner's symphonic art also extended into the realm of scholarship and textual criticism. During the latter part of Bruckner's life and in the years immediately following his death his pupils Ferdinand Löwe (1865–1925) and Franz Schalk (1863–1931) had made wholesale revisions to the composer's original scores; it was in these edited versions that the symphonies had entered the orchestral repertoire. However, in 1929 this situation began to change with the foundation of the Austrian-based Internationale Bruckner Gesellschaft under the principal editorship of

Gilliam, 'The Annexation of Anton Bruckner: Nazi Revisionism and the Politics of Appropriation', *Musical Quarterly*, vol. 78, no. 3 (Fall 1994), pp. 584–609. The article, minus Goebbels' speech, is reprinted in Timothy L. Jackson and Paul Hawkshaw, eds, *Bruckner Studies* (Cambridge: CUP, 1997), pp. 72–90.

46 *Blut und Boden* (Blood and Soil): the Nazi idea of common blood and soil which reflected the anti-urban ideals of the movement. Nazi racial theory stressed the advantages of originating from peasant stock. See Louis L. Snyder, ed., *Encyclopaedia of the Third Reich* (New York: McGraw-Hill, 1976), p. 33.

47 Although these plans were never fully implemented, the Linzer Reichs Bruckner Orchester and Bruckner Chor were established in 1942 and continued to perform until 1945. Furtwängler conducted the orchestra on one occasion only: Bruckner's Ninth Symphony on 11 October 1944 at the Abbey of St Florian. See Jackson and Hawkshaw, eds, *Bruckner Studies*, 75.

the musicologist Robert Haas.[48] The stated aim of the society was to promote the republication of Bruckner's scores in editions prepared in accordance with the manuscript sources. The government considered the preparation of 'authentic' editions of Bruckner's works to be of such importance, especially with its ideological subtext of musical purity and expulsion from the organic artwork of any impure elements, that Goebbels in his Regensburg address promised financial assistance for the endeavour:

> Anton Bruckner's works represent a national legacy for us. The Führer and his government regard it as a cultural debt of honour to do everything in their power to enable the entire German people to share in this blessed heritage, and, through encouragement and support of interest in Bruckner and his works, to see to it that this interest and its effects penetrate not only deeply but broadly. For these reasons they have decided to make a considerable annual contribution to the International Bruckner Society for the editions of the original versions of his symphonies, until the master's complete works are available in the form he envisioned.[49]

However, within this broad general remit the Bruckner Gesellschaft had a secondary musicological purpose: to present Bruckner as an accomplished composer in his own right (that is, the composer of organically cohesive, autonomous works) and thus to counter the accepted stereotype of the 'Wagnerian' symphonist, whose work represented little more than a symphonic distortion of Wagner's art. To this effect the president, Max Auer, published an article in the May 1937 issue of the *Zeitschrift für Musik* (the issue immediately preceeding the Regensburg ceremony) in which he drew attention to the stylistic differences between the two composers.[50] Auer's intention was to contrast Wagner's theatrical with Bruckner's ecclesiastical origins; but in so doing he contradicted the official, government-endorsed view of the composer as stated by Goebbels in his Regensburg address:

> After all, Bruckner's mastery first developed fully, and as a person he was most able to break free from external fetters, only when, at the age of almost

48 Robert Haas (1886–1960), Austrian musicologist and member of the Nazi party since 1933; head of the Music Collection of the Vienna Nationalbibliothek from 1922 to 1945. Haas was allegedly victimised as a National Socialist in pre-Anschluss Vienna and in the preparation of his Bruckner edition waged a difficult battle with 'Jewish business interests'. See Pamela Potter, *Most German of the Arts*, pp. 115–16.
49 Gilliam, 'The Annexation of Anton Bruckner', p. 608.
50 Max Auer, 'Anton Bruckner, die Orgel und Richard Wagner', *Zeitschrift für Musik*, vol. 104 (1937), pp. 477–81. See also Jackson and Hawkshaw, eds., *Bruckner Studies*, p. 77.

forty, he experienced the art of the great music dramatist Richard Wagner for the first time. This had an almost revolutionary effect on the sonority of his musical language [die klangliche Gestalt seiner Tonsprache], which only then assumed the character we recognise as the true Bruckner style. From that moment on the church musician disappears almost entirely and there emerges the distinctive symphonist.[51]

The official view is that the progression from organist to symphonist represented an elevation from the narrow confines of the organ loft to an idealised secular realm of music. This served Goebbels' domestic propaganda purposes in that the credit for Bruckner's artistic development could largely be attributed to the influence of the doyen of Nazi-approved composers: Richard Wagner. Conversely, Auer suggested that Bruckner's orchestral style, or 'Klang', resulted from his experience as an organist and thus remained ecclesiastical in origin. In attempting to separate Bruckner and Wagner, however, Auer was careful to disassociate himself from any implied criticism of the latter composer, for criticism of Wagner during the Third Reich was tantamount to criticism of the regime itself. This did not, however, alter the fact that Auer's view was in direct opposition to the officially endorsed reception of Bruckner as a symphonic scion of Wagner's art; the Internationale Bruckner Gesellschaft, in its evaluation of Bruckner as an independent and not a Wagnerian composer, was thus at odds with the National Socialists on ideological grounds. It was therefore with a degree of inevitability that, in the aftermath of the political Anschluss of March 1938, Goebbels dissolved the Vienna-based organisation, removed its Austrian identity, amalgamated the publishing house with its sister organisation in Leipzig, and reformed it as the Deutsche Bruckner Gesellschaft with Furtwängler as president.[52] The Deutsche Bruckner Gesellschaft therefore became an object of both artistic and political *Gleichschaltung* with Furtwängler, the leading German conductor with strong Austrian links through his work with the Vienna Philharmonic Orchestra, as the perceived representative of the co-ordinating process.[53]

51 Gilliam, 'The Annexation of Anton Bruckner', p. 607.
52 The *Gesamtausgabe*, originally published by the Musikwissenschaftlicher Verlag, was initially based in both Leipzig and Vienna. After the Anschluss in 1938 it was renamed the Bracknerverlag and its Viennese activities transferred to Leipzig. In 1947 the organisation was reformed in Wiesbaden and was responsible for the publication of Furtwängler's Symphony No. 2 in E minor (1952). The Musikwissenschaftlicher Verlag recommenced its Viennese publishing programme in 1947 and was again entrusted with the publication of the second *Gesamtausgabe* under the general editorship of Leopold Nowak.
53 See Prieberg, *Kraftprobe*, p. 351; Eng. edn, *Trial of Strength*, pp. 268–9; also Hans-Hubert Schönzeler, *Bruckner*, p. 172.

The foregoing account of the politicisation of Bruckner by the Nazi ideologues is necessary in order to contextualise the capacity in which Furtwängler spoke to the Deutsche Bruckner Gesellschaft in Vienna on 5 July 1939. The text of his address on this occasion is the most extensive piece of writing on the composer to come from his pen. The sources for this essay are problematic. The manuscript is a mass of crossings-out and alterations; the three typescripts (of which only the first is dated: 5 July 1939) appear to be drafts for the final printed version.[54] It is significant that in 1942 the essay, together with the essay on Brahms referred to in Chapter 5, was published in booklet form as *Johannes Brahms–Anton Bruckner: Mit einem Nachwort von Walter Riezler*.[55] Riezler's *Nachwort* is an example of official hagiography in the same vein as the first edition of Friedrich Herzfeld's *Wilhelm Furtwängler: Weg und Wesen* (1941). One of the typescripts, together with the 1942 printing, contains the following sentence in which Furtwängler makes specific reference to the ceremony in Regensburg:

> It is certainly true that in Germany today Bruckner is more widely accepted – an indication of this is the unveiling of his bust in Regensburg's 'Valhalla' before the inclusion of those of Schumann and Brahms, even though, historically speaking, the latter composers have undoubtedly had a greater effect on both German music and that of the world at large. This late recognition of Bruckner was initiated by the Führer himself with the specific intention of honouring this great son of his own native earth [Heimaterde].[56]

This sentence, together with its specific reference to the Führer, is excised from the later printed version of the essay which appears both in *Johannes Brahms and Anton Bruckner* (1952) – otherwise a reprinting of the 1942 publication – and *Ton und Wort* (1955). This is a clear example of how Furtwängler's writings were sanitised for post-war publication, with politically compromising statements such as that referring to the Führer carefully redacted.

Furtwängler's address begins by endorsing this appropriation of Bruckner as a model German artist:

> Bruckner's magnificent works have become an essential part of the life of Germans today. Perhaps this is due to their quality of timelessness for

---

54 The ms and typescript sources are all contained in the Zentralbibliothek Zürich, Nachl. W. Furtwängler: S 21. For the final printed version, see TW, pp. 102–20; Eng. edn, FM, pp. 105–16.

55 For the 1942 printing, see Zentralbibliothek Zürich, Nachl. W. Furtwängler: S 55. The Bruckner essay is on pp. 24–46 and Riezler's *Nachwort* on pp. 47–72.

56 Ibid., pp. 26–7.

they compel us to set aside historical methods when we attempt to evolve a direct relationship to the music of the past. Bruckner was indeed a product of his age; but whereas his contemporaries Wagner and Brahms were largely responsible for moulding and fashioning their epoch, the one striking out in new directions, the other consolidating the achievements of the past, Bruckner stood apart. He thought through his art only of eternity and created for that eternity.[57]

The notion of Bruckner's works somehow standing outside time is central to Furtwängler's view of the composer. He endorses Max Auer's view that Bruckner's music is absolute in origin, and in so doing identifies himself with the problematic status of Bruckner in Nazi Germany. Bruckner the church musician turned symphonist represented, albeit in a somewhat exaggerated form, an extreme example of the eternal 'otherness' of music in transcending space and time; Bruckner the Wagnerian symphonist, as identified in Goebbels' Regensburg address, associated the composer with the tendentious ideology that formed the basis of Nazi musical æsthetics.

Furtwängler's self-contradictory comments on the vexed question of the Bruckner editions are typical of this contradiction. For example, five years earlier, in 1934, he had noted with approval that:

It is clear that Löwe's edition of Bruckner's Ninth Symphony is an excellent piece of work, so good that some further explanation is necessary. First, he loosens up the instrumentation in such a way that the content can be more clearly heard and absorbed. Almost without exception his retouchings are the improvements of a practical man who had the advantage of numerous rehearsals at which he could try out and respond to the actual sound. The same applies to the dynamics, which he adapts in the same way while retaining Bruckner's ideas. Those fanatics who adhere to the letter will say that he has gone too far. However, I believe that if Bruckner had heard this real sound he would have been in agreement with it. Here is a good example of how imaginary dynamics, which we also find in Bach, can be realised. Crescendi and diminuendi can be highlighted according to the character of the instruments [concerned]. Thirdly, Löwe occasionally makes thematic recompositions, or rather transitions. Admittedly this represents distinct deviations from the original but I am of the opinion that – in view of the boundless admiration for the master which Löwe inspired, and in view of his fidelity to the work – he undertook these improvements with Bruckner's agreement, even though we do not know the details.

So for the foreseeable future Bruckner's Ninth Symphony will continue to live in Löwe's version. It is to be hoped that our entire musical wealth

57 TW, p. 102; FM, p. 105 (translations amended).

does not fall victim to the current vogue for the theoretical and literary 'original'. This is perhaps legitimate in the case of Beethoven and Chopin, but with Bruckner, as this case shows, it has a different result entirely.[58]

Bruckner's Ninth Symphony was first performed on 11 February 1903 in a version prepared by Löwe after the composer's death. Until 1932 this was the only version in which the work was known and it is to this version that Furtwängler refers. On 2 April 1932 Siegmund von Hausegger, conducting the Munich Philharmonic Orchestra, played the Löwe version and followed it immediately with the *Urfassung*, the score of which was edited by Alfred Orel and published in 1934. At this point in time Furtwängler is presumably championing and justifying the Löwe version at the expense of the recently published *Urfassung*. In his public statement of 1939 Furtwängler continues to praise the work of the early Bruckner enthusiasts such as Schalk and Löwe, yet he also endorses the *Gesamtausgabe* editions prepared by Robert Haas:

> We can never be too grateful to those of his contemporaries who took upon themselves the thankless task of bringing Bruckner's music to the attention of the public. How immense this task was, how wide the gulf that separated Bruckner's view of music from that which prevailed in Viennese cultural circles at the time, can be seen from a recent striking development. I am thinking here of the publication, forty years after Bruckner's death, of the original versions of the symphonies, which we owe to the selfless efforts of a number of scholars, most notably Robert Haas. [...]
>
> The differences lie partly in the orchestration, partly in the tempo markings, and in both respects the original versions have a greater simplicity, a greater sense of unity and directness which seems to correspond more closely to the expansiveness of Bruckner's nature. In the many instances where the cuts have been restored, we feel a sense of greater organic cohesion, not only in the particular, from one bar to another, but in respect of the movement as a whole.[59]

It is entirely consistent with Furtwängler's world-view that he regards the enhanced sense of organic cohesion to be one of the most praiseworthy aspects of the editions prepared by Haas. On 5 July 1939, the day of his address to the Deutsche Bruckner Gesellschaft, he demonstrated his support for Haas' work by including in the programme of a concert he gave with the Vienna Philharmonic Orchestra the first performance of the *Urfassung* of the Eighth Symphony. It seems reasonable to assume that the address was given in connection with this event. Whether this public sanctioning of Haas

58 Furtwängler, VMS, p. 13 (author's translation).
59 Furtwängler, TW, pp. 104–5; FM, pp. 106–7.

represented a genuine change of heart or whether it was motivated at least
in part by political expediency is not easy to determine. However, two years
later, in 1941, there is an entry in Furtwängler's private notebooks, which
sheds some further light on the matter; here he contradicts his earlier public
statement by privately censuring Haas and defending the altered texts of
Schalk and Löwe:

> They have found – it is said – setting copy. Haas says this has changed
> nothing. The fact remains. Violation of Bruckner by scholars. That could go
> a long way. One might sooner speak of violation of the public by the Haas
> myth. The fact is that it was not the *Gesamtausgabe* that made Bruckner
> famous, but the earlier edition. The question is even raised of whether the
> *Gesamtausgabe* would have made him quite so famous. I am not concerned
> with the literal Bruckner, the Bruckner of the 'scribes and Pharisees', but
> with the authentic Bruckner. And I cannot call only the *Original-Ausgabe*
> authentic if another print from a later period is available. This is why Haas'
> violation myth is necessary, and it is not authentic. It even contradicts the
> psychology of all great men. Only unproductive minds can seriously believe
> that a great productive artist can be 'put under pressure' for the duration
> of a depression. Depression and productivity are essential opposites, the
> former only ever a reaction, nothing more. The falsification that is done
> here to the character of Bruckner – Bruckner as a fool – is much greater
> than [that done] by the essays of the first scholars, Löwe and Schalk.[60]

Furtwängler's view of the Bruckner *Gesamtausgabe* is inconsistent. Publicly
he champions the editions prepared in accordance with the manuscript
sources, though with a retrospective acknowledgement of the importance of
the altered texts in making Bruckner's music known; privately he continues
to believe in the superiority of the editions prepared by Löwe and Schalk.
Ambivalent though his position may be, it is beyond question that in 1939
it was politically expedient to express approval of the *Gesamtausgabe*; public
support for the texts of Löwe and Schalk would have been seen as contra-
dicting the government-endorsed official position.

In Furtwängler's opinion the danger of an 'over-intellectual' approach
to Bruckner is that the spiritual message of the music may be obscured.
What matters to him is the importance of the composer's underlying
purpose rather than perfection of artistic detail. The quality of idealistic
transcendence, which was such an important feature of Bruckner's works,
must be paramount:

---

60 Furtwängler, AZN, pp. 220–1; NBKS, p. 135.

But there are other qualities to look for which we Germans, in particular, find more appropriate, more to the point. [...] No one who has genuinely experienced this music can fail to recognise its profundity, its purity, its sense of dedication. Its failings, moreover, seem somehow to be an integral part of the achievement as a whole. Bruckner is one of the few geniuses in the whole history of music whose appointed task was to express the transcendental in human terms, to weave the power of God into the fabric of human life. Be it in struggles against demonic forces, or in music of blissful transfiguration, his whole mind and spirit were infused with thoughts of the divine, of God above and God on earth.[61]

It is this idea, with its anti-intellectual subtext, which associates Furtwängler so strongly with aspects of Nazi ideology. The notion here expressed, that Bruckner's music represents the power of God at work in the fabric of human existence, can be seen as an extension of the Nazi concept of *Gottgläubigkeit*, or the belief in God as a mystical creative power rather than God as defined by the Catholic Church. This idea naturally formed the basis of Goebbels' explanation of the religious content of Bruckner's works:

We are far from any scholarly examination of his music, yet we let his works affect us simply and immediately as artistic revelations. We both sense and know that his deep religious faith has long since freed itself from all confines of doctrine, and that it has its roots in the same heroic feeling for the world which is the origin of all the truly great and eternal creations of German art.[62]

Furtwängler further develops this concept by associating Bruckner both with the rediscovery of a lost mythical spirituality and the prevailing metaphor of cultural rebirth. In his influential biography of the composer, Robert Haas compares Bruckner with such figures as Meister Eckart and Jacob Böhme, whose broad-based doctrines of mysticism strongly influenced the Nazi idea of a specifically Aryan Christianity.[63] It is probable that Furtwängler had Haas' work in mind when he drew a similar comparison:

He was, in fact, not a musician but a mystic, in the line of men like Meister Eckart and Jakob Böhme. Is it surprising that he walked the earth like a stranger, a man for whom the world in itself held no interest, had no

---

61 TW, p. 111; FM, pp. 110–11 (amended).
62 Gilliam, 'The Annexation of Anton Bruckner', p. 608 (amended).
63 Robert Haas, *Anton Bruckner* (Potsdam: Akademische Verlagsgesellschaft Athenaion, 1934), pp. 1 and 6. See also Jackson and Hawkshaw, eds, *Bruckner Studies*, pp. 96–7.

meaning? And is it not immaterial whether such a man is a cobbler – as Böhme was – or a choirmaster from Upper Austria?[64]

This idea of transcendental mysticism as a metaphor of cultural rebirth demanded nothing less than absolute submission on the part of the audience:

> A composer such as Bruckner demands from his listeners total dedication, total surrender. This then, in turn, yields its own priceless rewards.
>
> But the outside world has little idea what it is like for an artist to have such a cross to bear. We should at least preserve a sense of gratitude and humility, and be mindful of the fact that it is to divine providence that we, as a nation, owe the presence in our midst of such prophets, geniuses who hold up a mirror to mankind.[65]

The organic artwork required total surrender on the part of the listener in the same way that the organic state demanded the total allegiance and obedience of its constituent members. This idea is common to many of Furtwängler's writings; there are striking parallels between the passage quoted above and the notion of the kind of artistic hegemony he advocated in *Conversations about Music*.[66]

In Furtwängler's view Bruckner is a paradigmatic example of the artistic genius that emerges from the national spirit; in this respect he sees Bruckner as a model representative of the idealised community that gave rise to the doctrine of Blood and Soil (*Blut und Boden*):

> From a biological point of view, as I have already indicated, Bruckner represents a strange mixture [Biologisch betrachtet stellt Bruckner, wie ich schon andeutete, eine eigenartige Mischung dar]: peasant and child of the people on the one hand, sensitive musician, receptive to experiences of the most sublime exaltation on the other. Such a combination of rude earthiness and intense intellectuality is not all that rare among German composers. Haydn, Beethoven, Schubert, Brahms – these may be reckoned among his spiritual companions, though the extremes seem more pronounced in Bruckner.[67]

It is this unimpeachable pedigree as a product of *das Volk* that gives Bruckner his ultimate validity as an artistic genius; it is because of its essential *völkisch* simplicity that Bruckner's message reaches to the heart of human experience:

64 TW, p. 111; FM, p. 111.
65 TW, p. 112; FM, p. 111.
66 See present work, pp. 139–48.
67 TW, p. 112; FM, p. 111.

The universal validity of artistic expression was far greater in earlier, unsophisticated periods than it became later. As time went on and the consciousness of theoretical issues and artistic techniques grew, this validity becomes increasingly hard to find, until we reach the paradoxical state of affairs where it is no longer the man from the midst of the masses, the proverbial 'simple soul' ['einfache Gemüt'] mirroring the popular taste of this day, that gives expression to these universal truths in his nobility and his simplicity, but only the great and original genius. [...] He has become a necessity: through him we are able to regain or souls.[68]

The artistic genius leading his followers towards the goal of spiritual renewal once again seems intent on providing an allegory of the political process through which the Führer, in the person of Hitler, was reinventing the true nature of national greatness.

Furtwängler concludes his address by returning to the concept of artistic transcendence. It is this quality, together with the intrinsic power of the message, which gives Bruckner's art its timeless validity:

Ultimate experience can only be achieved when 'Above' and 'Below' have ceased to be irreconcilable opposites, when the nobility of divine nature manifests itself in the humble world of the common people, and when in his supreme moments of sublime inspiration the artist never loses the consciousness of standing with his feet firmly planted on the native soil [Mutterboden] of his beloved Earth.

Which returns us to Bruckner, for such an artist was he. [...] There is not a single note in his music that does not link us, and him, in some way to the world of the eternal. He has shown that even in the modern world it is still possible to strive for universal validity of expression, and that simplicity [Einfachheit], purity [Reinheit], greatness [Größe] and power of expression [Kraft des Ausdrucks] can still be a feature of art and life today.[69]

Despite the fact that the four qualities ascribed to Bruckner's music here were typically ascribed to the masterworks of the German canon by Nazi ideology, Furtwängler does not otherwise dwell on the aspects of his art which might have glorified the public face of the Nazi state, such as the ceremonial, architectonic and brass-dominated passages which were easily appropriated for militaristic and propaganda purposes.[70] The general flow

68 TW, pp. 114–15; FM, pp. 112–13.
69 TW, pp. 119–20; FM, pp. 115–16.
70 The finale of the Fifth Symphony and the closing passage from *Das Rheingold* were used to frame the Führer's speech at the Nuremberg Party Rally on 7 September 1937. The conductors were Siegmund von Hausegger and Peter Raabe. Furtwängler was invited to conduct but the authorities apparently overlooked the fact that he was

of his thought is concerned with loftier matters: the concept of artistic transcendence; the evocation of faith in music and in particular the supraecclesiastical *Gottglaubigkeit*; Bruckner as a model of the ideal German *Volk* and the associated concept of the development of artistic genius from such origins; the transmutation of the notion of artistic genius into the idea of an artistic hegemony; and finally the censure of intellectualism and the emphasis on the supra-rational, spiritual message enshrined in Bruckner's works.

In his consideration of the questions raised by Bruckner's art Furtwängler moves ever closer towards the ideology of National Socialism; his position is a continuation of that contained in Robert Haas' biography and Goebbels' Regensburg speech. Furtwängler's July 1939 address, though somewhat less strident in tone, parallels that of Goebbels in its tendentious appropriation of Bruckner as an icon of the prevailing *Zeitgeist*. It is in many respects a restatement of the sentiments expressed in his Brahms address of May 1933 that had so disturbed Alban Berg. Furtwängler's attempts to declare art and politics to be separate entities only served to underline the fact that, after six years of Nazi rule, they were so inextricably linked as to be virtually indistinguishable.

Furtwängler in World War II

Furtwängler concludes his address to the Deutsche Bruckner Gesellschaft by describing the heavenly homeland of the great master 'which today and tomorrow and in the future will never be lost to us'. He invokes this transcendent imagery by citing the second stanza of Goethe's nature poem 'Rainbow' ('Regenbogen'). 'For many thousands of years, the heavenly bow has spoken "Peace".'[71] Less than two months later, on 1 September 1939, German troops invaded Poland; for the second time in Wilhelm Furtwängler's lifetime, aggressive German nationalism provoked a conflict which was to bring about untold destruction in the European heartlands. Furtwängler continued much as before to conduct the Berlin and Vienna Philharmonic orchestras in programmes drawn mostly from the Austro-German canon. That he proved a useful cultural ambassador for the Nazi regime is beyond dispute. In the early months of the war he appeared as a guest conductor

---

already engaged to participate in the German Week of Culture at the World Exhibition in Paris which ran concurrently with the Party Rally. See Prieberg, *Kraftprobe*, p. 279; Eng. edn, *Trial of Strength*, p. 213.

71 Goethe, FA, vol. 2, p. 691; TW, p. 120. This postscript is not included in the English translation. It is ironic in view of subsequent events to note that in all sources the first line of the cited stanza misquotes Goethe's 'Frohe Zeichen' [Happy Signs] as 'Frohe Zeiten' [Happy Times].

in programmes of Beethoven, Schumann, Brahms and Richard Strauss in Switzerland (Winterthur, 8 November; Zurich, 14 November); and in Hungary (Budapest, 24–26 November). On 9 January 1940 Propaganda Minister Goebbels noted in his diary

> Furtwängler reports on his trips to Switzerland and Hungary. He met with triumphal success everywhere. We can put him to good use and at the moment he is very willing. He intends now to keep an eye on the music world in Vienna. And to go to Prague to raise our musical prestige. There it is an urgent necessity.[72]

Furtwängler appeared in Copenhagen (12 and 16 January 1940) and Oslo (1 April 1940). On 5 April he conducted again in Copenhagen; a further concert scheduled for 10 April was cancelled due to the German occupation of Denmark, although his work as cultural ambassador continued. On 5 October Goebbels recorded:

> Visit by Furtwängler: he has some worries because of his commitments abroad. I advise him against Switzerland for the moment. Particularly against Winterthur, where even now emigrés from Germany are still active. He is very helpful and offers to give a concert with the Berlin Philharmonic during my visit to Prague. This visit must be the consummation of our work of reconciliation. I shall give it a skilful build-up.[73]

Goebbels arrived in Prague on 5 November. 'Big reception. Local people still very cool.' The promised concert took place on 7 November.

> In the evening, Furtwängler gives a concert with the Berlin Philharmonic. *The Moldau, Eulenspiegel,* and Beethoven's Seventh. A solemn occasion with Hacha, the Neuraths, and the entire Czech government. Everybody of rank or name in Prague is there. *Moldau* indescribably beautiful. *Eulenspiegel* interesting. Ravishingly played. The public goes wild.[74]

'The Case of Wagner, freely after Nietzsche' (April 1941)

The placing of an icon of German art within the context of the prevailing political and cultural ideology is also a subtext running beneath the discursive surface of Furtwängler's most extensive piece of theoretical

72 *The Goebbels Diaries 1939–1941*, p. 90.
73 Ibid., p. 131.
74 Ibid., p. 168.

discourse, 'The Case of Wagner, freely after Nietzsche' ('Der Fall Wagner, frei nach Nietzsche'). The text was written in April 1941 during a period of forced inactivity following a skiing accident. The precise authorial purpose is unclear. It does not appear to be intended for publication in the manner of the Brahms and Bruckner addresses considered earlier which appeared in published form in 1942. It may to some extent be a working-out of Furtwängler's complex and ambivalent relationship to Nietzsche as there is abundant evidence throughout the discourse of a wide knowledge of Nietzsche's philosophical writings. The primary sources are in the portion of the Furtwängler Nachlass held in the Staatsbibliothek Berlin and consist of three typescripts. The first is clearly the working draft containing annotations and corrections with the date 'April 1941' superscripted in pencil in Furtwängler's hand. The original title was 'The Case of Wagner, freely after Nietzsche: A dispassionate Reflection' ('Der Fall Wagner, frei nach Nietzsche: ein nüchterne Betrachtung'). Significantly, Furtwängler amends this to 'The Case of Wagner, freely after Nietzsche: a contemporary Reflection' ('eine zeitgenössische Betrachtung'). The second typescript is a fair copy containing no annotations or corrections; the third is a carbon copy of the second. The printed version included in *Ton und Wort* omits the second limb of the title altogether.[75]

The title is adapted from Nietzsche's celebrated polemic, *Der Fall Wagner* (1888) together with a nod to Richard Strauss' tone poem *Also Sprach Zarathustra: Tondichtung für großes Orchester, frei nach Friedrich Nietzsche* (Op. 30, 1896). The essay is in one sense a dispassionate appraisal of the Wagner–Nietzsche relationship; in another sense it can be seen to be an extended critique of the prevailing cultural situation – hence Furtwängler's alteration of the original title. He bases his discussion on the question of why it is that Wagner, fifty years after his death, remains the most controversial figure in the entire history of the arts. In attempting an answer he returns to a familiar theme that defines the contradiction at the heart of Wagner's work and which is the principal cause of his own ambivalent attitude towards the composer: are Wagner's music dramas valid in their own right as organically cohesive artworks, or do they consist of little more than an artistic 'omnium gatherum', an amalgamation of a number of disparate elements and therefore a devaluation of music?

As he indicates in his title, Furtwängler follows the methodology of Friedrich Nietzsche: through this lens he scrutinises the relationship between the composer and the philosopher. The long and diffuse polemic

---

75 SPK Berlin, 55 Nachl. 13, W. Furtwängler, Kasten 45–6; TW, pp. 121–70; FM, pp. 66–96 (translations amended). See also Friedrich Nietzsche, *Der Fall Wagner* (1888).

9   Furtwängler skiing in the Arlberg, March 1941

can be reduced to two related questions: first, can Wagner's *Gesamtkunstwerk* constitute an artistically valid organic whole; secondly, does the organic principle and its associated concepts of musical structure serve a similar function as a central idea of Nietzsche's musical æsthetic? Not surprisingly, given the context in which he is writing, his discussion is heavily inclined towards Wagner's side of the equation, particularly when he considers the question of the idea of the organic totality of the artwork. Furtwängler reminds his readers early in his critique of Nietzsche that 'if we are to do justice to Wagner it is important to keep this totality in mind' ('dieses Ganze muß man ins Auge fassen').[76] Nietzsche's perceived inability to understand the importance of this concept is the principal critical weapon with which Furtwängler challenges the later Nietzsche's view of Wagner: 'Nietzsche appears not to recognise that music can create an organic, self-contained world with as absolute a validity as that created by Wagner in his *Gesamtkunstwerk*, of which music is only a part.'[77]

It is Nietzsche's inability to comprehend the central importance of organic cohesion in an artwork which, in Furtwängler's view, is the main cause of his critical failings:

> The target of his thrusts [in *Der Fall Wagner*] is now Wagner's music. What he admires in this music, he says, is the composer's skill in dealing with the particular, his attention to detail; in this respect Wagner is 'a master of the highest rank, the greatest miniaturist in music, who can compress an infinity of meaning and charm into the smallest of spaces'. Everything else he calls into question. The essence of this music lies in what he calls the external 'gesture'. [...] How awkward, how pitiful, he exclaims, are Wagner's attempts at musical development! The man has nothing in common with real composers, let alone with great composers, because he is incapable of creating an artistic whole; his music is wild, undisciplined, bereft of inner structure.[78]

We have seen that Furtwängler considered the theory of the *Gesamtkunstwerk* as the most problematic aspect of Wagner's work, and he identifies it as the object of the main thrust of Nietzsche's own critical approach. To Nietzsche, this is the cause of Wagner's decadence; his works rely for their effect on theatricality. However, Furtwängler points out: 'In truth Nietzsche was not concerned with the organic principle in music or with questions of structure.

---

76 TW, p. 131; FM, p. 72.
77 TW, p. 132; FM, p. 73.
78 TW, pp. 139–40; FM, p. 77.

What attracted him in music were its colours, its fragrance, its delicacy, its sensuous, morbid, transient, seductive qualities.'[79]

Furtwängler's analysis of Nietzsche's concept of decadence in Wagner prompts him to refer to the philosopher in this context as 'out of date and outmoded, who can see nothing around him but decadence'.[80] The huge demands made by Wagner had in themselves, Furtwängler suggests, resulted in the emergence of the phenomenon of the 'Wagnerite':

> So, what is a Wagnerite? He is a person who has taken up his position not on the outside of Wagner's work but in the midst of it, having been unable to gain his spiritual freedom and independence in the face of this music, to which he has surrendered himself body and soul.[81]

Wagner, who summons his works 'from the collective unconscious of the whole nation – even European people', is paradigmatic of this inseparability between art and life.[82] Art, as the phenomenon of the Wagnerite demonstrates, grows out of life. Furtwängler continues this line of thought by emphasising the poetic nature of Wagner's work. In so doing he is reaffirming his position of 1919: that the essential nature of Wagner's art is that of a poetic idea realised in music, and the more all-pervading the central idea the closer the work comes to fulfilling the organic ideal. It was this notion of the poetic idea growing from the collective unconscious of the German people and enshrined in artworks of such emotional and hypnotic potency that had made Wagner into such a powerful icon of Nazi ideology.

In the conclusion to his essay Furtwängler restates the contradiction at the centre of both Nietzsche's and his own relationship to Wagner:

> To conclude: in principle our relationship today [1941] to the works of Wagner has not advanced beyond the position adopted by Nietzsche [1888]. He embodies our two basic responses – on the one hand an unconditional surrender to Wagner's art, a declaration of total devotion; on the other hand a no less radical repudiation of everything he stands for, an expression of antipathy and deep distaste. But, like so many typical 'Wagnerians' [echte 'Wagnerianer'], Nietzsche allowed himself to become bogged down in matters relating to details of content. We must take the argument beyond this and discuss it in terms of the real Wagner, Wagner the poet, the dramatist, the composer – in short, of Wagner the artist. Only in this way shall we be able to discover a new and genuinely productive

79 TW, pp. 140–1; FM, p. 78.
80 TW, pp. 147–8; FM, p. 82.
81 TW, p. 155; FM, p. 87.
82 TW, p. 163; FM, p. 91.

relationship to his works. And only then shall we become aware who this artist really was.[83]

This chapter began with an account of Furtwängler's Wagnerian activities during the early years of the Third Reich. In this essay of 1941 Furtwängler is less critical of Wagner in a direct sense than he was in his earlier essay of 1919. The discussion, despite its prolixity, is on an altogether higher level; but for all its insights it remains in essence an attempt to justify and defend Wagner against Nietzsche's critique of 1888 and as such it represents a more complete acceptance of the 'totality' of Wagnerian ideology than was to be found in his earlier essay. Although 'The Case of Wagner' is largely free from the tendentiousness of the Brahms and Bruckner addresses previously considered, it occupies the same ideological territory. Thus the essay can be read as having the same underlying purpose as the analytical work of the Wagnerian analyst Alfred Lorenz (1868–1939): by analysing Wagner's operas in terms of music-poetic periods Lorenz sought to prove the organic, and thus ideological, validity of the *Gesamtkunstwerk* by demonstrating the same level of internal cohesion that Schenker identified in Beethoven.[84] Similarly, for Furtwängler Wagner is no longer the defiler of pure music who, in the spirit of Thomas Mann's Herr Edmund Pfühl,[85] he so passionately vilified in his youthful correspondence with Bertel von Hildebrand. By challenging Nietzsche he appropriates Wagner's *Gesamtkunstwerk* into his own organic world-view, and in so doing forges one more link in the chain that harnesses conservative values to the service of ideological ends.

The above reference to *Buddenbrooks* prompts comparison of this extended essay by Furtwängler with the earlier, subsequently famous public address on Wagner given in February 1933 by Thomas Mann, 'The Sufferings and Greatness of Richard Wagner'.[86] At the beginning of Nazi rule, Mann had warned of the dangers of political appropriation of Wagnerian ideology; in contrast, at the same critical point in history in May 1933, Furtwängler had extolled Brahms as a representative of the new *Zeitgeist* in a clear case of

83 TW, pp. 169–70; FM, pp. 95–6.
84 Alfred Lorenz, *Das Geheimnis der Form bei Richard Wagner*, 4 vols (Berlin: Max Hesse, 1924–33). For a detailed exegesis of Lorenz's work and his relationship to the Nazis, see Stephen McClatchie, *Analyzing Wagner's Operas: Alfred Lorenz and German Nationalist Ideology* (Rochester, NY: University of Rochester Press, 1998).
85 *Buddenbrooks*, p. 407.
86 Thomas Mann, 'Leiden und Grösse Richard Wagners', in Erika Mann, ed., *Wagner und unsere Zeit* (Frankfurt: Fischer, 1983), pp. 63–121; Eng. edn, *Thomas Mann: Pro and Contra Wagner* (London: Faber, 1985), pp. 91–148. See also 'Protest der Richard-Wagner Stadt München', *Münchener Neueste Nachrichten*, 16–17 April 1933; quoted in *Pro und Contra Wagner*, pp. 149–51.

the tendentious application of artistic ideology for political ends. Whereas Mann famously, and to some notoriously, defined Wagner's *Gesamtkunstwerk* as the product of a form of artistic dilettantism raised to the level of genius, Furtwängler, eight years later, defends the *Gesamtkunstwerk* from Nietzsche's, and by implication Mann's, criticisms and declares it to be an organically cohesive artistic concept unified by the governing poetic idea. Furtwängler was not one of the signatories to the 'Protest from Richard Wagner's Own City of Munich', published in response to Mann's perceived attack on Wagner and signed by such musical luminaries as Hans Knappertsbusch, Hans Pfitzner, Richard Strauss and Siegmund von Hausegger; but 'The Case of Wagner' might well have been in part a retrospective response to Mann's essay of 1933 in its defence of the ideal Wagner, the icon of National Socialist ideology.

Furtwängler's essay 'The Case of Wagner' dates from April 1941. The following year, on 26 February 1942, he gave a highly visible demonstration of the political potency of Richard Wagner by conducting a concert in the industrial setting of the AEG factory in Berlin. This was one of the *Strength through Joy* (*Kraft durch Freude*) concerts designed as propaganda exercises to raise morale. The programme consisted of Schubert's Symphony No. 8, the 'Unfinished', Richard Strauss' *Till Eulenspiegel* and the Prelude to *Die Meistersinger*. In bringing Wagner out of the opera house onto the factory floor the culture of *Gemeinschaft* visibly sustained the productive *Gesellschaft*. The propagandist filmed performance of the *Meistersinger* Prelude, together with the opening shots of the exterior of the industrial plant, is one of the most extended film sources of Furtwängler conducting. It is a newsreel-style film in the *Zeit im Bild* (*Time in Picture*) series, entitled 'Furtwängler dirigiert' (Furtwängler conducts). The iconography is extraordinary. Outsize Swastika banners are portentously draped behind the orchestra. Most indicative of all are the individual close-up shots of the supposedly enraptured audience: older factory workers, wounded military personnel, young men and women carefully identified as corresponding most closely with the Aryan racial archetype; all wear marmoreal expressions and are shown deeply absorbed in the music. There can be no more telling illustration of Richard Grunberger's description of the Nazi regime 'bathing the Reich in music as in a foetal fluid'.

Still more potent is the filmed extract of the closing moments of the performance of Beethoven's Ninth Symphony given a few weeks later on 19 April 1942 in honour of Hitler's birthday the following day. The Führer himself is not present, but serried ranks of the Nazi High Command, led by Goebbels, are prominently seated in the front of the audience. At the conclusion Goebbels is seen to shake Furtwängler by the hand. The question of who initiated the handshake is not important, although it should be noted that Goebbels approaches Furtwängler, who remains on the conductor's rostrum. Both these filmed examples are powerful reminders of the propaganda potential of high culture when the perceived heightened reality of music is associated in the public imagination with festive celebrations, known as 'Fest- und Feiertage'.[87] The concert hall and opera house, twin temples of high culture in which Furtwängler presided as High Priest, become irrevocably politicised spaces.[88]

The period following the composition of the essay 'Der Fall Wagner, frei nach Nietzsche' was a time during which Furtwängler became ever more firmly established as an important cultural figurehead for the increasingly embattled Nazi regime. Many of his performances were given in highly politicised contexts, telling examples of which are the wartime Bayreuth Festivals of 1943 and 1944, when *Die Meistersinger* was performed before audiences of military personnel on leave from active duties together with other servants of the state attending at the specific 'invitation' of the Führer. In addition, Furtwängler continued to serve as cultural ambassador for the regime by directing events such as the gala concert given by the Berlin Philharmonic in the occupied Czech capital of Prague on 16 March 1944. The programme of iconic symphonies by Dvorak (No. 9) and Beethoven (No. 5) was tendentiously symbolic of the Nazi 'co-ordination' of German and Czech culture and formed part of the celebrations, organised and attended by Goebbels, to mark the fifth anniversary of the occupation. Such events served both as cultural and propaganda statements and were intended to form a screen of normality behind which the uncertain international situation could be concealed.[89] As the war intensified, and the outlook for Germany became increasingly bleak, Furtwängler succeeded in maintaining a schedule of concerts with the Berlin and Vienna Philharmonic Orchestras which continued until January 1945. By this time, however, the political situation had deteriorated to such a point that it became expedient for him to leave Germany and take up permanent residence in neutral Switzerland, outside the borders and jurisdiction of the Reich.

---

87 See Rehding, *Music and Monumentality*, p. 171.
88 Both the *Meistersinger* Prelude and closing sequence of Beethoven's Ninth Symphony films are available on YouTube.
89 For an account of the wartime Bayreuth Festivals, see Spotts, *Bayreuth*, pp. 189–211. For an account of the Prague concert and Furtwängler's other wartime activities in occupied territories see Kater, *The Twisted Muse* (Oxford: OUP, 1997), p, 201; also René Trémine, *Wilhelm Furtwängler: Concert Listings 1906–1954* (Bezons: Productions Tahra, 1997), p. 55.

CHAPTER 7

REFLECTION AND REACTION: FURTWÄNGLER IN THE IMMEDIATE POST-WAR PERIOD (1945-50)

It is a serious omission of the [Faust] legend and poem that they do not connect Faust with *music*. He must have been musical; he must have been a musician. Music is the area of the daemonic. [...] It is the most calculated order and at the same time chaotic anti-reason, rich in fantastical and incantatory gestures, the magic of numbers, the most passionate of the arts and yet the furthest from reality, abstract and mythical. If Faust is to be the representative of the German soul, he must have been musical; for abstract and mythical (i.e. musical) is the relationship of things German to the world – the relationship of a professor with a touch of the daemonic, awkward and at the same time conditioned by his arrogant awareness of being superior to the world in 'depth'.[1]

But now where am I? Here's more trouble;
There was a path, and now its rubble.[2]

The circumstances surrounding Furtwängler's movements in the months of January and February 1945 together with his subsequent emigration are well documented and in the public domain. In brief, he spent the closing months of the war in Switzerland. In the aftermath of the total defeat of Germany he was prevented by the occupying powers from initiating or participating in any form of public music-making pending the investigation of his activities in Germany during the twelve-year period of Nazi rule. This in itself was a complex, protracted and strangely inconclusive process: in March 1946 Austria declared him to be untainted by Nazi collaboration, yet the hearing in Berlin was delayed until December of that year. Ultimately he was cleared of all charges; yet, for reasons which are not entirely clear, the judgement was

---

1   Thomas Mann, 'Germany and the Germans': see Appendix 2.
2   Goethe, *Faust*, Part II, lines 7801–2, tr. David Luke.

10　Furtwängler in Berlin, 1947

not finally ratified until 27 April 1947.[3] Whatever the pretext for this delay, it meant that Furtwängler was now free to resume his conducting activities in the public arena. On 25 May 1947 he made his first appearance in Berlin following the defeat of the Third Reich with his own Berlin Philharmonic Orchestra in an all-Beethoven programme which, by a strange irony, was the same as that of the concerts he gave in Vienna, Berlin and Hamburg following his concordat with the Nazi regime in early 1935: the Overture to *Egmont*, the Sixth Symphony and the Fifth Symphony. (As has already been noted, the Berlin concert on 3 May 1935 was attended by Hitler, Göring and Goebbels.) Furtwängler was afforded a tumultuous reception. The orthodox interpretation of this demonstration of public approbation is that these ovations were a spontaneous display of gratitude on the part of a culture-loving people, recently freed from oppression, towards a courageous individual who had resisted the tyranny of dictatorship; yet Erika Mann, daughter of Thomas Mann, declared that this was little more than a political demonstration in support of the defeated regime, a gesture of defiance against the occupying powers expressed through a reaffirmation of the cultural values of the Third Reich by one of its leading executive artists.[4] Erika Mann's testimony must itself be treated with caution. As the daughter of the exiled Thomas Mann she could hardly be described as a dispassionate witness; moreover, she had considerable histrionic talents and was strongly critical of the Germans in defeat. Nevertheless, these diametrically opposed interpretations of this event are indicative of the mixed reception that Furtwängler would face as he sought to re-establish himself as a performing artist.

Furtwängler generally based his concert programmes in the post-war period around the core works of the Austro-German canon together with the early Strauss tone poems *Tod und Verklärung* and *Till Eulenspiegel*. They are conservative in content and virtually indistinguishable from those of the pre-war and wartime periods; but subtle changes can be discerned in accordance with the changed political circumstances. The second series of Berlin concerts given on 31 May and 1–2 June 1947, not with the Berlin Philharmonic Orchestra but with the Berliner Staatskapelle Orchester, included Tchaikovsky's Symphony No. 6; Mendelssohn gradually makes a reappearance (Incidental music to *A Midsummer Night's Dream*, Violin Concerto, *Hebrides* Overture) together with rarities such as Stravinsky (*The Firebird*) and even an isolated

---

3   See Klaus Lang, *Wilhelm Furtwängler und seine Entnazifizierung* (Aachen: Shaker Media GmbH, 2012). For narrative accounts of the circumstances surrounding Furtwängler's emigration from Germany and of his subsequent de-Nazification trial see Schönzeler, *Furtwängler*, pp. 101–8 and Shirakawa, *The Devil's Music Master*, pp. 292–337.
4   Letter to the editor of the *New York Herald Tribune*, dated 31 May 1947, published 5 June 1947; also cited in Shirakawa, *The Devil's Music Master*, p. 340.

performance of Vaughan Williams' *Tallis Fantasia* given in London with the London Philharmonic Orchestra on 29 February 1948. Of particular note are two performances of Strauss' late *Metamorphosen*, completed on 12 April 1945 and given in Berlin on 26 and 27 October 1947. Furtwängler had hitherto paid scant attention to Strauss' later music and as he grew older increasingly confined himself to the three early tone poems: *Don Juan*, *Till Eulenspiegel* and *Tod und Verklärung*. These performances of Strauss' 1945 elegy make a powerful statement of longing for the certainties of a lost world now irretrievably buried under the surrounding ruins of Berlin.[5] Furtwängler was later to make a memorable return to late Strauss when on 22 May 1950 he gave the posthumous first performance of the *Four Last Songs* in London's Royal Albert Hall with Kirsten Flagstad as soloist.

This brief sketch of Furtwängler's position during the period immediately following the defeat of Nazi Germany puts into context the series of writings in which the extent of the historical and critical problems he poses becomes increasingly apparent. His constantly recurring theme is that of a clarion call for a return to the conservative culture of the Wilhelmine period. Furtwängler makes his appeal through acerbic and direct criticism of an over-intellectualised approach to music through constant recourse to the now familiar trope of the organic metaphor and its associated biological imagery; yet it is this all-pervasive use of the organic model which most powerfully indicates the continuing presence of conservative-nationalist ideological affinities. This implies a more complex position than that of a cultural conservative who was merely calling for a return to pre-Weimar values. The progressive nationalisation of this culture by the Nazis should have made such a return an ideological impossibility. What may be discerned in the related issues and themes which run as a subtext through the articles, lectures and compositions of his last years is not so much a process of personal rehabilitation but a process of realignment of an unaltered set of ideological convictions in a post-totalitarian context.

The Mendelssohn Centenary Address (1947)

Among this final series of writings is the text of an address given in Leipzig in 1947 as part of the celebrations honouring the centenary of Mendelssohn's death.[6] His central theme is that of Mendelssohn's 'Germanness'. Nazi racial

---

5   The performance of 27 October 1947 has survived on record (see Appendix 3).
6   On 4 November 1947 Furtwängler made a further contribution to these celebrations by directing the Leipzig Gewandhaus orchestra in a programme of works by Mendelssohn and Beethoven. See Trémine, *Wilhelm Furtwängler: Concert Listings 1906–1954*, p. 57.

doctrine had declared that the concepts of 'Jewishness' and 'Germanness' were antithetical: Jewish elements in art corrupted and polluted the expression of the pure German spirit. The Nazi censure of Mendelssohn was essentially a restatement of the central thesis of Wagner's 'Judaism in Music', in which the composer is cited as paradigmatic of undesirable Jewish influence in German art. Furtwängler had himself promulgated this line of thought when in 1933 he declared the Jewish composer Mahler incapable of composing a true folk melody on account of his Jewishness;[7] yet in 1947 he contradicts this earlier view by citing both Mahler (a composer he all but ignored in his post-war concert programmes) and Mendelssohn as quintessential German composers:

> It is not all that long ago that a bigoted racist doctrine denied that Mendelssohn was a German composer. [...] To be sure, unlike Mahler, who belongs in no less a degree to the German cultural scene, Mendelssohn does not belong in a narrow German frame of reference, for, during his lifetime, his presence was felt throughout Europe. [...] He belongs unquestionably to the history of German music. He is one of the most fertile, most striking examples of the symbiosis [Symbiose] of Germanness and Jewishness, and gives the lie to those theories which hold that such a symbiosis is impossible, or, if not impossible, then undesirable.[8]

Furtwängler's affirmation of the artistic merits of a symbiosis of Germanness and Jewishness, together with his positive reference to Mahler as a *bona fide* German composer is different in emphasis to sentiments expressed in his Brahms address given in the early months of Nazi rule, although it is consistent with his double vision evident in the open letter to Goebbels in which he had argued that true Jewish artists should be allowed to continue working in Germany.[9] He continues in eulogistic tone to honour Mendelssohn as the creator of this cultural synthesis, an important figure in the Romantic movement and an archetypal representative of the German tradition:

> The tradition that Mendelssohn represents is in a very special sense the tradition of German music. It was he who created that synthesis that arose from the foundations laid by Bach, Beethoven and the other German classical composers. The Leipzig Conservatoire, which he founded, dominated the nineteenth century, and its roots lay in that immortal

7   See present work, p. 121.
8   Wilhelm Furtwängler, 'Mendelssohn zu seinem 100-Jährigen Todestag', SPK Berlin, 55 Nachl. 13/C W. Furtwängler, Kasten 45–6; in VMS, pp. 114–17; Eng. edn, FM, pp. 59–61 (amended).
9   See especially the address 'Johannes Brahms' (1933), discussed in Chapter 5.

German music that has conquered the world. In the second half of the century the supremacy of the Mendelssohn school was continued by Joachim; he was praised by no less a man than Wagner as an outstanding musician both as performer and teacher, and behind him stood the figure of Brahms. It is also to Mendelssohn that we owe the rediscovery of Bach and the first performance of the *Matthäus Passion* since Bach's own day. Bach on the one side, Beethoven's symphonies on the other – such were his parameters, art at its greatest, relevant to the age, subject to timeless laws.[10]

The concept of tradition was, as we have seen, of paramount importance to Furtwängler; tradition seen as a continuous, organic process represented by the unbroken line of artistic continuity realised in the Austro-German symphonic canon. Two years previously, in 1945, he had written in his diary:

The step from Wagner to Schoenberg represents not progress but catastrophe. We are in the middle of this catastrophe. It is important to consider the natural powers of growth. This involves not allowing intelligence to become impertinent and sanctimonious. The artist must be allowed to develop naturally, to construct, instead of chasing after an unproductive, sensational originality.[11]

The continuance of the organic tradition which Furtwängler considered to have been so disastrously compromised by the innovations of Schoenberg and his school, and which he valued so highly, was now, in his view, partly attributable to Mendelssohn. Through his synthesis of Bachian polyphony and the Beethovenian sonata dialectic Mendelssohn had realised the principle of the universal laws of artistic creation – one of the central ideas which had occupied Furtwängler's mind since his earliest days:

What Mendelssohn found embodied in this music [Bach and Beethoven] was the principle of artistic laws, in the highest sense. The Leipzig Conservatoire taught laws – narrow laws, perhaps, but real laws nonetheless.

True, we must be under no illusion that such laws can be easily abused; pedants of all kinds have both done so and continue to do so. But today we have a different attitude towards these laws. Symbols of tradition, they represent a rejection, a fundamental rejection of individualism.[12]

Having thus praised Mendelssohn and his work as vital to the maintenance of tradition, Furtwängler concludes this short address by testifying to the

---

10 VMS, p. 116; FM, p. 60.
11 AZN, pp. 259–60; NBKS, p. 159.
12 VMS, p. 117; FM, pp. 60–1.

contribution made by individual Jews towards the nobility of German art: 'Mendelssohn, Joachim, Schenker, Mahler: Jewish-German in nationality. They testify that we Germans have every reason to see ourselves as a great and noble people. It is tragic that this has to be emphasised today.'[13] Furtwängler is now of the opinion that there is no qualitative difference between Jews and Germans: Jewishness and Germanness, far from being mutually exclusive, are seen as complementary and capable of symbiosis; the resulting synthesis is in itself crucial to the maintenance and continuity of artistic tradition.

In one sense this address can be seen as a call for a return to traditional values of nineteenth-century cultural conservatism as a central pillar of the artistic reconstruction of post-war Germany; the potency of this message is heightened by the context in which it is expressed, namely the rehabilitation of Mendelssohn as a composer worthy of inclusion in the German canon. In order to drive his message home more strongly Furtwängler is almost philo-Semitic in his appraisal of the contribution of German Jewry to the continuation of the organic tradition in art. Superficially, this appears as an attempt to redress the balance in Mendelssohn's favour after the denigration heaped upon him by the ideologues of Nazism. Yet it has a hollow ring: did Furtwängler welcome the opportunity to participate in these centennial celebrations for Mendelssohn as an act of artistic rehabilitation on behalf of a composer compromised by Nazism, or did he exploit the situation as an opportunity to rehabilitate himself in the eyes of the wider international artistic community by publicly denouncing the more exaggerated and extreme elements of Nazi artistic policy? Whatever his underlying purpose, the position he adopts is wholly Germanocentric.

'Heinrich Schenker: A Contemporary Problem' (1947)

This subtext is also apparent in a tribute which Furtwängler wrote in the same year to his erstwhile mentor: Heinrich Schenker.[14] In spite of the fact that the intention to write the essay is mentioned in a diary entry in the previous year, the authorial purpose is not entirely clear.[15] Nevertheless, this short but significant document is indicative of Furtwängler's view of the position in which he found himself during the post-war period; to an

---

13 VMS, p. 117; FM, p. 61 (amended).
14 Furtwängler, 'Heinrich Schenker, Ein zeitgemässes Problem', in TW, pp. 198–204. A translation of this essay by the author is to be found in Appendix 1.
15 See Furtwängler, AZN, p. 276; NBKS, p. 170.

increasing extent this is the writing of an artist who found himself more and more adrift in an alien cultural environment.

Furtwängler examines two of the central ideas of Schenker's theory: the concepts of the *Urlinie* (overarching line) and of *Fernhörens* (distance hearing).[16] In passing it may be noticed that in the course of the discussion Schenker is criticised for his 'talmudische' train of thought.[17] It is this over-fastidious aspect of Schenker's theory which prompts Furtwängler to question the entire concept of the *Urlinie*:

> The concept of the *Urlinie*, the theoretical idea of his last years, has not been completely thought through [...]. According to Schenker's thinking the *Meistersinger* Prelude was not an evolving composition but more of an operatic pot-pourri and a shining example of how the abandonment of the *Urlinie* caused disintegration of the overall artistic structure and cohesion. His portrayal of the *Urlinie* as a single unifying factor in a classical structure, e.g. the *Eroica*, lost itself in abstraction and was, by necessity of fate, before its time.[18]

The Schenkerian concept which is so important to Furtwängler is that of *Fernhörens*:

> What Schenker shows at the mid-point in the development of his thinking is the conception of the overview [Fernhörens] in music. [...] It is Schenker's historical significance that he was the first to investigate the biological implications of music. This concept of the overview, with all its interconnections and complexities, characterised for Schenker the great works of German classical music; this is the foundation of Schenker's ideas and why he never wearied of advocating the organic superiority and proven validity of these works.[19]

Here Furtwängler approaches a definition of his own conception of the internal processes of the organic artwork. In the case of the musical work it is the interconnectedness within the overall concept of time and musical space, both retrospective and forward-looking. This view recalls the Gestalt-inspired premise supporting the expressive æsthetic position articulated in the 1880s by Friedrich von Hausegger and seen again in Pfitzner's concept of inspiration (*Einfall*) in which works of art are conceived at a specific point

---

16 Usually translated as 'structural hearing'. See Felix Salzer, *Structural Hearing* (New York: Charles Boni, 1952).
17 Furtwängler, TW, p. 200.
18 Ibid., p. 201.
19 Ibid., pp. 201–2.

in time and then given actual form by the artist.[20] Furtwängler also identifies himself with the evolutionary aspects of Schenker's theories by describing the process of artistic conception as biological in origin. Furtwängler emphasises this point by comparing the relative artistic merits of a Beethoven symphony, with its superior musical logic, to what he considers to be the random organisation and arbitrariness of jazz:

> For some time in Switzerland a young man had expressed his enthusiasm for jazz;[21] he publicly declared it to be more up-to-date than Beethoven's symphonies because, in its refinements and complications, it was more relevant to contemporary man. The rhythmic and harmonic interrelationships in Beethoven's symphonies are childlike in comparison. In making this observation the young man was not totally wrong, for are not the melodic, harmonic and rhythmic elements in a Beethoven symphony so much more simple than in a jazz piece? The decisive difference is that jazz is lacking in overview. [...] Here is the crux of Schenker's wisdom. His perceptions are of a biological nature and increasingly point to new avenues of enquiry. We learn that the principles of modern biology can be applied elsewhere, above all in art. The ungainly, constricted, superficial and historically questionable understanding of the musical public must be replaced by an awareness of art and artistic worth. Schenker's wide-ranging conception of the overview will fulfil this need.[22]

In his censure of jazz, which during the period of Nazi rule was considered 'degenerate', and through his insistence that the principles of modern biology can be applied to art, Furtwängler seems to be advocating in the post-war period the conservative-nationalist discourses considered earlier. Although the use of biological metaphors is partly drawn from Goethe's scientific theories, by 1947 the notion of the biological implications of music and the associated organic superiority of the Austro-German tradition implied continuing advocacy of German cultural hegemony. Moreover, by paying tribute to Schenker he was again, as in the Mendelssohn essay, acknowledging the contribution made by an assimilated Jew to *German* culture. This in itself represents another curious twist in Furtwängler's attitude towards the Jews. His enthusiasm for Schenker was not manufactured from political expediency, which, as we have seen, was possibly the case with the Mendelssohn essay. It was born of genuine admiration for the theoretical achievements of a thinker who had considerably influenced his artistic

20 See Friedrich von Hausegger, *Die Musik als Ausdruck* (Vienna: Carl Konegen, 1887); also McClatchie, *Analyzing Wagner's Operas*, p. x.
21 Probably Rolf Liebermann (1910–99).
22 TW, pp. 202–4.

WILHELM FURTWÄNGLER

development. Yet, paradoxically, it is from Schenker himself that we learn that Furtwängler was capable of behaving as an 'undisguised anti-Semite'; a point given further purchase by Furtwängler's diagnosis of the theorist's apparently 'talmudic' pedantry evidenced above.[23]

Conversations about Music: An Additional Chapter (1947)

In the same year that the Mendelssohn and Schenker essays appeared, Furtwängler added an additional chapter to his *Conversations about Music*, the book in which, ten years previously, he had expounded and defined his musical æsthetic.[24] His anti-modernist agenda is apparent from his discussion of modern music within the framework of a highly tendentious argument asserting the supremacy of tonality over atonality. Crucial to Furtwängler's analysis of the cultural phenomenon of modern music is his understanding of the concept of progress. He rejects the claim that Wagner's *Tristan und Isolde* had 'expanded and developed chromatic harmony with a consistency unknown in the history of music until that date'; the modernist concept of progress in this case is defined as a specific process which creates a recognisable break with the past.[25] This is strongly countered by Furtwängler with the assertion that the evolution of the chromatic language of *Tristan* was not a deliberate compositional act but a consequence of Wagner's search for the most suitable means with which to realise the poetic content of his poem in musical terms:

> This theory leaves out of consideration, of course, the fact that in writing *Tristan*, Wagner had no intention at all of creating something 'new', of 'expanding the laws of harmony', of 'forcing' progress, but was solely and exclusively concerned with finding the most adequate and impressive language for his poetic vision, for his *Tristan* world. [...] The fact that in so doing he discovered the chromatic system which was of such significance for the future, was far from essential as far as he was concerned; it was a mere accident.[26]

This theory of progress as a consequence only of organic growth is central to Furtwängler's position and became ever more important in the cultural flux which followed the defeat of Nazism. He is strongly critical of the premises underpinning the idea of atonality: that is, the fact that the

23 See present work, p. 82.
24 See present work, pp. 139–48.
25 Furtwängler, GM, p. 110; CM, p. 81.
26 Ibid., pp. 110–11; pp. 81–2.

musical process is an intellectual construct rather than originating in human experience:

> To derive development from the substance and not from the human being searching for expression, to seek and to postulate not the 'beautiful' but the 'new'; this, as I have mentioned above, is the great novelty which was introduced into music at the turn of the century.[27]

In his subsequent account of his understanding of the concept of tonality Furtwängler reduces the idea to its prime fundamental: the cadence.

> The cadence is the basis of tonality, i.e. of the expression of music within the scope of definite keys. It is the cadence which determines the key. Its simplest progression, via the upper dominant to the lower dominant and then back to the tonic, covers a certain definite ground. This not only means that in such a progression each chord is connected with its neighbour, i.e. with the preceding or following chord, but – and this is the decisive point – a context is created on a higher plane, which connects all the links of the chain with each other from the starting point to the end. By means of this superimposed relationship, this 'area' [Raum] marked out by the cadence, no less than the decisive factor is achieved: music can take shape. It has found a point of departure, a course to run, a goal to attain.[28]

Such thinking is closely related to the ideas expressed in the essay on Schenker considered above, where Furtwängler explains his understanding of the concepts of musical space and time. In this particular case he is defining his parameters: the cadence serves as the main structural point, the function of which is to make the process of *Fernhören*, or structural hearing, possible.

Schenker is not the only musical thinker whose ideas are implicitly invoked in the content of this additional chapter to the *Gespräche über Musik*. Later, when drawing a parallel between the motion inherent in a musical work and the movement of the waves of the sea, Furtwängler seems to draw on the ideas of Ernst Kurth (1886–1946), whose concept of sound waves in Bruckner symphonies makes use of a similar metaphor:

> Thus, a tonal work looks rather like the sea: big waves carrying small waves, and small waves smaller waves still, etc. In this simile, waves correspond to cadence spans superimposed upon one another. We are therefore dealing with a system of separate forces running their course independently of our

27 Ibid., p. 111; p. 82.
28 Ibid., p. 111; p. 82.

intentions or wishes. It is not until our will of expression coincides with the will of expression of these forces that the work of art is born.[29]

It is not entirely surprising that the thought of Kurth is suggested in close proximity to a discussion of Wagner's *Tristan*. Kurth's seminal study *The Crisis of Romantic Harmony in Wagner's 'Tristan'* (*Romantische Harmonik und ihre Krise in Wagner's 'Tristan'*) was of crucial importance to the understanding and reception of the musical language of the opera and was followed in 1925 by a lengthy and detailed study of Bruckner. The concepts Furtwängler puts forward here represent a synthesis of the ideas of Kurth and Schenker within a broader framework of the notion of the ceaseless striving of the will, or the daemonic force, driving artistic creation. The moment of collision between the individual will to expression and the will to expression latent in the material is the moment of *Einfall*. This suggests the ideas of the philosopher whose work formed the foundation of so much nineteenth-century musical thought: Artur Schopenhauer. It is, perhaps, significant that in this critique of atonal music written in 1947 Furtwängler draws directly or indirectly on the ideas of the most influential yet conservatively minded thinkers on musical matters of the early years of the twentieth century, Schenker, Kurth and Pfitzner, and relates their thought to that of the philosopher whose work had such a profound impact on Wagner, Nietzsche and Thomas Mann. The fundamental premise of Furtwängler's musical æsthetic is that tonal music and the laws of tonality are natural, intrinsic and rooted in the laws of nature (or 'Art'); in the case of atonal music the laws are manufactured, extrinsic and imposed from without (or 'Artifice'). Thus atonal music is antithetical to the organic artwork. Tonality is not the 'past', but the 'future'.

Having established that tonal music is rooted in natural laws, Furtwängler proceeds to expand on how the principles of tonality are rooted in the human condition; in so doing he raises the question of to what extent the tonal or atonal material of music corresponds to the biological constitution of man: 'the fluctuation between tension [Spannung] and relaxation [Entspannung] represents the rhythm of life; there is not a moment, as long as we breathe, in which one or the other does not prevail'.[30] Furtwängler explains the properties of the triad and the cadence, which is built on this triad. He also stresses that it is the function of these musical processes within the context of the whole which is the overriding factor; in so doing he brings the reader back to what

29 Ibid., p. 114; pp. 83–4 (translation amended). See Ernst Kurth, *Romantische Harmonik und ihre Krise in Wagners 'Tristan'* (Bern: Paul Haupt, 1920); *Bruckner* (Berlin: Max Hesses Verlag, 1925); also Lee A. Rothfarb, ed. and tr., *Ernst Kurth, Selected Writings* (Cambridge: CUP, 1991).
30 GM, p. 119; CM, p. 87 (translation amended).

is the central and most important recurring motive in his writings from his earliest correspondence to his final essays, which by this time had gathered a thick crust of ideological accretions: the idea of organic cohesion in a sense that would be understood by Ferdinand Tönnies. Atonal music lacks this property; it is therefore deficient in essential biological and organic values:

> But when it is over one asks oneself what one has really heard: the full synthesis, the meaning of the whole, is all too often not apparent. It is sometimes astonishing what wealth of intelligence is to be found in the permutations and combinations of atonal music; as an achievement of the intellect it can in certain circumstances rank extremely high. But the price it must pay for this from the biological point of view is a lack of the vital values.[31]

A further important property of tonal music is its sense of spatial logic or 'location' at any given point within the flow of the musical process; it is this that enables tonal music to be 'independent' of external images or an extra-musical programme. The listener must always know where he 'is' in any particular movement; it is this 'feeling for locality' which has definite organic value, for 'the desire to know where one is and where one is going constitutes one of the earliest instincts of organic life to be developed in man and beast alike'.[32] Atonal music lacks this biological property; it can therefore only be regarded as inferior:

> We cannot escape from the conclusion that a type of music which dispenses with a device to regulate tension and relaxation, thereby sacrificing the spatial precision [Ortsbestimmtheit] of tonality, must be considered as biologically inferior [biologisch minderwertig]. It does not depict forces running their course. [...] It is this element of biological insufficiency implicit in the substance of atonal music [...] which is at the root of the insuperable, stubborn opposition offered to this kind of music by the vast majority of the public.[33]

The resonances of Social Darwinism here thinly encoded do not sit well with the fact that the chief protagonist of atonal music, Arnold Schoenberg, was Jewish. Furtwängler considers that the phenomenon of atonal music resulted from the erroneous notion that artistic progress can be achieved through a complete break with past ideas rather than through a natural process of organic development. In expanding this point he arrives at the fundamental

---

31 Ibid., pp. 121–2; p. 89.
32 Ibid., pp. 122–3; p. 89.
33 Ibid., pp. 124–5; pp. 90–1.

reason why he believes tonality to be superior to atonality: tonality is in itself rooted and grafted in human experience.

> Not only is the art of antiquity and that last flower of the culture of antiquity, Christianity, absolutely convinced of the decisive importance of the human being, of the immortal soul of each individual, but all the art of more recent periods, down to modern times, takes it for granted. [...] Tonality is, as it were, a late child of this view of the world, and the masterpieces of tonal music have become the last and sweetest flower of the creative cultural genius of Europe.[34]

This view of the world, with its interest in the culture of antiquity and emphasis on the importance of the place of the individual within the world, was prototypical of the late-nineteenth-century culture of *Bildungsbürgertum*. Furtwängler's obsession with the idea that the laws of tonality are biological in origin, and his consequent use of biological metaphor, is a development of the all-pervading concept of the 'organic'. In this respect he shares similar premises to those on which Schenker constructed the theories which continued to exert such a potent and pervasive influence on Furtwängler's thought in the aftermath of the defeat of Nazism. The all-pervasive use of the biological metaphor itself is redolent of the ideas of Social Darwinism that nourished Schenker's notion of the hegemony of the Austro-German tradition. Furtwängler's censure of atonal music as a complex intellectual construct, which lacks foundation in the principles of organic growth, retains strong overtones of the non-rational censure of 'degenerate' art by the Nazis. Thus, in this additional chapter to his pre-war work of ten years earlier, Furtwängler follows an increasingly conservative, not to say reactionary, agenda. His defence of tonality notwithstanding, the intellectual affinities of the argument irrevocably reveal their roots in the conservative-nationalist discourses of the Wilhelmine Empire, which had gradually but inexorably transmuted into the cultural bedrock of National Socialism.

Furtwängler's essays on Mendelssohn and Schenker, the additional chapter of the *Conversations about Music*, together with his Second Symphony and its written exegesis 'Observations of a Composer' (to be considered in the next chapter), all originated in the period immediately following the fall of the Third Reich. They reveal the deeply conservative world-view of an increasingly embattled artist who found a degree of security and purpose through constantly reaffirming, almost to the point of obsession, the ideas of the late-nineteenth-century epoch from which he originated. The fact that

34 Ibid., pp. 126–8; p. 92.

this conservative-nationalist tradition, especially the organic world-view with its evolutionary and biological associations, became so closely intertwined and associated with National Socialism did not in any way help to distance Furtwängler from this ideology. On the contrary, although he was eventually exonerated by the de-Nazification tribunal and cleared of direct collaboration with the regime, he remained in his post-war writings a persuasive advocate of ideas whose dark side had been so relentlessly exploited by the Nazis. By reasserting the ideals of the 'other' Germany Furtwängler was ironically promoting the selfsame organic and biological world-view which had proved such a powerful tool in the hands of the ideologues from whom it was now politically expedient that he should appear to try to disassociate himself. The values of the 'other' Germany, of which he was so passionate an advocate, were those on which Nazi ideology was founded.

'On the Works of Hans Pfitzner' (14 August 1948)

It is apparent from surviving letters and writings that in the immediate post-war period the by now elderly and infirm Hans Pfitzner was a constant presence in the embattled Furtwängler's mind.[35] It is unclear why Furtwängler's early enthusiasm for Pfitzner's works, so evident in the letters concerning *Palestrina* and *Von deutscher Seele* considered earlier, did not result in their frequent inclusion in his concert or opera programmes during the years when he was effectively Germany's *Generalmusikdirektor*. It is puzzling that Pfitzner's hymn to conservative nationalism, *Von deutscher Seele*, virtually disappears from Furtwängler's programmes after his initial performances and was not given at all during the Nazi years. He gave a single performance of the death-haunted cantata *Das dunkle Reich* on 24 November 1930 and then appears to have dropped the piece. The *Palestrina* Preludes make occasional appearances in orchestral programmes; the opera *Das Herz* is included in the repertoire of the State Opera in the 1931/2 season; but Pfitzner's later instrumental works are confined to isolated individual performances. Furtwängler's attitude to Pfitzner during the Nazi years is ambivalent. In 1933, at the outset of the Nazi era, an entry in his Notebooks describes Pfitzner as 'a great living composer – *Palestrina* his greatest work';[36] on 2 February 1938 he took part in the founding of the Hans Pfitzner Society in Berlin when he shared the

---

35 For possible reasons, including the matter of a proposed government pension for Pfitzner, see Michael H. Kater, *Composers of the Nazi Era: Eight Portraits* (New York: OUP, 2000), pp. 170–1.
36 AZN, p. 93; NBKS, p. 55.

conducting with the composer. Yet following the defeat of Nazism a notebook
entry in 1946 rather disingenuously diagnoses in 'Pfitzner's particular style a
desire forcibly to impose an intellectual picture [geistiges Bild] on the external
world! There is something "National Socialist" in the very tendency.'³⁷ Yet
despite this cooling of the relationship, contact was never completely broken
off. In a letter to Helmut Grohe dated 12 February 1947 Furtwängler writes:
'I am very interested in what you say about Pfitzner. Everything to do with
German culture is so inexpressibly sad that it hardly bears mention. But for
Pfitzner and his art, his day will surely come again.'³⁸ On 30 August 1948,
to the same correspondent, Furtwängler asks: 'Is it right that Pfitzner is
composing again? How is he otherwise?'³⁹ At this point the aged Pfitzner was
indeed composing again: he was sketching a choral cantata setting for soloists,
chorus and orchestra of Goethe's darkly sibylline poem *Urworte, Orphisch*,
which deals with the daemonic as the source of created form.⁴⁰

In 1948, while Pfitzner was still alive, Furtwängler wrote a short article
simply entitled 'On the works of Hans Pfitzner'.⁴¹ This is a revealing
document for, as is often the case with Furtwängler's formally composed
essays, it tells us a good deal more about its author than about its subject.
It shows Furtwängler attempting to come to terms with the very different
context of the post-war years by reconnecting with his earlier artistic
influences, not to say ideologies. The immediate authorial agenda is unclear
but Furtwängler's autobiographical intention is apparent from the outset.

> The name of Hans Pfitzner will always for us Germans be linked with
> one work: the dramatic legend *Palestrina*. Hardly ever has a creative artist
> represented the position of the artist within his time, depicted his nature,
> his struggles, his suffering, indeed himself as perceptively and unsparingly
> as Pfitzner had done in *Palestrina*. This work is an autobiography, but one
> (otherwise than in the works of Strauss such as *Heldenleben* and *Intermezzo*)
> in which everything purely biographical appears absorbed and related back
> to something more essential which underlies it.

Furtwängler praises Pfitzner for ensuring that technique does not obscure
the 'spirit and sense of a work'. He sets Pfitzner up as an example of the

---

37 AZN, p. 274; NBKS, p. 168 (amended).
38 SPK Berlin, 55 Nachl. 13, W. Furtwängler, Kasten 18; *Briefe*, p. 155.
39 Ibid.; *Briefe*, pp. 186–7.
40 The work was incomplete at Pfitzner's death; the sketches were subsequently
    completed by Pfitzner's pupil Robert Rehan.
41 'Zu den Werken Hans Pfitzners', Zentralbibliothek Zürich, Nachl. W. Furtwängler:
    S 15; also in VMS, pp. 118–22. A translation of the complete essay is included in
    Appendix 1.

age when *Einfall* or musical inspiration was the source of musical creation. '"Musical inspiration" [Einfall] plays a larger role in his works than in those of his contemporaries.' Resonances of Spengler's excoriation of 'post-Faustian' music (discussed in Chapter 4) as overblown and manufactured are clearly evident in Furtwängler's praise of Pfitzner for 'never succumbing to the temptation of gigantism [Mammutismus], the excessive scale which the age of Strauss, Reger and Mahler honoured'. Moreover, 'not even the most brilliant development of musical "material" means anything unless it runs in parallel with an underlying expressive need'. The spirit pervading Pfitzner's works is the 'spirit of German music. Like Bruckner and Reger, Pfitzner is and remains in the narrower sense a "German" phenomenon.'

Hans Pfitzner died on 22 May 1949 while Furtwängler was on a concert tour of Italy. He responded by including as a tribute the three Preludes from *Palestrina* in the programmes of a tour of southern and western Germany he made with the Berlin Philharmonic in early June; he also conducted Pfitzner's *Symphony* (Op. 46) together with Bruckner's Eighth Symphony at the Salzburg Festival on 7 August 1949. On 9 June he wrote to Pfitzner's widow Mali:

> I think you know that I am and will always remain one of the staunchest and most passionate admirers of the great musician Pfitzner. That the relationship between us was tarnished in recent years is not a cause for reproach as I am certain he knew how much I admired both him and his music. [...] I have included the *Palestrina* Preludes in the individual concerts of the tour of the Berlin Philharmonic I am presently leading in south and west Germany. They are the most beautiful memorial for the dead that can be imagined. They make as profound an impression on the public as on us musicians. The spirit that emerges from these works is imperishable.[42]

In the following year, in a letter to Max Brockhaus of 11 April 1950, Furtwängler wrote: 'I regarded Pfitzner, if not the most purely musical, then one of the most significant composers of his generation – the generation of Strauss, Reger, Mahler and Pfitzner.' In a striking echo of Spengler he goes on to say:

> It is curious how the works of the previous generation, that of Brahms and Bruckner, are so much more lively and substantial. This is surely because they were less manufactured in design and intention and more the result of natural processes [Einfall].[43]

42 SPK Berlin, 55 Nachl. 13, W. Furtwängler, Kasten 25.
43 SPK Berlin, 55 Nachl. 13, W. Furtwängler, Kasten 7; *Briefe*, pp. 208–9.

When Wilhelm Furtwängler wrote that letter in 1950, four years before his own death in 1954 at the age of sixty-eight, he had completed his own Second Symphony and was engaged on the composition of a third – two extensive symphonic works in which the compositional voice of Pfitzner can clearly be heard. As will become apparent in the next chapter, Furtwängler's symphonies are romantic symphonies in a post-romantic age that nevertheless do, it seems, 'succumb to the temptations of gigantism'.

In considering Furtwängler from the converging perspectives of Pfitzner's *Palestrina* and Spengler's *Decline of the West* we can see these driving the longing for a return to an actual or imagined golden age of the past. The palpable sense of *Weltschmerz*, or world-weariness, arises not only from the immediate chaos caused by the defeat of Nazi Germany but from the notion that the thousand-year cultural cycle identified by Spengler had come to an end. It is clear that Furtwängler did not share the view of Goethe's Faust, that:

> the spirit of an earlier time,
> to us it is a seven-sealed mystery;
> And what you learned gentleman would call
> Its spirit, is its image, that is all,
> Reflected in your own mind's history.[44]

The image of that earlier time was reflected in the history of Furtwängler's mind as a lost reality. In 1945, in his lecture 'German and the Germans', as we saw at the beginning of this chapter, Thomas Mann said with reference to Goethe's *Faust*: 'It is a great omission of the legend and the poem, that they do not connect Faust with music. Faust must have been musical; he must have been a musician.' Furtwängler and Pfitzner were the embodiment of Mann's identification of the Faustian spirit and the daemonic with music. They shared many of the assumptions of Spengler's pessimistic historiography as defined in *The Decline of the West*: they were both 'Faustian' musicians in Spengler's 'post-Faustian' age, now compromised by an extreme and perverted form of Faustian ideology. Furtwängler in his Swiss refuge and Pfitzner in his old people's home in a suburb of Munich might be described as musical Spenglers. It must have seemed to them as though Spengler's apocalyptic prophecies of a post-cultural 'winter of discontent' had indeed come about.

---

44 die Zeiten der Vergangenheit / Sind uns ein Buch mit sieben Siegeln; / Was ihr den Geist der Zeiten heißt, / Das ist im Grund der Herren eigner Geist, / In dem die Zeiten sich bespiegeln. (*Faust*, Part 1, lines 574–9, tr. David Luke).

CHAPTER 8

FURTWÄNGLER AS SYMPHONIST

Tonality is not the past but the future.[1]

At this point it is appropriate to break off from tracing the progress of Furtwängler's thought through his writings and consider the significance and possible ideological implications of his return to active composition in the late 1930s when he was at the height of his prestige as conductor. Furtwängler is one of a significant group of composer/conductors that emerged in the immediate aftermath of Wagner. This was the age in which the workmanlike figure of the old-style court Kapellmeister (of which Hans Richter and Hermann Levi were among the last and most illustrious representatives) gave way to the figure of the star conductor as initially represented by Arthur Nikisch and later Arturo Toscanini. It is Nikisch and Toscanini, perhaps, who were the true precursors of the autocratic power-brokers of the podium later personified by Furtwängler's successor in Berlin: Herbert von Karajan. Furtwängler belonged to a much older tradition that traced its origins back to Wagner and even to Mendelssohn: artists in the broadest sense to whom the act of composition and performance were part of an indivisible creative process. Representatives of this tradition would include Weber as well as Mendelssohn; and then such luminaries as Hans von Bülow, to be followed by Gustav Mahler, Felix Weingartner, Richard Strauss, Hans Pfitzner, Alexander von Zemlinsky and Oskar Fried.

The young Wilhelm Furtwängler began to compose at a very early age; his first extant composition, *Ein Stückche* [*sic*] *von den Tieren* (A Little Piece about Animals) is dated 30 June 1893 and dedicated to his father. The manuscript sources of Furtwängler's entire output are all in the portion of the Furtwängler Nachlass held in the Zentralbibliothek Zürich. This collection contains the manuscripts of 120 compositions, ranging from an outpouring of youthful songs, piano pieces, choral works and so on, to three grandiose

---

1   Furtwängler, AZN, p. 304; NBKS, p. 188.

symphonies composed during the last fifteen years of his life. Furtwängler's earliest musical ambition was first and foremost to be a composer. He included a Symphonic Adagio in B minor of his own composition in his very first concert with the Kaim Orchestra of Munich in 1906; but as his career as a performer burgeoned from the time of his appointment in Lübeck onwards, his compositional ambitions were tempered by the increasing demands of his concert-giving activities. It was not until the late 1930s, following his accommodation with the Nazi regime in the wake of the Hindemith affair, that he began to compose again.

Furtwängler's return to active composition after a gap of some thirty years requires explanation. There are several possible reasons. There is the obvious factor that following his resignation from all his official posts in ostensible protest against Nazi cultural policy he was once again free to follow the path of the freelance artist and allow himself more time to compose. In his book *Lies and Epiphanies: Composers and their Inspiration*, Chris Walton has argued that a stronger motivation was that by the late 1930s his conservative, quasi-Brucknerian style was now ideologically acceptable and consonant with the prevailing spirit of the times.[2] The appropriation of Bruckner at the Regensburg 'Valhalla' ceremony in 1938 (described in Chapter 6) made the direction of Nazi cultural policy regarding music abundantly clear: 'progressive' music of the Second Viennese School of Schoenberg and his followers, and that of the *Neue Sachlichkeit* as represented by Hindemith and others, was un-German and degenerate.

Earlier in his career Furtwängler's youthful essays in symphonic form had been subjected to savage critical mauling. Adverse criticism was never well received by the hypersensitive Furtwängler, and the poor reception given to his early compositions may have been a factor in his decision to give priority to his career as a performing artist. By the late 1930s, however, the cultural climate seemed to have bypassed the experimentations of early modernism in the first decade of the century, and the tide of critical reception was now flowing in his favour. Hostility to anything that accorded with Nazi cultural values had effectively been silenced. Furtwängler's response was therefore to return to active composition. His Violin Sonata No. 1 in D minor, composed over an extended period between 1916 and 1935, was first performed in Leipzig on 4 March 1937, followed later in the same year by the premiere in Munich of the Symphonic Concerto for Piano and Orchestra with Edwin Fischer as soloist (26 October 1937). The alternative hypothesis that composition represented a form of inner emigration into a retreat from restrictions

---

2   Chris Walton, *Lies and Epiphanies: Composers and their Inspiration from Wagner to Berg*, esp. Ch. 4, 'Wilhelm Furtwängler and the Return of the Muse', pp. 94–109.

placed on him under a totalitarian regime is less convincing. The available documentary and circumstantial evidence does not support any idea that Furtwängler withdrew into some kind of inner world of his own creation, but rather that he responded to the more favourable prevailing circumstances. In July 1937 he wrote in an unpublished, untitled Memorandum reflecting further on the Hindemith case that:

> The underground Bolshevisation of music today, two years after the ban on Hindemith made him a martyr, which he by no means deserves to be, is nearly complete. It is hardly possible any more for someone like me, who stands for and writes a different kind of music, seriously to be heard.

Furtwängler became far more critical of Hindemith's music than in his 1934 published article discussed in Chapter 5. He now found Hindemith's music 'narrow in scope and spiritually empty'. In his view performances of Hindemith should nevertheless be permitted again. 'That is, as I know from many years of my own activity, the only way to counter these efforts: i.e. to reduce them to absurdity in the eyes of the world' through the judgement of the *Volk*.[3] Walton's hypothesis that Furtwängler's conservative idiom now accorded more directly with the cultural mores of the time is persuasive.[4]

Symphony No. 1 in B minor (1905–40)[5]

Furtwängler initially completed his First Symphony in B minor in 1940, although it is clear from the sources that he continued to work on the score for a further seven years. Furtwängler never himself gave a public performance and the symphony did not see the light of day during his lifetime. It must be assumed that he was never fully satisfied with the revisions and felt that the work remained 'unfinished'. The extensive first movement had its origins in 1906 as the piece Furtwängler chose to include in his first orchestral concert as his Symphonic Adagio in B minor. It begins with more than a passing resonance of Tchaikovsky's Sixth Symphony, also in B minor; the underlying fundamental structure broadly follows the Brucknerian binary pattern of

3   Zentralbibliothek Zürich, Nachl. W. Furtwängler: S 126, 2, TS, 'Der Fall Hindemith tritt jetzt', Bayreuth, July 1937.
4   For more on the notion of inner emigration, or survival through compromise, see John Williamson, *The Music of Hans Pfitzner*, Ch. 8. See also Thomas Mann, *The Genesis of a Novel*, tr. Richard and Clara Winston (London: Secker & Warburg, 1961), pp. 113–14.
5   Zentralbibliothek Zürich, Nachl. W. Furtwängler: WF 110b; Full Score (Berlin: Ries & Erler, 2001).

statement and restatement plus a coda, the restatement being a continuous development of material from the first through a process of dense and often over-repetitive motivic working. The extended *Bogen* profile, or arch form, reaches a climactic point at bar 558 before subsiding into a coda (*sehr ruhig*) which, with its prominent writing for bassoon, somewhat improbably recalls the close of *Die Meistersinger*, Act II. The second movement, again in B minor, is less obvious in its allegiances, being a rapid *perpetuum-mobile*-style scherzo driven by pounding motor-rhythms; but oddly there is no clearly defined contrasting trio section in the manner of its Brucknerian antecedents. The third movement (*Molto adagio*) in the tertiary related key of G major is headed by the portentous direction 'con devozione'. The movement opens with an expansive melodic idea for the strings:

Ex. 1   Furtwängler, Symphony No. 1, third movement, bars 1–7

With its prominent woodwind and polyphonic string writing, this is a thinly disguised attempt to recreate the grand Brucknerian symphonic adagio; the climax of the movement at Bar 209 bears the same harmonic stamp as that of the Adagio of Bruckner's Ninth Symphony, the work Furtwängler conducted at his first orchestral concert some three decades earlier in 1906. The Bruckner paradigm is continued in the prolix finale. Again the underlying teleological structure of statement and restatement plus coda is evident; the restatement eventually arrives in bar 659 on the tonic major (B major), in preparation for the expected and perhaps inevitable brass-dominated bombast of a closing statement recalling the chorale-like opening gesture. Furtwängler's First Symphony is certainly problematic: it is generally too long to sustain the developmental potential of the musical material; the motivic working is often excessively dense and over-repetitive; the quasi-Brucknerian 'Gesangsperiode' make attempts at lyrical invention but are often artificial and overwritten. It only rarely rises above the level of quotidian and contrived Kapellmeister music. It is perhaps indicative of a general dissatisfaction with the work that Furtwängler never programmed and performed his First Symphony in public, despite plentiful opportunities to do so.

Symphony No. 2 in E minor (1944–18 October 1945)[6]

In contrast, the Second Symphony in E minor became something of a signature work of Furtwängler's last years, occupying a significant place in his concert programmes and generating a studio recording. The autograph is catalogue WF119 and a study score was published in 1952 by Brucknerverlag Wiesbaden, the only orchestral score of Furtwängler to be so treated. The work was initially composed between an unspecified date in 1944 and, according to a letter to John Knittel, 18 October 1945.[7] The first performance took place in Berlin on 22 February 1948 under Furtwängler's own direction. In the manner of the First Symphony, it is an extensive work in four movements that takes approximately seventy-five minutes in performance. It again follows the romantic 'darkness to light' paradigm, beginning in a murky E minor and concluding with what the musicologist Deryck Cooke describes with reference to Bruckner as a 'blaze-up' in E major.[8] The tonic key of E minor immediately suggests Brahms' Fourth, and perhaps more remotely Tchaikovsky's Fifth Symphony, while the relatively modest instrumental forces required are those of a slightly expanded Brahms orchestra: triple woodwind plus cor anglais. Noticeably absent given the symphony's apparent Brucknerian lineage are the eight horns, four of which double with a quartet of Wagner tubas as called for by Bruckner in his last three symphonies. A strong musical voice is undoubtedly that of Hans Pfitzner. There is a striking resemblance between some of Furtwängler's thematic material and that of Pfitzner's Symphony in C major Op. 46 (1940), although at no point does Furtwängler achieve the formal cohesion and terse concision of Pfitzner's symphony. A further point of interest is how Furtwängler specifies the *Hauptstimme* and *Nebenstimme* [leading voice and secondary voice] with signs familiar from Schoenberg's scores, together with footnoted instructions to the conductor. It must be said, however, that he is not always consistent is his use of these signs, an unfortunate habit that can lead to confusion in trying to understand the music.

The first movement follows the sonata paradigm in that there are discernible divisions into exposition and development with a return of the opening material signifying a recapitulation. Schoenberg's terminology of principal and subordinate groups is more helpful here than any attempts to

6   Zentralbibliothek Zürich, Nachl. W. Furtwängler: WF119; Full score (Berlin: Ries & Erler, 2001); Study score (Wiesbaden: Brucknerverlag, 1952).
7   SPK Berlin, 55 Nachl. 13, W. Furtwängler, Kasten 22; *Briefe*, p. 116.
8   Deryck Cooke, 'Anton Bruckner', in *The Pelican History of the Symphony*, vol. 1 (Harmondsworth: Penguin Books, 1968), p. 291.

identify first and second subjects;[9] from the outset the music is in a state of continuous development through the use (one might say overuse) of familiar devices of sequence, fragmentation and all the rest of the late tonal period compositional toolkit. Tonally the movement is unusual in that rather than the expected dominant or tertiary opposition there is a strong pull towards the subdominant as the subordinate tonal area; indeed what might be termed the subordinate theme initially appears in the subdominant major (bar 43) and the tonality eventually settles over an extended pedal on A before the general pause signifying the end of the exposition (bar 228). The resolution of this tonal displacement comes in the recapitulation in the tonic major (bar 449) – thus signifying the ambiguity of mode between major and minor as an important compositional device. Although there is a clear ternary pattern at what might, in Schenkerian terms, be termed the middleground level, the fundamental structure, or *Ursatz*, is again better described in binary terms as statement and restatement plus a coda – or an extended A–A1 structure in which the restatement is an extended development of the statement, encompassing the tonal resolution required by the initial move to the subdominant but at the same time continuing to build to a grandiose restatement of subordinate group material over a chord of the tonic major (bar 596) before leading to an identifiable climax over a dominant pedal point (bar 622). This then subsides into a *tranquillo* coda (bar 641) beginning with material from the subordinate group recapitulated over a tonic pedal before ending with an explosive statement of the original and inverted versions of the opening theme counterpointed in contrary motion.

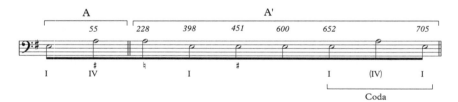

Ex. 2a   Furtwängler, Symphony No. 2, first movement, extended
tonal profile and binary structure: A (Statement) and A1 (Restatement)
plus Coda reaffirming tonic/subdominant polarity

9   See Arnold Schoenberg, *Fundamentals of Musical Composition* (London: Faber & Faber, 1967); see esp. Ch. 20, pp. 199–213.

Ex. 2b   Furtwängler, Symphony No. 2, first movement, bars 1–228, Statement, or First Model. Principal harmonic events and disposition of thematic material

The debt to Bruckner is apparent in the large-scale binary pattern under-pinning the movement; the four-square rhythmic patterns and rather contrived development of the material are, however, quite un-Brucknerian in character and there are no long-breathed 'Gesangsperioden' familiar from Bruckner's mature symphonic style. There are also distinct echoes of Richard Strauss and even Mahler, especially in the treatment of the horns and in some of the string writing.

The second movement, *Andante semplice (tranquillo)* has a far less clearly defined pedigree. Given its obvious debt to Bruckner, it is puzzling that this symphony lacks a 'grand Adagio' after the Brucknerian model. Rather the movement begins in the tertiary related key of C major and has the distinct character of a Brahmsian Romanze: the lyrical a clarinet melody in irregular rhythm over a pizzicato string accompaniment.

Ex. 2c   Furtwängler, Symphony No. 2, second movement, bars 1–5

This is followed by a second theme clearly derived from the principal theme of the first movement.

Ex. 2d   Furtwängler, Symphony No. 2, second movement, bars 14–20

Again the movement follows a clearly identifiable binary structure with the restatement (bar 113), an extensive development of the statement leading to a climax (bar 206), followed by a coda which is tonally open in preparation for the following movement. The musical processes here are very similar to the first movement, being best described as a continuous development almost on the Lisztian model of transformation of themes. This is the shortest and it may be said the most successful movement of the symphony: the movement is not too long for the musical substance.

The third movement in A minor continues the pattern of keys related by descending thirds while further emphasising the pull towards the subdominant as a primary tonal event of the symphony. It is ferociously energetic with a clear overall ternary structure; but rather than simply repeating the Scherzo after the trio there is a contracted restatement in which the two principal thematic elements are combined, to be followed by a brief coda (bar 801) that recalls the richly romantic central (or trio) section before ending with an explosion of energy. The Scherzo itself is based on two independent thematic ideas heard at the outset and at bar 140 – and, following the subdued beginning, the music is in constant motion driven by frenetic energy of almost Shostakovich-like ferocity.

Ex. 2e   Furtwängler, Symphony No. 2, third movement, bars 1–6

Ex. 2f   Furtwängler, Symphony No. 2, third movement, bars 140–5

From the point of view of outline structure the third movement is clear and relatively unproblematic. The same cannot, however, be said for the multisectioned finale. This movement is a lumbering symphonic behemoth, taking nearly half an hour in performance. Even the Furtwängler hagiographer and apologist Hans-Hubert Schönzeler admits that the length might be out of proportion to the musical substance.[10] Thematically, it is closely based on material from the preceding three movements. A notable feature is the solemn chorale intoned at the outset by brass and strings.

10 Schönzeler, *Furtwängler*, p. 146.

Ex. 2g Furtwängler, Symphony No. 2, finale, bars 5–8

This is followed by a broad melodic idea that, unsurprisingly in view of its strong Brucknerian pedigree, will end both the movement and the symphony in a coruscating blaze of E major, thus inevitably recalling the close of Bruckner's Seventh Symphony.

Ex. 2h Furtwängler, Symphony No. 2, finale, bars 13–17

A further idea is the equivalent of the Brucknerian 'Gesangsperiode' or long-breathed string melody.

Ex. 2i Furtwängler, Symphony No. 2, finale, bars 341–8

The overall structure is again based on a discernible binary foundation with the restatement beginning with the opening material in the dominant and consisting entirely of further development of material from the statement. Thus the first, second and fourth movements share a common structural foundation derived from the Brucknerian binary model.

Here, then, is a large-scale symphonic artefact composed during the later stages of the war and first presented to the public in 1947. Structurally it adheres most closely to the Brucknerian model, but in style and content there are clearly discernible influences of Richard Strauss, Pfitzner and even Mahler. There are three primary sources contemporaneous with the composition and first performance of the Second Symphony that are helpful in understanding the compositional intention: Furtwängler's *Notebooks*, the programme note he wrote for the first performance ('Observations of a

Composer')[11] and the seventh and final chapter of *Conversations about Music* (*Gespräche über Musik*), added in 1947 (considered in the previous chapter). The two 'red threads' that recur to the point of obsession throughout Furtwängler's writings, the organic and the biological, are readily apparent in his exegesis of his own music. We have seen that Furtwängler was heavily influenced by the ideas of Schenker, particularly those formulated during the 1920s. To Furtwängler the intrinsic value of an artwork was not novelty, experimentation or innovation, but the extent to which it conformed to the organic ideal. The question confronting the composer was, simply put: 'How do we create a whole?'[12] He also shared the Schenkerian assumption of the governance of the cadence: 'The cadence is a structural element, defining the organic form, with a beginning, a middle and an end.'[13]

> The cadence is the basis of tonality, i.e. the expression of music within the scope of definite keys. It is the cadence which determines the key. Strictly tonal music can indeed be described as a closed series of cadences. A Bach fugue or a movement of a Beethoven symphony – such as the first movement of Symphony No. 9 – literally represents a cadence on a gigantic scale.[14]

The biological metaphor is much more problematic and difficult to deal with but, as with so much of Furtwängler's thinking, it derives in part from Goethe's *On Morphology* and its continuation in nineteenth-century humanistic thought rather than the specious science of the Social Darwinists and Houston Stewart Chamberlain.

> It is sometimes astonishing what wealth of intelligence is to be found in the permutations and combinations of atonal music; as an achievement of the intellect it can in certain circumstances rank extremely highly. But the price it must pay for this from the biological point of view is a lack of the vital values. The lack of orientation in atonal music renders it *biologically inferior*. It does not depict forces running their course.[15]

Later he goes on to say that 'the substance of music arranged according to the laws of tonality manifests *biological* fact – not physical or cosmic fact'.[16]

---

11 Furtwängler, TW, pp. 205–8; FM, pp. 23–4 (translations amended).
12 Ibid., p. 206; p. 24.
13 Ibid., p. 207; p. 24.
14 GM, p. 113; CM, p. 83 (translations amended).
15 Ibid., p. 124; p. 90.
16 Ibid., p. 129; p. 94.

What might Furtwängler have meant by the entry in his notebook, 'tonality is not the past but the future'? To say that Furtwängler was a basilisk-like reactionary who was opposed on principle to any form of atonal music is not entirely supported by the evidence; but he did have very serious reservations that he expressed in stronger and more uncompromising terms as he grew older. 'It is a reality, and none the less so if it manifests itself, as some people think, more in formulas and designs evolved by theoreticians than in great achievements.'[17] What is abundantly clear from his writings is that to Furtwängler the decline of tonality was indicative of the cultural disintegration identified by Oswald Spengler in *Decline of the West*. The future of music must rest securely on tonal foundations.

Symphony No. 3 in C sharp minor (1946–54)[18]

The Symphony No. 3 in C sharp minor occupied Furtwängler intermittently from 1946 until his death on 30 November 1954. The choice of C sharp minor as the governing tonality recalls not only Beethoven's late String Quartet Op. 131 (a work which Furtwängler, following Wagner, held in particularly high esteem) but also Hans Pfitzner's Symphony Op. 36a (1932), derived from his slightly earlier String Quartet in C sharp minor Op. 36 (1925). The Third Symphony occupies the same territory as its immediate precursor, but at the same time there is an element of concision and concentrated expression absent from the first two symphonies. The first movement lasts a mere 147 bars. The dark, brooding opening (marked *Largo mesto, pesante*) generates a process of dense motivic development that gives way at Bar 41 to a broad, elegiac string melody which extends into an almost Tchaikovskian episode with strong resonances of the *Symphony Pathétique*, a work which, as we have seen, Furtwängler included in his Berlin programmes following his return to concert-giving in Germany.[19] The characteristic process of motivic intensification reaches the climactic point of the movement at bar 120 before subsiding into a coda (bars 127–47) ending on an unresolved dominant (G sharp). There follows another *perpetuum mobile* movement of ferocious

17 Ibid., p. 109; p. 80.
18 Zentralbibliothek Zürich, Nachl. W. Furtwängler: WF 120; Full Score (Berlin: Ries & Erler, 2001).
19 Furtwängler appears to have had a strong affinity with Tchaikovsky's Symphony No. 6. In November 1938 he made a studio recording with the Berlin Philharmonic. It is one of his most highly regarded pre-war studio recordings. There is also a recording of a performance given in Cairo with the Berlin Philharmonic, 19 or 22 April 1951. See John Ardoin, *The Furtwängler Record* (Portland, OR: Amadeus Press, 1994), pp. 189–90.

energy with a more lightly scored contrasting central section. As with the
second movement of the Second Symphony, the return of the opening is not
a literal reprise but a varied and intensified reworking of the same musical
material which reaches a climactic point at bar 546 before coming to a
sudden and abrupt halt.

The third movement in the relative major E major (*Adagio, sehr langsam*)
is probably the most successful movement in all three symphonies: in a
relatively compact ternary structure of only 154 bars, it reaches a sustained
level of compositional invention only sporadically achieved elsewhere in
Furtwängler's symphonic output. Again there are strong resonances of the
slow finale of Tchaikovsky's Sixth Symphony in the opening interrogative
antecedent string gesture, which is almost Mahlerian in its intensity.

Ex. 3a   Furtwängler, Symphony No. 3, third movement, bars 1–5

The terse consequent phrase over a tonic pedal articulated in triplets by
divisi string basses (bars 13–16) is scored for divisi violas (à 4) and cellos
(à 3) that recalls the disposition of instrumental voices in Richard Strauss'
Metamorphosen (1945).

Ex. 3b   Furtwängler, Symphony No. 3, third movement, bars 13–14

The second musical paragraph is dominated by a grand Adagio melody first introduced in bar 70.

Ex. 3c   Furtwängler, Symphony No. 3, third movement, bars 70–3

This is further developed from bar 82 onwards towards a brass-dominated rhetorical gesture at the climactic point (bar 105). The opening string theme returns at bar 125 in a contracted reprise before the movement subsides into a serene E major coda recalling the closing bars of the Adagio of Bruckner's Ninth.

Once again strong compositional influences are discernible: in common with all Furtwängler's symphonic movements the overall structure is again evident of its Brucknerian lineage; the melodic writing owes a good deal to Tchaikovsky and Mahler in its elegiac lyricism; there are even traces of the Sibelius of *En Saga* in some of the antiphonal writing for strings and woodwind in thirds (bar 42) and of *Tapiola* in the sombre sonorities of divisi violas and cellos (see Ex. 3b). Nevertheless, the individual musical voice here rises above the level of the derivative and is unmistakably Furtwängler's own. There is a palpable sense of world-weariness (*Weltschmerz*). This sense of loss and longing for a world now irretrievably lost shares much in common with Richard Strauss *Metamorphosen*, a work which, as we have seen, Furtwängler conducted infrequently but memorably in the post-war period.

Furtwängler was at work on revisions to the finale at the time of his admission to the Ebersteinberg clinic near Baden-Baden on 12 November 1954. He evidently did not regard the symphony as entirely finished. It was first performed in Berlin on 26 January 1955 in tribute to its recently deceased composer as a three-movement work, rather in the manner of Bruckner's Ninth, and conducted by Furtwängler's younger contemporary, Joseph Keilberth. In this form it was given occasional performances and presented by Wolfgang Sawallisch on 7 January 1980, in commemoration of the twenty-fifth anniversary of Furtwängler's death. It was only later that the unrevised finale was made available to enable the work to be given in its four-movement form. The wisdom of this decision is open to question. At nearly 900 bars in length the finale is once again out of proportion to the rest of the symphony. The familiar gestures of the chorale-like theme, the *immer ruhig* cross reference to the third movement, and the grand rhetorical closing statement are all there and bound together with a degree of rhythmic monotony that quickly seems to exhaust the developmental potential of the musical material. At no point does it reach the level of compositional invention sporadically achieved in the first two movements and largely sustained throughout the Adagio.

Although Furtwängler's compositional achievement across these three symphonies is at best inconsistent and at worst no more than workmanlike, the Adagio of the Third Symphony reaches the same level as that of a more recognised composer such as his contemporary Hans Pfitzner. His intentions can be discerned from the titles for the four separate movements noted in his diary but subsequently omitted from the autograph: 1. Das Verhängnis (Fate); 2. Im Zwang zum Leben (The Life Force); 3. Jenseits (Beyond); 4. Der Kampf geht weiter (The struggle goes on). In respect of his Second Symphony, Furtwängler had previously noted: 'With this work I sought to provide neither a mythical and mathematical construction, nor an ironic and sceptical consideration of the age, but nothing more or less than a tragedy.'[20] In the Adagio of the Third Symphony, this threnody for a lost Faustian world of striving for transcendence, he may be said to have succeeded.

Furtwängler's three large-scale symphonic utterances, which reached their final form between 1940 and 1954, are among the last generic examples of the Romantic symphony. No matter what the level of compositional invention, there are clearly discernible features shared by all three works: the ubiquitous structural device of statement and restatement is clearly Brucknerian in origin, as are the moments of heightened lyrical intensity invoking Bruckner's long-breathed 'Gesangsperioden'. In all three symphonies the music tends to emerge out of silence rather than opening with a strong symphonic gesture in the manner of Brahms. Unsurprisingly, the harmonic language is relatively conservative; there is only a limited attempt to engage with the chromatic idioms of the later Wagner, especially *Tristan* and *Parsifal*, or the enhanced dissonances of Strauss in *Elektra* and the pre-atonal Schoenberg. Furtwängler's harmonic language, while chromatically inflected, is rooted in secure tonal foundations. It is almost as if within this outwardly Brucknerian framework Furtwängler is recalling the earlier German romantic world of Schubert, Weber and Schumann.

For Furtwängler music must be imbued with a vital force of organic origin that can only manifest itself in tonality. Thus in the last decade of his life he produced in his Second and Third Symphonies two large-scale works composed entirely according to tonal principles in defiance of what he regarded as the disintegration of the culture that formed him. Here comparisons with Strauss' *Metamorphosen* are instructive. As is the case with

20 Furtwängler, AZN, p. 344; NBKS, p. 213.

Metamorphosen these symphonies might be seen not only as a reaffirmation of Wilhelmine conservative-nationalist values but also as indicative of the hopes Furtwängler initially had for Nazi Germany as signalling a return to the certainties of Bismarckian authoritarianism and its reverence of high culture; hopes that finally vanished for ever in the catastrophe of 1945.

It becomes clear with increasing study and familiarity that, with the possible exception of the second movement of Symphony No. 2 (Andante) and the third movement of Symphony No. 3 (Adagio), the level of compositional invention is not consistently equal to the expectations and demands of the genre. The musical spaces are simply too large to be filled by the developmental potential of the musical material, much of which is distinctly mundane in character. Within the overarching binary structure already identified, Furtwängler does not follow the Brucknerian practice of presenting his musical material in blocks; rather his excessive use of the familiar devices of development through sequential repetition and intensification through motivic fragmentation and contraction give the impression that, come what may, he will at all costs create 'an organic entity, a whole'. There are, however, long sections in all three symphonies where the treatment of the material sounds distinctly contrived rather than the result of the naturally self-generating organic process that was Furtwängler's compositional ideal for the creation of a living rather than synthetic artwork. Like Hans Pfitzner in his polemic 'On Musical Inspiration' (Über musikalische Inspiration, 1940), Furtwängler considered inspiration – *Einfall* – to be the essence of all music. The difficulty here is that, as Shelley so aptly put it in the lines inscribed by Elgar over the score of his Second Symphony that Furtwängler so derided, the 'spirit of delight' came but rarely.[21] It is almost as if Furtwängler's subconscious compositional drivers are not the generative properties latent in his invented musical material, 'inspiration' in Pfitzner's sense, but the instinctive, deeply experienced responses to musical line and gesture that conditioned his hearing of Beethoven, Brahms, Wagner, Bruckner and, as evidenced in these symphonies, the later Tchaikovsky and Richard Strauss. In Furtwängler's case, composition and performance cannot be divided into two separate acts but were part of the same indivisible, organic and supra-rational intuitive musical process, as he might have found it: the daemonic. The lasting value of these symphonies is therefore not so much as symphonic utterances in their own right, but as guides to the creative musical energies

---

21 SPK Berlin, 55 Nachl. 13, W. Furtwängler, Kasten 27; *Briefe*, p. 242. Furtwängler dismissively makes a disparaging comparison between the 'barren routine of E. Elgar' and the music of a 'truly great Master'.

that made Furtwängler's performances of the central Austro-German repertory so compelling.

The by now all too familiar usages of the ubiquitous organic and biological metaphors in the conservative discourses of the Wilhelmine Empire and Weimar Republic invoke the idea of retrospective cultural memory that engages directly with the grand Austro-German symphonic tradition of the nineteenth century. The moments of lyrical intensity that occur to a greater or lesser extent throughout all three works, and which in the Adagio of the Third Symphony reach a level of musical expression unique in Furtwängler's output, are irrevocably associated with ideas of loss and abandonment. The romantic symphony as a genre invoked the certainties of a past authoritarian age that had been irretrievably swept away by the ideological storms that convulsed Germany in the first half of the twentieth century. Furtwängler's last two symphonies are distant echoes of a lost culture that had now disappeared beyond recall. These symphonic statements in the grand style are giving a musical voice to the very experience of cultural disintegration: the irony is that in so doing they undermine the tradition they superficially sought to maintain.[22]

22 I am very grateful to my Oxford colleagues Laurence Dreyfus and David Maw for their helpful comments and feedback on an earlier version of this chapter.

CHAPTER 9

'ALL GREATNESS IS SIMPLICITY' (1951-54)

Those, I think, who have looked so long and deeply into the complexities of the spirit ask of outward things merely that they should possess one quality above all: simplicity.[1]

The final period of Furtwängler's life was a time during which he gradually regained a measure of his pre-war prestige both at home and abroad, in spite of the fact that the ambivalence of his public position during the years of Nazi rule continued to be a hotly debated and highly contentious issue. From 1948 onwards he became a regular visitor to the annual Salzburg Festival where the operas he conducted included Beethoven's *Fidelio* (1948); Mozart's *Die Zauberflöte* and Verdi's *Otello* (1951), *Don Giovanni* (1954) and Weber's *Der Freischütz* (1954). With *Don Giovanni*, *Fidelio* and *Der Freischütz* Furtwängler returned to three works with which he had begun his career as Hofkapellmeister in Mannheim in 1915.

On 29 July 1951 Furtwängler directed Beethoven's Ninth Symphony as part of the reopening ceremony of the Bayreuth Festival after a six-year silence.[2] This iconic event was in many ways a 'Reconsecration of the House' after the years of American occupation. It linked back directly in the historical memory not only to the performance conducted by Wagner himself on 22 May 1872 when Furtwängler's mentor, the young Arthur Nikisch, was among the orchestral violinists; but also in more recent times to the appropriation of the work by the Nazis, as exemplified by the performance Furtwängler conducted in Berlin on 19 April 1942, the eve of Hitler's birthday.[3] The reopening of Bayreuth was therefore an event of considerable political as well as cultural significance. Winifred Wagner, daughter-in-law of the composer, Intendant

---

1 Thomas Buddenbrook, in *Buddenbrooks*, pp. 537–8.
2 See Spotts, *Bayreuth*, pp. 207–9 and Ch. 7; Hans Mayer, *Richard Wagner in Bayreuth* (Zurich and London: Belser, 1976), pp. 177–85; Geoffrey Skelton, *Wieland Wagner: The Positive Sceptic* (London: Gollancz, 1971), pp. 98–9; Richard Osborne, *Herbert von Karajan: A Life in Music* (London: Chatto & Windus, 1998), pp. 300–3.
3 See present work, pp. 167–8.

during the Nazi period and close personal friend of Hitler, was forbidden by the occupying powers from taking any further part in the running of the festival. A new administration was formed under the artistic direction of Winifred's eldest son Wieland, whose austere, psychoanalytical productions were in marked contrast to the portentous stagings of Tietjen and Preetorius which had adorned the Festspielhaus stage during the Nazi years. Wieland's productions appeared to signal a break with the festival's immediate past. However, all was not as it seemed. In a wide-ranging article the historian Neil Gregor interrogates the received view that the festival administration wanted to move on from the years of Nazi patronage.[4] Gregor's central argument, that there was a strong but covert agenda of continuity with the past, is supported by the roster of conductors recruited to preside in the covered orchestra pit. Furtwängler, who as we have seen, had conducted regularly at the festival during the Nazi period, was invited to return as chief conductor. He eventually declined but did agree to direct the opening performance of Beethoven's Ninth Symphony. The choice of the festival administration then fell on Hans Knappertsbusch (1888–1965), who although ostensibly out of favour with the Nazis, had conducted on high-profile occasions such as Hitler's birthday celebrations in 1943. The second conductor was the figure who more than any other had risen to fame as a result of the Nazi politicisation of music: Herbert von Karajan (1908–89).

Furtwängler's 1951 Bayreuth performance of the Ninth Symphony is preserved on record and has long been considered an iconic item in the Furtwängler discography. It is worth noting that this was also the period during which he began to realise the potential of the gramophone record as a means of preserving his recreative art. The majority of the recordings for which he is best remembered, and which subsequently proved to be the foundation on which his posthumous fame rests, date from the early 1950s.[5] In a letter in early 1953 to the recording company His Master's Voice, Furtwängler wrote:

When I finally heard my recording of *Tristan* in its entirety, I was astonished at its effect. Without the problems of staging, it becomes ever more apparent just how extraordinary are the musical cohesion and tireless inspiration of this unique work. Although records can never be a substitute for the communal experience of music in the concert hall, in Wagner's case the effect of the music can be just as powerful as in a stage performance.[6]

---

4   Neil Gregor, 'Beethoven, Bayreuth and the Origins of the Federal Republic of Germany', in *English Historical Review*, vol. 126, no. 521, pp. 835–77.
5   E.g. Wagner, *Tristan und Isolde* (1952).
6   SPK Berlin, 55 Nachl. 13, W. Furtwängler, Kasten 20; *Briefe*, 239.

'Bach' (1951)

Two further essays dating from the same year as the reopening of Bayreuth are indicative of Furtwängler's continuing championship of conservative ideology. In March of that year he published an article entitled simply 'Bach', which sheds considerable light on his position relative to the question of Bach reception in post-war Germany.[7] The history of Bach reception in the nineteenth century is complex.[8] Bach's first biographer, J. N. Forkel (1749–1818), who wrote his biography of the composer in 1802 at a time when stirrings of national identity were emerging as a potent artistic force, appropriated the composer (in a move strikingly prescient of the Nazi adoption of Bruckner in 1937) as an icon of the newly emergent cultural nationalism and search for a national identity. As we saw in Chapter 1, he wrote: 'And this man, the greatest musical poet and the greatest musical orator that ever existed, and probably ever will exist, was a German. Let his country be proud of him; let it be proud, but, at the same time, worthy of him!'[9] Later in the century Richard Wagner, in his essay 'Was ist Deutsch' (1865), written at the time of the composition of *Die Meistersinger*, described Bach as 'the musical wonderman, Sebastian Bach'. He continued:

> If, however, we wish to account for the amazing rebirth of the German spirit in the field of poetic and philosophical literature we can do so only by learning from Bach what the German spirit is in truth, where it dwelt and how it restlessly shaped itself anew when it seemed to have vanished altogether from the world.[10]

In the period immediately following the defeat of Nazism German musical life sought to rediscover and reinvent itself; as part of this process Bach was promoted as an ideal of German music. Furtwängler's opening remarks share the same idealised view of Bach:

> Of all great composers, Bach, since the rediscovery of his music at the beginning of the nineteenth century, must be the one whose standing has been subject to the least fluctuation. He remains today what he has always

7   Furtwängler, 'Bach'; Zentralbibliothek Zürich, Nachl. W. Furtwängler: S 20; published in *Deutsche Rundschau* (Gelsenkirchen, 1951), pp. 249–52; TW, pp. 214–20; FM, pp. 27–31.
8   See Bernd Sponheur, 'Reconstructing Ideal Types of the "German" in Music', in Applegate and Potter, eds, *Music and German National Identity*, pp. 48–52.
9   Forkel, 'On Johann Sebastian Bach's Life, Genius and Works', *The Bach Reader*, eds David and Mendel, 353.
10 GSD, vol. 10, pp. 36–53; Eng. edn, PW, vol. 4, pp. 151–69.

been – the divine creator on his throne above the clouds, beyond the reach of all others.[11]

Bach came to be regarded (quite unhistorically) as an unimpeachable absolute of music; in endowing the composer with ultimate musical authority Furtwängler invokes the by now all too familiar tropes of earlier discourses.

> Here concentration on the moment is combined with underlying breadth; the fulfilment of the temporal with a truly sovereign view of the whole. Bach's music has a simultaneous sense of proximity and distance; a realisation of the here and now; a mastery of structure and a fundamental awareness of the power of the whole. It combines 'close, lived through experience' [Nah-Erleben] with 'distance hearing' [Fernhörens]; as such it is an example of biological certainty such as we seldom find elsewhere in all of music.[12]

The idea of 'Nah-Erleben', or 'near-experiencing', is enclosed in quotation marks in both typescript sources and printed sources. Furtwängler's use of the term here is sufficiently close in meaning to construct a hypothesis that it is most likely a reference to Dilthey's idea of 'Nach-Erleben' or 're-experiencing'. For Dilthey, 'Nach-Erleben' is a means of experiencing after the event something that is actively creative rather than reproductive, such as the idea of the organic unity of a work of art. In literary terms *nacherleben* is a creative understanding that may go beyond the original. Its task is to understand a text as an unfolding continuity whereby the fragments of life that an author selects are articulated into a unified theme.[13] The term 'Fernhören' is a clear and unequivocal reference to Schenker's concept of distance hearing considered in Chapter 7.

As is by now expected, the ultimate measure against which Furtwängler evaluates Bach's music is the familiar trope of the 'whole'. In the course of the remainder of the essay, Bach is praised for his ability to create an entity, for his 'inexhaustible, free-ranging imagination', and for creating in the *Matthäus Passion* a work dominated by a single ethos and comparable 'only to that colossal achievement of the romantic period: Wagner's

---

11 TW, p. 214; FM, pp. 27–8.
12 TW, p. 215 (author's translation). See also FM, p. 28. Ronald Taylor's translation conveys the sense of this passage admirably; but in the process the resonances of Dilthey and the reference to Schenker are lost.
13 See Rudolf A. Makkreel, *Dilthey: Philosopher of the Human Studies* (Princeton: Princeton UP, 1975), pp. 329 and 361. Also Jacob Owensby, *Dilthey and the Narrative of History*, pp. 155–9.

Tristan'.[14] Furtwängler's view of Bach is essentially that of the romantic, of the expressive æsthetic of Friedrich von Hausegger. He acknowledges as much himself when he writes: 'Seen from one angle, Bach is the greatest of the Romantics. The image that we have of him today was created by the Romantics. Subsequent ages may have broadened that image but they have not changed it.'[15]

'Beethoven and Us' (1951)

The process of advancing the cause of the romantic æsthetics of the previous century in the very different intellectual climate of the post-war period continued in a lecture entitled 'Beethoven and Us' ('Beethoven und Wir').[16] In the evaluation of Furtwängler's post-war thought this essay occupies an especially significant place. Here, within the framework of an extended analytical exegesis of the first movement of Beethoven's Fifth Symphony, Furtwängler draws together the threads of the system which had energised his creative activity for almost half a century. In the course of this the extent of his adherence to the conservative ideology of the Wilhelmine era is once again apparent. In his Bach essay he historicised the composer as a manifestation of the expressive æsthetic of the previous century; in 'Beethoven and Us' he historicises himself by demonstrating the deeply conservative, not to say reactionary, reception of Beethoven which found such potent, and to Furtwängler such persuasive, support in Schenkerian thought.

Furtwängler's supra-rational position is a recurring motive in his later writings. What matters to him, as he believes it did for Beethoven, is the 'sound' of the music rather than any implied intellectual construct:

> Beethoven puts the sound first. For him music is something to be listened to, not something thought out. This is an important point for us musicians today. To Beethoven, what mattered above all was the process of listening as an immediate, biologically-conditioned experience [biologisch bedingter Ablauf]. Music that was not heard, no matter how 'correct' it might be, simply did not exist as far as he was concerned.[17] In his eyes the grasp of

---

14 TW, p. 218; FM, p. 29.
15 TW, p. 220; FM, p. 30.
16 'Beethoven und Wir: Bermerkungen über den Ersten Satz der Fünften Symphonie', given on 20 August 1951 in the Salzburg 'Mozarteum'. SPK Berlin, 55 Nachl. 13: Schriften Furtwänglers, Kasten 45; TW, pp. 221–52; FM, pp. 40–58.
17 This calls to mind the mischievous quip attributed to Sir Thomas Beecham: 'A musicologist is a man who can read music but who can't hear it.' See Atkins and Newman, *Beecham Stories*, p. 68.

the formal structure of a work was an absolute precondition for a grasp of the meaning of that work as a whole, and as these opening bars of the Fifth Symphony show, clarity of structure was among his first and unconditional demands. That meant that it was not sufficient for the structure just to be latent in the work as it stood – which it was anyway in the whole of European music in Beethoven's time; it had to be directly felt and heard, had to get 'in one's blood', so to speak.[18]

The biological metaphor is again evident, and in addition Furtwängler touches on an issue which is of crucial importance in conditioning his reception of Beethoven: by making an appeal for Beethoven to be heard through the ears of the early nineteenth century he is historicising the act of listening. He seems to suggest that Beethoven's music should be heard as if through Beethoven's ears.

'Beethoven and Us' is unusual among Furtwängler's writings in that it concerns itself with a detailed exegesis of a specific musical object. By now his explanation of musical process in terms of his organic world-view is predictable, if not inevitable. In this essay, however, he additionally and significantly introduces the notion of 'periodisation' (*Periodisierung*) as a means of revealing the underlying musical structure:

> It reflects a fundamental biological need of all creation. The periodisation of music was not just a matter of intellectual concern, a way of helping people to understand a piece, but something that corresponded to a basic, elemental need felt throughout the whole of existence. The modern view that non-periodic music, with its irrational rhythms, was a feature of an earlier, more natural phase of musical thought and feeling has nothing to commend it. Historically, irregular, irrational rhythms have always been countered by the strict periodisation of ratio. Put another way: behind irregular rhythms lies the euphoric spirit of freedom that scorns the discipline of structure, whereas rational structure aims at the creation of form, which seeks to absorb and give expression to all the forces of life, including those of freedom and irrationality.[19]

Furtwängler's discussion of periodisation calls to mind the work of the Wagnerian analyst, Alfred Lorenz (1869–1939), whose 'discovery' of extended

---

18 TW, pp. 225–6; FM, p. 42 (amended). In the original German text the final phrase reads: 'Sie muß sozusagen "ins Blut gehen"'. The ideological resonances suggested by this turn of phrase are not immediately apparent in translation. As with Schenker, Furtwängler's texts can unwittingly become 'sanitised' through the process of translation.

19 TW, p. 231; FM, pp. 45–6.

periods as a means of explaining the form of Wagner's operas was highly influential. Although there is no specific reference to Lorenz in this essay his influence is clearly discernible. Indeed, Lorenz shared Furtwängler's biological conception of musical form when he wrote: 'Form is the breath of a work of art, and the method of its breathing the deepest expression of its inner life. The constructive framework of a piece of music is its spirit.'[20]

In 'Beethoven und Wir' Furtwängler makes his clearest and most direct acknowledgement of Schenker and his analytical method. The following passage, with its references to the Lorenzian concept of periodisation and the Schenkerian concepts of foreground (*Vordergrund*) and background (*Hintergrund*) merits extended quotation in that it both represents a cogent synthesis of the two analytical methods and provides a telling analogy of musical form and process as ideology:

I have already pointed out that it is the changing periodisation that constitutes the 'action' of the movement, the 'foreground' so to speak. On the broader front the movement can be divided into larger, regular periods and groups of periods that give scope for further correlations and analogies, making up the background. This background provides the network of links between the parts. Thus each time a theme reappears, whether in the middle of a movement or at the end, its nature has changed, because it now bears with it further associations of the past and presents itself in a new light. The construction of a whole, as for example in the first movement of the Fifth Symphony, is only possible because this background is constantly and uninterruptedly present in the listener's mind. It is this background which gives all Beethoven's works, whose foreground seems dominated by violent outbursts and eruptions, their coherence and which shrouds them in an atmosphere of peace and serenity. As the foundation of the structure as a whole, it allows the stream of intensity to build up into climaxes, while at the same time acknowledging the interplay between tension and relaxation [Spannung und Entspannung] that is an inborn feature of all existence. Such a work is thus a simultaneous presentation of a foreground of spontaneous action governed by a fundamental background, a nexus of interconnections from which the foreground derives its freedom of action and its meaning.

I would like to make a passing observation. I have referred a great deal to periodisation in music, specifically Beethoven's music, perhaps implying that nothing else matters. Certainly, the structural aspect is of fundamental importance, particularly in so-called 'absolute' music, and one will never get to the heart of this music if one does not make structure the point of

20 Alfred Lorenz, 'Betrachtungen über Beethoven's Eroica-Skizzen: Ein Beitrag zur Psychologie des Schaffens', *Zeitschrift für Musikwissenschaft*, vol. 7 (1924–25), p. 420; quoted in Stephen McClatchie, *Analyzing Wagner's Operas*, p. 24.

departure. At the same time, the structural web of abstract tensions and relaxations by no means constitutes the whole content of this music, for these tensions are human in origin and presented as objects for human experience.[21]

Furtwängler continues his exegesis of the movement in the manner so characteristic of him: Beethoven's music is the result of a self-generating, creative process in which even the composer himself is reluctant to interfere. As a development of this concept he extends his use of the biological metaphor by attributing to the musical materials masculine and feminine characteristics:

> To a greater degree than any other composer, not excluding Mozart and Bach, he assigned each melody, each motif, each subject its individual place. The masculine [Männliche] and the feminine [Weibliche], the strong-willed and the gentle, the tiniest detail and the all-embracing panorama – everything comes together to form a harmonious unity that defies understanding. Beethoven is the great 'lawgiver' [Gesetzgeber] of music.[22]

Furtwängler proceeds to present Beethoven as the paradigm of the absolute musician. Beethoven's music exists only within its own terms of reference and evolves from exclusively musical data. Yet the form is no accident of the musical process; rather it is the result of the refinement and simplification of the musical material. There is a clearly discernible line of descent traceable from the position stated in Furtwängler's early correspondence with Bertel von Hildebrand to this utterance of fifty years later.[23] The idealistic and conservative mindset of this essay becomes even more apparent when he further explains Beethoven's creative process by evoking Goethe's thought patterns:

> His aim was clearly to find the simplest way of formulating his thoughts, the 'created form' [geprägte Form] of which Goethe wrote. A simplicity of this kind is no everyday phenomenon. It has what one might be tempted to call the power of redemption.
>   For anybody who does not understand what is at stake, the path from complexity to simplicity may look like the path from wealth to voluntary poverty. And whoever fails to understand the meaning of the process of liberation and purification to which Goethe's couplet points will fail to recognise the blessings that this simplicity has brought.[24]

---

21 TW, pp. 231–2; FM, pp. 46–7 (amended).
22 Ibid., p. 238; p. 50.
23 See present work, pp.35–8.
24 TW, p. 241; FM, pp. 51–2.

Furtwängler thus invokes in his discussion of Beethoven the most powerful literary and philosophical influence on the formation of his world-view: Goethe. The couplet in question, from the poem *Urworte: Orphische*, which Furtwängler quotes verbatim, reads:

> Und keine Zeit und keine Macht zerstückelt
> Geprägte Form, die lebend sich entwickelt.
>
> No time, no power can destroy
> Created form in its living development.[25]

The Wagnerian resonances implicit in the concepts of redemption, liberation and purification are also significant, given their later history. He completes his triumvirate of literary and intellectual forebears by invoking the spirit of Friedrich Nietzsche in his application of the metaphor of the Apolline and the Dionysian to Beethoven:

> In Beethoven the Dionysian and the Apolline, ecstatic abandon and cool sobriety, find common cause. He sweeps us off our feet by his powers of persuasion. He cannot contemplate a musical utterance that is not brought to a balanced, unequivocal conclusion; but nor can he contemplate one that confines itself to the intellectual realm, to a satisfaction with intellectual achievement alone.[26]

For the historian this invocation of the thought of these central figures of nineteenth-century culture only serves to heighten the ideological paradox of Furtwängler's situation at this time. In the Bach and Beethoven essays he was attempting to reinvigorate the discourses of Wilhelmine cultural conservatism in a wholly different context; yet it was these ideas that had been politically appropriated and distorted in the intervening period of totalitarian rule. In this process of association they had acquired such a thick ideological crust that they could not simply be presented anew in a different context devoid of their recent associations.

---

25 TW, p. 238; FM, p. 50. The Goethe reference is explained by Ronald Taylor in an illuminating footnote to his translation of 'Beethoven und Wir': 'The influence of Goethe's concepts and thought patterns can be felt throughout this essay. Words such as "liberation" and "purification" [both meanings are implied in the German word "Läuterungsprozesses"] recall the principle of "Stirb und werde" – "Die and be born again" – in the poem *Selige Sehnsucht*, the power of unceasing metamorphosis embedded in the processes of all organic life. The image of the organic evolution of man towards a state of harmony and perfection is also one to which Furtwängler has frequent recourse.'
26 TW, p. 250; FM, p. 57.

It is this musical idealist in Furtwängler, the high priest of the podium
and practical exponent of Dilthey's triangle of 'Experience (Erlebnis) –
Expression (Ausdruck) – Understanding (Verstehen)', the musician to whom
music was a holy art and a sacred trust, who finds his ultimate justification
and authority in Beethoven. Beethoven is the creator of the 'community
[Gemeinde] of the faithful', the audience, in which may be seen a now
explicit microcosm of the organic state:

> Beethoven takes his public seriously, extremely seriously. He is not out
> to preach at them or overwhelm them, let alone to browbeat them into
> submission by one or other of the means that have become so fashionable in
> recent times. Any such methods he would indignantly reject. His insistence
> on a strictly logical pattern of musical argument [unbedingter Logik des
> Ablaufs] in which there can be no break, even for a single moment, shows
> how he sees his relationship to his listeners, whom he sets out to convince
> and by whom he wishes to be properly understood – a relationship based
> on a communion of minds. They are his partners, his equals. Not only does
> he take them seriously, as seriously as he takes himself – he sees them as his
> neighbours, whom it is his responsibility, as the Bible says, to love as himself.
> He both assumes the presence of an audience of equals and helps to create
> such an audience. Indeed, his music is virtually responsible for the creation
> of the modern concert-going public and for the development of musical
> life as we know it. With each performance there comes into existence a
> kind of ideal community [Daher schafft jede richtige Aufführung eines
> Beethovenschen Werkes ideell gesprochen so etwas wie eine Gemeinde].[27]

Furtwängler concludes by contrasting Beethoven's achievement with the
strident attitude adopted by so many contemporary composers and members
of the musical avant-garde. He deplores the iconoclasm and lack of respect
for the past which is characteristic of so many exponents of modernism;
then, in what seems to be a thinly veiled apologia for the authoritarian state
as representative of the ideal community referred to above, he suggests his
prescription for the resolution of this problem:

> Small wonder, therefore, that the intimidation formerly practised in certain
> quarters – and still being energetically pursued in those quarters today
> – should have provoked the state, at that time in its authoritarian form
> [den Staat zumal in seiner autoritären Form], to reply with its own form of
> intimidation, namely with its proscription of what it called 'degenerate' art
> ['entartete' Kunst].[28]

---

27 Ibid., p. 249; p. 57.
28 Ibid., p. 251; p. 58.

'Form and Chaos' (1954)

During what was to be the last year of his life, 1954, Furtwängler wrote two substantial essays which may be said to be representative of his legacy or *Vermächtnis*. The first, 'Form and Chaos' ('Chaos und Gestalt'), was originally published under the title 'The Musician and his Public' ('Der Musiker und sein Publikum'); it is a deeply reactionary essay which is essentially a protracted restatement of the ideas contained in the supplementary chapter added to *Conversations about Music* in 1947.[29] The substance of the essay is strongly, almost stridently, anti-intellectual and begins by deploring the fact that so much modern music represents little more than a cerebral construct which follows the prescribed dictates of critics and theoreticians:

> Musical life today is characterised by a massive increase in theorising and a corresponding decline in actual music-making. In fact we have almost reached the point where a composer scarcely dares to write a note without seeking justification in some fashionable ideology, or in some programme or system on which he can call to prove his credentials as a genuinely 'contemporary' composer.[30]

The result of this ideological dislocation is that music, especially in this case that of the Second Viennese School, has lost contact with its roots: in addition this essay, in its analysis of the relationship between the creative artist and his public, is shot through with a strong element of *völkisch* thinking and the ideological distinction between *Gemeinschaft* and *Gesellschaft*: 'Without the presence of a community [Gemeinschaft], a society in the background, a work of music – a communal work [Gemeinschaftswerk] in the truest sense, cannot survive.'[31] It is in his understanding of the inner nature of this public, the receptor of the art of music, that this *völkisch* content of Furtwängler's thought is at its most apparent:

> Who and what is this public? In the sense in which the question is asked, the public forms part of the great 'Thou', the great world outside ourselves, to which the artist addresses his activity. Whether it is a middle-class [bürgerliches] public or a working-class [Arbeiterpublikum] is of

29 'Der Musiker und sein Publikum: Ein Vortrag, der in der Bayerischen Akademie der schönen Künste gehalten werden sollte' (Zürich, 1955). The typescript of this essay is merely headed 'Vortrag'; the title was added later by the publisher, Martin Hürlimann. It appears in VMS as 'Chaos und Gestalt', pp. 131–63; Zentralbibliothek Zürich, Nachl. W. Furtwängler: S 22, 1, 1a and 2; also FM, pp. 140–59.
30 VMS, p. 131; FM, p. 140 (translations amended).
31 Ibid., p. 135; p. 142.

no account, nor is its nationality. Even a nation ethnically [blutmäßig] so different from ourselves as the Japanese today shows itself responsive to European music. We are talking here about a public, a body of people which feels as a community [Gemeinschaft] and reacts as a community, not as a mass of individuals. This is a significant distinction. Experts have repeatedly discovered, to their surprise, that however mistaken, even stupid an individual's opinions may be, those of the public at large can often be rational and sharp-witted.[32]

Such a notion of the 'will' of the community shares a similar conceptual premise to that of the organic state. Moreover, Furtwängler proceeds to develop the associated idea, itself rooted in the discourses of the previous century, that music functions as a means by which a community is formed; the work of art is a living symbol of the symbiotic relationship between creator and audience, for the artist is both a product and a servant of the organic community:

> Today, however, it is clear that the deep-rooted, if unspoken mutual confidence which existed between composer and public in the nineteenth century, despite many conflicts and differences of opinion, has been shaken. Little is left of that feeling of being bound together into an ideal community, of trusting the public and serving it, which Wagner still had, and Strauss too. The modern composer now confronts his listeners with a set of demands; no longer does he subordinate himself to their wishes but expects them to submit to his authority. He has ceased to be in the community and is now above it.[33]

A further consequence of this over-intellectualisation of music is the loss of the concept of the transcendent nature of the artistic experience:

> At the same time modern man has to understand that it is not the function of music to speak to his soul – this is just a hangover from the romantic past. [...]
> Of one thing I am certain. If composers no longer conceive of the public as a source of divine judgement, as the voice of nature, as the spokesman for mankind, and if the God-given partnership, the voluntary community of affection, between artist and public no longer exists, then we are facing the final collapse of everything that has hitherto been called art, everything that has been truly creative.[34]

---

32 Ibid., p. 136; p. 143.
33 Ibid., pp. 137–8; p. 144.
34 Ibid., pp. 142–4; pp. 147–8.

It is Furtwängler's contention that modern musical development is concerned with technical matters and not with the soul of man; he considers the claim that modern music can also represent the soul as symptomatic of the way in which man is in danger of being 'locked in the prison of his own intelligence' (im Gefängnis unseres eigenen Verstandes befinden).[35] Modern music, and in particular twelve-tone music with its emphasis on intellectual constructs, is thus incompatible with the Romantic ideal of the transcendent æsthetic.

Towards the end of his essay Furtwängler categorically states that the 'vicious circle that links ideological propaganda [ideologischer Propaganda] and abstract, intellectual, unheard music must be recognised'.[36] He apparently fails to recognise the parallel which suggests itself between this notion and the position of art in the Third Reich when the musical master-works, of which he was so persuasive a champion, were inextricably linked to the pernicious ideological propaganda of the organic state. By 1954, when this essay was written, the position had become curiously inverted for Furtwängler. Ideological propaganda now attempted to make music intel-ligible; the ideology served the music, albeit of a spurious kind. In the Third Reich music had served ideology; it not only gave the regime credibility but helped sustain the hubris.

That 'Form and Chaos' is the work of a nineteenth-century cultural conservative is nowhere more clearly apparent than in the concluding remarks on the nature of musical form. Modern music does not represent the imposition of form upon the chaos of raw materials in the way that tonal music represents the operation of the rational principle:

> Form cannot emerge without the interplay – the struggle [Kampf] even – between composer and public, between the creator and the world in, and for which, he creates. [...]
> From the standpoint of modern man, with his peculiar attraction to chaos, form provides a way of overcoming and controlling this chaos, starting with the vision of the work as a whole and reaching down to every little detail. Brought thus under the control of the formal principle, chaos can be found equally in the overall vision of a symphony and in the concen-trated moment of an individual melody from that symphony.[37]

The public is therefore essential to the act of creation: form cannot emerge without this interplay between composer and public. It is also interesting to note in passing how strongly Furtwängler's thinking is still imbued with the

35 Ibid., p. 151; p. 152.
36 Ibid., p. 159; p. 157.
37 Ibid., p. 161; p. 158.

principles of Gestalt psychology, previously discussed, and how such ideas influenced his concept of musical form.[38] In brief, Furtwängler's argument may be summarised thus: form controls chaos; therefore for art to emerge chaos must be subject to the formative principle. This application of the dialectical process produces a defining example of the notion of form as ideology which in itself is an illustration of the subtext which permeates this entire essay.

Read in a particular way 'Chaos und Gestalt' can be seen as a portentous and rather cumbersome diatribe against the inadequacies of modern music from the standpoint of one whose cultural outlook was formed by the supra-rational thought of the previous century and who found himself increasingly isolated in the alien cultural climate of post-war Europe; read as text it represents an impassioned plea for a return to the cultural values of the Wilhelmine era which, in 1954, had distinct, not to say reactionary ideological overtones. Nevertheless, an ideal view of man as humanistic ideal is never entirely submerged, as is apparent from his concluding remarks:

> The essential factor is, and remains: Man. Behind all art is Man. It is Man that Art expresses, and Art is Man, who creates it. As long as my present faith in man persists – not that tense, hidebound creature locked in the prison of his own thought processes but modern man in all his breadth and depth, in the warmth of his love and the compass of his knowledge – I shall not allow my belief and hope in his art to perish.[39]

'All Greatness is Simplicity' (1954)

It is a discussion of this quality of so-called humanism and its associated anti-intellectualism which provides the substance for Furtwängler's final essay, 'All Greatness is Simplicity' ('Alles Große ist einfach').[40] In many ways this essay draws together the constants which had permeated Furtwängler's thought patterns throughout his life; it is not therefore surprising that he begins by explaining his title through an exegesis of the ideas of the 'whole', the 'daemonic' and how they relate to the organic world.

---

38 The ideas of Gestalt psychology are so much in evidence throughout this essay that it is probably reasonable to suggest that this debt is acknowledged in the title 'Chaos und Gestalt'.

39 VMS, p. 163; FM, p. 159 (amended).

40 Zentralbibliothek, Zürich, Nachl. W. Furtwängler: S 33. First published as 'Freiwild Kunst', *Die Kultur*, 15 November 1954; TW, pp. 253–68; FM, pp. 160–8.

'Greatness is Simplicity' ['Alles Große ist einfach'] because, in the first place, the word 'simple' ['einfach'] assumes the existence of an entity, a whole. The whole in this sense is not only a separate, independent part of the world but also, as such, a reflection of this world in its wholeness. 'In wholeness lies the Daemonic' ['Im Ganzen liegt das Dämonische'] said the 'artist' ['Künstler'] Goethe. The inorganic world is ignorant of such a concept of wholeness because that world is infinite, has no limits. The term wholeness in our sense is relevant only by virtue of the fact that we, as human beings, are part of organic life. We think as organisms, we feel as organisms, and every organism – every plant, every animal – constitutes for us something whole. Every whole, however, must be simple in its own way, and by seeing it as a whole we are making it simple. Thus 'Greatness is Simplicity' also appears to signify that what we feel to be great is at the same time part of the organic world.[41]

The idea of the 'daemonic' represents the irresistible force which, in characters such as Werther and Faust, drives the individual towards his destiny and against which it is useless to struggle. Moreover, he pursues the organic metaphor as an allegory of the contemporary situation pertaining in artistic life: what he perceives to be artistic decline is a result of art being too strongly influenced by the inorganic:

The artist lives by creating, by giving expression in organic, finite form, in work upon work, to the infinite power of creative nature ['unendlich'-schöpferische Natur]. What he requires is, on the one hand, the intuitive vision of a 'whole' [die Intuition eines 'Ganzen'], on the other hand the tenacity to give this vision flesh and blood, to convert it into a modern experience of reality. But science pays scant heed to the artistic intuition that gives birth to the individual work of art, still less to the artist's fanatical attempts to give form and reality to his vision.[42]

In Furtwängler's view rational scientific method is by definition anti-artistic, for the only valid form of artistic creation is rooted in nature, as understood by Goethe. The supra-rational content of 'All Greatness is Simplicity' here becomes more focused than that of 'Form and Chaos': it consists of a rejection of any form of scientific method and a restricted view of science as an antithetical concept to Art as 'an overestimation of outer appearances, an over-indulgence in the sensory attractions of the physical life'.[43] Furtwängler is of the view that the artistic vision of the organic 'whole' is

41   TW, p. 254; FM, p. 160 (amended and with emphases restored).
42   Ibid., p. 255; p. 161.
43   Ibid., p. 255; p. 161.

intuitive, supra-rational and not explicable empirically by means of scientific scrutiny. Moreover, he goes further and suggests that what he perceives to be the crisis in contemporary musical life is the direct result of a predominance of positivist, scientific thinking over artistic intuition: 'For the crisis that faces musical life today has arisen because the "scientific" mode of thought [das "wissenschaftliche" Denken] has come to predominate at the expense of everything else.'[44] That positivist mode of thinking was also apparent in the manner in which composers were relegated to the status of historical phenomena rather than paradigms of transcendent reality. This new artistic historicism, this historical treatment of art, Furtwängler believed to be a product of modern scientific thinking, which discourages direct artistic experience in the sense in which he described it in 'Form and Chaos' as 'speaking to the soul':

> I would explain the situation in this way. Formerly Beethoven – one could name many others in his place – was seen as a great composer, a divine creator, a source of divine grace, who awoke in us the consciousness of belonging to the world of divine nature that surrounded us. He was what might be called a fragment of religious reality. This is what he signified for Wagner, for Brahms, for Mahler – but much less so today. [...] Beethoven is now seen primarily as one of the 'First Viennese School', an historical phenomenon [ein 'Wiener Klassiker', eine historische Erscheinung] with an undoubted importance in his day but no longer of much immediate relevance to us in the present age. [...]
>
> Today the importance of the historical perspective for our understanding of reality is fully realised. We are constantly striving to take a bird's-eye view of things [aus der Vogelperspektive zu sehen]. Rather than experience a work of art directly, surrendering ourselves to its message, we set out to try and understand it, explain it, thus bring it under our control. This is the method of modern science.[45]

It is interesting to note in passing that in his repudiation of scientific method and positivist artistic historicism Furtwängler anticipates the arguments that would in due course be used against the authentic performance movement, the first stirrings of which were becoming apparent in 1954. What matters to him is the Gestalt-inspired notion of the direct apprehension of a work of art through *Einfall* as a living entity, an organic whole, not an historical artefact. The historicist approach bypasses the need for the individual to confront the artwork; the process of reception becomes less

---

44 Ibid., p. 257; p. 162.
45 Ibid., p. 259; p. 163.

interactive and the act of listening becomes entirely passive. The artwork is treated as a historical artefact – the approach to it is not concerned with the personality of the composer and the content of his message but with the context of the work:

> In performances today the public looks not so much for an interpretation that goes to the heart of the work and its message as for one that follows certain general guidelines based on the abstract, speculative tendencies fashionable at the present time. 'Classical' works must be played in an appropriate 'period style' ['stilvoll'] – which can mean anything except personally coming to grips with those works as a man of the twentieth century.[46]

To Furtwängler this modern æsthetic of performance does not sufficiently take into account the possibility of inner experience of the artwork in Dilthey's sense of 'Nach-Erleben'. Furtwängler makes his point by drawing a comparison between contemporary attitudes and Wagner's ecstatic reception of Beethoven: '"Ecstasy" ["Verzückung"] is considered in any case an "un-modern" ["nicht mehr an der Zeit"] way of responding to a work of art, appropriate rather to the Romantic nineteenth century that modern man believes himself to have left behind.'[47]

A further consequence of the growth of the historical approach is the supposed loss of artistic freedom, spontaneity and intuition – the very qualities which were fundamental to Furtwängler's æsthetic of performance; he cites as a specific example the fact that it is not possible to indicate inflexions of articulation and phrasing in a score: this can only be the result of spontaneous artistry, or improvisation. Furthermore, he considers that the increasing prevalence of the mechanical reproduction of music is resulting in contrived, superficial performances (artifice), which as 'art' are lacking in depth and meaning:

> Next to the problem of phrasing comes that of form, of structure, perhaps the most pressing question facing music today but one which we seem largely to have lost sight of. Besides this, the overly critical attitude encouraged by listening too often to radio and records, has led to soulless, mechanical, superficial performances, when what is needed is something quite different.[48]

---

46 Ibid., p. 259; pp. 163–4.
47 Ibid., p. 261; p. 164.
48 Ibid., p. 262; p. 165.

Furtwängler takes the notion of individuality as his artistic measure; this quality, so central to his beliefs, is in danger of being crushed under the levelling interests of contemporary theoretical dogma. The prevalence of intellectual argument over what he, following Dilthey, describes as directly experienced reality ('erlebten Wirklichkeit') is, he says, a major cause of artistic decline. Furthermore, he regards the increasing influence of critics as both arbiters and moulders of public taste and judgement to be a further symptom of this process:

> Take those none-too-rare cases where an audience's reaction differs from that of the critics, with their fixed theories and principles. We are left with the impression that although there was an audience present – someone has to fill the hall – they have lost their right to an opinion. The immediate emotional impact of the music is being consistently played down, especially in Germany; indeed, it is often not taken into account at all, in response to new theories of composition.[49]

It is stressed that in a great work there is no separation of mind and emotion, nor can there be; indeed, it is the dialectical tension between these two poles which produces the equilibrium, balance and synthesis essential to a great work of art. Herein lies the problem. The twelve-tone system is non-intuitive: the predominance of compositional method precludes any possibility of transcendent artistic experience and expression:

> Twelve-tone music is not only taken seriously by musicians and scholars but generally accepted without question. One side of the coin is to historicise, play down, devalue the music of the past; the other is to stake one's claims for a music of the future based on pre-stated theories and dogmas. The result is a totally different attitude to music, to art of all kinds. No longer is the artist a recipient of God's grace; no longer is his activity a source of awe and wonder.[50]

Furtwängler concludes his essay by reducing its argument to that of a conflict between the dominance of theoretical concepts and the antithetical notion of artistic expression. The fact that science is becoming an ersatz religion, usurping the place previously occupied by art, is for him a matter of life and death for music: artistic individuality must come before the dictates of historical development:

49 Ibid., p. 265; p. 167.
50 Ibid., p. 266; p. 167.

By all means let our intellectuals use their historical perspective as a guide but not as a means of trying to control developments; they must learn to put the individual work of art, the phenomenon that is of direct concern to us, before matters of historical development. Above all, they must relearn what it is to revere true greatness, to love it passionately, unreservedly, unconditionally. The situation is like that in Wagner's *Parsifal* – the only way to heal the wound is through the spear that caused it. The only way we can transcend the terrible effects of the warped thinking with which we are plagued is by recourse to a universal, all-embracing mode of thinking, thinking that moves on a higher plane. True art can flourish only in an atmosphere of – relative – naiveté. Let us hope that all those in positions of responsibility will come to realise that this naiveté is the naiveté of wisdom, the recaptured naiveté that befits our culture [Kultur].[51]

This closing reference to *Parsifal* significantly draws attention to the notion of a community or individual detached from its roots, which is precisely the situation in which Furtwängler now found himself. Ideas of the supra-rational 'daemonic', Schenkerian organicism and a preoccupation with the idea of the artistic whole, come together as elements of a conservative world-view that had little in common with the astringent positivist intellectual climate of the 1950s. This cultural dysfunction expresses itself in the strong attack which Furtwängler mounts on twelve-tone music in particular and modern music in general; moreover, it is combined with an impassioned plea for a return to the principles of *Gemeinschaft* culture. Stressing the importance of naiveté and simplicity in art, he overlooks the fact that it was these very qualities to which he assigns such importance that proved such a potent force in the realisation of the dark side of the world-view of which he was so late and committed a representative.

Concurrently with these two final essays Furtwängler continued to work on his Third Symphony. As discussed in Chapter 8, the Second Symphony (1944–45), with its fusion of Brahmsian lyricism and Brucknerian structural complexity, could be seen as a powerful restatement of the supremacy of the Austro-German symphonic tradition when the culture which gave rise to that tradition was in a state of disintegration; the Third Symphony both attempts to realise in musical terms the ideas textualised in 'Form and Chaos' and 'All Greatness is Simplicity' while acting as a lament for the destruction of the culture to which he had dedicated his creative life.

These two essays from the last year of Furtwängler's life, together with the stated compositional intent of the Third Symphony, represent a world-view that remained essentially unchanged since it was formed in the very different

51 Ibid., pp. 267–8; p. 168 (amended).

11   Furtwängler in 1954.

context of the closing years of the nineteenth and early years of the twentieth century. Furtwängler believed passionately in the power and capacity of a musical artwork to transcend the limits of the 'here and now'; this was the daemonic force that nourished his world-view until the end of his life and it is this quality which to him 'modern' music so conspicuously lacked. Contained within this cast of mind is a supra-rational emphasis on the importance of spontaneity and intuition, of lived experience over rational thought and emotional reaction over intellectual rigour. It was these tendencies, which he continued to advocate, which had reached their most extreme and perverted form in the Germany of Hitler and National Socialism.

Right up to the end of his life Furtwängler appeared to be in denial about the ideological associations of his ideas and their recent historical affiliations. The 'non-political' man thought he could rise above the political through the practice of his art: yet it was precisely this supra-rational quality of transcendence which had politicised art and fuelled the politics of extremism to the point where the institutions, systems and public face of that culture became a powerful expression of political ideology. Furtwängler himself was a notable function of this process. At no point in the writings of his last years does he acknowledge that it was the daemonic power, which he so strongly advocates as essential to artistic creativity, that had unleashed the forces which had destroyed the world he now laments. In his view atonal music was artistically deficient because it lacked the daemonic. He does not appear to realise that the music he so dislikes might be culturally and historically determined or that its overt anti-romanticism might have been a deliberate reaction against the destructive forces latent within the *Gemeinschaft* ideologies of *Bürgertum*.

Such was the ideological background to the closing stages of Wilhelm Furtwängler's career as a conductor. On 9 August 1954 he conducted Beethoven's Ninth Symphony at Bayreuth; in July and August he appeared with the Vienna Philharmonic Orchestra conducting opera at the Salzburg Festival. By a strange irony his penultimate operatic performance of all was of a work he had included in his opening season as Court Kapellmeister at Mannheim in 1915: Carl Maria von Weber's *Der Freischütz*. Furtwängler shared with Pfitzner an abiding love of the German romantic world of Weber and Schumann; *Freischütz* was a work he held in particularly high regard. Weber's *Singspiel* takes its subject matter from the pre-industrial, supernatural world of the old German forests so vividly portrayed by the Brothers Grimm and so beloved of the *Bildungsbürger* as a utopian expression of true German values. In a brief essay, probably written in 1950, and in conversations with students at the Berlin Hochschule für Musik, Furtwängler describes *Freischütz* as 'sui generis': he praises its simplicity, its melodic inventiveness and its capacity to restore the naivety of childhood.[52] *Der Freischütz* is for Furtwängler just as much a matter of cultural memory as are his Second and Third Symphonies.

On 22 August 1954 at the Lucerne Festival Furtwängler gave his final performance of what might be regarded as the defining work of his career: Beethoven's Ninth Symphony. His last act as a conductor was to make a studio recording of Wagner's *Die Walküre*, completed in Vienna on 6 October 1954. Shortly afterwards he contracted pneumonia and entered the clinic Ebersteinberg near Baden-Baden for treatment. Wilhelm Furtwängler died on 30 November 1954. His funeral service (Trauerfeier) took place on 4 December in the Church of the Holy Spirit in Heidelberg followed by burial in the Bergfriedhof.

In his 1933 essay 'The Sufferings and Greatness of Richard Wagner', Thomas Mann had warned of the direction in which an uncritical assimilation of supra-rational Wagnerian ideology might lead. Furtwängler's unconditional acceptance of and adherence to the supra-rational was uncritical in the way that Mann described. At the end of his life, he exemplified so much of what Mann perceived, with ironic detachment, to be its tragic outcome.[53]

---

52 TW, pp. 212–13.
53 'The Sufferings and Greatness of Richard Wagner', in *Thomas Mann: Pro and Contra Wagner*.

CHAPTER 10

AFTERWORD

By the time of his death in November 1954 Wilhelm Furtwängler was already an historical figure. Born and raised in the Wilhelmine Empire, he lived through the Weimar Republic and the Third Reich, and then experienced de-Nazification in the very different context of post-war *Bundesrepublik* restoration overshadowed by the unfolding narrative of the Nazi Holocaust. Yet in spite of these seismic political and ideological upheavals, his world-view remained unchanged and governed by the conservative-nationalist ideologies of *Bürgertum*. He remained a figure of the nineteenth century. He can only be understood against this background.

As became clear in the previous chapter, Furtwängler effectively historicised himself through the writings, compositions and concert-giving activities of his last years. An historical period and its associated world-view was represented in him and by him. Romantic idealism with its view of music as a transcendent art form; the organic world-view with its assumption of artistic hegemony; the supra-rational form of anti-intellectualism which became such a feature of Nazi ideology – all are combined to a greater or lesser degree in this complex and highly problematic individual. In as far as he can be said to adopt any specific æsthetic position, it represents a heady mixture of seemingly contradictory positions of Hanslick's formalism and the expressive ideas of Schopenhauer and Wagner beaten out on the anvil of Schenkerian organicism. What emerges most strongly, however, in any attempt to follow the development of Furtwängler's thought, is that there is a palpable sense in which, with the qualified exception of a modification of his attitude towards Wagner's work, his core ideas were firmly established by his late twenties and did not in essence change until his death at the age of sixty-eight.

In many respects Furtwängler's writings and his later compositions can be seen as fragments of a grand Schenkerian process of 'composing out' of the conservative intellectual agenda first defined in 'Timely Reflections of a Musician' (1915), the purpose of which was to justify and defend this position against the influence of what he regarded as increasing artistic degeneracy. It is the central paradox of his career that a particularly tendentious, not to say perverted, form of this conservative, supra-rational world-view ultimately became the intellectual justification of so much Nazi ideology. This may be seen at its most explicit in Furtwängler's constant, almost obsessive reference to the motif which runs as an interconnecting thread throughout his writings from 'Timely Reflections of a Musician' to his 1954 essay 'All Greatness is Simplicity': that of the application of the organic metaphor to a work of art through the creation of a 'whole'. It is through the wider implications and applications of this organic world-view that non-political artistic idealism merges so seamlessly into tendentious political ideology.

It is in this context that a comparison between the respective positions of Furtwängler and Thomas Mann is at its most instructive. Furtwängler's 1915 'Timely Reflections of a Musician' and Mann's 1918 *Reflections of a Non-Political Man* were both written in a time of intense nationalistic fervour engendered by World War I, and share a good deal of common ideological ground. However, by the time of the establishment of the totalitarian state in 1933 their positions had begun to diverge: Mann initially left his homeland in consequence of the restrictions placed on his intellectual freedom; Furtwängler remained in Germany as a leading exponent of 'heil'ge deutsche Kunst'. Furtwängler and Thomas Mann were never to be reconciled. In a strongly worded letter of 11 March 1947 Mann wrote to his fellow German emigré Manfred George, founder and editor-in-chief of the New York German-Jewish newspaper *Aufbau*, what amounted to an attack on the case for the defence presented at Furtwängler's de-Nazification proceedings. 'I see from Furtwängler's defence, as from so many other documents, what an abyss lies between our experience and that of the people who remained in Germany. Communication across this abyss is completely impossible.'[1] In an undated letter to Mann written at some point in late June 1947 Furtwängler suggested that the two should meet to discuss 'questions relating to Germany'.[2] Mann replied on 1 July that such a discussion would make little sense; he defended his position put forward in his address 'Germany and the Germans' that there were not two Germanys, but that wicked Germany was good Germany gone astray.

> There are not two Germanys, an evil and a good, but only one, the best of which turned out as evil through devilish cunning. The evil Germany is the good one gone to the bad, the good one in misfortune, in guilt and in ruin. It is therefore impossible for a German-born spirit to deny completely the evil, guilt-laden Germany and to declare: 'I am the good, the noble and the

---

1 Thomas Mann, *Briefe*, ed. Erika Mann, 3 vols (Frankfurt: S. Fischer Verlag, 1961–65), vol. 2, *Briefe 1937–47* (1963), p. 529.
2 Furtwängler, *Briefe*, p. 165.

just Germany in my white garment; I leave it to you to eradicate the evil one.' Nothing that I have tried to say or fleetingly to indicate to you about Germany has come out of alien, cold or detached knowledge; it is all within me, I have experienced it all in my own person.[3]

The rift between the literary-inclined musician and the musically inclined man of letters was wide indeed. It would remain an open wound.

The concept of the 'Great Conductor', the interpreter of genius, was a convenient and potent tool in the hands of Nazi ideologues and iconographers. The high priest of the podium who exercised absolute authority over the orchestra, that microcosmic paradigm of the organic state, represented a synthesis of the nineteenth-century concept of creative genius and the idea of the strong leader which was so central to Nazi ideology. The idealised figure of the conductor became the artistic and highly visible embodiment of the *Führerprinzip*.[4] Therefore, while a sceptical intellectual with a sharply honed critical facility such as Thomas Mann found himself displaced in the restrictive cultural climate of the organic state, Furtwängler, the suprarational artist, found himself essential to its continued existence.

Furtwängler regarded himself, in an almost metaphysical sense, as part of the *Gemeinschaft* community from which he had originated. The *völkisch*-inspired idea that art creates an ideal community through what may loosely be termed the spirituality of belonging found a persuasive advocate in him. It was this that inspired his nationalism. Furtwängler's reported anti-Semitism may also be considered in the same light. As we have seen, prior to the Nazi period anti-Semitism was an almost universal construct in the minds of educated Germans; but its eliminationist implications were not yet apparent. The Jewish composer Arnold Schoenberg, writing immediately after the war in 1946, defined such a position as follows:

> I agree with you about Furtwängler. I am sure he was never a nazi. He was one of those old-fashioned Deutschnationale from the time of Turnvater Jahn, when you were national because of those Western states who went

3 Thomas Mann 'Germany and the Germans': see Appendix 2. For a full discussion of the respective positions of Mann and Furtwängler in the post-war period together with transcriptions of the correspondence and associated documentation see Klaus Kanzog, *Offene Wunden: Wilhelm Furtwängler und Thomas Mann* (Würzburg: Königshausen & Neumann, 2014).

4 This idea has continued to fascinate long after the demise of fascism. For an interesting corollary see Richard Osborne's account of a meeting in 1984 between Herbert von Karajan and Margaret Thatcher in *Herbert von Karajan: A Life in Music*, pp. 694–5. Apparently the conversation was concerned with 'the nature of power and the exercise of authority'.

with Napoleon. This is more an affair of Studentennationalismus, and it differs very much from that of Bismarck's time and later on, when Germany was not a defender, but a conqueror. Also I am sure that he was no anti-Semite – or at least no more than any non-Jew. And he is certainly a better musician than all these Toscaninis, Ormandys, Kussevitzkis [sic], and the whole rest. And he is a real talent, and he *loves* music.[5]

Schoenberg is mistaken in that Furtwängler's conservative nationalism was very much that of 'Bismarck's time and later on'; yet the point about the old-fashioned allegiance to an earlier form of pre-industrial search for national identity is perceptive in that it succinctly identifies the ideals of *Bildung* that formed Furtwängler's world-view. Whatever perspective is adopted and no matter how the problem is nuanced, the inescapable and indisputable fact remains: Furtwängler stayed in Germany to protect German culture and in so doing he played an important and high-profile public role in constructing the cultural totality which was National Socialism. As a result, he became mired in an ideological quicksand of his own making from which he can never be fully extricated.

Furtwängler will always be a perplexing, not to say controversial figure. His lasting stature as an artist supreme in the interpretation of the Austro-German canon is widely acknowledged and assured. At the same time, his role in the cultural aggrandisement of a barbaric and criminal regime cannot be denied, excused or ignored. Yet neither should it be exaggerated. As can be seen so clearly in his writings, as an embodiment of what may be termed the 'problem' of Germany, he became caught in the web of his own contradictions. It is this, rather than any blunt-edged attempts to measure degrees of collaboration or resistance, guilt or innocence, that will always cast a shadow over his historical reputation. No writer has expressed this dichotomy with more penetrating subtlety than Thomas Mann. Mann's own highly individual and time-specific 1947 reworking of the 'Faust' legend, in his novel *Doctor Faustus*, charts the horrifying price the central character in the person of the imaginary composer Adrian Leverkühn has to pay for creative achievement. As Erich Heller succinctly states in his commentary on the novel, 'how imperceptibly smooth is the transition from art as salvation to art as damnation'.[6] The organic world-view in both its artistic and political

5   Schoenberg to Kurt List (written in English), *Listen* magazine, New York, 24 January 1946; quoted in Erwin Stein, ed., *Arnold Schoenberg: Letters* (London: Faber & Faber, 1964), pp. 237–8.
6   Erich Heller, *The Ironic German: A Study of Thomas Mann* (London: Secker & Warburg, 1958), p. 261. See also Patrick Carnegy, *Faust as Musician* (London: Chatto & Windus, 1973), pp. 143–67, esp. p. 149.

form is one way in which 'the connection between the destiny of a German genius and the politics of the German tyranny' becomes apparent and can be understood.[7] *Doctor Faustus*, described by Mann as 'something like a belated return and homecoming to the old-fashioned German and musical sphere of *Buddenbrooks*' is an allegory of the tragedy of Germany in the first half of the twentieth century, which runs both in parallel and in counterpoint to the career of the subject of the novel, the fictitious composer, Adrian Leverkühn.[8] Furtwängler's historical significance lies in the fact that it is not so much as an allegory of Germany but as a representative German that he can offer insights into how and why the 'sense' (*Sinn*) of nineteenth-century ideals of *Bildung* transmuted into the 'coinage' (*Prägungen*) of twentieth-century ideology.[9]

7 Heller, *The Ironic German*, p. 264.
8 Thomas Mann, *The Genesis of a Novel*, p. 58.
9 Thomas Mann, *Doctor Faustus*, p. 84. For usage of the German terms, see *Doktor Faustus*, p. 117.

TWO FURTWÄNGLER ESSAYS

Heinrich Schenker: A Contemporary Problem (1947)[1]

Heinrich Schenker was a music theorist who died in the 1930s. In his youth he experienced the later years of Brahms and Verdi; he was contemporary with Richard Strauss, Pfitzner, Reger, Mahler, Schoenberg, Debussy, Stravinsky and the young Hindemith. He merits our attention for he possessed a wideranging and deep musicality. It was because of his rich humanity that he was able to grasp the various worlds with equal dedication. He knew Wagner's *Ring* in no less detail than the Brahms symphonies or the B Minor Mass of Bach. He maintained an open view of Verdi and Debussy, knew Strauss, Reger and Mahler, but his main preoccupation was almost exclusively with German classical music. Schenker possessed a unique, sharp-edged intellect in the field of music theory. In the years following World War I he published in Vienna, his home town and the town of his work, a periodical entitled *Der Tonwille*.[2] In it he expressed a passion for German music, up to and including Brahms and Wagner. In the years following World War I the Germans experimented with every kind of internationalism and Europeanism in art, but Schenker remained traditionally German. It was strange how a pure and passionate Jew – for this was Schenker – could feel so at ease in German culture. It was only later, when the first sinister rumblings of Nazism began to make themselves felt, that Schenker feared that his pro-German sympathies could be politically misunderstood so he thereafter refrained from comment.

The first work that became widely known was a monograph on Beethoven's Ninth Symphony. This book fell into my hands in Lübeck in 1911 when I was beginning my career as a Kapellmeister and immediately aroused my passionate interest. Whenever I disagreed with him in matters of

---

1   Neither of the archive holdings in Berlin and Zurich contains a primary source for this essay. The text here is taken from TW, pp. 198–204. Translation by Brian Hitch and Roger Allen.

2   *Der Tonwille*, 10 vols (Vienna, 1921–24).

detail, whenever the polemical position was questionable, the overview and cast of mind that formulated the answers to these questions was so unusual and expressed itself in a way which was so different from the usual style of musical writing, that I was deeply moved. Here for the first time there were no hermeneutics, no irrelevances, but the question was put, simply and directly, what really stands before us in Beethoven's Ninth Symphony? No questions regarding the formal structure were asked, which today are the cause of so much misunderstanding; there was no attempt made to place the work in historical context; rather the composer's creative process was examined. It is this which is the source of the organic cohesion of the work as a whole and which so profoundly affects us all.[3]

When later I came to Vienna I visited Schenker and this resulted in many lively, rich and unique experiences. His theoretical observations stimulated discussion and provoked many searching questions. His answers were always constructive and personal in a way that was not influenced by preconceived theoretical ideas. Schenker believed that the questions arising from the study of the great musical masterworks were above all founded and rooted in real life and human experience.

I will not at this point attempt to summarise Schenker's work. Such a task is very difficult, for Schenker, with all his exceptional intelligence, was not given to expressing himself in a clear and intelligible way, as was desirable. It may have been that an oversubtle, exaggerated talmudish train of thought came to the foreground in his later years. It may have been that the extraordinary isolation and loneliness, the sense that he was a voice crying in the wilderness, prevented him from speaking out clearly. The conception of the *Urlinie*, the theoretical idea of his last years, has not yet been completely thought through, even though he had some remarkable pupils who tried to continue his work. To me personally it seemed questionable, as if Schenker, in his impulse towards the absolute, was somewhat wide of the mark. According to Schenker's thinking the *Meistersinger* Prelude was not an evolving composition but more of an opera potpourri and a shining example of how the abandonment of the *Urlinie* caused disintegration of the overall artistic structure and cohesion. His portrayal of the *Urlinie* as a single unifying factor in a classical structure, e.g. the *Eroica*, lost itself in abstraction and was, by necessity of fate, before its time. Nevertheless, and this is the main point, when considered in context it can be seen that Schenker's work was not in vain. On the contrary, the necessity for his questionings becomes clear.

What Schenker shows at the midpoint in the development of his thinking is the conception of structural hearing [Fernhörens] in music. In order to

3   Schenker, *Beethoven's Ninth Symphony* (1912).

make these ideas comprehensible I must take a spatial view of the concept of time. We know that all life has a certain cohesion and at the centre of this condition in organic life is a subconscious awareness of space and time. This is evident in the first utterances of infants and remains throughout life. There are no incoherences in these concepts as each action is both retrospective and forward-looking. At any given point we have an instinctive awareness of origin and destination. These orientations first made organic life possible and are of singular origin rather than being a synthesis of disparate elements. Each and every one has a foundation and a consequence which apparently exist on many different levels. These causes and effects can only exist within a wider spatial context. Precisely because causes and effects occur across a broad spectrum, an awareness of the total time span is essential in order that concepts may fully penetrate the consciousness. It is Schenker's historical significance that he was the first to investigate the biological implications of music. The concept of the overview with all its interconnections and complexities characterised for Schenker the great works of German classical music; this is the foundation of his ideas and the reason why he never wearied of advocating the organic superiority and proven validity of these works. With his idea of the overview Schenker not only established for himself a platform but reinforced the idea that objectivity exists as the obverse of subjective taste; it is this that will become an integral part of the scientific understanding of our time.

For some time in Switzerland a young man had expressed his enthusiasm for jazz and publicly declared it to be more up to date than Beethoven's symphonies because in its refinements and complications it was more relevant to contemporary man.[4] The rhythmical and harmonic interrelationships in Beethoven's symphonies are childlike in comparison. In making this observation the young man was not entirely mistaken for are not the melodic, harmonic and rhythmic elements in a Beethoven symphony so much more simple than in a jazz piece? The decisive difference is that jazz is lacking in overview. The complications are of the moment and the way is as through a thick jungle where from right to left there are always new nuances and rhythms which act like creepers until suddenly, when the matter is ended, we step out again into freedom. In contrast, in a Beethoven symphony the first bar prepares for the fifteenth, eighteenth, twentieth, thirtieth and so it continues until the end. The individual bar is simple but in its thematic and rhythmic interrelationships, the hundredfold variations and equivalents, the increases in tension and diminutions, it surpasses all that jazz can offer and as a living organism it exceeds in complexity any machine created by man. And

4   The identity of this young man is not revealed: probably Rolf Liebermann.

here is the crux of Schenker's wisdom. His perceptions are of a biological nature and increasingly point to new avenues of enquiry. We learn that the principles of modern biology can be applied elsewhere, above all in art. The ungainly, constricted, superficial and historically questionable understanding of the musical public must be replaced by an awareness of art and artistic worth. Schenker's wide-ranging conception of structural hearing will fulfil this need.

On the Works of Hans Pfitzner (1948)[5]

The name of Hans Pfitzner will always for us Germans be linked with one work: the Dramatic Legend *Palestrina*. Hardly ever has a creative artist represented the position of the artist within his time, his nature, his struggles, his sufferings, indeed himself, as perceptively and unsparingly as Pfitzner has done in *Palestrina*. This work is an autobiography, but one – otherwise than in the works of Strauss such as *Heldenleben* and *Intermezzo* – in which everything purely biographical appears absorbed and related back to something more essential which underlies it. It is a portrayal of its time, a portrayal of the artist in his time, a portrayal of art at this present juncture. Hardly ever has the power of artistic intuition, the loneliness of the creator, the gulf, distance and hostility that prevails between real art and the 'real' world, assumed a more shocking form than in this work. For the first and only time since Wagner, and yet in a completely different way, the poet and musician seem in Pfitzner's work to participate equally. *Palestrina* is Pfitzner and Pfitzner is *Palestrina*. Here the musician has raised a monument to the artist in such a way as was only possible in our hypersensitive [überwachen] age. In the face of this great artistic self-sacrifice the clamour of the day must fall silent.

■ ■ ■ ■ ■

What differentiates Pfitzner from other leading musicians of his time, from Strauss, Reger, Mahler, Debussy? It strikes me at once that he was cast in a special mould [daß er aus besonderem Holz geschnitzt ist], even if, in saying this, we do not think of his unique feeling for life that he has so often expressed in his writings – the feeling of the loner, of one living against his time. Even as a musician he approaches his task differently from his contemporaries. He

5   Hans Pfitzner (1869–1949). Source: Zentralbibliothek Zürich, Nachl. W. Furtwängler: S 15, typescript dated 14 August 1948; also published in VMS, pp. 118–22. Translation by Brian Hitch and Roger Allen.

scorns the superstructure [Überbau] of an unrestrained counterpoint, which Strauss and Reger introduced in order to create their personal style. He takes care that technique should not obscure the spirit and sense of a work. He avoids both Strauss' use of leitmotif together with its massive effects, which harks back to Wagner, as well as Reger's instrumental music – pseudo-Bachian and quite often harmonically and contrapuntally over-nourished. He never succumbed to the temptation of gigantism [Mammutismus], the excessive scale which the age of Strauss, Reger and Mahler honoured. He stands by the themes that he invents, i.e. he shows himself unconcerned, as he is, even at the risk that his all-too-clever and blasé contemporaries [daß allzu Kluge und blasierte Zeitgenossen] find him naive and unoriginal. Almost alone in his generation he constantly maintains a lively sense that in order to create a work spiritual experience and purely musical conditions must coincide, that even the most noble wish of the mind has no continued existence without the relevant musical realisation and that above all not even the most brilliant development of musical 'material' means anything unless it runs in parallel with an underlying expressive need. Thus Pfitzner constantly rejects what for the other composers constitutes a large part of musical-historical meaning: the creation of a 'style'. This was in no way advantageous to the effect of his work and for its 'acceptance' [Durchsetzen] in today's world. He does, of course, have his own style, but this is intimately connected with the content of each and every work. Intuition, or – as he has termed it – 'musical inspiration' ['Einfall'] plays a relatively larger role in his works than in those of his contemporaries. He places himself before the listener more openly, more unconcernedly, more honestly. Above all he believes in the content of his work and in the themes that he invents. He believes in himself, however he may be, i.e. in this case – and this is significant – he believes in what one is, in the spirit, not in what one represents, in the style. This spirit is admittedly the spirit of German music. Like Bruckner and Reger, Pfitzner is and remains in the narrower sense a 'German' phenomenon.

■ ■ ■ ■

A further word concerning Pfitzner's later years. Pfitzner himself, if we are to believe him, seems not to have the highest regard for the works of his 'later style' ['Altersstils'] as he calls it, and is almost surprised that it is so highly regarded in certain quarters. We are not speaking here of what these works mean in themselves, but what Pfitzner as an old man wishes to teach us through them.

Special circumstances apply to the old age of an artist; the increasing independence of the ageing person from his surroundings allows him to live more in accordance with his true inner needs than was possible for him at other stages of his life. This is not contradicted by the fact that the artist often returns in his old age to the beginnings and starting points of his youth. False directions and adaptations, which do not correspond to his true talents, melt away. The significant point about the work of Pfitzner's old age appears to me to be above all its complete 'naturalness' ['Natürlichkeit']. Pfitzner is of the opinion that a sequence of notes with no natural course – 'natural' in the logical development of harmony, natural in the interaction of melody, harmony and rhythm, natural in the unfolding and ultimate completion of form – has no right to exist [Lebensberechtigung]. Even the most esoteric must be natural and must, as it were, be brought back to nature by the artist if it is to be art, or a creation of universal validity. Pfitzner believes in naturalness (as Bach, Mozart, Beethoven, Wagner, etc., believed in it) right up to the present day.

Fifty years ago this belief would hardly have been worth mentioning. Today it brings whoever holds it into opposition with the greater part of his surroundings. Today there is nothing less self-evident than the self-evident, i.e. the 'Natural'. Precisely because being natural means no more and no less than being oneself – always supposing something not at all self-evident, namely that one is something [daß man etwas ist] – precisely for this reason old age, which does not need to take into account the all-too-presumptuous demands of the world around us, seems to be the period of one's life enjoying internal and external honesty. Being and wishing to appear like everyone else is not relevant in this case: i.e. as an artist somewhat progressive and clever. But intellectual courage is relevant – such as Pfitzner has had in great measure all his life – if, as a normal, intelligent man of today, one is to attach importance to things which not only have to do with cleverness and progressiveness but also with being 'honest' ['ehrlich'], 'upright' ['aufrichtig'] and 'affectionate' ['liebevoll']: in other words, if one is to value genuineness and inner truth above outward conformity.

THOMAS MANN, 'GERMANY AND THE GERMANS' (1945)[1]

Ladies and Gentlemen, as I stand here before you, a seventy-year-old, and however improbably, for several months an American citizen, speaking English, or at least attempting to, as a guest, no, as an official member of an American State institute which has invited you to hear me, – as I stand here, I have the feeling that life is such stuff as dreams are made on.[2] All is so strange, so little credible, so unexpected. In the first instance I never thought that I would reach the patriarchal age [of three score years and ten], although in theory I have long thought this to be desirable. I thought and said that once one was in the world it would be good and honourable to stay the course, to lead a full and regular life [kanonisches Leben] and, as an artist, to be characteristically productive at all stages of my life. But I had little confidence in my own biological competence and efficiency, and the stamina which I have nonetheless shown, seems to me less as proof of my own vital patience, than of the patience which the genius of life has had with me, as an addition, as grace. But grace is always astonishing and unexpected. Whoever experiences it thinks he is dreaming.

It seems to me dreamlike that I am and where I am. I do not need to be a poet for this to strike me as self-evident. One only needs a little fantasy to

---

1   Source: Thomas Mann, 'Deutschland und die Deutschen', in *Sorge um Deutschland* (Stockholm: S. Fischer Verlag, 1957), pp. 73–93. Address drafted between 27 February and 18 March 1945; given in English in the Coolidge Auditorium of the Library of Congress, Washington, on 29 May 1945 to mark the author's seventieth birthday on 6 June 1945. Published separately in English as *Germany and the Germans* (Washington, DC: Library of Congress, 1945); translator not identified. Republished in book form in *Thomas Mann's addresses delivered at the Library of Congress, 1942–1949* (Washington, DC: Library of Congress, 1963). Here newly translated from the German by the late Brian Hitch and Roger Allen. We are very grateful to Reinhard Strohm for his comments on and suggested revisions to an early draft of this translation.
2   William Shakespeare, *The Tempest*, Act IV, Scene 1, lines 156–7.

find life fantastic. How did I get here? Which dream-wave [Traumwelle] cast me from the furthest corner of Germany, where I was born, and where in the last analysis I belong, into this hall, onto this podium, that I stand here as an American, speaking to Americans? Not that it seems wrong to me. On the contrary, it has my complete approval. As everything stands today, my kind of Germanness is preserved most fittingly in a hospitable cosmopolitan environment, the multiracial and multinational universe that is America. Before I became an American, I was allowed to be a Czech; that was highly commendable and I was grateful, but it had no rhyme or reason. All the same, I only have to imagine that I had by chance become a Frenchman, an Englishman or an Italian, to realise with satisfaction how much more fitting it is that I became an American. Everything else would have meant too narrow and specific an alienation of my existence. As an American I am a citizen of the world – as is by nature the German, in spite of the caution of the world which at the same time is part of him, of his timidity of the world, about which it is hard to say whether it is actually based on arrogance or inborn provincialism, of an inferiority complex within the society of nations. Probably both.

It is about Germany and the Germans that I am to speak to you this evening – a foolhardy undertaking; not only because the subject is so complex, so multifaceted, so inexhaustible, but also in view of the passion which it arouses today. *Sine ira et studio* [without anger or partiality], to treat the subject from a purely psychological point of view could appear almost immoral, in view of the unspeakable things this unhappy people has done to the world. Should a German avoid this theme today? But then I would hardly have known what I could have chosen instead for this evening. More than that, a conversation transcending the private that does not almost inevitably turn on the German problem is scarcely conceivable today, the riddle in the character and destiny of this people, who have undeniably given the world so much greatness and beauty and yet at the same time has repeatedly been so fateful a burden to the world. The gruesome destiny of Germany, the monstrous catastrophe to which its modern history has now led, compels our interest, even if this interest does not command our sympathy. To try to arouse sympathy, to defend and to excuse Germany would certainly not be a fitting intention for a native German today. To play the judge out of compliance towards the immeasurable hatred which his people has been able to arouse, to curse and damn his people and to commend himself as the 'good Germany' completely in contrast to the wicked one over there with which one has nothing at all to do, that doesn't seem to me to be particularly becoming. One *has* to be concerned with German destiny and German guilt if one is born a German.[3] Critical distance should not be interpreted as disloyalty. Truths, which one aspires to speak about one's own people, can only be the product of self-examination.

I have already, without rightly knowing how, slipped into the complex world of German psychology with the remark about the combination of international inadequacy and shyness of the world [Weltscheu], of cosmopolitanism and provincialism in the German nature. I think I am looking at this in the right way, I believe I have experienced it from my childhood onwards. A journey from the Reich across Lake Constance into Switzerland was a journey from the provincial into the world, – however strange it may seem that Switzerland, a narrow country in comparison to the broad and mighty German Reich and its huge cities, could be perceived as the 'World'.[4] It was, and is, however, its justification: Switzerland, neutral, multilingual, French-influenced, breathing in the air of the West, was indeed, despite her diminutive size, much more the 'World', the European stage, than the political colossus in the North, where the word 'international' had long since become an insult and an arrogant provincialism had spoiled the atmosphere and made it musty.

That was the modern – nationalistic form of the German alienation from the world, German unworldliness, a profound world-clumsiness, which in earlier times together with a type of petty-bourgeois [spießbürgerlich][5] universalism, a cosmopolitanism in a nightcap as one might say [einem Kosmopolitismus in der Nachtmütze sozusagen], had made up the image of the German soul. Something scurrilous and supernatural, something secretive and sinister, something quietly daemonic had always attached to this image, to this unworldly and provincial German cosmopolitanism. My personal origins may have been exceptionally helpful to me in understanding this. I think back to the corner of Germany, out of which the dream-wave of life cast me here, and which formed the first framework of my existence: it was the old Lübeck, near the Baltic, once the Bailiwick of the Hansa, founded before the middle of the twelfth and elevated by Barbarossa in the thirteenth century to the status of a free imperial city.[6] The extraordinarily beautiful Town Hall, which my father frequented as a Senator, was completed in the year in which Martin Luther nailed his theses to the gate of the castle church in Wittenberg; i.e. at the onset of the modern era. Just as Luther, the

3 Mann's italics: Man *hat* zu tun mit dem deutschen Schicksal und deutscher Schuld, wenn man als Deutscher geboren ist.
4 Mann's emphasis.
5 Library of Congress translates this term as 'Philistine'.
6 See Neil MacGregor, 'The Baltic Brothers', in *Germany: Memories of a Nation* (London: Allen Lane, 2014), pp. 231–47.

reformer, was in his manner of thinking and in his soul very much a man of the Middle Ages and wrestled with the Devil all his life, in the same way one could stroll in the Protestant Lübeck that had become a republican member of Bismarck's Reich, and still move in the atmosphere of the gothic Middle Ages. In saying this I am thinking not only of the steepled image of a town with gates and walls, of the humorously macabre shudderings evoked by the Death-Dance painting in the Marienkirche, the crooked, enchanted alleys which were often named after the old craftsmen's guilds, the bell-founders, butchers and of the picturesque town houses. No, in its very atmosphere something had remained of the state of mind of that time: let's say of the last decades of the fifteenth century, the hysteria of the closing years of Middle Ages, something of a latent spiritual epidemic. A strange thing to say of a rational, sober, modern commercial city, but one could imagine that suddenly a children's procession, a St Vitus Dance, an excitement over a miracle of the cross with mystical movement of the people or something of the sort might break out here, – in short, an old-fashioned neurotic undertow was traceable, a secret disposition of the soul expressed in the many 'originals' always to be found in such a town, strange people and harmless semi-lunatics. They live within its walls and in the same way as the old buildings belong to the local scene: a certain type of 'old woman' with rheumy eyes and a walking stick, half jokingly suspected of witchcraft; a modest pensioner with a purple wart on his nose and a kind of nervous tic, ludicrous habits and a stereotypical and compulsive bird-like cry; a female person with a crazy hairstyle who, in an old-fashioned long dress and accompanied by dogs and cats, meanders her way through the town with her nose in the air. To this scene also belong the children, the street urchins, who come along behind these figures, mock them and, if they turn around, run away in superstitious panic.

I do not even know why I am conjuring up these earlier memories here today. Is it because I first experienced Germany, visually and spiritually, in the shape of this strange and venerable cityscape and because to me it suggests a secret link between the German spirit and the daemonic, a link that is a matter of my own inner experience but is not easy to justify? Our greatest poem, Goethe's *Faust*, has as its hero a man at the boundary of the Middle Ages and [the age of] Humanism, a God-fearing man who out of presumptuous drive for knowledge gives himself to magic and the Devil. Where the pride of intellect joins with the spiritually obsolete and with ancient bonds, there is the Devil. And the Devil, Luther's Devil, Faust's Devil, I want to see as a very German figure, and the pact with him, signed and sealed, to gain for a while all the treasures and power of the world at the cost of his soul's salvation, as something peculiarly close to the German nature. A solitary thinker and searcher, a theologian and philosopher in his cell, who, wishing to enjoy and rule the world, signs away his soul to the Devil, – is this not just the right moment to see Germany in this light, today, where Germany is literally being carried off by the Devil?

It is a serious omission of the legend and the poem, that they do not connect Faust with *music*.[7] He must have been musical, he must have been a musician. Music is the domain of the daemonic[8] – Søren Kierkegaard, a great Christian, put it at its most convincing in his painful and enthusiastic essay about Mozart's *Don Juan*. Music is Christian art with a negative prefix [Vorzeichen]. It is the most calculated order and at the same time chaotic anti-reason [Wider-Vernunft], rich in fantastical and incantatory gestures, the magic of numbers, the art which is furthest from reality and at the same time the most passionate, abstract and mythical. If Faust is to be the representative of the German soul, he must have been musical; for the relationship of things German to the world is abstract and mythical, i.e. musical, – the relationship of a professor with a touch of the daemonic, awkward and at the same time conditioned by his arrogant awareness of being superior to the world in 'depth'.

Of what does this depth comprise? Precisely the musicality of the German soul, what might be called its inwardness [Innerlichkeit], that is to say: the antithesis of the speculative and the socio-political element in human energy and the complete prevalence of the first over the second. Europe has always felt this and experienced the monstrous and unfortunate side of it. In 1839 Balzac wrote: 'the Germans, even if they don't know how to play the great instruments of freedom, of course know how to play all the instruments of music'. That is well observed, and is not the only pertinent remark of this kind that the great novelist made. In *Cousin Pons* he says of the German musician Schmucke, a wonderful figure: 'Schmucke, who like all Germans was very strong in harmony, orchestrated the scores, the vocal line of which Pons provided.' Balzac was right: the Germans are above all else musicians of the vertical, not the horizontal; greater masters of harmony, in which Balzac includes counterpoint, rather than of melody; instrumentalists rather than ennoblers of the human voice; more devoted by far to the scholarly and spiritual in music than singing to please the public. They have given the West – I will not say its most beautiful and socially most binding but its deepest and most meaningful music, and the West has not withheld its thanks and

7 Mann's italics.
8 As we saw in Chapter 1, *dämonisch* cannot adequately be translated by the English word 'demon', nor by any other. In addition to its normal meaning, it carries resonances given to it by the *Sturm und Drang* writers of the late eighteenth century, particularly Goethe. It was used like the Greek '*daimon*', to mean the genius, or obsession, driving the dynamic, creative man.

recognition for this. At the same time the West has detected, and today detects more strongly than ever, that such musicality of the soul costs dear in another sphere, – in the political sphere, that of human coexistence.

Martin Luther, a gigantic incarnation of the German nature, was extraordinarily musical. I openly confess that I do not like him. Germanness in its primary state, the separatist anti-Roman alienates and frightens me even in the guise of evangelical freedom and spiritual emancipation; the specifically Lutheranish (the choleric and brutish) [Cholerisch-Grobianische]; the scolding, spitting and raging; forthright rudeness coupled with a tender soul and the most massive belief in demons, incubi and persons afflicted with the goitre [Kielkröpfe])[9] arouses my instinctive antipathy. I would not have liked to be Luther's guest at table: I would probably have felt as little at home with him as with an ogre and am convinced that I would have got along much better with Leo X, Giovanni de Medici, the friendly humanists, whom Luther called 'the Devil's Sow, the Pope'. Nor do I recognise the contradiction between popular force and cultured behaviour, the antithesis between Luther and the fastidious pedant Erasmus, as at all necessary. Goethe transcends this contradiction and reconciles it. He is the completely *cultured* and popular force,[10] the urbane daemonic, simultaneously spirit and blood, namely art. With him Germany took a powerful step forward in human culture – or should have done; for in reality it kept itself closer to Luther than to Goethe. And who would deny that Luther was an immensely great man, great in the most German manner; great and German, too, in his ambiguity as a force at once liberating and reactionary, a conservative revolutionary. He not only restored the Church; he saved Christianity. We are in Europe accustomed to reproach the German nature with being unchristian and heathen. That is highly contestable. Germany took its Christianity extremely seriously. In Luther German Christianity took itself deeply seriously in a childlike and bucolic way at a time when it was no longer doing so elsewhere. Luther's revolution conserved Christendom – rather as the New Deal is intended to conserve the capitalist system – even if capitalism is unwilling to understand this.

Let nothing be said against the greatness of Martin Luther! Not only did he through his powerful translation of the Bible first create a proper German language, which Goethe and Nietzsche then perfected, he also, by bursting the scholastic fetters and reviving conscience, gave a powerful impulse to

9 *Der Kielkropf* – person afflicted with the goitre (London: Cassell's New German English/English German dictionary, 1909).
10 Mann's italics.

freedom of enquiry, criticism and philosophical speculation.[11] By restoring the immediacy of man's relationship to God, he promoted European democracy, since 'every man his own priest' is democracy. German idealistic philosophy, the refinement of psychology through pietistic searchings of conscience, finally the self-conquest of Christian morality by morality, by the strictest adherence to the truth – for that was the deed, or misdeed, of Nietzsche – all this comes from Luther. He was the champion of freedom, but in German style, for he understood nothing of freedom. I do not now mean the freedom of the Christian, but political freedom, freedom of the citizen. The latter not only left him cold, but its stirrings and pretensions were deeply repugnant to him. Four hundred years after him the first President of the German Republic, a Social Democrat, said, 'I hate revolution like sin'. That was genuinely Lutheran, genuinely German. Luther hated the Peasants Revolt which, inspired as it was by Protestantism, would (had it been successful) have given a happier turn to the whole of German history, a turn towards freedom. But Luther saw in this revolt only a tangled compromising of spiritual liberation; he therefore spat on it and cursed it as only he could. He ordered the peasants to be killed like mad dogs and announced to the princes that one could now get to heaven by slaughtering and strangling the peasantry. Luther, the German man of the people, must take a good deal of the responsibility for the sad outcome at this first attempt at a German revolution, for the victory of the princes and for all its consequences.

At that time there lived in Germany a man who has my especial sympathy, Tilman Riemenschneider: a pious artist, a sculptor and woodcarver, very famous for the faithful and expressive integrity of his works, elaborate altar pictures and chaste sculptures, which were much sought after and adorned places of worship throughout Germany.[12] The master had won high regard, both as man and citizen, among his immediate circle in the city of Würzburg, and belonged to its town council. He had never thought to involve himself in high politics and world affairs. That was originally far removed from his natural modesty and love of free, peaceable creativity. He had nothing of the demagogue [about him]. But his heart, which beat for the poor and oppressed, forced him to take up the peasants' cause, which he regarded as just and godly, against the lords, the bishops and princes, whose humanistic benevolence he could easily have retained; moved by the great and fundamental contrasts of the time, he was compelled to leave his purely intellectual and aesthetic civic life as an artist and become a champion of freedom and

---

11 For more on Luther, see 'A Language for all Germans', in MacGregor, *Germany: Memories of a Nation*, pp. 90–110.
12 See 'Sculpting the Spirit', in MacGregor, *Germany: Memories of a Nation*, pp. 214–29.

justice. He gave up his own freedom and the dignified calm of his existence for this cause which meant more to him than spiritual peace. It was chiefly his influence that decided the city of Würzburg to refuse its military support to the 'Burg', the Prince-Bishop, against the peasants and, in general, to take a revolutionary stand against him. He paid a fearful price for this. For after the defeat of the Peasants' Revolt the victorious historical powers that he had opposed took the most cruel revenge on him; they imprisoned and tortured him, and he emerged a broken man, henceforth incapable of awakening beauty from wood and stone.

Such things happen in Germany, and have always happened. But they are not what is specifically and monumentally German. This [latter] is repre-sented by Luther, the musical theologian. In politics he went no further than declaring both parties to be wrong, the princes and the peasants, an attitude that could not fail soon to lead him to put the blame on the peasants – and that with uncontrolled fury. Inwardly he adhered entirely to the Pauline saying 'Be subject to authority, which has authority over you!' But that had referred to the authority of the Roman Empire, which was the precon-dition and the political framework for Christian world-religion, whereas in Luther's case we are dealing with the petty, reactionary authority of German princes. His antipolitical obsequiousness, this product of musical-German inwardness and unworldliness, has not only determined for centuries the submissive attitude of Germans towards their princes and all state authority; has not only in part favoured and in part created the German dualism of boldest speculation and political immaturity. It is above all representative in a monumental and defiant way of that essentially German separation of *national* impulse and the ideal of political freedom. For the Reformation, as later the rising against Napoleon, was a *nationalistic* movement for freedom.

Let us for a moment speak of freedom: the curious reversal which this concept has undergone with such an important people as the Germans, and still undergoes today, gives good grounds for reflection. How was it possible, that even National Socialism, now ending in disgrace, could adopt the name of a German freedom movement, – when the general feeling is that it is impossible that such a perversion could have anything to do with freedom. In this title was expressed not only challenging audacity, but a fundamental misinterpretation of the concept of freedom, a psychological law which has always had its effects in German history. Freedom, politically understood, is above all a moral, internally political concept. A people that is not internally free and responsible for itself does not deserve external freedom; it has no say concerning freedom, and if it uses this resonant term, it uses it wrongly. The German concept of freedom was always directed only outwards; it meant the right to be German and nothing beyond that; it was a protesting concept of self-centred defence against everything which wanted to condition and limit popular egotism, to tame it and keep it in the service of the community and of humanity. Outwardly a defiant individualism in relation to the world, Europe and civilisation; inwardly it conducted itself with an alienating lack of freedom, immaturity and dull subservience. It was militant servility, and National Socialism took this disparity between this external and internal need for freedom to the extreme of contemplating world enslavement by a people as unfree at home as the Germans.

Why must the German urge for freedom always end up as inner enslavement? Why had it finally to become a conspiracy against the freedom of all others, on freedom itself? The reason is that Germany has never had a revolution and has never learnt to unite the concept of the nation with that of freedom. The 'nation' was born in the French Revolution; it is a revolutionary and libertarian idea that includes the humanitarian, and in an internal, political sense it means freedom and in an external political sense, Europe. Everything advantageous in the French political spirit rests on this fortunate unity; everything constricting and depressing in German patriotic enthusiasm rests on this unity never having come about. It might be said that the idea of 'nation' itself, in its historical connection with that of freedom, is foreign to Germany. It might be regarded as erroneous to call the Germans a nation, whether they or others are doing the calling. It is a mistake to apply the word 'nationalism' to their passion for their Fatherland. It represents the misuse of a French idea and creates misunderstandings. The same name should not be applied to two different things. The German idea of freedom is 'völkisch'[13] and anti-European; it is always very close to the barbaric, even if it doesn't explode into open and declared barbarity, as in our day. But the æsthetically repellant and uncouth, already to be found in its standard bearers as early as the Wars of Liberation, in the student associations [Burschenschaftswesen] and in such types as Jahn and Massman, attests to its unhappy character. Goethe was certainly no stranger to popular culture and had written not only the classic *Iphigenie*, but also such quintessentially German things as *Faust I*, *Götz* and *Sprüche in Reimen*.[14] However, to the embitterment of all patriots his attitude towards the wars against Napoleon was one of complete coldness, – not only out of loyalty to his equal, the great Prince, but also because he must have found the barbaric 'völkisch' element in this uprising repulsive. The painful isolation of this great man, who approved of all that is broad and great (the supernational, Germany in the world, world literature) cannot in the Germany of his time, excited as

13 Library of Congress version gives 'racial'.
14 Aphorisms in Rhymes.

it was by patriotism and freedom, be sufficiently appreciated. The decisive and dominating ideas, on which everything turned for him, were culture and barbarism, – and it was his fate to belong to a people to whom the idea of freedom, because it is directed only outwards against Europe and against culture, became barbarism.

A curse prevails here, a continuing tragedy, that expresses itself in the fact that even Goethe's negative attitude to political Protestantism and cheap popular democracy, – that even this attitude has exercised on the nation and especially on its intellectually influential element, the German *Bürgertum*,[15] essentially the effect of confirming and deepening the Lutheran dualism between intellectual and political freedom and that this attitude has prevented the German concept of culture from assimilating the political element. It is very difficult to determine how far great men make their imprint on the character of a people and model it – and how far they are its personification and expression. It is certain that the relationship of the German disposition to politics is a non-relationship, an uncalled-for relationship. Historically it finds expression in the fact that all German revolutions failed: that of 1525, 1813, the 1848 revolution which collapsed due to the political impotence of the German *Bürgertum*, and finally that of 1918. But it also finds expression in the awkward and sinister misunderstanding into which the idea of politics so easily deteriorates with the Germans whenever ambition drives them to engage in it.

Politics has been called the 'Art of the Possible' and it is indeed a sphere similar to art, in so far as, like art, it stands as creative intermediary between spirit and life, idea and reality, the desirable and the necessary, conscience and deed, morality and power. It includes much that is hard, necessary, amoral, much of 'expediency' and concessions to the material, much that is all-too-human [Allzumenschlich] and trapped in the vulgar, and it is difficult to imagine that there ever was a politician or statesman who achieved something great without having to ask himself afterwards whether he could still be accounted a decent man. And yet, just as man does not belong only to the realm of nature, so politics does not belong only to the realm of evil. Without degenerating into the diabolical and destructive, and without becoming an enemy of humanity and perverting its often compromised creativity into shameful and criminal sterility, it can never completely escape from its ideal element, never completely deny the moral and decent part of its nature and descend just to the immoral and vulgar, to lies, murder, deception and force. That would no longer be art and creatively mediating or enabling

---

15 Library of Congress version gives 'leaders', but as this does not convey the resonance of Mann's German text, the term has been left untranslated (see Chapter 1).

irony but blind and dehumanised nonsense, which can establish nothing real, but enjoy only fleeting, frightening success, while already in the shorter term having a world-exterminating, nihilistic and even self-destructive effect; for the completely immoral is also that which is opposed to life.

For peoples who are called and born to politics instinctively know, at least subjectively, how to maintain the political unity between conscience and deed, between mind and power; they engage in politics as an art of life and power which cannot be continued without the intervention of the evil which is useful to life and the all-too-earthy, but as an art which never completely leaves out of account the higher things, the idea, the humane, the decent and moral: it is precisely in this engagement that they feel politically and come to terms with the world and with themselves. Coming to terms with life on the basis of such a compromise seems to the German like hypocrisy. He is not born to come to terms with life and he proves his lack of political vocation by misunderstanding politics in a clumsily honest manner. Being by nature not evil at all but rather inclined to the spiritual and ideal, he considers politics to be nothing more than lies, murder, deceit and force, as something completely unclean; if he engages in it from worldly ambition he pursues it in accordance with this philosophy. The German, as politician, believes he must conduct himself in such a way that humanity is dumbfounded – that is what he considers politics. For him it is evil – and so he thinks he is right to become the devil on its behalf.

We have experienced it. Crimes have been committed which no psychology can help to excuse, and least of all, can their superfluity serve as an excuse. They were irrelevant; Germany could have spared itself them. It could have pursued its plans for power and conquest without them. In a world with trusts and exploitation, the thought of monopolistically exploiting all other peoples through the Göring concern was not entirely alien. Its painful aspect was that it thoroughly compromised all too readily the prevailing system by blatant exaggeration. Moreover, as an idea it simply came too late – today, when humanity is striving for economic democracy and fighting for a higher stage of social maturity. The Germans always came too late. They are late, as is music – which is always the last of all the arts to give expression to a universal condition – when this universal condition is understood to be in decline. They are also abstract and mystical – like this, the art most dear to them – both to the point of criminality. Their crimes, I say, did not necessarily belong to their belated exploitative undertakings. They were an addition, a luxury, which they allowed themselves from their inclination to be theoretical, in honour of an ideology, a racial phantasm. If it did not sound as a monstrous glossing-over, it might be said that they committed their crimes from unworldly idealism.

Sometimes, and not least when we look at German history, we have the impression that the world is not the sole creation of God but a co-operative enterprise with someone else. We would like to ascribe to God the gracious fact that good can come out of evil. That evil so often comes out of good is apparently the contribution of the other party. The Germans might well ask why their good turns out evil, why it becomes evil in their hands. Take their original universalism and cosmopolitanism, their inner lack of boundaries, which may be understood as a spiritual appurtenance of their old supra-national empire, the Holy Roman Empire of the German nation. [This is] a highly valuable, positive inclination which, however, was turned into evil through a type of dialectical inversion. The Germans allowed themselves to be seduced into basing their claim to European hegemony – indeed to world rule – on their innate cosmopolitanism; in this way their claim became its exact opposite, the most presumptuous and threatening nationalism and imperialism. In the process they themselves noticed that they had once again come too late to nationalism, that it had outlived its time. So they replaced it with something more modern: the slogan of race – which promptly led them to monstrous crimes and plunged them into deepest misfortune.

Or take what is perhaps the most famous quality of the Germans, that which we designate with the near-untranslatable word 'Innerlichkeit' (inwardness): tenderness, a deep feeling for the heart, unworldly reverie, a piety towards nature, a most pure seriousness of thought and conscience; in short all traits of higher lyricism are involved and not even today can the world forget what it owes to this German 'Innerlichkeit': German metaphysics, German music, and in particular the miracle of the German Lied – something nationally quite unique and incomparable, these are the fruits of German 'Innerlichkeit'. The great historical act of German 'Innerlichkeit' was Luther's Reformation – we have called it an act of liberation – and therefore it had its good side. But it is obvious that the devil had a hand in it. The Reformation brought a religious split of the West, a manufactured misfortune, and it brought for Germany the Thirty Years War, which depopulated it and dealt a fatal blow to its culture, and through vice and scourge probably made something different and worse of German blood than it may have been in the Middle Ages. Erasmus of Rotterdam, who wrote the *Praise of Folly*, a sceptical humanist of little 'Innerlichkeit', was well aware of the implications of the Reformation. 'When you see terrible disorder arising in the World', he said 'then remember that Erasmus predicted them.' But the venerable boor of Wittenberg was no pacifist. He was full of German affirmation of tragic destiny and declared himself ready 'to take the blood that would flow "on his own shoulders"'.

What is German *Romanticism* other than an expression of that most beautiful German attribute: German 'Innerlichkeit'. Much that is nostalgic and dreamlike, fantastic and spectral, profound and absurd, a high artistic refinement, an all-embracing irony are bound up with the concept of Romanticism. But this is not really what I am thinking of when I speak of German Romanticism. It is much more a certain dark powerfulness and piety – one could even say antiquatedness – of the soul that feels very close to the chthonian, supra-rational and daemonic forces, i.e. to the actual sources of life; it offers to a purely rational view of the world and its ways the opposite view of deeper knowledge and a deeper connection with the sacred. The Germans are a people of romantic counter-revolution against the philosophical intellectualism and rationalism of the Enlightenment – of a rebellion of music against literature, of mysticism against clarity. Romanticism is anything but sickly imaginings; it is depth perceiving itself as strength and fullness, a pessimism of honesty which prefers the existing, the real and the historical to criticism and meliorism, preferring, in short, insight into the spirit and thinking precious little of any rhetorical virtue and idealistic beautification. Here is the connection between Romanticism and that realism and Machiavellianism that celebrated its victories over Europe in Bismarck, the only political genius ever produced by Germany. The German drive towards unification and empire, which Bismarck directed along Prussian lines, would be misunderstood were one to see in it the usual model of a national-democratic unification movement. It had once, around about 1848, tried to be just that, although even then the discussion of Greater Germany in the St Paul's Parliament had an aura of medieval imperialism and memories of the Holy Roman Empire. But it transpired that the usual European national-democratic way to unification was not the German way. Essentially Bismarck's Reich had nothing to do with democracy or anything to do with nation in the democratic sense of the word. It was a pure power construct aiming towards European hegemony and, regardless of all modernity and sober efficiency, the empire of 1871 associated itself with memories of medieval glory and the age of the Saxon and Swabian rulers. What was both characteristic and threatening in this was the mixture of robust timeliness, efficient modernity and nostalgia, i.e. a highly techno-logical form of Romanticism. Having come into existence through wars the Unholy German Empire of the Prussian nation could only be an empire of war. As such it has lived, a thorn in the flesh of the world, and as such it is now destroyed.

The merits of the German Romantic counter-revolution in intel-lectual history are invaluable. Hegel himself had the most important share in it, in that his dialectic philosophy bridged the gulf which the rational Enlightenment and the French Revolution had opened up between reason and history. His reconciliation of the rational with the real gave a powerful impulse to historical thought and actually created the science of history which hitherto had hardly existed. Romanticism is essentially an immersion, particularly a self-immersion, into the past; it is the longing for the past, and at the same time a realistic recognition of all that has actually existed in its own right with its local colour and atmosphere – no wonder that it was particularly well suited to historiography or that it inaugurated the discipline in its modern form.

The contributions of Romanticism to the realm of the beautiful, as science and æsthetic doctrine, are rich and fascinating. Positivism and intellectual enlightenment have no knowledge of the nature of poetry; Romanticism alone taught it to a world which was collapsing from boredom in virtuous academicism. The Romantic poeticised ethics by proclaiming the right of individuality and spontaneous passion. It raised treasures of fairy tale and song out of the depths of folk-history and was the principal intellectual patron of folklore, which in its colourful light appears as a deviant form of exoticism. The preference which it gave to the emotional over the rational (even to the emotional in its distant forms of mystical ecstasy and Dionysiac intoxication) brings it into a particular and psychologically highly fruitful relationship to disease – just as the late Romantic Nietzsche, himself a spirit carried aloft by disease into the realm of genius and death, could not sufficiently acclaim the value of disease as a means of acquiring knowledge. In this sense even psychoanalysis, which represents a great advance towards the understanding of man from the viewpoint of illness, is an offshoot of Romanticism.

Goethe gave the laconic definition of the Classical as healthy and the Romantic as diseased; a painful formulation for anyone who loves the Romantic with all its sins and vices.[16] But it is not to be denied that in its fairest, most ethereal but at the same time popular and sublime manifestations it carries within itself the seed of disease, like the rose bears the worm; its innermost nature is seduction, and what is more, seduction to death. This is its confusing paradox: while it revolutionarily advocates irrational life forces against abstract reason and shallow humanity, it possesses a deep affinity with death precisely through its devotion to the irrational and the past. In Germany, its real homeland, it has most strongly retained this iridescent ambiguity, as the glorification of the vital against the merely moral and at the same time as affinity with death. As the German spirit and as a Romantic counter-revolution, it has given deep and lively impulses to European thought; but it was beneath its pride in life and death to accept any corrective teachings from Europe, from the spirit of European humanistic religion or from European democracy. In its *Realpolitik* form, as Bismarckism,

16 See Furtwängler, AZN, p. 230; NBKS, p. 141.

as the German victory over France, over civilisation, and by the creation of the German Imperial Empire, seemingly resplendent and in the most robust health, it elicited the astonishment of the world, but at the same time confused and depressed it. As soon as the genius himself no longer ruled this empire it kept the world in a constant state of unease.

Moreover, this unified imperial power was a cultural disappointment. Nothing spiritually great came out of Germany, which had formerly been the teacher of the world. Now it was only strong. But in this strength and with all Germany's organised efficiency the Romantic seed of disease and death survived and worked away. Historical misfortune, the sufferings and humiliation of a lost war, nourished this seed. And, reduced to the miserable level of the masses, the level of Hitler, German Romanticism broke out into hysterical barbarism, in an intoxication and convulsion of arrogance and crime, which is now finding its hideous end in national catastrophe, in an unparalleled physical and psychical collapse.

What I have told you in brief fragments, ladies and gentlemen, is the history of German 'Innerlichkeit'. It is a melancholy history – I call it thus and do not speak of 'tragedy', for misfortune should not boast. This story should convince us of one thing: that there are not two Germanys, an evil and a good, but only one, the best of which turned out as evil through devilish cunning. The evil Germany is the good Germany gone astray, the good one in misfortune, in guilt and in ruin. It is therefore impossible for a German-born spirit simply to deny completely the evil, guilt-laden Germany and to declare: 'I am the good, the noble and the just Germany in my white garment; I leave it to you to eradicate the evil one.' Nothing that I have tried to say or fleetingly to indicate to you about Germany has come out of alien, cold or detached knowledge; it is all within me, I have experienced it all in my own person.

In other words: what I have tried to give within the limits of time, was [is] a piece of German self-criticism – and truly, I could not have followed German tradition more faithfully than by so doing. The tendency to self-criticism, often to the point of self-disgust, to self-denigration, is quintessentially German, and it will remain forever incomprehensible, how a people so inclined to self-knowledge could at the same time conceive the idea of world domination. The quality most necessary for world domination is above all naivety, a blissful limitation and even lack of intention, but not an extreme inner life like the German, in which arrogance is coupled with remorse. Nothing that a Frenchman, an Englishman or even an American has thrown in the face of his people can be compared to the stark home truths which great Germans such as Hölderlin, Goethe or Nietzsche have levelled against Germany. In conversation, at least, Goethe went so far as to wish for a

German Diaspora. 'Like the Jews', he said, 'the Germans must be transplanted and scattered over the world!' And he added, 'In order to develop the mass of good that lies in them, fully and to the benefit of the nations.'

The mass of good – it really does exist, but in the traditional form of the national state it could not fulfil itself. The immigration legislation of other states will put a definite stop to the scattering throughout the world that Goethe wished for his Germans and to which they may be strongly inclined after this war. But does the hope not remain, in spite of all drastic warnings against exaggerated expectations which *Machtpolitik* imposes on us, that inevitably and of necessity after this catastrophe the first tentative steps will be taken in the direction of a world order in which the national individualism of the nineteenth century will dissolve, indeed finally disappear, and which will offer the 'mass of good' within the German nature more fortunate possibilities to prove itself than did the now untenable old world order. It could indeed be that the liquidation of Nazism has opened the way to social reform in the world that offers the greatest possibilities of happiness for Germany's innermost inclinations and needs. World economy, the reduced importance of political boundaries, a certain depoliticising of the state, the awakening of humanity to awareness of its practical unity, its first contemplation of a world state – how can all this social humanism which transcends bourgeois democracy, the humanism which is the object of great contention, be alien and repugnant to the German character? In the seclusion of the German there was always so much longing for the world [Weltverlangen];[17] in the solitude that made him evil is the wish, as we all know, to love and be loved. In the final analysis the German misfortune is only the paradigm of human tragedy in general. We all need the grace that Germany so sorely needs.

17 Library of Congress version gives 'companionship'.

AUDIO AND VISUAL SOURCES

The following is not in any sense a discography of Furtwängler recordings. For a full listing see René Trémine, *Wilhelm Furtwängler: A Discography* (Bezons: Tahra Productions, 1997). Below are listed selected audio CD and DVD sources associated with documents and historical events discussed above. Recordings are conducted by Furtwängler unless otherwise stated. Most are now widely available. They are regularly reissued in various formats and can usually be traced without difficulty via an Internet search. Only dates are therefore given below. See also John Ardoin, *The Furtwängler Record* (Oregon: The Amadeus Press, 1994).

Chapter 2

Wilhelm Furtwängler (composer), *Te Deum*; *Religiöser Hymnus*; *Schwindet, ihr dunklen Wölbungen*; *Lieder*, Frankfurt a. d. Oder Philharmonic Orchestra und Singakademie, conducted by Alfred Walter, 1993

Chapter 3

Hans Pfitzner, *Palestrina* (complete), Julius Patzak (Palestrina), Hans Hotter (Borromeo), conducted by Robert Heger, live performance, 24 July 1951, Prinzregententheater, München

Chapter 4

Hans Pfitzner, *Von deutscher Seele* (Op. 28), *Das dunkle Reich* (Op. 38), Chor und Symphonieorchester des Bayerischen Rundfunks, conducted by Eugen Jochum

There are no known recordings of Furtwängler or Toscanini conducting Beethoven's *Eroica* contemporaneous with Toscanini's appearances in Berlin in May 1930. The following later performances are given by way of comparison:

Beethoven, Symphony No. 3 in E flat major, *Eroica*, Op. 55
NBC Symphony Orchestra, conducted by Toscanini, 28 October 1939
Vienna Philharmonic Orchestra, conducted by Furtwängler, 19 December 1944

Chapter 5

Hindemith, *Sinfonie Mathis der Maler*, Bamberger Symphoniker, conducted by Karl Anton Rickenbacher

DVD, Hindemith: A Pilgrim's Progress, film by Tony Palmer

Chapter 6

Wagner, *Lohengrin*, extracts from Act III recorded at the Bayreuth Festival, 19 July 1936

Wagner, *Die Walküre*, Act III (complete), recorded at the Royal Opera House, Covent Garden, London, 26 May 1937

Beethoven, Symphony No. 9, recorded in the Philharmonie, Berlin, 22 March 1942

Wagner, *Die Meistersinger von Nürnberg* (almost complete; some material missing, including the Act III Quintet), recorded at the Bayreuth Festival, 15 July 1943

Bruckner, Symphony No. 8, Vienna Philharmonic *Magnetofonkonzert*, recorded 17 October 1944

DVD, *The Reichsorchester*, a film by Enrique Sánchez Lansch. Includes footage of the closing moments of the performance of Beethoven's Ninth Symphony given on 19 April 1942; also the complete *Kraft durch Freude* film of Furtwängler conducting the *Meistersinger* Prelude, 26 February 1942

Chapter 7

Beethoven, Symphonies Nos. 5 and 6, Berlin Philharmonic Orchestra, 25 May 1947, Berlin

Richard Strauss, *Metamorphosen*, Berlin Philharmonic Orchestra, 27 October 1947, Berlin

Mendelssohn, Violin Concerto, with Yehudi Menuhin, Berlin Philharmonic Orchestra, 25–6 May 1952, Berlin

Hans Pfitzner, *Palestrina, Three Preludes*, Berlin Philharmonic Orchestra, 10 June 1949, Wiesbaden

Hans Pfitzner, Symphony (Op. 46), Vienna Philharmonic Orchestra, 7 August 1949, Wiesbaden

Richard Strauss, *Four Last Songs*, with Kirsten Flagstad, Philharmonia Orchestra, 22 May 1950, London)

Film (YouTube)

Brahms, Symphony No. 4, rehearsal of the second part of the fourth movement with the Berlin Philharmonic Orchestra in London, 2 or 3 November 1948 (see present work, p. xi)

Chapter 8

Wilhelm Furtwängler's works

Symphony No. 1 in B minor, Czecho-Slovak State Philharmonic, conducted by Alfred Walter

Symphony No. 2 in E minor
Radio-Sinfonie-Orchester Stuttgart, 30 March 1954, conducted by Furt-wängler
Chicago Symphony Orchestra, conducted by Daniel Barenboim, studio recording, 2002

Symphony No. 3 in C sharp minor
Bayerische Staatsorchester, conducted by Wolfgang Sawallisch, first to third movements, 7 January 1980
Staatskapelle Weimar, conducted by George Alexander Albrecht, complete, 2000

Chapter 9

Beethoven, *Fidelio*, Kirsten Flagstad, Julius Patzak, Salzburg Festival, 5 August 1950

Bach, *Brandenburg Concerto No. 5*, with Furtwängler on piano, 31 August 1950

Beethoven, Symphony No. 9, Bayreuth Festival, 29 July 1951

Wagner, *Tristan und Isolde*, London, June 1952

Bach, *Matthäus Passion*, Vienna, 14–17 April 1954

Beethoven, Symphony No. 5, Berlin, 23 May 1954

Weber, *Der Freischütz*, Salzburg Festival, 26 July 1954

Beethoven, Symphony No. 9, Lucerne, 22 August 1954

Wagner, *Die Walküre*, Vienna, October 1954

Film (YouTube)

Richard Strauss, *Till Eulenspiegel*, Berlin, 1951

Mozart, *Don Giovanni*, Overture, Salzburg, 1954

BIBLIOGRAPHY

Unpublished Sources

The Furtwängler Nachlass is held in two locations:
- Musikabteilung, Zentralbibliothek Zürich (Nachlass W. Furtwängler)
- Furtwängler Nachlass der Staatsbibliothek zu Berlin – Preußischer Kulturbesitz (SPK), Musikabteilung mit Mendelssohn-Archiv, (Signatur 55, Nachl. 13)

Abbreviations used below

MS   Manuscript
TS   Typescript

Items consulted in the Furtwängler Nachlass, Zentralbibliothek Zürich

S 3, 'Anmerkung zu Beethoven's Musik', in *Der Tag*, 5 March 1918

S 4, 'Anmerkungen zur Musik von Wagners *Ring des Nibelungen*', in *Mannheimer Theaterjahrbuch*, 1919

S 5, 'Anton Bruckners achte Sinfonie', newspaper cutting of indeterminate origin, 1917

S 7, 'Bach', TS, in *Deutsche Rundschau*, Gelsenkirchen, March 1951

S 14, 'Bermerkungen eines Komponisten: Geleitwort zur Uraufführung der II. Sinfonie', in *Universitas*, vol. 3, 1948

S 18, 'Johannes Brahms: Festvortrag für das Johannes Brahms-Fest, Wien, 16–21 May 1933', TS, in *Deutsche Allgemeine Zeitung*, 28 May 1933 and *Neue Freie Presse*, 28 May 1933; *Johannes Brahms–Anton Bruckner: mit einem Nachwort von Walter Riezler* (Leipzig, 1942; Stuttgart, 1952); see also Item S 55

S 21, 'Anton Bruckner', 5 July 1939, MS, TS, in *Deutsche Allgemeine Zeitung*, 16 July 1939, as 'Über das Wesen Anton Bruckners'; *Johannes Brahms–Anton Bruckner: mit einem Nachwort von Walter Riezler* (Leipzig, 1942; Stuttgart, 1952); see also Item S 55

S 22, 'Chaos und Gestalt: Anmerkungen zur Musik der Gegenwart', fragments, TS, 1 1a 2 sketches for the essay of the same title in *Vermächtnis*, pp. 131–63

S 31, 'Der Fall Hindemith', in *Deutsche Allgemeine Zeitung*, 25 November 1934

S 33, 'Freiwild Kunst' ('Alles Grosse ist Einfach'), in *Die Kultur*, 15 November 1954

S 44, *Gespräche über Musik*, various TS versions, annotated by Furtwängler, of drafts of the conversations which comprise the published book

S 51, 'Improvisation: Dirigent und Orchester', in *Weser Kurier*, Bremen, 25 January 1951; extract from *Gespräche über Musik*, pp. 55–6, 59–61

S 53, 'Interpretation: Eine Musikalische Schicksalsfrage', TS, in *Atlantisbuch der Musik*, Berlin, 1934

S 55, *Johannes Brahms–Anton Bruckner: Mit einem Nachwort von Walter Riezler*, setting copy (Druckvorlage) for publication in book form (Leipzig, 1942)

S 58, 1, 'Die Klassiker in der Musik-Krise', MS, in *Unterhaltungsblatt der Vossischen Zeitung*, 19 April 1932 and *Allgemeine Musikzeitung*, 29 April 1932

S 63, 'Max von Schillings', TS, 31 August 1933

S 67, 'Die Musik Ludwig van Beethovens', in *Universitas*, vol. 5, 1950; extract from *Gespräche über Musik*, pp. 34–7, 38–41, 44–50

S 76, 'Musikalisches Gesetz oder dichterische Idee in Beethoven's Schaffen?', in *Das Musikleben*, vol. 1, 1948; extract from *Gespräche über Musik*, pp. 44–50

S 95, 'Toscanini: Beitrag zur wahren Situation des deutschen Musizierens im Jahre 1933', TS

S 107, 'Um Bayreuths Zukunft', in *Unterhaltungsblatt der Vossischen Zeitung*, 28 June 1932

S 121, 'Zeitgemässe Betrachtungen eines Musikers', offprint of indeterminate origin. Published in *Vermächtnis*, pp. 57–82 and dated 1915

S 126, 2, 'Der Fall Hindemith tritt jetzt', TS, Bayreuth, July 1937

S 129, 5, 'Als ich meinen Artikel über Hindemith schrieb', TS, January–March 1935

S 130, Fragments, including a heavily amended MS draft of Furtwängler's letter to Goebbels, 11 April 1933

S 132, Taschenkalender (*Aufzeichnungen*)
   1. 14 Taschenkalender, 1924, 1925, 1927–34
   2. 26 Taschenkalender, 1935–45
   3. 10 Taschenkalender, 1946–54)
   Microfilm only. Originals held in SPK Berlin, 55 Nachl. 13, W. Furtwängler, Kasten 44

Compositions, MS sources

WF 57, *Erinnerungen*, Op. 4 No. 1, 28 June 1897
WF 75, *Ganymed*, 1898, fragment
WF 88, *Wanderers Nachtlied*, November 1900, fragment
WF 90, *Auf dem See*, 1900
WF 100, *Herbstgefühl*, April–June 1902
WF 106, *Religiöser Hymnus*, 1903
WF 110b, *1. Sinfonie in b-moll*, 1906–40
WF 119, *2. Sinfonie in e-moll*, 1944–18 October 1945
WF 120, *3. Sinfonie in Cis*, 1946–54

Items consulted in the Furtwängler Nachlass, Staatsbibliothek zu Berlin, Preußischer Kulturbesitz

Kasten 6, 7, 9, 10, 12, 13, 18, 20, 22, 25, 27, 31, 33 and 44–6, 'Der Fall Wagner, frei nach Nietzsche', TS, April 1941
Correspondence as detailed in footnotes

Furtwängler's Published Writings and Compositions

Gespräche über Musik [GM] (Zürich: Atlantis, 1948); Eng. edn, *Concerning Music* [CM], tr. L. J. Lawrence (London: Boosey and Hawkes, 1953)
Ton und Wort: Aufsätze und Vorträge 1918–1954 [TW] (Wiesbaden: F. A. Brockhaus, 1955)
Vermächtnis: Nachgelassene Schriften [VMS] (Wiesbaden: F. A. Brockhaus, 1956)
Wilhelm Furtwängler: Briefe, ed. Frank Thiess (Wiesbaden: F. A. Brockhaus, 1964; Vierte Auflage, 1980)
Aufzeichnungen [AZN], eds Elisabeth Furtwängler and Günter Birkner (Wiesbaden: Brockhaus, 1980); Eng. edn, *Notebooks* [NBKS], tr. Shaun Whiteside, ed. Michael Tanner (London: Quartet Books, 1989)
Furtwängler on Music [FM], tr. and ed. Ronald Taylor (Aldershot: Scolar Press, 1991)
1. Sinfonie in b-moll (Berlin: Ries & Erler, 2001)
2. Sinfonie in e-moll (Wiesbaden: Brucknerverlag, 1952; Berlin: Ries & Erler, 2001)
3. Sinfonie in Cis (Berlin: Ries & Erler, 2001)

Other Primary Sources

Bent, Ian, David Bretherton and William Drabkin, eds, *Heinrich Schenker: Selected Correspondence* (Woodbridge: The Boydell Press, 2014)

Federhofer, Hellmut, *Heinrich Schenker nach Tagebüchern und Briefen in der Oswald Jonas Memorial Collection* (Hildesheim: Georg Olms Verlag, 1985)

Huch, Friedrich, *Enzio: Ein musikalischer Roman* (Leipzig: Josef Singer Verlag, 1910)

Hürlimann, Martin, ed., *Wilhelm Furtwängler. Im Urteil seiner Zeit* (Zürich: Atlantis, 1955)

Kanzog, Klaus, *Offene Wunden: Wilhelm Furtwängler und Thomas Mann* (Würzburg: Königshausen & Neumann, 2014)

Lang, Klaus, *Wilhelm Furtwängler und seine Entnazifizierung* (Aachen: Shaker Media, 2012)

Mann, Thomas, 'Deutschland und die Deutschen', in *Sorge um Deutschland* (Stockholm: S. Fischer Verlag, 1957), pp. 73–93; Eng. tr. Brian Hitch and Roger Allen in Appendix 2

Schenker Documents Online <http://www.schenkerdocumentsonline.org> (accessed 16 November 2017)

Trémine, René, *Wilhelm Furtwängler: Concert Listings 1906–1954* (Bezons: Tahra Productions, 1997)

——, *Wilhelm Furtwängler: A Discography* (Bezons: Tahra Productions, 1997)

Narrative Biographies

Herzfeld, Friedrich, *Wilhelm Furtwängler: Weg und Wesen* (Leipzig: Wilhelm Goldmann, 1941, rev. edn, München: Goldmann Verlag, 1950)

Riess, Curt, *Wilhelm Furtwängler: Musik und Politik* (Berne: Scherz, 1953); tr. Margaret Goldsmith, *Wilhelm Furtwängler: A Biography* (London: Frederick Muller, 1955)

Schönzeler, Hans-Hubert, *Furtwängler* (London: Duckworth, 1990)

Shirakawa, Sam H., *The Devil's Music Master: The Controversial Life and Career of Wilhelm Furtwängler* (New York and Oxford: OUP 1992)

Wessling, Berndt, *Furtwängler: Eine kritische Biographe* (Stuttgart: Deutsche Verlags-Anstalt, 1985)

Stage Play

Ronald Harwood, *Taking Sides* (1995), published as *Collaboration & Taking Sides* (London: Faber & Faber, 2008)

General Bibliography of Works Consulted

Adorno, Theodor W., 'Die Meisterschaft des Maestro', in *Musikalische Schriften I–III, Gesammelte Schriften* (Frankfurt: Suhrkamp, 1978), vol. 16, pp. 52–67

——, *Philosophy of Modern Music*, tr. A. G. Mitchell and W. V. Bloomster (New York: Seabury Press, 1973)

——, *Versuch über Wagner* (Frankfurt: Suhrkamp, 1952); Eng. edn, *In Search of Wagner*, tr. Rodney Livingstone (London: Verso, 1981)

Allen, Roger, tr. and ed., *Richard Wagner's 'Beethoven' (1870)* (Woodbridge: The Boydell Press, 2014)

Alperson, Philip, ed., *What is Music? An Introduction to the Philosophy of Music* (Pennsylvania: Pennsylvania State UP, 1994)

Ancelet-Hustache, Jeanne, *Master Eckhart and the Rhineland Mystics* (New York and London: Harper, 1957)

Anderson, Benedict, *Imagined Communities* (New York and London: Verso, 1983)

Anderson, Martin, ed., *Klemperer on Music* (London: Toccata Press, 1986)

Applegate, Celia, 'How German Is It? Nationalism and the Idea of Serious Music in the early Nineteenth Century', *19th Century Music*, vol. 21 (Spring 1998), pp. 274–96

Applegate, Celia, and Pamela Potter, eds, *Music and German National Identity* (Chicago and London: University of Chicago Press, 2003)

Ardoin, John, *The Furtwängler Record* (Portland, OR: Amadeus Press, 1994)

Atkins, Harold, and Archie Newman, *Beecham Stories* (London: Robson Books, 1978)

Attfield, Nicholas, *Challenging the Modern: Conservative Revolution in German Music 1918–1933* (Oxford: OUP, 2017)

Auer, Max, *Anton Bruckner: Sein Leben und Werk* (Wien: Musikwissenschaftlicher Verlag, 1932)

Bachmann, Robert C., *Karajan: Notes on a Career*, tr. Shaun Whiteside (London: Quartet Books, 1990)

Beddow, Michael, *Thomas Mann, Dr Faustus* (Cambridge: CUP, 1994)

Beecham, Thomas, *A Mingled Chime: Leaves from an Autobiography* (London: Hutchinson & Co., 1944)

Bekker, Paul, *Beethoven* (Stuttgart and Berlin: Deutsch Verlags-Anstalt, 1911); Eng. edn, tr. M. M. Bozman (London: J. M. Dent, 1925)

Bennett, Alan, *The History Boys* (London: Faber & Faber, 2004)

Berg, Alban, *Briefe an seine Frau* (München and Wien: Albert Langen, Georg Müller, 1965); Eng. edn, ed. and tr. Bernard Grun, *Alban Berg: Letters to his Wife* (London: Faber & Faber, 1971)

Berlin, Isaiah, *Concepts and Categories* (Oxford: OUP, 1980)

——, *The Crooked Timber of Humanity* (London: Fontana, 1991)

Biancolli, Louis, *The Flagstad Manuscript* (London: William Heinemann, 1953)

Birkin, Kenneth, *Hans von Bülow: A Life for Music* (Cambridge: CUP, 2011)

Bonds, Mark Evan, *Absolute Music: The History of an Idea* (Oxford: OUP, 2014)

Brown, Hilda Meldrum, *The Quest for the Gesamtkunstwerk & Richard Wagner* (New York: OUP, 2016)

Bujić, Bojan, ed., *Music in European Thought, 1815–1912* (Cambridge: CUP, 1988)

Bullock, Alan, *Hitler: A Study in Tyranny* (London: Odhams Press, 1952)

Burkhardt, Max, *Führer durch Richard Wagners Musikdramen* (Berlin: Globus Verlag, n.d., handwritten inscription, 1910)

Burleigh, Michael, *The Third Reich: A New History* (London: Macmillan, 2000)

Busch-Salmen, Gabriele, and Günther Weiss, *Hans Pfitzner: Münchner Dokumente, Bilder und Bildnisse* (Regensburg: Bosse, 1990)

Butler, Eliza, *The Fortunes of Faust* (Cambridge: CUP, 1952; pbk reprint, Stroud, Gloucs.: Sutton Publishing Ltd, 1998)

Cardinal, Roger, *German Romantics in Context* (London: Studio Vista, 1975)

Cardus, Neville, *Autobiography* (London: Collins, 1947)

——, *Cardus on Music*, ed. Donald Wright (London: Hamish Hamilton, 1988)

——, *Full Score* (London: Cassell, 1970)

——, *Sir Thomas Beecham* (London: Collins, 1961)

Carnegy, Patrick, *Faust as Musician* (London: Chatto & Windus, 1973)

——, *Wagner and the Art of the Theatre* (New Haven and London: Yale UP, 2006)

Chamberlain, Houston Stewart, *Das Drama Richard Wagners: Eine Anregung* (Leipzig: Breitkopf & Härtel, 1892)

——, 'Einleitung', *Richard Wagner: Auswahl seiner Schriften* (Leipzig: Insel-Verlag, 1910), pp. v–xvi

——, *Goethe* (München: F. Bruckmann AG, 1912; Ungekürzte Volksausgabe zum Goethe-Jahr, 1932)

——, *Die Grundlagen des neunzehnten Jahrhunderts* (München: F. Bruckmann AG, 1899; 4th edn, 1903); Eng. edn, *The Foundations of the Nineteenth Century*, tr. John Lees, 2 vols (London: The Bodley Head, 1910)

——, *Immanuel Kant* (München: Verlagsanstalt F. Bruckmann AG, 1905); Eng. edn, tr. Lord Redesdale, 2 vols (London: The Bodley Head, 1914)

——, *Politische Ideale* (München: F. Bruckmann, 1915)

——, *Richard Wagner* (München: Verlagsanstalt für Kunst und Wissenschaft, 1896)

Collins, Diana, *Partners in Protest: Life with Canon Collins* (London: Victor Gollancz Ltd, 1992)

Cook, Nicholas, *Beethoven: Symphony No. 9* (Cambridge: CUP, 1993)

——, 'The Conductor and the Theorist: Furtwängler, Schenker and the first Movement of Beethoven's Ninth Symphony', in *The Practice of Performance: Studies in Musical Interpretation* (Cambridge: CUP, 1995), pp. 105–25

——, 'Heinrich Schenker, Polemicist: a reading of the Ninth Symphony Monograph', *Music Analysis*, vol. 14, no. 1 (1995), pp. 89–105

——, *The Schenker Project: Culture, Race and Music Theory in Fin-de-Siècle Vienna* (New York: OUP 2007)

Cooke, Deryck, 'Anton Bruckner', in *The Pelican History of the Symphony*, vol. 1 (Harmondsworth: Penguin Books, 1968), pp. 283–306

Dahlhaus, Carl, *Grundlagen der Musikgeschichte* (Cologne: Musikverlag Hans Gerig, 1977); Eng. edn, *Foundations of Music History*, tr. J. Bradford Robinson (Cambridge: CUP, 1983)

——, *Die Musik des 19. Jahrhunderts* (Wiesbaden: Laaber, 1980); Eng. edn, *Nineteenth-Century Music*, tr. J. Bradford Robinson (Berkeley and London: University of California Press, 1989)

Dahlhaus, Carl, and John Deathridge, *The New Grove Wagner* (London: Macmillan, 1984)

Darwin, Charles, *The Origin of the Species* (1859; pbk edn, Oxford: OUP, 1996)

David, Hans T., and Arthur Mendel, *The Bach Reader* (New York: W. Norton, 1945)

Dilthey, Wilhelm, *Von Deutscher Dichtung und Musik* (Berlin: Teubner, 1933)

——, *Das Erlebnis und die Dichtung* (Leipzig and Berlin: Teubner, 1913)

——, *Das Wesen der Philosophie* (Stuttgart: Philipp Reclam Jun., 1984)

Dunwell, Wilfrid, *Music and the European Mind* (New York: T. Yoseloff, 1962)

Ehrenfels, Christian von, Über Gestaltqualitäten', *Vierteljahrschrift für wissenschaftliche Philosophie*, vol. 14 (1890), pp. 249–92; Eng. tr., Barry Smith, ed., *Foundations of Gestalt Theory* (München and Wien: Philosophia Verlag, 1988), pp. 82–123

Einstein, Alfred, *Greatness in Music*, tr. César Saerchinger (New York and London: OUP, 1941)

Elkin, Robert, *Royal Philharmonic: Annals of the Royal Philharmonic Society* (London: Rider & Co., 1946)

Evans, Richard, *The Coming of the Third Reich* (London: Allen Lane, 2003)

——, 'Playing for the Devil: How Much did Furtwängler really resist the Nazis?', *Times Literary Supplement* (London), 13 November 1992, pp. 3–4

——, ed., *Society and Politics in Wilhelmine Germany* (London: Croom Helm Ltd, 1978), especially Ch. 4, Robin Lenman, 'The State and the Avant-Garde in Munich 1886–1914' and Ch. 5, Geoff Eley, 'The Wilhelmine Right: How it changed'

Fichte, J. G., *Sämmtliche Werke*, vol. 7 (Berlin: Veit und Comp., 1845–46)

Field, Geoffrey, *Evangelist of Race: The Germanic Vision of Houston Stewart Chamberlain* (New York: Columbia UP, 1981)

Fifield, Christopher, *True Artist and True Friend: A Biography of Hans Richter* (Oxford: OUP, 1993)

Fischer-Dieskau, Dietrich, *Nachklang* (München: Deutsche Verlags-Anstalt, 1987); Eng. edn, *Reverberations*, tr. Ruth Hein (New York: Fromm, 1990)

——, *Wagner und Nietzsche: Der Mystagoge und sein Abtrünniger* (München: Deutsche Verlags-Anstalt, 1974); Eng. edn, *Wagner and Nietzsche*, tr. Joachim Neugroschel (London: Continuum Publishing Group, 1976)

Franklin, Peter, 'Audiences, Critics and the Depurification of Music: Reflections on a 1920s Controversy', *Journal of the Royal Musical Association*, vol. 114, Part 1 (1989), pp. 80–91

Friedell, Egon, *Kulturgeschichte der Neuzeit: Der Krisis der Europäischen Seele von der Schwarzen Pest bis zum Ersten Weltkrieg*, 3 vols (München: C. H. Beck, 1927–31; combined edn in one volume, München: C. H. Beck, 1931)

Friedenthal, Richard, *Goethe: His Life and Times* (London, 1963; pbk edn, London: Weidenfeld, 1993)

Friedländer, Saul, *Nazi Germany and the Jews: The Years of Persecution 1933–39* (London: Weidenfeld & Nicolson, 1997)

Furtwängler, Elisabeth, *Über Wilhelm Furtwängler* (Wiesbaden: Brockhaus, 1979)

Garratt, James, *Music, Culture and Social Reform* (Cambridge: CUP, 2010)

Geissmar, Berta, *The Baton and the Jackboot* (London: Hamish Hamilton, 1944); German edn, *Musik im Schatten der Politik* (Zürich: Atlantis, 1945); 4th edn with an introduction by Fred K. Prieberg (Zürich, 1985); republished as *Taktstock und Schaftstiefel: Erinnerungen an Wilhelm Furtwängler und Sir Thomas Beecham* (Köln: Dittrich-Verlag, 1996)

Gilliam, Bryan, 'The Annexation of Anton Bruckner: Nazi Revisionism and the Politics of Appropriation', *Musical Quarterly*, vol. 78, no. 3 (1994), pp. 584–609

——, *Music and Performance during the Weimar Republic* (Cambridge: CUP, 1994)

Gillies, A., *Herder* (Oxford: Blackwell, 1945)

Goebbels, Joseph, *The Goebbels Diaries 1939–1941*, tr. and ed. Fred Taylor (London: Hamish Hamilton, 1982)

Goehr, Lydia, *The Imaginary Museum of Musical Works: An Essay in the Philosophy of Music* (Oxford: Clarendon Press, 1992)

Goethe, Johann Wolfgang von, *Faust*, Parts I and II (1808 and 1832); Eng. edn, tr. David Luke (Oxford World's Classics: OUP, 1987 and 1994)

——, *Goethe: The Penguin Poets*, tr. David Luke (Harmondsworth: Penguin Books, 1964)

——, *Sämtliche Werke. Briefe, Tagebücher und Gespräche*, 40 vols (Frankfurt am Main: Deutscher Klassiker Verlag, 1985–2013)

Goldberg, David, and John Rayner, *The Jewish People: Their History and Religion* (London: Penguin, 1989)

Goldhagen, Daniel Jonah, *Hitler's Willing Executioners: Ordinary Germans and the Holocaust* (New York: Alfred A. Knopf, 1996)

Greenfeld, Liah, 'The Final Solution of Infinite Longing: Germany', *Nationalism: Five Roads to Modernity* (Cambridge, MA: Harvard UP, 1992)

Gregor, Neil, 'Beethoven, Bayreuth and the Origins of the Federal Republic of Germany', *English Historical Review*, vol. 126, no. 521

Grey, Thomas, ed., *The Cambridge Companion to Wagner* (Cambridge: CUP, 2008)

Grunberger, Richard, *A Social History of the Third Reich* (London: Weidenfeld & Nicolson, 1971)

Gutman, Robert, *Richard Wagner: The Man, His Mind and His Music* (New York: Harcourt, Brace & World, 1968; pbk edn, Harmondsworth: Penguin Books, 1971)

Haas, Michael, *Forbidden Music: Jewish Composers banned by the Nazis* (New Haven and London: Yale UP, 2013)

Haas, Robert, *Anton Bruckner* (Potsdam: Akademische Verlagsgesellschaft Athenaion, 1934)

Haeckel, Ernst, *Die Welträthsel* (Bonn: Emil Strauss, 1900); Eng. edn, *The Riddle of the Universe at the Close of the Nineteenth Century*, tr. Joseph McCabe (New York: Harper & Brothers, 1900)

Haffner, Sebastian, *Anmerkungen zu Hitler* (München: Kindler Verlag, 1978); Eng. edn, *The Meaning of Hitler*, tr. Ewald Osers (Cambridge, MA: Harvard UP, 1979)

Halm, August, *Von zwei Kulturen der Musik* (München: Miller, 1913); extract in Lippmann, *Musical Aesthetics*, vol. 3, pp. 51–69

Hanslick, Eduard, *Vom Musikalisch-Schönen* (1854); Eng. edn, *On the Musically Beautiful*, tr. and ed. Geoffrey Payzant (Indianapolis: Hackett Publishing Company, 1986)

Hartog, Howard, ed., *European Music in the Twentieth Century* (London: Routledge, 1957; pbk edn, Harmondsworth: Penguin Books, 1961)

Hausegger, Friedrich von, *Die Musik als Ausdruck* (Vienna: Carl Konegen, 1887)

Hayman, Ronald, *Thomas Mann* (New York: Scribner, 1995; pbk edn, London: Bloomsbury, 1997)

Hegel, G. W. F., *Æsthetics: Lectures on Fine Art*, tr. and ed. T. M. Knox (Oxford: OUP, 1975)

——, *Grundlinien der Philosophie des Rechts* (1821); Eng. edn, *Philosophy of Right*, tr. S. W. Dyde (London: G. Bell, 1896)

Heiber, Helmut, *Goebbels-Reden* (Düsseldorf: Droste Verlag, 1971)

Heilbut, Anthony, *Thomas Mann: Eros and Literature* (New York: Alfred A. Knopf, 1995; London: Macmillan, 1996; pbk edn, London: Papermac, 1997)

Heller, Erich, *The Disinherited Mind* (London, 1952; pbk edn, Harmondsworth: Penguin Books, 1961)

——, *The Ironic German: A Study of Thomas Mann* (London: Secker & Warburg, 1958)

Hensellek, Werner, 'Wilhelm Furtwängler: Phenomenon of a Crisis', *Music Review*, vol. 34 (1973), pp. 124–31

Heyworth, Peter, ed., *Conversations with Klemperer* (London: Littlehampton Book Services, 1973)

——, *Otto Klemperer: His Life and Times*, 2 vols (Cambridge: CUP, 1983 and 1996)

Hitler, Adolf, *Mein Kampf* (München: Franz Eher, 1925 and 1927; Gesamtauflage, München: Franz Eher, 1940)

Höcker, Karla, *Die nie vergessenen Klänge: Erinnerungen an Wilhelm Furtwängler* (Berlin: Arani Verlag, 1979)

——, *Sinfonische Reise* (Gütersloh: C. Bertelsmann Verlag, 1954)

——, *Wilhelm Furtwängler: Begegnungen und Gespräch* (Gütersloh: C. Bertelsmann Verlag, 1956)

——, *Wilhelm Furtwängler: Dokumente, Berichte, Bilder und Aufzeichnungen* (Berlin: Rembrandt Verlag, 1968)

Holden, Raymond, *The Virtuoso Conductors: The Central European Tradition from Wagner to Karajan* (New Haven and London: Yale UP, 2005)

Honderich, Ted, ed., *The Oxford Companion to Philosophy* (Oxford: OUP, 1995)

Huller, Helene, 'Der Schriftsteller Friedrich Huch: Studien zu Literatur und Gesellschaft um die Jahrhundertwende' (Inaugural Dissertation zur Erlangung des Doktorgrades der Philosophischen Fakultät der Ludwig-Maximilians-Universität zu München, 1974)

Hunt, John, 'The Furtwängler Sound: Discography' (4th edn), in Ardoin, *The Furtwängler Record*, pp. 303–68

Hust, Christoph, '"How desolating to have to say that he is and will be the premier conductor of our time!": Heinrich Schenker and Wilhelm Furtwängler', in *Journal of Schenkerian Studies*, vol. 4 (2010), pp. 3–14

Jackson, Timothy, and Paul Hawkshaw, eds, *Bruckner Studies* (Cambridge: CUP, 1997)

Kaminsky, Jack, *Hegel on Art* (New York: State University of New York Press, 1962)

Kant, Immanuel, *Critique of Judgement*, tr. J. C. Meredith (Oxford: Clarendon Press, 1952)

——, *Critique of Pure Reason*, tr. J. M. D. Meiklejohn (London: Dent, 1934)

Kater, Michael H., *Composers of the Nazi Era: Eight Portraits* (New York: OUP, 2000)

——, *The Twisted Muse: Musicians and Their Music in the Third Reich* (New York and Oxford: OUP, 1997)

Kaufmann, Walter, *Nietzsche: Philosopher, Psychologist, Antichrist* (Cleveland: World, 1950)

Kemp, Ian, *Oxford Studies of Great Composers: Hindemith* (Oxford: OUP, 1970)

Klemperer, Victor, *Ich will Zeugnis ablegen bis zum letzen* (Berlin: Aufbau Verlag, 1995); Eng. edn, *I Shall Bear Witness: The Diaries of Victor Klemperer 1933–41*, tr. and abridged Martin Chalmers (London: Weidenfeld & Nicolson, 1998)

——, *LTI* (= Lingua Tertii Imperii, 1946; Halle: Reclam, 1957)

Köhler, Joachim, *Friedrich Nietzsche und Cosima Wagner* (Berlin: Rowohlt, 1996); Eng. edn, *Nietzsche and Wagner: A Lesson in Subjugation*, tr. Ronald Taylor (New Haven: Yale UP, 1998)

Krahnert, Sebastian, ed., *Furtwängler-Studien I* (Berlin: Ries & Erler, 1998)

Kropfinger, Klaus, *Wagner und Beethoven* (Regensburg: Bosse, 1974); Eng. edn, *Wagner and Beethoven: Richard Wagner's Reception of Beethoven*, tr. Peter Palmer (Cambridge: CUP, 1991)

Kurth, Ernst, *Bruckner* (Berlin: Max Hesses Verlag, 1925)

——, *Romantische Harmonik und ihre Krise in Wagners 'Tristan'* (Bern: Paul Haupt, 1920)

——, *Selected Writings*, ed. and tr. Lee A. Rothfarb (Cambridge: CUP, 1991)

Laqueur, Walter, *Fascism: A Reader's Guide* (Berkeley and Los Angeles: University of California Press, 1976)

Large, David C., and William Weber, eds, *Wagnerism in European Culture and Politics* (Ithaca and London: Cornell UP, 1984)

Le Huray, Peter, and James Day, *Music Aesthetics in the Eighteenth and Early Nineteenth Centuries* (Cambridge: CUP, 1981)

Lebrecht, Norman, *When the Music Stops* (London: Simon & Schuster, 1996)

Leppert, Richard, and Susan McClary, eds., *Music and Society: The Politics of Composition, Performance and Reception* (Cambridge: CUP, 1987)

Levi, Erik, *Music in the Third Reich* (London: Palgrave Macmillan, 1994)

Lindsay, J. M., *Thomas Mann* (Oxford: Basil Blackwell, 1954)

Lippmann, E. A., ed., *Musical Aesthetics: A Historical Reader*, 3 vols (New York: Pendragon, 1986–90), vol. 2, *The Nineteenth Century* (1988), vol. 3, *The Twentieth Century* (1990)

Lorenz, Alfred, *Das Geheimnis der Form bei Richard Wagner*, 4 vols (Berlin: Max Hesse, 1924–33)

Lucas, John, *Reggie: The Life of Reginald Goodall* (London: Julia MacRae Books, 1993)

MacGregor, Neil, *Germany: Memories of a Nation* (London: Allen Lane, 2014)

Makkreel, Rudolf A., *Dilthey: Philosopher of the Human Studies* (Princeton: Princeton UP, 1975)

Mann, Erika, ed., *Thomas Mann: Wagner und Unsere Zeit. Aufsätze, Betrachtungen, Briefe* (Frankfurt: Fischer, 1983); Eng. edn, *Thomas Mann: Pro and Contra Wagner*, tr. Allan Blunden (London: Faber, 1985)

Mann, Golo, *Deutsche Geschichte des 19. und 20. Jahrhunderts* (Frankfurt: S. Fischer Verlag, 1958); Eng. edn, *The History of Germany Since 1789*, tr. Marian Jackson (London: Chatto & Windus, 1968; pbk reprint, 1996)

Mann, Heinrich, *Der Untertan* (Leipzig: Kurt Wolff Verlag, 1918; Eng. edn, *Man of Straw* (London: Hutchinson & Co., 1946)

Mann, Klaus, *Mephisto*, tr. Robin Smyth (New York, 1977; Harmondsworth: Penguin Books, 1983; repr. 1995)

Mann, Thomas, *Betrachtungen eines Unpolitischen* (Berlin: S. Fischer Verlag, 1918); Eng. edn, *Reflections of a Nonpolitical Man*, tr. Walter D. Morris (New York: Frederick Ungar, 1983)

——, *Briefe*, ed. Erika Mann, 3 vols (Frankfurt: S. Fischer Verlag, 1961–65), vol. 2, *Briefe 1937–47* (1963)

——, *Buddenbrooks: Verfall einer Familie* (Berlin: S. Fischer Verlag, 1901); Eng. edn, tr. H. T. Lowe-Porter (London: Secker & Warburg, 1924)

——, *Doktor Faustus* (Stockholm: Fischer Verlag, 1947); Eng. edn, *Doctor Faustus*, tr. H. T. Lowe-Porter (London: Martin Secker & Warburg, 1949; pbk reprint, Minerva Books, 1996)

——, *The Genesis of a Novel*, tr. Richard and Clara Winston (London: Secker & Warburg, 1961)

——, *Letters of Thomas Mann 1889–1955*, selected and tr. Richard and Clara Winston (London: Secker & Warburg, 1970; pbk edn, Harmondsworth: Penguin Books, 1975)

——, *Der Zauberberg* (Berlin: S. Fischer Verlag, 1924); Eng. edn, *The Magic Mountain*, tr. John E. Woods (New York: Alfred A. Knopf, 1995). Everyman's Library, 2005

Matzner, Joachim, *Furtwängler: Analyse, Dokument, Protokoll* (Zürich and Gräfelfing: Atlantic Verlag, 1986)

Mayer, Hans, *Richard Wagner in Bayreuth* (Zürich and London: Belser, 1976)

McClatchie, Stephen, *Analyzing Wagner's Operas: Alfred Lorenz and German Nationalist Ideology* (New York: University of Rochester Press, 1998)

Montgomery, David L., 'The Myth of Organicism: From Bad Science to Great Art', *Musical Quarterly*, vol. 76 (1992), pp. 17–66

Montgomery, Marshall, *Studies in the Age of Goethe* (Oxford and London: OUP, 1931)

Müller, Ulrich, and Peter Wapnewski, eds, *Richard-Wagner-Handbuch* (Stuttgart: Alfred Kröner Verlag, 1986); Eng. edn, *The Wagner Handbook*, ed. John Deathridge (London and Cambridge, MA: Harvard UP, 1992)

Muck, Peter, *Dr Karl Muck: Ein Dirigentleben in Briefen und Dokumenten* (Tutzing: Verlegt bei Hans Schneider, 2003)

Newman, Ernest, *The Life of Richard Wagner*, 4 vols (London: Cassell, 1933–47; pbk reprint, Cambridge: CUP, 1976)

——, *The Unconscious Beethoven* (New York: Alfred A. Knopf, 1927)

——, *Wagner as Man and Artist*, 2nd edn (London: The Bodley Head, 1925)

Nicholls, Angus, *Goethe's Concept of the Daemonic: After the Ancients* (Rochester, NY: Camden House, 2006)

Nietzsche, Friedrich, *Beyond Good and Evil* (1886), tr. R. J. Hollingdale (London: Penguin, 1973)

——, *Ecce Homo* (1888), tr. R. J. Hollingdale (London: Penguin, 1968)

——, *Der Fall Wagner* (1888) in *The Birth of Tragedy and the Case of Wagner*, tr. Walter Kaufmann (New York: Vintage, 1967), pp. 152–92

——, *Die Geburt der Tragödie* (1872); Eng. edn, *The Birth of Tragedy*, tr. Shaun Whiteside (London: Penguin, 1993)

——, *Untimely Reflections* (1873–76); Eng. edn, tr. R. J. Hollingdale (Cambridge: Cambridge Texts in the History of Philosophy, 1997)

Oboussier, Robert, ed. Martin Hürlimann, *Berliner Musik-Chronik 1930–1938: Ausgewählte Rezensionen und Essays* (Zürich: Atlantis, 1969)

Oehlmann, Werner, *Das Berliner Philharmonische Orchester* (Kassel: Bären-reiter Verlag, 1974)

Osborne, Richard, *Conversations with Karajan* (Oxford: OUP, 1989)

——, *Herbert von Karajan: A Life in Music* (London: Chatto & Windus, 1998)

Owensby, Jacob, *Dilthey and the Narrative of History* (Ithaca and London: Cornell UP, 1994)

Papen, Franz von, *Memoirs*, tr. Brian Connell (London: Andre Deutsch, 1952)

Pascal, Roy, *From Naturalism to Expressionism: German Literature and Society 1880–1918* (London: Weidenfeld & Nicolson, 1973)

Pfitzner, Hans, *Die neue Aesthetik der musikalischen Impotenz* (München: Verlag der Süddeutschen Monatshefte, 1920)

Pirie, Peter, *Furtwängler and the Art of Conducting* (London: Duckworth, 1980)

Plato, *Phaedo*, tr. and with commentary by R. Hackforth (Cambridge: CUP, 1955)

Potter, Pamela, *Most German of the Arts: Musicology and Society from the Weimar Republic to the End of Hitler's Reich* (New Haven: Yale UP, 1998)

——, 'Musicology under Hitler: New Sources in Context', *Journal of the American Musicological Society* (Spring 1996), pp. 70–113

Prater, Donald, *Thomas Mann: A Life* (Oxford: OUP, 1995)

Prieberg, Fred K., *Kraftprobe: Wilhelm Furtwängler im Dritten Reich* (Wiesbaden: F. A. Brockhaus, 1986); Eng. edn, *Trial of Strength: Wilhelm Furtwängler and the Third Reich*, tr. Paul Dolan (London: Quartet Books, 1991)

——, *Musik im N.S. Staat* (Frankfurt: Fischer Verlag, 1982)

Pulzer, Peter, *Germany 1870–1945: Politics, State Formation, and War* (Oxford: OUP, 1997)

Rehding, Alexander, *Music and Monumentality: Commemoration and Wonderment in Nineteenth-Century Germany* (New York: OUP, 2009)

Reich-Ranicki, Marcel, *Thomas Mann and his Family*, tr. Ralph Mannheim (London: Collins, 1989)

Reid, Charles, *Thomas Beecham* (London: The Readers' Union, 1962)

Reiss, H. S., tr. and ed., *Political Thought of the German Romantics 1793–1815* (Oxford: Basil Blackwell, 1955)

Remak, Joachim, ed., *The Nazi Years, A Documentary History* (Englewood Cliffs, NJ: Prentice Hall, Inc, 1969)

Riezler, Walter, *Beethoven* (Berlin and Zürich: Atlantis, 1936); Eng. edn, tr. G. D. H. Piddock (London: M. C. Forrester, 1938)

Robertson, Ritchie, *Goethe: A Very Short Introduction* (Oxford: OUP, 2016)

Rose, Paul Lawrence, *Wagner: Race and Revolution* (London: Faber & Faber, 1992)

Rosenberg, Alfred, *Der Mythus des 20. Jahrhunderts* (München: Hoheneichen-Verlag, 1930)

Russell, John, *Erich Kleiber* (London: Andre Deutsch, 1957)

Russell, Thomas, *Philharmonic* (London: Hutchinson, 1942)

——, *Philharmonic Decade* (London: Hutchinson, 1944)

Salzer, Felix, *Structural Hearing* (New York: Charles Boni, 1952)

Schenker, Heinrich, *Beethovens neunte Sinfonie* (Wien, 1912); Eng. edn, *Beethoven's Ninth Symphony*, tr. John Rothgeb (New Haven and London: Yale UP, 1992)

——, *Harmonielehre* (Stuttgart, 1906); Eng. edn, *Harmony*, ed. and annotated Oswald Jonas, tr. Elisabeth Mann Borgese (Chicago: Chicago UP, 1954, pbk reprint, Cambridge, MA: MIT Press, 1973)

——, 'The Music of Today' (1894), tr. Jonathan Dunsby, *Music Analysis*, vol. 7, no. 2 (1988), p. 134

——, *Neue musikalische Theorien und Phantasie*, vol. 3, *Der freie Satz* (Wien: Universal Edition, 1935); Eng. edn, *Free Composition*, tr. Ernst Oster (New York: Schirmer Books, 1979)

——, 'Rameau or Beethoven? Paralysis or Spiritual Life in Music?'; extract from *Das Meisterwerk in der Musik III* (München, 1930), in Lippmann, *Musical Aesthetics*, vol. 3, pp. 71–87

Schiller, Friedrich, *On the Aesthetic Education of Man*, tr. Reginald Snell (London: Routledge, 1954; reprinted Bristol: Thoemmes Press, 1994)

Schlink, Bernhard, *The Reader*, tr. Carol Brown Janeway (London: Phoenix House, 1997)

Schoenberg, Arnold, *Arnold Schoenberg: Letters*, ed. Erwin Stein (London: Faber & Faber, 1964)

——, *Fundamentals of Musical Composition* (London: Faber & Faber, 1967)

——, *Style and Idea*, tr. Leo Black, ed. Leonard Stein (London: Faber & Faber, 1975)

Schonberg, Harold C., *The Great Conductors* (London: Victor Gollancz, 1968)

Schönzeler, Hans-Hubert, *Bruckner* (London: Calder & Boyars, 1970)

——, ed., *Of German Music* (New York and London: Barnes & Noble, 1976)

Schopenhauer, Artur, *Die Welt als Wille und Vorstellung* (1819); Eng. edn, *The World as Will and Representation*, tr. E. J. F. Payne, 2 vols (New York: Dover Books 1966)

Schwarzkopf, Elizabeth, *On and Off the Record: A Memoir of Walter Legge* (London: Faber & Faber, 1982)

Schweizer, Werner R., *Vom Deutschen Geist der Neuzeit* (Cambridge: CUP, 1926)

Scruton, Roger, *The Aesthetics of Music* (Oxford: Clarendon Press, 1997)

——, *Kant* (Oxford: OUP, 1982)

Shirer, William L., *Berlin Diary* (New York: Alfred A. Knopf, 1941)

——, *The Rise and Fall of the Third Reich* (London: Secker & Warburg, 1960)

Siegel, Heidi, ed., *Schenker Studies* (Cambridge: CUP, 1990)

Simpson, Robert, *The Essence of Bruckner* (London: Gollancz, 1977)

Singer, Peter, *Hegel* (Oxford: OUP Past Masters, 1983)

Skelton, Geoffrey, *Wagner at Bayreuth* (London: Barrie & Rockliff, 1965)
——, *Wieland Wagner: The Positive Sceptic* (London: Gollancz, 1971)
Smith, Barry, ed., *Foundations of Gestalt Theory* (München: Philosophia, 1988)
Snarrenberg, Robert, *Schenker's Interpretive Practice* (Cambridge: CUP, 1997)
Snyder, Louis L., ed., *Encyclopaedia of the Third Reich* (New York: McGraw-Hill, 1976)
Solie, Ruth, 'The Living Work: Organicism and Musical Analysis', *19th Century Music*, vol. 4 (1980), pp. 147–56
Speer, Albert, *Inside the Third Reich*, tr. Richard and Clara Winston (London: Macmillan, 1970)
Spengler, Oswald, *Der Untergang des Abendlandes: Umrisse einer Morphologie der Weltgeschichte. Erster Band, Gestalt und Wirklichkeit* (München: C. H. Beck'sche Verlagsbuchhandlung, 1918); *Zweiter Band, Welthistorische Perspektiven* (1922). Annotated English translation in one volume by C. F. Atkinson, *The Decline of the West* (London: George Allen & Unwin, 1932)
Spotts, Frederic, *Bayreuth: A History of the Wagner Festival* (New Haven and London: Yale UP, 1994)
Stengel, Theo, and Herbert Gerigk, *Lexikon der Juden in der Musik* (Berlin: Hahnefeld, 1941)
Stern, Fritz, *The Failure of Illiberalism: Essays on the Political Culture of Modern Germany* (New York and Oxford: Columbia UP, 1955; republished with a new preface, 1992)
——, *The Politics of Cultural Despair: A Study in the Rise of Germanic Ideology* (Berkeley: University of California Press, 1961)
Storr, Anthony, *Music and the Mind* (London: HarperCollins, 1992)
Strunk, Oliver, *Source Readings in Music History* (New York and London: W. Norton, 1998)
Tanner, Michael, *Nietzsche* (Oxford: OUP, 1994)
——, *Schopenhauer: Metaphysics and Art* (London: Orion Publishing, 1998)
——, 'The Total Work of Art', in Peter Burbidge and Richard Sutton, eds, *The Wagner Companion* (London: Faber & Faber, 1979), pp. 140–224
——, *Wagner* (London: HarperCollins, 1996)
Taruskin, Richard, 'Resisting the Ninth', *19th Century Music*, vol. 12 (1989), pp. 241–56; *Text and Act* (New York and Oxford: OUP, 1995), 235–61
Thaler, Lotte, *Organische Form in der Musiktheorie der 19. und beginnenden 20. Jahrhunderts* (München and Salzburg: Katzbichler, 1984)
Thärichen, Werner, *Paukenschläge: Furtwängler oder Karajan?* (Berlin and Zürich: M & T Verlag, 1987)
Thyssen, Fritz, *I Paid Hitler*, tr. César Saerchinger (New York and London: Hodder & Stoughton, 1941)

Toland, John, *Hitler* (New York: Doubleday, 1976; repr. 1997)

Tönnies, Ferdinand, *Gemeinschaft und Gesellschaft* (Leipzig, 1887); Eng. edn, *Community and Civil Society*, tr. and ed. Jose Harris and Margaret Hollis (Cambridge: CUP, 2001)

Trümpi, Fritz, *The Political Orchestra: The Berlin and Vienna Philharmonics in the Third Reich*, tr. Kenneth Kronenberg (Chicago and London: Chicago UP, 2016)

Vazsonyi, Nicholas, ed., *The Cambridge Wagner Encyclopedia* (Cambridge: CUP, 2013)

Vondung, Klaus, ed., *Das wilhelminische Bildungsbürgertum: Zur Sozialgeschichte seiner Ideen* (Göttingen: Vandenhoek & Ruprecht, 1918)

Wagner, Cosima, *Cosima Wagner's Diaries 1869–1883*, tr. and ed. Geoffrey Skelton, 2 vols (London, 1978–80)

Wagner, Gottfried, *He Who Does Not Howl With The Wolf*, tr. Della Couling (London: Sanctuary Publishing Limited, 1998)

Wagner, Richard, 'Beethoven' (1870); Eng. edn, tr. E. Dannreuther (London: Willima Reeves, 1903); see also Allen, Roger

——, *Gesammelte Schriften und Dichtungen* [GSD], 10 vols (Leipzig: Fritzsch, 1871–83); Eng. edn, *Richard Wagner's Prose Works* [PW], tr. W. Ashton Ellis, 8 vols (London: Kegan Paul, Trench, Trübner & Co., 1892–99)

——, *Letters of Richard Wagner*, selected and ed. Wilhelm Altmann, tr. M. M. Bozman, 2 vols (London: J. M. Dent, 1927)

——, *Selected Letters of Richard Wagner*, tr. and ed. Stewart Spencer and Barry Millington (London: J. M. Dent, 1987)

——, 'Über das Dirigiren' (1869); Eng. edn, 'On Conducting', tr. E. Dannreuther (London: William Reeves, 1887)

Walker, Alan, *Hans von Bülow: A Life and Times* (New York: OUP, 2010)

Walter, Bruno, *Thema und Variationen* (Stockholm: Bermann-Fischer, 1947); Eng. edn, *Theme and Variations*, tr. James A. Galston (London: Hamish Hamilton, 1947)

——, *Von der Musik und vom Musizieren* (Frankfurt: S. Fischer, 1957); Eng. edn, *Of Music and Music Making*, tr. Paul Hamburger (London: Faber & Faber, 1961)

Walton, Chris, *Lies and Epiphanies: Composers and their Inspiration from Wagner to Berg* (New York: University of Rochester Press, 2014)

——, 'Wilhelm Furtwänglers Apologia pro vita sua', *Dissonanz*, vol. 51 (February 1997), pp. 16–24

Walton, Chris, Jürg Stenzl *et al.*, eds, 'Wilhelm Furtwängler in Diskussion', in *Werkverzeichnis Wilhelm Furtwängler* (Winterthur, 1996), pp. 7–83

Waterhouse, Gilbert, *A Short History of German Literature* (London: Methuen 1942; rep. with corrections, 1952)

Watkins, Holly, *Metaphors of Depth in German Musical Thought* (Cambridge: CUP, 2011)

Watson, Derek, *Bruckner* (London: Dent, 1975)

Weber, William, *Music and the Middle Class: The Social Structure of Concert Life in London, Paris and Vienna* (Farnham: Ashgate, 1975)

Wessling, Berndt W., ed., *Bayreuth im Dritten Reich: Richard Wagners politische Erben. Eine Dokumentation* (Weinheim und Basel: Beltz, 1983)

Westernhagen, Curt von, *Wagner* (Zürich: Atlantis, 1979); Eng. edn., *Wagner*, tr. Mary Whittall (Cambridge: CUP, 1981)

———, *Wagner, Sein Werk, Sein Wesen, Seine Welt* (Zürich: Atlantis, 1956)

Williamson, John, *The Music of Hans Pfitzner* (Oxford: OUP, 1992)

Wooldridge, David, *Conductor's World* (London: Barrie & Jenkins, 1970)

Zippel, Adolph, *Lohengrin: Richard Wagners Oper vom philosophisch-esoterischen Standpunkte aus betrachtet* (Württemberg: Karl Rohm, 1913)

INDEX